❦ ❦ ❦ THE PRE-RAPHAELITES

D1714136

❦ ❦ ❦ THE PRE-RAPHAELITES

EDITED WITH AN INTRODUCTION BY

JEROME H. BUCKLEY   HARVARD UNIVERSITY

ACADEMY
CHICAGO

First published in 1986 by Academy Chicago Publishers
This edition published by Academy Chicago Publishers
An imprint of Chicago Review Press
814 North Franklin Street
Chicago, IL 60610

ISBN 978-0-89733-2378

Library of Congress Cataloging-in-Publication Data
Buckley, Hamilton Jerome-editor
   The Pre-Raphaelites: An Anthology of Poetry Dante
Rossetti and Others
Reprint. Originally published: New York : Modern Library,
1968.
   Includes indexes.
   1. Preraphaelitism—Poetry. 2. English poetry—19th
century. I. Buckley, Jerome Hamilton.
PR1195.P66P74   1986   821'.8'08   86-22187

Cover Design: Natalya Balnova

Printed in the United States of America
5 4 3 2 1

CONTENTS

CHRISTINA ROSSETTI 197

WILLIAM MORRIS ❧ 257

ALGERNON CHARLES SWINBURNE ❧ 289

GEORGE MEREDITH ❧ 347

MINOR PRE-RAPHAELITE POETS

WILLIAM MICHAEL ROSSETTI ❧ 375

THOMAS WOOLNER ❧ 379

ELIZABETH SIDDAL ROSSETTI ❧ 388

INTRODUCTION

In the summer of 1848 three young painters, Dante Gabriel
Rossetti, William Holman Hunt, and John Everett Millais,
each impatient with the artifices and conventions pre-
scribed by the Royal Academy, joined with four friends to
establish the Pre-Raphaelite Brotherhood, a loosely organ-
ized society for the informal study of art and poetry and
the promotion—through their own work—of "truth to na-
ture" in both. All seven, with more of boyish enthusiasm
than informed judgment, professed to admire the bold en-
ergy of early Italian painting, a freedom lost, they thought,
in the schools *after* Raphael, which, like the Academy,
were intent upon reproducing by fixed rules the achieve-
ments of the past. Yet none assigned any precise denota-
tion to the Pre-Raphaelite label; each indeed took a con-
spiratorial delight in the enigmatic monogram "PRB," the
significance of which remained for a while a closely
guarded secret.

The original Brotherhood disbanded after four years of
shared exuberance, intermittent creativity, and frequent
altercation. But the term "Pre-Raphaelite," as it passed
into the hands of associates and followers, became only the
vaguer and more elusive. The movement left a deep im-
press on the literature and the graphic art of middle and
late Victorian England, but apart from Rossetti's dynamic
personality, apparent from first to last, it is difficult to find
any single common denominator of subject matter, idiom,
or manner for the various Pre-Raphaelite groups. Ros-
setti's own style in both painting and poetry was by no
means constant or consistent: there is little real similarity
between the startling simplicity of his early brightly lit
"Annunciation" and his later ornate portraits of Jane Mor-

ris, her heavy hair in somber shadows; there is great disparity in diction and rhetoric between "My Sister's Sleep" and the baroque, richly connotative sonnets of *The House of Life*. The distance, in terms of effect, between the literal "truth to nature" of the early Millais and the elaborate artifice of Edward Burne-Jones is striking and decisive. And the difference in tone between Swinburne's verse in his Pre-Raphaelite phase and that of Christina Rossetti is no less conspicuous.

Nevertheless, we may still speak of a Pre-Raphaelite quality. We may still assemble an exhibition of Pre-Raphaelite paintings and drawings or, as in the present volume, an anthology of Pre-Raphaelite poems. For uniformity of method among the Pre-Raphaelites is of far less consequence than a certain community of spirit. Each of the painters and poets, in his own way or in more than one way, raised his protest against the comfortable assumptions of a matter-of-fact world. Each sought to recover the sense of wonder and mystery, the dream beyond the commonplaces of an order increasingly devoted to the mechanization of human life. Each strove to make of his art the vehicle of a fresh intuition. Pre-Raphaelitism involved a peculiar intimacy, conveyed by a close observation of specifics, especially visual details, or a close analysis of moods —the peculiar heightening of individual impression and emotion. The quality was to be experienced rather than defined. Its literary expression became only gradually known as the poetry slowly emerged from private circles, but its presence was immediately distinct and disturbing to the public first confronted by the paintings.

In his engaging autobiography, *Father and Son,* the Edwardian critic Edmund Gosse tells how as a boy in the early 1860s he was taken to a public showing in a nearby Devonshire town of Holman Hunt's "Finding of Christ in the Temple." Though attracted to the familiar subject of "the large and uncompromising picture," the townsmen were astonished and distressed by the "Pre-Raphaelite" treatment, the harsh bright lighting that brought every detail of costume and setting into sharpest focus. But the child—rightly—saw no great difference in technique between the painting and his father's closely delineated scientific sketches. "Indeed," Gosse remarks, "if anything, the exact, minute and hard execution of Mr. Hunt was in sympathy with the methods we ourselves were in the habit of using when we painted butterflies and seaweeds, placing perfectly pure pigments side by side, without any nonsense about chiaroscuro."

Gosse's father, as a biologist, was devoted to accurate observation. Though he fervently rejected the idea of evolution, he shared with Darwin and other Victorian scientists a strong empirical bias, the habit of painstaking measurement, the will to analyze each particular object in itself and so perhaps to wring yet another secret from nature's close reserve. And Hunt's impulse was remarkably similar. To perceive intensely and to paint with absolute "truth to nature" were the first principles of his Pre-Raphaelite creed. Hunt strove accordingly to make his religious paintings indubitably authentic in every last detail. "The Light of the World," which depicted Christ in a moonlit orchard knocking at a barred door, was painted night after chilly night in a moonlit orchard; "The Scapegoat" was modeled by a real goat tethered in woebegone thirst by the actual shore of the Dead Sea; and the background of "The Triumph of the Innocents" was drawn with photographic fidelity on the very road from Jerusalem to Bethlehem. The Gosses, father and son, could be assured of the verifiable correctness of the temple robes and mitres and phylacteries.

Reviewing the large Millais exhibition at the Royal Academy more than a century after Hunt's one-picture show, David Thompson in his report to the *New York Times* commented on the "almost illusionistic detail" that characterized Pre-Raphaelite paintings; but, he added, "it is detail not so much 'actually seen' as unblinkingly stared at, and rendered with such passionate literalness and abnormal clarity that it comes out with a strange, poetic intensification of its own." Millais indeed, rather than Hunt, was the first of the Pre-Raphaelites to bring this mode of lidless staring to public attention, the first to excite general alarm by his studied realism. His "Christ in the House of His Parents," shown in June, 1850, derived the hard firm outlines of its setting from an actual carpenter's shop in Oxford Street, assigned to Joseph's arms the muscles of a real carpenter, and exposed the grain of each cedar plank to unrelenting scrutiny. The canvas was immediately attacked, by those who failed to detect its poetic intensity, as "a pictorial blasphemy . . . repulsive and revolting." Few knew or cared to know that they might have found the sanction for such practice in *The Germ*, the little magazine issued by the Pre-Raphaelites that after four issues had expired quietly in April of the same year.

For the cover of *The Germ* William Michael Rossetti wrote a sonnet expounding—not very lucidly—the primary assumptions of the Brotherhood, which he served as secretary. Every original idea in art, his poem suggested, deserved original expression, and the proper question to ask of every fresh work was simply "Is this truth?" The search for new truth beyond existing stereotypes, he explained several years later, even accounted for the odd name of the coterie. The Pre-Raphaelites, he said, had no intention of imitating the methods of the early painters:

> Let there be no mistake about what Pre-Raphaelitism means. It has nothing to do with the technical deficiencies, or technical practice, or choice of subjects, of painters who lived before Raphael, but with the condition of mind which actuated them to represent whatever was in hand—whether typically or naturally—with a resolute adherence to truth of feeling and truth of fact, and a resolute disregard of all mere grace and all mere dexterity which would interfere with the first or affect the second. Pre-Raphaelitism, at its lowest, is reverent faith in Nature, whether seen with the poet's eye or with the catalogue-compiler's, whether rendered with the artist's hand or with the transcriber's. At its highest . . . this faith in Nature takes a far wider range; involving that sincerity of thought which shall always invent something specific

and new in conception—something truly natural in idea, as well as express this through a medium of visible nature studied with that love of observance which cannot but catch, out of her infinity, beauties ever fresh and individual.

William Michael's own verses "Fancies at Leisure" suggest the transcriber rather than the artist; but a respect for fact—a "reverent faith in Nature"—clearly prompts his description of a dead dog floating in a stagnant pool as much as it inspires Millais' more adroit delineation of the cedar planks.

Though they developed their credos independently, all the original Pre-Raphaelites knew and admired Ruskin's *Modern Painters,* and all could have cited with approval Ruskin's admonition to go to nature, to "walk with her laboriously and trustingly, having no other thought but how best to penetrate her meaning; rejecting nothing, selecting nothing, and scorning nothing." But though Ruskin meant such homage to fact to be but the beginning of art, the Pre-Raphaelites, especially Millais and Hunt, sometimes seemed to regard it as the proper end. Still, in their best work, single simple detail, stared at fixedly, grew incandescent with the suggestion of extra meaning. In effect, their realism became surrealistic, and it is not surprising that Salvador Dali could see a kinship between their paintings and his own. Ruskin himself perceived the psychological effect of rendering detail so precisely. In Hunt's "Awakening Conscience" he saw countless tiny objects thrusting themselves forward "with a ghastly and unendurable distinctness, as if they would compel the sufferer to count, or measure, or learn them by heart." And this presentation, he thought, was appropriate to the intensity of the scene depicted, for "nothing is more notable than the way in which the most trivial objects force themselves upon the attention of a mind which has been fevered by violent and distressful excitement."

In his simply etched lyric "The Woodspurge" Dante Gabriel Rossetti demonstrated this truth. In a moment of complete despair, the poet apprehends the wild flower with preternatural clarity, and he remembers the configuration of its design when he has forgotten the occasion of his distress. Unlike Hunt, however, Rossetti here and elsewhere in his work is less concerned with "truth of fact" (to use William Michael's categories) than with "truth of feeling." The fact of the flower is, of course, intensely vivid, but only because it is brooded upon by the quickened subjective consciousness.

Both as painter and as poet, Rossetti, though attentive always to detail, was more literary than literal, interested first of all in the psychology of moods, the analysis of states of soul, and eager to depict the life of an imagination nourished on books and private reverie. The work of Elizabeth Siddal, who wrote and painted in his shadow, as it were, kept at best a very frail hold on outward reality. But Rossetti's own life and art respected a strong sensuousness as the element essential to give his dream-world force and substance. Nonetheless, his subject matter must always have seemed remote and rarefied. Few of his pictures were in any way contemporary or typical. His poems seldom touched on the political crises that preoccupied most of the major Victorians; and when they concerned modern English society at all, the allusions, as in "The Burden of Nineveh," were characteristically oblique and ironic. He considered the large issues of love and time and death (the themes of *The House of Life*) of abiding importance to the artist, but he had no respect for propagandistic poetry or painting of didactic purpose. For the most part he was quite uninterested in current events, and he steadily deplored an absorption in which he once called "the momentary momentousness and eternal futility of many of our noisiest questions." Throughout his life he had a genius for friendship and a capacity for instilling intense loyalty in his disciples; but he shrank from the outside world, sold his pictures privately, withheld his poetry for years from publication, and was in general content to have his work and person seem strange and enigmatic. Both his strengths and his weaknesses may be ascribed to his distance from any large public; both bear the mark of an alienated sensibility.

Accordingly, though the leader of each successive Pre-Raphaelite group, Rossetti spoke only to those whose imaginations he could fire with new visions of a more or less esoteric beauty. He had little sympathy with the middle-class economy of his time, the standards of material progress and the complacent conventions of success. In its inception the PRB, with Rossetti the chief enthusiast, was essentially a revolt; it was, as Gerard Manley Hopkins understood it, a radical questioning, a breaking apart. Ruskin, who appreciated its motives, found—as he comments ironically in *Pre-Raphaelitism*—"little cause for surprise that pictures painted in a temper of resistance, by exceedingly young men, of stubborn instincts and positive self-trust . . . should not be calculated, at first glance, to win us from works enriched by plagiarism, polished by convention, invested with all the attractiveness of artificial grace, and recommended to our respect by established authority."

It mattered little that the rejection of the establishment often prompted retreat to an older tradition, an archaic convention, or that the quest for the natural involved new affectations; the Pre-Raphaelites achieved their difference by repudiating the world that was too much with their contemporaries. To the mechanical standardization of parts they opposed the fresh apprehension of detail. To the quantitative measurement of large impersonal things, they preferred the qualitative analysis of their own intense perceptions. Rossetti described a sonnet as a "moment's monument," that is, the enshrining of a single mood or impression or intuition snatched from the onrushing flux of time; and all Pre-Raphaelite art—both poetry and painting—aspires to such intensity: the discovery of the significant gesture at the moment of crisis. Far more anxiously than his disciples, Rossetti sought to make the sharp sense impression the avenue to mystical revelation; a quasi-mystical overtone is the individual hallmark of his work. But the quality of his imagination spread contagiously from group to group, animating many who did not share his psychological need for the reassurance of eternity.

Rossetti the man and the poet, rather than simply the painter, was the one link between the several Pre-Raphaelite circles. By 1852 the original Brotherhood had scattered, as his sister amusingly explained in her sonnet "The P.R.B." But five years later he found himself at the center of a lively and talented Oxford group (at first known as the Birmingham Set), which included William Morris, Edward Burne-Jones, and Richard Watson Dixon. Morris had recently been chief sponsor of *The Oxford and Cambridge Magazine* (1856), a sort of second *Germ,* which had warmly praised Rossetti's short story "Hand and Soul" and printed three of his poems, "The Blessed Damozel," "The Burden of Nineveh," and "The Staff and Scrip." With the ebullient aid of these new admirers Rossetti now launched what he called his "jovial campaign" to decorate the walls of the Oxford Union. Amid general hilarity each sought to execute his own Arthurian designs in brilliant colors. It was an ill-fated venture since neither Rossetti nor his young companions knew anything of the technique of preparing surfaces to give the murals permanence, and the scenes of a bright Camelot receded rapidly into the damp grayness. Yet it was a memorable encounter, too, insofar as the force of Rossetti's personality gave Burne-Jones the inspiration to devote the rest of his life to Pre-Raphaelite painting and determined the direction of Morris' manifold concern with the graphic arts. But the advent of the young Swinburne and later, as the group moved to London, of George Meredith assured that the main Pre-Raphaelite emphasis would now fall on poetry rather than painting. Rossetti's verse, the little of it that they could know, was a decisive influence on Dixon and Morris, even in minute particulars; the Saint Mary Magdalene of the one, for example, in gesture and helpless yearning is remarkably like the Guenevere of the other, and both are closely akin to the Blessed Damozel. Dedicated to Rossetti, Morris' *Defence of Guenevere and Other Poems,* almost completely ignored on publication, was actually the first Pre-Raphaelite volume and as a whole the nearest in treatment of detail to the practice in painting of the original PRB. *Christ's Company* by Dixon, Meredith's *Modern Love,* and Christina Rossetti's *Goblin Market* (for which Dante Gabriel did two illustrations) followed early in the 1860s; though only the last of these attracted much attention, all were to some degree Pre-Raphaelite in mood and coloring. Then in 1866, Swinburne's *Poems and Ballads* (which despite its defiant originality showed a measurable indebtedness to Rossetti) exploded upon the world, the most notorious book of verse of the whole Victorian period—and one of the most exciting.

By 1870, when Rossetti's own volume at last appeared, yet another circle of disciples was beginning to form. This third group—more derivative and less vitally creative than the second—included Arthur O'Shaughnessy, Philip Bourke Marston, and the perverse but gifted painter Simeon Solomon. Robert Buchanan, whose polemic, as we shall see, redounds to his own discredit, was absurdly hysterical in attacking Rossetti as the leader of the Fleshly School of Poetry, devoted to the wanton destruction of all reticence and decency. But he was not mistaken in associating with him not only Morris and Swinburne but also a good many younger and lesser poets of the time. For Rossetti, though he remained withdrawn from public events, was proving a more distinct force than any other in the shaping of the new poetry. His impact in the seventies ranged well beyond the relatively narrow confines of his private experience. Yet until the end he was able to inspire devotion in personal friends such as Theodore Watts-Dunton and the young journalist T. Hall Caine, who came in the last months to serve as his confidant and his Boswell. And the force of his presence remained altogether overpowering to at least one late admirer, Thomas Dixon, a cork cutter and would-be poet of Sunderland, who died, we are told, from the "excitement and exaltation" of an interview with the master.

After Rossetti's own death, Pre-Raphaelite graphic art

persisted with variations into the 1890s, when it influenced directly the intricate drawings of Aubrey Beardsley and more generally the practice of the *Art nouveau.* Pre-Raphaelite poetry helped determine the approach of Gerard Manley Hopkins, the resolute dedication of the young Yeats, and later the Imagists' preoccupation with precise impressions. But the Pre-Raphaelite movement as a whole—if the loosely associated groups can be thought of as a single force—reached even further in more elusive directions. It did much to establish the autonomy of art and the independence of the artist from didactic purpose and sectarian demand; it made clear the importance of the vivid detail and the symbolic overtone of the sharp perception; and by its stress on the quality rather than the variety of experience it ultimately did more than a little to quicken the aesthetic sensibility of a whole culture.

Jerome H. Buckley

BIBLIOGRAPHICAL NOTE

GENERAL   *Pre-Raphaelitism: A Bibliocritical Study* (1965), by William E. Fredeman, is an excellent guide to the Pre-Raphaelite movement, stimulating in its critical commentary and useful in its bibliographical listings. There are also helpful chapters on Pre-Raphaelite scholarship in *The Victorian Poets: A Guide to Research*, edited by Frederic E. Faverty, by Howard Mumford Jones in the first edition (1956) and by W.E. Fredeman in the second (1968).

EDITIONS   William Michael Rossetti reissued *The Germ* of 1850 in 1901 with his own notes and prepared many other standard Pre-Raphaelite editions, including *Family Letters* (2 vols., 1895), *Ruskin: Rossetti: Pre-Raphaelitism* (1899), *Rossetti Papers, 1862-1870* (1903), *The Works of Dante Gabriel Rossetti* (1911), and *The Poetical Works of Christina Rossetti* (1904). *The Germ* was reprinted by Robert S. Hosman in 1970. Paull F. Baum prepared a critical edition of *The House of Life* (1928), and Oswald Doughty and J.R. Wahl issued *Letters of Dante Gabriel Rossetti* (4 vols., 1965-66). May Morris edited the *Collected Works of William Morris* (24 vols., 1910-15), and Norman Kelvin is currently editing the Morris *Letters* (1984 +). G.M. Trevelyan's *Poetical Works of George Meredith* (1912) was the standard edition till Phyllis B. Bartlett's in 1977, and C.L. Cline's is the definitive edition of the Meredith *Letters* (3 vols., 1970). The Bonchurch Swinburne (20 vols., 1925-27), edited by Edmund Gosse and T.J. Wise should be supplemented by *The Swinburne Letters* (6 vols., 1959-62), presented with gusto by Cecil Lang.

BIOGRAPHY AND CRITICISM   Popular introductions to the PRB, such as Francis L. Bickley's *The Pre-Raphaelite Comedy* (1932) and William Gaunt's *The Pre-Raphaelite Tragedy* (1942), still entertaining in their gossipy detail, have been followed by more substantial scholarly studies, such as G.H. *Fleming's Rossetti and the Pre-Raphaelite Brotherhood* (1967), John Dixon Hunt's *The Pre-Raphaelite Imagi-*

nation (1969), and Lionel Stevenson's survey, *The Pre-Raphaelite Poets* (1970). Oswald Doughty's *Dante Gabriel Rossetti* (1960) offers a detailed biography of the enigmatic poet-painter, whom Stanley Weintraub's *Four Rossettis* (1978) skillfully places in a family context. Among the many critical monographs on the principal Pre-Raphaelite we should mention Robert Cooper's *Lost on Both Sides: Rossetti, Critic and Poet* (1970), David Sonstroem's *Rossetti and the Fair Lady* (1970), Joseph F. Vogel's *Dante Gabriel Rossetti's Versecraft* (1971), Ronnalie Roper Howard's *The Dark Glass: Vision and Technique in the Poetry of Rossetti* (1972), and the double issue of *Victorian Poetry* (Autumn-Winter, 1982), devoted entirely to Rossetti, profusely illustrated, edited by William E. Fredeman.

Lona Mosk Packer's *Christina Rossetti* (1963) and Georgina Battiscombe's *Christina Rossetti: A Divided Life* (1981) offer new perspectives on the Pre-Raphaelite Sister. J.W. Mackail's standard *Life of William Morris* (1899) may be supplemented by Philip Henderson's *William Morris, his Life, Work and Friends* (1967), E.P. Thompson's *William Morris, Romantic to Revolutionary* (1977), Frederick Kirchhoff's *William Morris* (1979), and Carole Silver's *Romance of William Morris* (1982). Lionel Stevenson's *The Ordeal of George Meredith* (1953) remains the best balanced Meredith biography. Georges Lafourcade's *Swinburne* (1932) has not been superseded but may be supplemented by Philip Henderson's *Swinburne: Portrait of a Poet* (1974). One of the few sustained modern defences of Swinburne's art is the critique in dialogue form by Jerome J. McGann, *Swinburne: An Experiment in Criticism* (1972).

Among the volumes devoted to the minor Pre-Raphaelites, the following, though mostly long since out of print, may be noted: *Thomas Woolner, R.A., Sculptor and Poet* (1917), by Amy Woolner; *William Allingham: A Diary* (1907), edited by Helen Allingham and D. Radford; *A Poet Hidden: The Life of Richard Watson Dixon* (1962), by James Sambrook; *Arthur O'Shaughnessy: His Life and His Work* (1894) by Louise Moulton Chandler; and Charles C. Osborne's *Philip Bourke Marston* (1926).

As painters the Pre-Raphaelites, once virtually ignored by art historians, have received considerable recent attention. Virginia Surtees in 1971 compiled a splendid two-volume "catalogue raisonné," *Dante Gabriel Rossetti, 1828-1882: The Paintings and Drawings*, with a full descriptive text and over five hundred plates.

Maryan Wynn Ainsworth and her associates at Yale University Art Gallery prepared a monograph, *Dante Gabriel Rossetti and the Double Work of Art* (exploring the relationships between the poetry and the painting) for a 1976 exhibition. And Julian Treuherz in 1980 issued the handsomely illustrated *Pre-Raphaelite Painters*, describing the large collection at the Manchester City Art Gallery. Two good picture books may also be recommended: *Pre-Raphaelite Painters* (1948), edited by Robin Ironside, and *I Prerafaelliti* (1969, published in Milan), edited by Renato Barilli.

Finally, Max Beerbohm's volume of affectionate caricatures, *Rossetti and His Circle* (1922), must be regarded as virtually a primary source for any study of the Pre-Raphaelites.

MAJOR PRE-RAPHAELITE

POETS

DANTE GABRIEL ROSSETTI

(1828–1882)

Though the center of each successive Pre-Raphaelite circle, Dante Gabriel Rossetti remained otherwise aloof from the concerns and conflicts of nineteenth-century England. The son of an Italian patriot, who had fled from Naples in 1824 and taken refuge in London as a language teacher, he was far more interested in his father's close knowledge of Dante's poetry than in the political intrigues that had led to exile. As a child he amused himself drawing fantastic pictures "out of his head," reading Gothic novels and adventure tales, and playing literary games with his brother, William, and his two sisters, Maria and Christina. One of their favorites, *bouts rimés,* consisted of composing sonnets to assigned rhymes.

Encouraged to develop his gift for graphic art, Rossetti was enrolled at the Royal Academy—but only briefly. He soon left to study under Ford Madox Brown, whose bold realism seemed far less stereotyped than the academic exercises. With Hunt and Millais he discovered the virtues of early Italian painting, worked out a new aesthetic credo, and in 1848 organized the PRB. He exhibited one painting in 1849, one in 1850, but rarely thereafter, and contributed several poems and the prose "Hand and Soul" to *The Germ* of 1850. In many respects the fifties proved his most fruitful period both as a poet and as a graphic artist. In that decade he produced his finest drawings (many of them more vividly suggestive than the later oil paintings), wrote some of his best sonnets and ballads, found vigorous new disciples at Oxford, where he conducted his "jovial campaign" to decorate the Union, and experienced alternate elation and misery in his long courtship of Elizabeth Siddal, whom he married at last in May, 1860. The following year he published *The Early Italian Poets,* translations of Dante and his predecessors which he had been making ever since his boyhood. Though the anthology reached only a small audience, it was well enough received by friends and reviewers to persuade Rossetti that he might venture a collection of his own poems. The suicide of his wife, however, in February, 1862, left him without hope or ambition, and in a gesture of despair he buried his manuscripts with her. He then moved to Tudor House at 16 Cheyne Walk in Chelsea, where he resumed his career as a painter in a strange ménage of literary friends and an even stranger menagerie of pet animals. When he finally returned to poetry, his friends induced him to order the exhumation of the manuscripts and to prepare from them and from a number of new pieces the book published as *Poems* in 1870. The reception accorded this volume was in general most enthusiastic until the appearance of Robert Buchanan's "Fleshly School of Poetry" in the *Contemporary Review* (October, 1871). But in Rossetti's eyes the one attack annulled all previous praise; already nervously debilitated, he now felt relentlessly persecuted by a whole Philistine world he had never cared to understand. Henceforth he was increasingly subject to delusive fears and more or less constant insomnia. Nonetheless, despite his illness, he continued to write with undiminished power and to attract new admirers, and his literary reputation grew steadily wider and more secure. His last volume, *Ballads and Sonnets* (1881), not only brought to completion his masterpiece, *The House of Life,* it also evinced a sustained command of lyric form and a new freedom in handling narrative verse. By the time of his death a few months later, his dedicated life in art, no less than his poetry and painting, had become a legend and an ideal to the intense young men of the Aesthetic Movement.

THE BLESSED DAMOZEL

[handwritten: → damsel]

The blessed damozel leaned out
   From the gold bar of Heaven;
Her eyes were deeper than the depth
   Of waters stilled at even;
She had three lilies in her hand,
   And the stars in her hair were seven. *[handwritten: classical planets]*

Her robe, ungirt from clasp to hem,
   No wrought flowers did adorn,
But a white rose of Mary's gift, *[handwritten: reference to]*
   For service meetly worn; *[handwritten: Christianity &]* 10
Her hair that lay along her back *[handwritten: the Virgin Mary]*
   Was yellow like ripe corn.

[handwritten left margin: motion ↑ myth]

Herseemed she scarce had been a day *[handwritten: she has been in]*
   One of God's choristers; *[handwritten: Heaven for ten years]*
The wonder was not yet quite gone
   From that still look of hers;
Albeit, to them she left, her day
   Had counted as ten years.

(To one, it is ten years of years. *[handwritten: new perspective, her]*
   . . . Yet now, and in this place, *[handwritten: lover speaks]* 20
Surely she leaned o'er me—her hair *[handwritten: mourns for her]*
   Fell all about my face. . . .
Nothing: the autumn-fall of leaves.
   The whole year sets apace.)

It was the rampart of God's house
   That she was standing on;
By God built over the sheer depth
   The which is Space begun;

So high, that looking downward thence
  She scarce could see the sun.   30

It lies in Heaven, across the flood
  Of ether, as a bridge.
Beneath, the tides of day and night
  With flame and darkness ridge
The void, as low as where this earth
  Spins like a fretful midge.

the distance between them is vast

Around her, lovers, newly met
  'Mid deathless love's acclaims,
Spoke evermore among themselves
  Their heart-remembered names;
And the souls mounting up to God
  Went by her like thin flames.   40

the reunited lovers around her cause her anguish

And still she bowed herself and stooped
  Out of the circling charm;
Until her bosom must have made
  The bar she leaned on warm,
And the lilies lay as if asleep
  Along her bended arm.

From the fixed place of Heaven she saw
  Time like a pulse shake fierce   50
Through all the worlds. Her gaze still strove
  Within the gulf to pierce
Its path; and now she spoke as when
  The stars sang in their spheres.

she speaks but we do not know what she says

The sun was gone now; the curled moon
  Was like a little feather
Fluttering far down the gulf; and now
  She spoke through the still weather.
Her voice was like the voice the stars
  Had when they sang together.   60

"The Blessed Damozel," painting by Dante Gabriel
Rossetti, completed in 1877, to illustrate the poem.
Courtesy of the Fogg Art Museum, Harvard University,
Grenville L. Winthrop Bequest

(Ah sweet! Even now, in that bird's song,
   Strove not her accents there,
Fain to be hearkened? When those bells
   Possessed the mid-day air,
Strove not her steps to reach my side
   Down all the echoing stair?)

many sounds remind the love of his lost damsel

"I wish that he were come to me,
   For he will come," she said.
"Have I not prayed in Heaven?—on earth,
   Lord, Lord, has he not pray'd?   70
Are not two prayers a perfect strength?
   And shall I feel afraid?

we finally hear the damsel speak

"When round his head the aureole clings,
   And he is clothed in white,
I'll take his hand and go with him
   To the deep wells of light;
As unto a stream we will step down,
   And bathe there in God's sight.

she imagines ... that they'll do once her lover i[s] able to join h[er] in heaven.

"We two will stand beside that shrine,
   Occult, withheld, untrod,   80
Whose lamps are stirred continually
   With prayer sent up to God;
And see our old prayers, granted, melt
   Each like a little cloud.

"We two will lie i' the shadow of
   That living mystic tree
Within whose secret growth the Dove
   Is sometimes felt to be,
While every leaf that His plumes touch
   Saith His Name audibly.   90

"And I myself will teach to him,
   I myself, lying so,

The songs I sing here; which his voice
  Shall pause in, hushed and slow,
And find some knowledge at each pause,
  Or some new thing to know."

(Alas! we two, we two, thou say'st!
  Yea, one wast thou with me
That once of old. But shall God lift
  To endless unity   100
The soul whose likeness with thy soul
  Was but its love for thee?)

"We two," she said, "will seek the groves
  Where the lady Mary is,
With her five handmaidens, whose names
  Are five sweet symphonies,
Cecily, Gertrude, Magdalen,
  Margaret and Rosalys.

"Circlewise sit they, with bound locks
  And foreheads garlanded;   110
Into the fine cloth white like flame
  Weaving the golden thread,
To fashion the birth-robes for them
  Who are just born, being dead.

"He shall fear, haply, and be dumb;   *She imagines the Virgin*
  Then will I lay my cheek   *approving of their love*
To his, and tell about our love,   *and devotion to each*
  Not once abashed or weak: *other and offering to*
And the dear Mother will approve   *grant a request*
  My pride, and let me speak.   120

"Herself shall bring us, hand in hand,
  To Him round whom all souls
Kneel, the clear-ranged unnumbered heads
  Bowed with their aureoles:
And angels meeting us shall sing
  To their citherns and citoles.

"There will I ask of Christ the Lord
   Thus much for him and me:—
Only to live as once on earth
   With Love,—only to be,
As then awhile, for ever now
   Together, I and he."

*she imagining meeting
with Christ and
asking a request of
him*

130

She gazed and listened and then said,
   Less sad of speech than mild,—
"All this is when he comes." She ceased.
   The light thrilled towards her, fill'd
With angels in strong level flight.
   Her eyes prayed, and she smil'd.

(I saw her smile.) But soon their path
   Was vague in distant spheres:
And then she cast her arms along
   The golden barriers,
And laid her face between her hands,
   And wept. (I heard her tears.)

140

(1847 *f.*)*

MY SISTER'S SLEEP

She fell asleep on Christmas Eve.
   At length the long-ungranted shade
   Of weary eyelids overweigh'd
The pain nought else might yet relieve.

Our mother, who had leaned all day
   Over the bed from chime to chime,
   Then raised herself for the first time,
And as she sat her down, did pray.

* Dates in italic type refer to the date or approximate date of com-
position; those dates that are not italic refer to the date of publication.

Her little work-table was spread
   With work to finish. For the glare   *10*
   Made by her candle, she had care
To work some distance from the bed.

Without, there was a cold moon up,
   Of winter radiance sheer and thin;
   The hollow halo it was in
Was like an icy crystal cup.

Through the small room, with subtle sound
   Of flame, by vents the fireshine drove
   And reddened. In its dim alcove
The mirror shed a clearness round.   *20*

I had been sitting up some nights,
   And my tired mind felt weak and blank;
   Like a sharp strengthening wine it drank
The stillness and the broken lights.

Twelve struck. That sound, by dwindling years
   Heard in each hour, crept off; and then
   The ruffled silence spread again,
Like water that a pebble stirs.

Our mother rose from where she sat:
   Her needles, as she laid them down,   *30*
   Met lightly, and her silken gown
Settled: no other noise than that.

"Glory unto the Newly Born!"
   So, as said angels, she did say:
   Because we were in Christmas Day,
Though it would still be long till morn.

Just then in the room over us
   There was a pushing back of chairs,
   As some who had sat unawares
So late, now heard the hour, and rose.   *40*

With anxious softly-stepping haste
    Our mother went where Margaret lay,
    Fearing the sounds o'erhead—should they
Have broken her long watched-for rest!

She stooped an instant, calm, and turned;
    But suddenly turned back again;
    And all her features seemed in pain
With woe, and her eyes gazed and yearned.

For my part, I but hid my face,
    And held my breath, and spoke no word: 50
    There was none spoken; but I heard
The silence for a little space.

Our mother bowed herself and wept:
    And both my arms fell, and I said,
    "God knows I knew that she was dead."
And there, all white, my sister slept.

Then kneeling, upon Christmas morn
    A little after twelve o'clock,
    We said, ere the first quarter struck,
"Christ's blessing on the newly born!"   60

                                        (1847 f.)

THE PORTRAIT

This is her picture as she was:
    It seems a thing to wonder on,
As though mine image in the glass
    Should tarry when myself am gone.
I gaze until she seems to stir,—
Until mine eyes almost aver
    That now, even now, the sweet lips part
    To breathe the words of the sweet heart:—
And yet the earth is over her.

Alas! even such the thin-drawn ray   *10*
   That makes the prison-depths more rude,—
The drip of water night and day
   Giving a tongue to solitude.
Yet only this, of love's whole prize,
Remains; save what in mournful guise
   Takes counsel with my soul alone,—
   Save what is secret and unknown,
Below the earth, above the skies.

In painting her I shrined her face
   'Mid mystic trees, where light falls in   *20*
Hardly at all; a covert place
   Where you might think to find a din
Of doubtful talk, and a live flame
Wandering, and many a shape whose name
   Not itself knoweth, and old dew,
   And your own footsteps meeting you,
And all things going as they came.

A deep dim wood; and there she stands
   As in that wood that day: for so
Was the still movement of her hands   *30*
   And such the pure line's gracious flow.
And passing fair the type must seem,
Unknown the presence and the dream.
   'Tis she: though of herself, alas!
   Less than her shadow on the grass
Or than her image in the stream.

That day we met there, I and she
   One with the other all alone;
And we were blithe; yet memory
   Saddens those hours, as when the moon   *40*
Looks upon daylight. And with her
I stooped to drink the spring-water,
   Athirst where other waters sprang:
   And where the echo is, she sang,—
My soul another echo there.

But when that hour my soul won strength
  For words whose silence wastes and kills,
Dull raindrops smote us, and at length
  Thundered the heat within the hills.
That eve I spoke those words again   *50*
Beside the pelted window-pane;
  And there she hearkened what I said,
  With under-glances that surveyed
The empty pastures blind with rain.

Next day the memories of these things,
  Like leaves through which a bird has flown,
Still vibrated with Love's warm wings;
  Till I must make them all my own
And paint this picture. So, 'twixt ease
Of talk and sweet long silences,   *60*
  She stood among the plants in bloom
  At windows of a summer room,
To feign the shadow of the trees.

And as I wrought, while all above
  And all around was fragrant air,
In the sick burthen of my love
  It seemed each sun-thrilled blossom there
Beat like a heart among the leaves.
O heart that never beats nor heaves,
  In that one darkness lying still,   *70*
  What now to thee my love's great will
Or the fine web the sunshine weaves?

For now doth daylight disavow
  Those days—nought left to see or hear.
Only in solemn whispers now
  At night-time these things reach mine ear;
When the leaf-shadows at a breath
Shrink in the road, and all the heath,
  Forest and water, far and wide,
  In limpid starlight glorified,   *80*
Lie like the mystery of death.

Last night at last I could have slept,
   And yet delayed my sleep till dawn,
Still wandering. Then it was I wept:
   For unawares I came upon
Those glades where once she walked with me,
And as I stood there suddenly,
   All wan with traversing the night,
   Upon the desolate verge of light
Yearned loud the iron-bosomed sea.   90

Even so, where Heaven holds breath and hears
   The beating heart of Love's own breast,—
Where round the secret of all spheres
   All angels lay their wings to rest,—
How shall my soul stand rapt and awed,
When, by the new birth borne abroad
   Throughout the music of the suns,
   It enters in her soul at once
And knows the silence there for God!

Here with her face doth memory sit   100
   Meanwhile, and wait the day's decline,
Till other eyes shall look from it,
   Eyes of the spirit's Palestine,
Even than the old gaze tenderer:
While hopes and aims long lost with her
   Stand round her image side by side,
   Like tombs of pilgrims that have died
About the Holy Sepulchre.

                                        (*1847 †.*)

AVE

Mother of the Fair Delight,
Thou handmaid perfect in God's sight,
Now sitting fourth beside the Three,
Thyself a woman-Trinity,—
Being a daughter born to God,

Mother of Christ from stall to rood,
And wife unto the Holy Ghost:—
Oh when our need is uttermost,
Think that to such as death may strike
Thou once wert sister sisterlike!   10
Thou headstone of humanity,
Groundstone of the great Mystery,
Fashioned like us, yet more than we!

Mind'st thou not (when June's heavy breath
Warmed the long days in Nazareth,)
That eve thou didst go forth to give
Thy flowers some drink that they might live
One faint night more amid the sands?
Far off the trees were as pale wands
Against the fervid sky: the sea   20
Sighed further off eternally
As human sorrow sighs in sleep.
Then suddenly the awe grew deep,
As of a day to which all days
Were footsteps in God's secret ways:
Until a folding sense, like prayer,
Which is, as God is, everywhere,
Gathered about thee; and a voice
Spake to thee without any noise,
Being of the silence:—"Hail," it said,   30
"Thou that art highly favourèd;
The Lord is with thee here and now;
Blessed among all women thou."

Ah! knew'st thou of the end, when first
That Babe was on thy bosom nurs'd?—
Or when He tottered round thy knee
Did thy great sorrow dawn on thee?—
And through His boyhood, year by year
Eating with Him the Passover,
Didst thou discern confusedly   40
That holier sacrament, when He,
The bitter cup about to quaff,

Should break the bread and eat thereof?—
Or came not yet the knowledge, even
Till on some day forecast in Heaven
His feet passed through thy door to press
Upon His Father's business?—
Or still was God's high secret kept?

   Nay, but I think the whisper crept
Like growth through childhood. Work and play,   *50*
Things common to the course of day,
Awed thee with meanings unfulfill'd;
And all through girlhood, something still'd
Thy senses like the birth of light,
When thou hast trimmed thy lamp at night
Or washed thy garments in the stream;
To whose white bed had come the dream
That He was thine and thou wast His
Who feeds among the field-lilies.
O solemn shadow of the end   *60*
In that wise spirit long contain'd!
O awful end! and those unsaid
Long years when It was Finishèd!

   Mind'st thou not (when the twilight gone
Left darkness in the house of John,)
Between the naked window-bars
That spacious vigil of the stars?—
For thou, a watcher even as they,
Wouldst rise from where throughout the day
Thou wroughtest raiment for His poor;   *70*
And, finding the fixed terms endure
Of day and night which never brought
Sounds of His coming chariot,
Wouldst lift through cloud-waste unexplor'd
Those eyes which said, "How long, O Lord?"
Then that disciple whom He loved,
Well heeding, haply would be moved
To ask thy blessing in His name;

And that one thought in both, the same
Though silent, then would clasp ye round   *80*
To weep together,—tears long bound,
Sick tears of patience, dumb and slow.
Yet, "Surely I come quickly,"—so
He said, from life and death gone home.
Amen: even so, Lord Jesus, come!

But oh! what human tongue can speak
That day when Michael came* to break
From the tir'd spirit, like a veil,
Its covenant with Gabriel
Endured at length unto the end?   *90*
What human thought can apprehend
That mystery of motherhood
When thy Beloved at length renew'd
The sweet communion severèd,—
His left hand underneath thine head
And His right hand embracing thee?—
Lo! He was thine, and this is He!

Soul, is it Faith, or Love, or Hope,
That lets me see her standing up
Where the light of the Throne is bright?   *100*
Unto the left, unto the right,
The cherubim, succinct, conjoint,
Float inward to a golden point,
And from between the seraphim
The glory issues for a hymn.
O Mary Mother, be not loth
To listen,—thou whom the stars clothe,
Who seëst and mayst not be seen!
Hear us at last, O Mary Queen!
Into our shadow bend thy face,   *110*
Bowing thee from the secret place
O Mary Virgin, full of grace!

(1847 ƒ.)

* A Church legend of the Blessed Virgin's death. [Rossetti's note]

AUTUMN SONG

Know'st thou not at the fall of the leaf
How the heart feels a languid grief
    Laid on it for a covering,
    And how sleep seems a goodly thing
In Autumn at the fall of the leaf?

And how the swift beat of the brain
Falters because it is in vain,
    In Autumn at the fall of the leaf
    Knowest thou not? and how the chief
Of joys seems—not to suffer pain?   *10*

Know'st thou not at the fall of the leaf
How the soul feels like a dried sheaf
    Bound up at length for harvesting,
    And how death seems a comely thing
In Autumn at the fall of the leaf?

                          (1848)

MARY'S GIRLHOOD

(For a Picture)

I

This is that blessed Mary, pre-elect
  God's Virgin. Gone is a great while, and she
  Dwelt young in Nazareth of Galilee.
Unto God's will she brought devout respect,
Profound simplicity of intellect,
  And supreme patience. From her mother's knee
  Faithful and hopeful; wise in charity;
Strong in grave peace; in pity circumspect.

So held she through her girlhood; as it were
  An angel-watered lily, that near God   *10*
    Grows and is quiet. Till, one dawn at home

She woke in her white bed, and had no fear
  At all,—yet wept till sunshine, and felt awed:
    Because the fulness of the time was come.

I I

These are the symbols. On that cloth of red
  I' the centre is the Tripoint: perfect each,
  Except the second of its points, to teach
That Christ is not yet born. The books—whose head
Is golden Charity, as Paul hath said—
  Those virtues are wherein the soul is rich: 20
  Therefore on them the lily standeth, which
Is Innocence, being interpreted.

The seven-thorn'd briar and the palm seven-leaved
  Are her great sorrow and her great reward.
    Until the end be full, the Holy One
Abides without. She soon shall have achieved
  Her perfect purity: yea, God the Lord
    Shall soon vouchsafe His Son to be her Son.

                            (*1848*)

ON REFUSAL OF AID BETWEEN NATIONS

Not that the earth is changing, O my God!
  Nor that the seasons totter in their walk,—
  Not that the virulent ill of act and talk
Seethes ever as a winepress ever trod,—
Not therefore are we certain that the rod
  Weighs in thine hand to smite thy world; though now
  Beneath thine hand so many nations bow,
So many kings:—not therefore, O my God!—

But because Man is parcelled out in men
  To-day; because, for any wrongful blow   10
    No man not stricken asks, "I would be told

Why thou dost thus;" but his heart whispers then,
  "He is he, I am I." By this we know
    That our earth falls asunder, being old.

(1849)

PLACE DE LA BASTILLE, PARIS

How dear the sky has been above this place!
  Small treasures of this sky that we see here
  Seen weak through prison-bars from year to year;
Eyed with a painful prayer upon God's grace
To save, and tears that stayed along the face
  Lifted at sunset. Yea, how passing dear,
  Those nights when through the bars a wind left clear
The heaven, and moonlight soothed the limpid space!

So was it, till one night the secret kept
  Safe in low vault and stealthy corridor   *10*
    Was blown abroad on gospel-tongues of flame.
  O ways of God, mysterious evermore!
How many on this spot have cursed and wept
    That all might stand here now and own Thy Name.

(1849)

FOR A VENETIAN PASTORAL

BY GIORGIONE

(In the Louvre)

Water, for anguish of the solstice:—nay,
  But dip the vessel slowly,—nay, but lean
  And hark how at its verge the wave sighs in
Reluctant. Hush! beyond all depth away
The heat lies silent at the brink of day:
  Now the hand trails upon the viol-string
  That sobs, and the brown faces cease to sing,

Sad with the whole of pleasure. Whither stray
Her eyes now, from whose mouth the slim pipes creep
    And leave it pouting, while the shadowed grass   *10*
        Is cool against her naked side? Let be:—
Say nothing now unto her lest she weep,
    Nor name this ever. Be it as it was,—
        Life touching lips with Immortality.

                                (1849)

WORLD'S WORTH

'Tis of the Father Hilary.
    He strove, but could not pray; so took
    The steep-coiled stair, where his feet shook
A sad blind echo. Ever up
    He toiled. 'Twas a sick sway of air
    That autumn noon within the stair,
As dizzy as a turning cup.
    His brain benumbed him, void and thin;
    He shut his eyes and felt it spin;
    The obscure deafness hemmed him in.   *10*
He said: "O world, what world for me?"

He leaned unto the balcony
    Where the chime keeps the night and day;
    It hurt his brain, he could not pray.
He had his face upon the stone:
    Deep 'twixt the narrow shafts, his eye
    Passed all the roofs to the stark sky,
Swept with no wing, with wind alone.
    Close to his feet the sky did shake
    With wind in pools that the rains make: *20*
    The ripple set his eyes to ache.
He said: "O world, what world for me?"

He stood within the mystery
    Girding God's blessed Eucharist:
    The organ and the chaunt had ceas'd.

The last words paused against his ear
   Said from the altar: drawn round him
   The gathering rest was dumb and dim.
And now the sacring-bell rang clear
   And ceased; and all was awe,—the breath   *30*
   Of God in man that warranteth
   The inmost utmost things of faith.
He said: "O God, my world in Thee!"

                       (*1849*)

THE CARD-DEALER

Could you not drink her gaze like wine?
   Yet though its splendour swoon
Into the silence languidly
   As a tune into a tune,
Those eyes unravel the coiled night
   And know the stars at noon.

The gold that's heaped beside her hand,
   In truth rich prize it were;
And rich the dreams that wreathe her brows
   With magic stillness there;   *10*
And he were rich who should unwind
   That woven golden hair.

Around her, where she sits, the dance
   Now breathes its eager heat;
And not more lightly or more true
   Fall there the dancers' feet
Than fall her cards on the bright board
   As 'twere a heart that beat.

Her fingers let them softly through,
   Smooth polished silent things;   *20*
And each one as it falls reflects
   In swift light-shadowings,

Blood-red and purple, green and blue,
   The great eyes of her rings.

Whom plays she with? With thee, who lov'st
   Those gems upon her hand;
With me, who search her secret brows;
   With all men, bless'd or bann'd.
We play together, she and we,
   Within a vain strange land: *30*

A land without any order,—
   Day even as night, (one saith,)—
Where who lieth down ariseth not
   Nor the sleeper awakeneth;
A land of darkness as darkness itself
   And of the shadow of death.

What be her cards, you ask? Even these:—
   The heart, that doth but crave
More, having fed; the diamond,
   Skilled to make base seem brave;   *40*
The club, for smiting in the dark;
   The spade, to dig a grave.

And do you ask what game she plays?
   With me 'tis lost or won;
With thee it is playing still; with him
   It is not well begun;
But 'tis a game she plays with all
   Beneath the sway o' the sun.

Thou seest the card that falls,—she knows
   The card that followeth: *50*
Her game in thy tongue is called Life,
   As ebbs thy daily breath:
When she shall speak, thou'lt learn her tongue
   And know she calls it Death.

                    (1849)

A LAST CONFESSION

(*Regno Lombardo-Veneto, 1848*)*

Our Lombard country-girls along the coast
Wear daggers in their garters: for they know
That they might hate another girl to death
Or meet a German lover. Such a knife
I bought her, with a hilt of horn and pearl.

Father, you cannot know of all my thoughts
That day in going to meet her,—that last day
For the last time, she said;—of all the love
And all the hopeless hope that she might change
And go back with me. Ah! and everywhere,   *10*
At places we both knew along the road,
Some fresh shape of herself as once she was
Grew present at my side; until it seemed—
So close they gathered round me—they would all
Be with me when I reached the spot at last,
To plead my cause with her against herself
So changed. O Father, if you knew all this
You cannot know, then you would know too, Father.
And only then, if God can pardon me.
What can be told I'll tell, if you will hear.   *20*

I passed a village-fair upon my road,
And thought, being empty-handed, I would take
Some little present: such might prove, I said,
Either a pledge between us, or (God help me!)
A parting gift. And there it was I bought
The knife I spoke of, such as women wear.

That day, some three hours afterwards, I found
For certain, it must be a parting gift.
And, standing silent now at last, I looked

* In the duchies of Lombardy and Venetia the Italians in 1848 were
in revolt against their Austrian overlords.

Into her scornful face; and heard the sea   30
Still trying hard to din into my ears
Some speech it knew which still might change her heart,
If only it could make me understand.
One moment thus. Another, and her face
Seemed further off than the last line of sea,
So that I thought, if now she were to speak
I could not hear her. Then again I knew
All, as we stood together on the sand
At Iglio, in the first thin shade o' the hills.

   "Take it," I said, and held it out to her,   40
While the hilt glanced within my trembling hold;
"Take it and keep it for my sake," I said.
Her neck unbent not, neither did her eyes
Move, nor her foot left beating of the sand;
Only she put it by from her and laughed.

   Father, you hear my speech and not her laugh;
But God heard that. Will God remember all?

   It was another laugh than the sweet sound
Which rose from her sweet childish heart, that day
Eleven years before, when first I found her   50
Alone upon the hill-side; and her curls
Shook down in the warm grass as she looked up
Out of her curls in my eyes bent to hers.
She might have served a painter to pourtray
That heavenly child which in the latter days
Shall walk between the lion and the lamb.
I had been for nights in hiding, worn and sick
And hardly fed; and so her words at first
Seemed fitful like the talking of the trees
And voices in the air that knew my name.   60
And I remember that I sat me down
Upon the slope with her, and thought the world
Must be all over or had never been,
We seemed there so alone. And soon she told me

Her parents both were gone away from her.
I thought perhaps she meant that they had died;
But when I asked her this, she looked again
Into my face and said that yestereve
They kissed her long, and wept and made her weep,
And gave her all the bread they had with them,   70
And then had gone together up the hill
Where we were sitting now, and had walked on
Into the great red light; "and so," she said,
"I have come up here too; and when this evening
They step out of the light as they stepped in,
I shall be here to kiss them." And she laughed.

   Then I bethought me suddenly of the famine;
And how the church-steps throughout all the town,
When last I had been there a month ago,
Swarmed with starved folk; and how the bread was
     weighed   80
By Austrians armed; and women that I knew
For wives and mothers walked the public street,
Saying aloud that if their husbands feared
To snatch the children's food, themselves would stay
Till they had earned it there. So then this child
Was piteous to me; for all told me then
Her parents must have left her to God's chance,
To man's or to the Church's charity,
Because of the great famine, rather than
To watch her growing thin between their knees.   90
With that, God took my mother's voice and spoke,
And sights and sounds came back and things long since,
And all my childhood found me on the hills;
And so I took her with me.
                 I was young,
Scarce man then, Father: but the cause which gave
The wounds I die of now had brought me then
Some wounds already; and I lived alone,
As any hiding hunted man must live.
It was no easy thing to keep a child
In safety; for herself it was not safe,   100

And doubled my own danger: but I knew
That God would help me.
                          Yet a little while
Pardon me, Father, if I pause. I think
I have been speaking to you of some matters
There was no need to speak of, have I not?
You do not know how clearly those things stood
Within my mind, which I have spoken of,
Nor how they strove for utterance. Life all past
Is like the sky when the sun sets in it,
Clearest where furthest off.
                          I told you how   110
She scorned my parting gift and laughed. And yet
A woman's laugh's another thing sometimes:
I think they laugh in Heaven. I know last night
I dreamed I saw into the garden of God,
Where women walked whose painted images
I have seen with candles round them in the church.
They bent this way and that, one to another,
Playing: and over the long golden hair
Of each there floated like a ring of fire
Which when she stooped stooped with her, and when she
          rose   120
Rose with her. Then a breeze flew in among them,
As if a window had been opened in heaven
For God to give His blessing from, before
This world of ours should set; (for in my dream
I thought our world was setting, and the sun
Flared, a spent taper;) and beneath that gust
The rings of light quivered like forest-leaves.
Then all the blessed maidens who were there
Stood up together, as it were a voice
That called them; and they threw their tresses back,   130
And smote their palms, and all laughed up at once,
For the strong heavenly joy they had in them
To hear God bless the world. Wherewith I woke:
And looking round, I saw as usual
That she was standing there with her long locks
Pressed to her side; and her laugh ended theirs.

For always when I see her now, she laughs.
And yet her childish laughter haunts me too,
The life of this dead terror; as in days
When she, a child, dwelt with me. I must tell   *140*
Something of those days yet before the end.

I brought her from the city—one such day
When she was still a merry loving child,—
The earliest gift I mind my giving her;
A little image of a flying Love
Made of our coloured glass-ware, in his hands
A dart of gilded metal and a torch.
And him she kissed and me, and fain would know
Why were his poor eyes blindfold, why the wings
And why the arrow. What I knew I told   *150*
Of Venus and of Cupid,—strange old tales.
And when she heard that he could rule the loves
Of men and women, still she shook her head
And wondered; and, "Nay, nay," she murmured still,
"So strong, and he a younger child than I!"
And then she'd have me fix him on the wall
Fronting her little bed; and then again
She needs must fix him there herself, because
I gave him to her and she loved him so,
And he should make her love me better yet,   *16‹›*
If women loved the more, the more they grew.
But the fit place upon the wall was high
For her, and so I held her in my arms:
And each time that the heavy pruning-hook
I gave her for a hammer slipped away
As it would often, still she laughed and laughed
And kissed and kissed me. But amid her mirth,
Just as she hung the image on the nail,
It slipped and all its fragments strewed the ground:
And as it fell she screamed, for in her hand   *170*
The dart had entered deeply and drawn blood.
And so her laughter turned to tears: and "Oh!"
I said, the while I bandaged the small hand,—
"That I should be the first to make you bleed,

Who love and love and love you!"—kissing still
The fingers till I got her safe to bed.
And still she sobbed,—"not for the pain at all,"
She said, "but for the Love, the poor good Love
You gave me." So she cried herself to sleep.

 Another later thing comes back to me.   *180*
'Twas in those hardest foulest days of all,
When still from his shut palace, sitting clean
Above the splash of blood, old Metternich
(May his soul die, and never-dying worms
Feast on its pain for ever!) used to thin
His year's doomed hundreds daintily, each month
Thirties and fifties. This time, as I think,
Was when his thrift forbad the poor to take
That evil brackish salt which the dry rocks
Keep all through winter when the sea draws in.   *190*
The first I heard of it was a chance shot
In the street here and there, and on the stones
A stumbling clatter as of horse hemmed round.
Then, when she saw me hurry out of doors,
My gun slung at my shoulder and my knife
Stuck in my girdle, she smoothed down my hair
And laughed to see me look so brave, and leaped
Up to my neck and kissed me. She was still
A child; and yet that kiss was on my lips
So hot all day where the smoke shut us in.   *200*

 For now, being always with her, the first love
I had—the father's, brother's love—was changed,
I think, in somewise; like a holy thought
Which is a prayer before one knows of it.
The first time I perceived this, I remember,
Was once when after hunting I came home
Weary, and she brought food and fruit for me,
And sat down at my feet upon the floor
Leaning against my side. But when I felt
Her sweet head reach from that low seat of hers   *210*

So high as to be laid upon my heart,
I turned and looked upon my darling there
And marked for the first time how tall she was;
And my heart beat with so much violence
Under her cheek, I thought she could not choose
But wonder at it soon and ask me why;
And so I bade her rise and eat with me.
And when, remembering all and counting back
The time, I made out fourteen years for her
And told her so, she gazed at me with eyes   220
As of the sky and sea on a grey day,
And drew her long hands through her hair, and asked me
If she was not a woman; and then laughed:
And as she stooped in laughing, I could see
Beneath the growing throat the breasts half-globed
Like folded lilies deepset in the stream.

    Yes, let me think of her as then; for so
Her image, Father, is not like the sights
Which come when you are gone. She had a mouth
Made to bring death to life,—the underlip   230
Sucked in, as if it strove to kiss itself.
Her face was pearly pale, as when one stoops
Over wan water; and the dark crisped hair
And the hair's shadow made it paler still:—
Deep-serried locks, the dimness of the cloud
Where the moon's gaze is set in eddying gloom.
Her body bore her neck as the tree's stem
Bears the top branch; and as the branch sustains
The flower of the year's pride, her high neck bore
That face made wonderful with night and day.   240
Her voice was swift, yet ever the last words
Fell lingeringly; and rounded finger-tips
She had, that clung a little where they touched
And then were gone o' the instant. Her great eyes,
That sometimes turned half dizzily beneath
The passionate lids, as faint, when she would speak,
Had also in them hidden springs of mirth,
Which under the dark lashes evermore

Shook to her laugh, as when a bird flies low
Between the water and the willow-leaves,   250
And the shade quivers till he wins the light.

  I was a moody comrade to her then,
For all the love I bore her. Italy,
The weeping desolate mother, long has claimed
Her sons' strong arms to lean on, and their hands
To lop the poisonous thicket from her path,
Cleaving her way to light. And from her need
Had grown the fashion of my whole poor life
Which I was proud to yield her, as my father
Had yielded his. And this had come to be   260
A game to play, a love to clasp, a hate
To wreak, all things together that a man
Needs for his blood to ripen; till at times
All else seemed shadows, and I wondered still
To see such life pass muster and be deemed
Time's bodily substance. In those hours, no doubt,
To the young girl my eyes were like my soul,—
Dark wells of death-in-life that yearned for day.
And though she ruled me always, I remember
That once when I was thus and she still kept   270
Leaping about the place and laughing, I
Did almost chide her; whereupon she knelt
And putting her two hands into my breast
Sang me a song. Are these tears in my eyes?
'Tis long since I have wept for anything.
I thought that song forgotten out of mind;
And now, just as I spoke of it, it came
All back. It is but a rude thing, ill rhymed,
Such as a blind man chaunts and his dog hears
Holding the platter, when the children run   280
To merrier sport and leave him. Thus it goes:—

    La bella donna   [She wept, sweet lady,*
    Piangendo disse: And said in weeping:

    * Rossetti's translation of the song.

"Come son fisse
Le stelle in cielo!
Quel fiato anelo
Dello stanco sole,
Quanto m' assonna!
E la luna, macchiata
Come uno specchio   *290*
Logoro e vecchio,—
Faccia affannata,
Che cosa vuole?

"Che stelle, luna, e sole,
Ciascun m' annoja
E m' annojano insieme;
Non me ne preme
Nè ci prendo gioja.
E veramente,
Che le spalle sien franche
E le braccia bianche   *301*

E il seno caldo e tondo.
Non me fa niente.
Che cosa al mondo
Posso più far di questi
Se non piacciono a te, come
        dicesti?"

La donna rise
E riprese ridendo:—
"Questa mano che prendo
E dunque mia?   *310*
Tu m' ami dunque?
Dimmelo ancora,
Non in modo qualunque,
Ma le parole

"What spell is keeping
The stars so steady?
Why does the power
Of the sun's noon-hour
To sleep so move me?
And the moon in heaven,
Stained where she passes
As a worn-out glass is,—
Wearily driven,
Why walks she above me?

"Stars, moon, and sun too,
I'm tired of either
And all together!
Whom speak they unto
That I should listen?
For very surely,
Though my arms and shoul-
        ders
Dazzle beholders,
And my eyes glisten,
All's nothing purely!
What are words said for
At all about them,
If he they are made for
Can do without them?"

She laughed, sweet lady,
And said in laughing:
"His hand clings half in
My own already!
Oh! do you love me?
Oh! speak of passion
In no new fashion,
No loud inveighings,

Belle e precise   But the old sayings
Che dicesti pria.   You once said of me.

'Siccome suole   "You said: 'As summer
La state talora   318   Through boughs grown
                            brittle,

(Dicesti) *un qualche istante*   Comes back a little
Tornare innanzi inverno,   Ere frosts benumb her,—
Così tu fai ch' io scerno   So bring'st thou to me
Le foglie tutte quante,   All leaves and flowers,
Ben ch' io certo tenessi   Though autumn's gloomy
Per passato l'autunno.   To-day in the bowers.'

"Eccolo il mio alunno!   "Oh! does he love me,
Io debbo insegnargli   When my voice teaches
Quei cari detti istessi   The very speeches
Ch' ei mi disse una volta!   He then spoke of me?
Oime! Che cosa dargli,"   Alas! what flavour
(Ma ridea piano piano   330   Still with me lingers?"
Dei baci in sulla mano,)   (But she laughed as my kisses
"Ch' ei non m'abbio da   Glowed in her fingers
      lungo tempo tolta?"   With love's old blisses.)
                               "Oh! what one favour
                               Remains to woo him,
                               Whose whole poor savour
                               Belongs not to him?"]

    That I should sing upon this bed!—with you
To listen, and such words still left to say!
Yet was it I that sang? The voice seemed hers,
As on the very day she sang to me;
When, having done, she took out of my hand
Something that I had played with all the while
And laid it down beyond my reach; and so
Turning my face round till it fronted hers,—   340
"Weeping or laughing, which was best?" she said.

But these are foolish tales. How should I show
The heart that glowed then with love's heat, each day
More and more brightly?—when for long years now
The very flame that flew about the heart,
And gave it fiery wings, has come to be
The lapping blaze of hell's environment
Whose tongues all bid the molten heart despair.

Yet one more thing comes back on me to-night
Which I may tell you: for it bore my soul   350
Dread firstlings of the brood that rend it now.
It chanced that in our last year's wanderings
We dwelt at Monza, far away from home,
If home we had: and in the Duomo there
I sometimes entered with her when she prayed.
An image of Our Lady stands there, wrought
In marble by some great Italian hand
In the great days when she and Italy
Sat on one throne together: and to her
And to none else my loved one told her heart.   360
She was a woman then; and as she knelt,—
Her sweet brow in the sweet brow's shadow there,—
They seemed two kindred forms whereby our land
(Whose work still serves the world for miracle)
Made manifest herself in womanhood.
Father, the day I speak of was the first
For weeks that I had borne her company
Into the Duomo; and those weeks had been
Much troubled, for then first the glimpses came
Of some impenetrable restlessness   370
Growing in her to make her changed and cold.
And as we entered there that day, I bent
My eyes on the fair Image, and I said
Within my heart, "Oh turn her heart to me!"
And so I left her to her prayers, and went
To gaze upon the pride of Monza's shrine,
Where in the sacristy the light still falls
Upon the Iron Crown of Italy,

On whose crowned heads the day has closed, nor yet
The daybreak gilds another head to crown.   380
But coming back, I wondered when I saw
That the sweet Lady of her prayers now stood
Alone without her; until further off,
Before some new Madonna gaily decked,
Tinselled and gewgawed, a slight German toy,
I saw her kneel, still praying. At my step
She rose, and side by side we left the church.
I was much moved, and sharply questioned her
Of her transferred devotion; but she seemed
Stubborn and heedless; till she lightly laughed   390
And said: "The old Madonna? Aye indeed,
She had my old thoughts,—this one has my new."
Then silent to the soul I held my way:
And from the fountains of the public place
Unto the pigeon-haunted pinnacles,
Bright wings and water winnowed the bright air;
And stately with her laugh's subsiding smile
She went, with clear-swayed waist and towering neck
And hands held light before her; and the face
Which long had made a day in my life's night   400
Was night in day to me; as all men's eyes
Turned on her beauty, and she seemed to tread
Beyond my heart to the world made for her.

  Ah, there! my wounds will snatch my sense again:
The pain comes billowing on like a full cloud
Of thunder, and the flash that breaks from it
Leaves my brain burning. That's the wound he gave,
The Austrian whose white coat I still made match
With his white face, only the two grew red
As suits his trade. The devil makes them wear   410
White for a livery, that the blood may show
Braver that brings them to him. So he looks
Sheer o'er the field and knows his own at once.

  Give me a draught of water in that cup;
My voice feels thick; perhaps you do not hear;

But you *must* hear. If you mistake my words
And so absolve me, I am sure the blessing
Will burn my soul. If you mistake my words
And so absolve me, Father, the great sin
Is yours, not mine: mark this: your soul shall burn   420
With mine for it. I have seen pictures where
Souls burned with Latin shriekings in their mouths:
Shall my end be as theirs? Nay, but I know
'Tis you shall shriek in Latin. Some bell rings,
Rings through my brain: it strikes the hour in hell.

    You see I cannot, Father; I have tried,
But cannot, as you see. These twenty times
Beginning, I have come to the same point
And stopped. Beyond, there are but broken words
Which will not let you understand my tale.   430
It is that then we have her with us here,
As when she wrung her hair out in my dream
To-night, till all the darkness reeked of it.
Her hair is always wet, for she has kept
Its tresses wrapped about her side for years;
And when she wrung them round over the floor,
I heard the blood between her fingers hiss;
So that I sat up in my bed and screamed
Once and again; and once to once, she laughed.
Look that you turn not now,—she's at your back: 440
Gather your robe up, Father, and keep close,
Or she'll sit down on it and send you mad.

    At Iglio in the first thin shade o' the hills
The sand is black and red. The black was black
When what was spilt that day sank into it,
And the red scarcely darkened. There I stood
This night with her, and saw the sand the same.

             *   *   *   *   *   *

    What would you have me tell you? Father, Father,
How shall I make you know? You have not known

The dreadful soul of woman, who one day   450
Forgets the old and takes the new to heart,
Forgets what man remembers, and therewith
Forgets the man. Nor can I clearly tell
How the change happened between her and me.
Her eyes looked on me from an emptied heart
When most my heart was full of her; and still
In every corner of myself I sought
To find what service failed her; and no less
Than in the good time past, there all was hers.
What do you love? Your Heaven? Conceive it spread
For one first year of all eternity   461
All round you with all joys and gifts of God;
And then when most your soul is blent with it
And all yields song together,—then it stands
O' the sudden like a pool that once gave back
Your image, but now drowns it and is clear
Again,—or like a sun bewitched, that burns
Your shadow from you, and still shines in sight.
How could you bear it? Would you not cry out,
Among those eyes grown blind to you, those ears   470
That hear no more your voice you hear the same,—
"God! what is left but hell for company,
But hell, hell, hell?"—until the name so breathed
Whirled with hot wind and sucked you down in fire?
Even so I stood the day her empty heart
Left her place empty in our home, while yet
I knew not why she went nor where she went
Nor how to reach her: so I stood the day
When to my prayers at last one sight of her
Was granted, and I looked on heaven made pale   480
With scorn, and heard heaven mock me in that laugh.

    O sweet, long sweet! Was that some ghost of you,
Even as your ghost that haunts me now,—twin shapes
Of fear and hatred? May I find you yet
Mine when death wakes? Ah! be it even in flame,
We may have sweetness yet, if you but say
As once in childish sorrow: "Not my pain,

My pain was nothing: oh your poor poor love,
Your broken love!"
            My Father, have I not
Yet told you the last things of that last day   *490*
On which I went to meet her by the sea?
O God, O God! but I must tell you all.

   Midway upon my journey, when I stopped
To buy the dagger at the village fair,
I saw two cursed rats about the place
I knew for spies—blood-sellers both. That day
Was not yet over; for three hours to come
I prized my life: and so I looked around
For safety. A poor painted mountebank
Was playing tricks and shouting in a crowd.   *500*
I knew he must have heard my name, so I
Pushed past and whispered to him who I was,
And of my danger. Straight he hustled me
Into his booth, as it were in the trick,
And brought me out next minute with my face
All smeared in patches and a zany's gown;
And there I handed him his cups and balls
And swung the sand-bags round to clear the ring
For half an hour. The spies came once and looked;
And while they stopped, and made all sights and sounds
Sharp to my startled senses, I remember   *511*
A woman laughed above me. I looked up
And saw where a brown-shouldered harlot leaned
Half through a tavern window thick with vine.
Some man had come behind her in the room
And caught her by her arms, and she had turned
With that coarse empty laugh on him, as now
He munched her neck with kisses, while the vine
Crawled in her back.
           And three hours afterwards,
When she that I had run all risks to meet   *520*
Laughed as I told you, my life burned to death
Within me, for I thought it like the laugh
Heard at the fair. She had not left me long;

But all she might have changed to, or might change to,
(I know nought since—she never speaks a word—)
Seemed in that laugh. Have I not told you yet,
Not told you all this time what happened, Father,
When I had offered her the little knife,
And bade her keep it for my sake that loved her,
And she had laughed? Have I not told you yet?   530

   "Take it," I said to her the second time,
"Take it and keep it." And then came a fire
That burnt my hand; and then the fire was blood,
And sea and sky were blood and fire, and all
The day was one red blindness; till it seemed,
Within the whirling brain's eclipse, that she
Or I or all things bled or burned to death.
And then I found her laid against my feet
And knew that I had stabbed her, and saw still
Her look in falling. For she took the knife   540
Deep in her heart, even as I bade her then,
And fell; and her stiff bodice scooped the sand
Into her bosom.
         And she keeps it, see,
Do you not see she keeps it?—there, beneath
Wet fingers and wet tresses, in her heart.
For look you, when she stirs her hand, it shows
The little hilt of horn and pearl,—even such
A dagger as our women of the coast
Twist in their garters.
         Father, I have done:
And from her side she now unwinds the thick   550
Dark hair; all round her side it is wet through,
But, like the sand at Iglio, does not change.
Now you may see the dagger clearly. Father,
I have told all: tell me at once what hope
Can reach me still. For now she draws it out
Slowly, and only smiles as yet: look, Father,
She scarcely smiles: but I shall hear her laugh
Soon, when she shows the crimson steel to God.

                     (1849 ƒ.)

THE SEA-LIMITS

Consider the sea's listless chime:
   Time's self it is, made audible,—
   The murmur of the earth's own shell.
Secret continuance sublime
   Is the sea's end: our sight may pass
   No furlong further. Since time was,
This sound hath told the lapse of time.

No quiet, which is death's,—it hath
   The mournfulness of ancient life,
   Enduring always at dull strife.   10
As the world's heart of rest and wrath,
   Its painful pulse is in the sands.
   Last utterly, the whole sky stands,
Grey and not known, along its path.

Listen alone beside the sea,
   Listen alone among the woods;
   Those voices of twin solitudes
Shall have one sound alike to thee:
   Hark where the murmurs of thronged men
   Surge and sink back and surge again,—   20
Still the one voice of wave and tree.

Gather a shell from the strown beach
   And listen at its lips: they sigh
   The same desire and mystery,
The echo of the whole sea's speech.
   And all mankind is thus at heart
   Not anything but what thou art:
And Earth, Sea, Man, are all in each.

(1849 f.)

A YOUNG FIR-WOOD

These little firs to-day are things
   To clasp into a giant's cap,
   Or fans to suit his lady's lap.
From many winters many springs
   Shall cherish them in strength and sap
   Till they be marked upon the map,
A wood for the wind's wanderings.

All seed is in the sower's hands:
   And what at first was trained to spread
   Its shelter for some single head,—   *10*
Yea, even such fellowship of wands,—
   May hide the sunset, and the shade
   Of its great multitude be laid
Upon the earth and elder sands.

                         (*1850*)

THE MIRROR

She knew it not:—most perfect pain
   To learn: this too she knew not. Strife
      For me, calm hers, as from the first.
      'Twas but another bubble burst
   Upon the curdling draught of life,—
My silent patience mine again.

As who, of forms that crowd unknown
   Within a distant mirror's shade,
      Deems such an one himself, and makes
      Some sign—but when the image shakes   *10*
   No whit, he finds his thought betray'd,
And must seek elsewhere for his own.

                         (*1850*)

THE STAFF AND SCRIP

"Who rules these lands?" the Pilgrim said.
  "Stranger, Queen Blanchelys."
"And who has thus harried them?" he said.
  "It was Duke Luke did this:
      God's ban be his!"

The Pilgrim said: "Where is your house?
  I'll rest there, with your will."
"You've but to climb these blackened boughs
  And you'll see it over the hill,
      For it burns still."   10

"Which road, to seek your Queen?" said he.
  "Nay, nay, but with some wound
You'll fly back hither, it may be,
  And by your blood i' the ground
      My place be found."

"Friend, stay in peace. God keep your head,
  And mine, where I will go;
For He is here and there," he said.
  He passed the hill-side, slow,
      And stood below.   20

The Queen sat idle by her loom:
  She heard the arras stir,
And looked up sadly: through the room
  The sweetness sickened her
      Of musk and myrrh.

Her women, standing two and two,
  In silence combed the fleece.
The Pilgrim said, "Peace be with you,
  Lady;" and bent his knees.
      She answered, "Peace."   30

Her eyes were like the wave within;
   Like water-reeds the poise
Of her soft body, dainty thin;
   And like the water's noise
     Her plaintive voice.

For him, the stream had never well'd
   In desert tracks malign
So sweet; nor had he ever felt
   So faint in the sunshine
     Of Palestine.   40

Right so, he knew that he saw weep
   Each night through every dream
The Queen's own face, confused in sleep
   With visages supreme
     Not known to him.

"Lady," he said, "your lands lie burnt
   And waste: to meet your foe
All fear: this I have seen and learnt.
   Say that it shall be so,
     And I will go."   50

She gazed at him. "Your cause is just,
   For I have heard the same,"
He said: "God's strength shall be my trust.
   Fall it to good or grame,
     'Tis in His name."

"Sir, you are thanked. My cause is dead.
   Why should you toil to break
A grave, and fall therein?" she said.
   He did not pause but spake:
     "For my vow's sake."   60

"Can such vows be, Sir—to God's ear,
   Not to God's will?" "My vow

Remains: God heard me there as here,"
  He said with reverent brow,
    "Both then and now."

They gazed together, he and she,
  The minute while he spoke;
And when he ceased, she suddenly
  Looked round upon her folk
    As though she woke.   70

"Fight, Sir," she said; "my prayers in pain
  Shall be your fellowship."
He whispered one among her train,—
  "To-morrow bid her keep
    This staff and scrip."

She sent him a sharp sword, whose belt
  About his body there
As sweet as her own arms he felt.
  He kissed its blade, all bare,
    Instead of her.   80

She sent him a green banner wrought
  With one white lily stem,
To bind his lance with when he fought.
  He writ upon the same
    And kissed her name.

Weak now to them the voice o' the priest
  As any trance affords;
And when each anthem failed and ceas'd,
  It seemed that the last chords
    Still sang the words.   90

"Oh what is the light that shines so red?
  'Tis long since the sun set;"
Quoth the youngest to the eldest maid:
  " 'Twas dim but now, and yet
    The light is great."

Quoth the other: " 'Tis our sight is dazed
  That we see flame i' the air."
But the Queen held her brows and gazed,
  And said, "It is the glare
    Of torches there."   *100*

"Oh what are the sounds that rise and spread?
  All day it was so still;"
Quoth the youngest to the eldest maid:
  "Unto the furthest hill
    The air they fill."

Quoth the other: " 'Tis our sense is blurr'd
  With all the chants gone by."
But the Queen held her breath and heard,
  And said, "It is the cry
    Of Victory."   *110*

The first of all the rout was sound,
  The next were dust and flame,
And then the horses shook the ground:
  And in the thick of them
    A still band came.

She sent him a white shield, whereon
  She bade that he should trace
His will. He blent fair hues that shone,
  And in a golden space
    He kissed her face.   *120*

Born of the day that died, that eve
  Now dying sank to rest;
As he, in likewise taking leave,
  Once with a heaving breast
    Looked to the west.

And there the sunset skies unseal'd,
  Like lands he never knew,

Beyond to-morrow's battle-field
  Lay open out of view
    To ride into.   *130*

Next day till dark the women pray'd:
  Nor any might know there
How the fight went: the Queen has bade
  That there do come to her
    No messenger.

The Queen is pale, her maidens ail;
  And to the organ-tones
They sing but faintly, who sang well
  The matin-orisons,
    The lauds and nones.   *140*

Lo, Father, is thine ear inclin'd,
  And hath thine angel pass'd?
For these thy watchers now are blind
  With vigil, and at last
    Dizzy with fast.

"Oh what do ye bring out of the fight,
  Thus hid beneath these boughs?"
"Thy conquering guest returns to-night,
  And yet shall not carouse,
    Queen, in thy house."   *150*

"Uncover ye his face," she said.
  "O changed in little space!"
She cried, "O pale that was so red!
  O God, O God of grace!
    Cover his face."

His sword was broken in his hand
  Where he had kissed the blade.
"O soft steel that could not withstand!
  O my hard heart unstayed,
    That prayed and prayed!"   *160*

His bloodied banner crossed his mouth
  Where he had kissed her name.
"O east, and west, and north, and south,
  Fair flew my web, for shame,
    To guide Death's aim!"

The tints were shredded from his shield
  Where he had kissed her face.
"Oh, of all gifts that I could yield,
  Death only keeps its place,
    My gift and grace!"   *170*

Then stepped a damsel to her side,
  And spoke, and needs must weep:
"For his sake, lady, if he died,
  He prayed of thee to keep
    This staff and scrip."

That night they hung above her bed,
  Till morning wet with tears.
Year after year above her head
  Her bed his token wears,
    Five years, ten years.   *180*

That night the passion of her grief
  Shook them as there they hung.
Each year the wind that shed the leaf
  Shook them and in its tongue
    A message flung.

And once she woke with a clear mind
  That letters writ to calm
Her soul lay in the scrip; to find
  Only a torpid balm
    And dust of palm.   *190*

They shook far off with palace sport
  When joust and dance were rife;

And the hunt shook them from the court;
　For hers, in peace or strife,
　　　Was a Queen's life.

A Queen's death now: as now they shake
　To gusts in chapel dim,—
Hung where she sleeps, not seen to wake,
　(Carved lovely white and slim),
　　　With them by him.   *200*

Stand up to-day, still armed, with her,
　Good knight, before His brow
Who then as now was here and there,
　Who had in mind thy vow
　　　Then even as now.

The lists are set in Heaven to-day,
　The bright pavilions shine;
Fair hangs thy shield, and none gainsay
　The trumpets sound in sign
　　　That she is thine.   *210*

Not tithed with days' and years' decease
　He pays thy wage He owed,
But with imperishable peace
　Here in His own abode,
　　　Thy jealous God.

　　　　　　　　　　　　　　(1851–1852)

A MATCH WITH THE MOON

Weary already, weary miles to-night
　I walked for bed: and so, to get some ease,
　I dogged the flying moon with similes.
And like a wisp she doubled on my sight
In ponds; and caught in tree-tops like a kite;
　And in a globe of film all liquorish
　Swam full-faced like a silly silver fish;—

Last like a bubble shot the welkin's height
Where my road turned, and got behind me, and sent
   My wizened shadow craning round at me,   *10*
   And jeered, "So, step the measure,—one two three!"—
And if I faced on her, looked innocent.
But just at parting, halfway down a dell,
She kissed me for good-night. So you'll not tell.

                                                      (1854)

SUDDEN LIGHT

    I have been here before,
        But when or how I cannot tell:
    I know the grass beyond the door,
        The sweet keen smell,
The sighing sound, the lights around the shore.

    You have been mine before,—
        How long ago I may not know:
    But just when at that swallow's soar
        Your neck turned so,
Some veil did fall,—I knew it all of yore.   *10*

    Has this been thus before?
        And shall not thus time's eddying flight
    Still with our lives our love restore
        In death's despite,
And day and night yield one delight once more?

                                                      (1854)

ON THE *VITA NUOVA* OF DANTE

As he that loves oft looks on the dear form
   And guesses how it grew to womanhood,
   And gladly would have watched the beauties bud
And the mild fire of precious life wax warm:

So I, long bound within the threefold charm
   Of Dante's love sublimed to heavenly mood,
   Had marvelled, touching his Beatitude,
How grew such presence from man's shameful swarm.

At length within this book I found portrayed
   Newborn that Paradisal Love of his,   *10*
And simple like a child; with whose clear aid
   I understood. To such a child as this,
Christ, charging well His chosen ones, forbade
   Offence: "for lo! of such my kingdom is."

                                            (1852)

PENUMBRA

I did not look upon her eyes,
(Though scarcely seen, with no surprise,
'Mid many eyes a single look,)
Because they should not gaze rebuke,
At night, from stars in sky and brook.

I did not take her by the hand,
(Though little was to understand
From touch of hand all friends might take,)
Because it should not prove a flake
Burnt in my palm to boil and ache.   *10*

I did not listen to her voice,
(Though none had noted, where at choice
All might rejoice in listening,)
Because no such a thing should cling
In the wood's moan at evening.

I did not cross her shadow once,
(Though from the hollow west the sun's
Last shadow runs along so far,)
Because in June it should not bar
My ways, at noon when fevers are.   *20*

They told me she was sad that day,
(Though wherefore tell what love's soothsay,
Sooner than they, did register?)
And my heart leapt and wept to her,
And yet I did not speak nor stir.

So shall the tongues of the sea's foam
(Though many voices therewith come
From drowned hope's home to cry to me,)
Bewail one hour the more, when sea
And wind are one with memory.   30

(1853)

THE HONEYSUCKLE

I plucked a honeysuckle where
    The hedge on high is quick with thorn,
    And climbing for the prize, was torn,
And fouled my feet in quag-water;
    And by the thorns and by the wind
    The blossom that I took was thinn'd,
And yet I found it sweet and fair.

Thence to a richer growth I came,
    Where, nursed in mellow intercourse,
    The honeysuckles sprang by scores,   10
Not harried like my single stem,
    All virgin lamps of scent and dew.
    So from my hand that first I threw,
Yet plucked not any more of them.

(1853)

SISTER HELEN

"Why did you melt your waxen man,
                        Sister Helen?
To-day is the third since you began."

"The time was long, yet the time ran,
                    Little brother."
                    (*O Mother, Mary Mother,*
Three days to-day, between Hell and Heaven!)

"But if you have done your work aright,
                    Sister Helen,
You'll let me play, for you said I might."   *10*
"Be very still in your play to-night,
                    Little brother."
                    (*O Mother, Mary Mother,*
Third night, to-night, between Hell and Heaven!)

"You said it must melt ere vesper-bell,
                    Sister Helen;
If now it be molten, all is well."
"Even so,—nay, peace! you cannot tell,
                    Little brother."
                    (*O Mother, Mary Mother,*   *20*
O what is this, between Hell and Heaven?)

"Oh the waxen knave was plump to-day,
                    Sister Helen;
How like dead folk he has dropped away!"
"Nay now, of the dead what can you say,
                    Little brother?"
                    (*O Mother, Mary Mother,*
What of the dead, between Hell and Heaven?)

"See, see, the sunken pile of wood,
                    Sister Helen,   *30*
Shines through the thinned wax red as blood!"
"Nay now, when looked you yet on blood,
                    Little brother?"
                    (*O Mother, Mary Mother,*
How pale she is, between Hell and Heaven!)

"Now close your eyes, for they're sick and sore,
                    Sister Helen,

And I'll play without the gallery door."
"Aye, let me rest,—I'll lie on the floor,
    Little brother."   *40*
     (O Mother, Mary Mother,
What rest to-night, between Hell and Heaven?)

"Here high up in the balcony,
     Sister Helen,
The moon flies face to face with me."
"Aye, look and say whatever you see,
     Little brother."
     (O Mother, Mary Mother,
What sight to-night, between Hell and Heaven?)

"Outside it's merry in the wind's wake,   *50*
     Sister Helen;
In the shaken trees the chill stars shake."
"Hush, heard you a horse-tread as you spake,
     Little brother?"
     (O Mother, Mary Mother,
What sound to-night, between Hell and Heaven?)

"I hear a horse-tread, and I see,
     Sister Helen,
Three horsemen that ride terribly."
"Little brother, whence come the three,   *60*
     Little brother?"
     (O Mother, Mary Mother,
Whence should they come, between Hell and Heaven?)

"They come by the hill-verge from Boyne Bar,
     Sister Helen,
And one draws nigh, but two are afar."
"Look, look, do you know them who they are,
     Little brother?"
     (O Mother, Mary Mother,
Who should they be, between Hell and Heaven?)   *70*

"Oh, it's Keith of Eastholm rides so fast,
     Sister Helen,
For I know the white mane on the blast."
"The hour has come, has come at last,
     Little brother!"
     (O Mother, Mary Mother,
Her hour at last, between Hell and Heaven!)

"He has made a sign and called Halloo!
     Sister Helen,
And he says that he would speak with you."   *80*
"Oh tell him I fear the frozen dew,
     Little brother."
     (O Mother, Mary Mother,
Why laughs she thus, between Hell and Heaven?)

"The wind is loud, but I hear him cry,
     Sister Helen,
That Keith of Ewern's like to die."
"And he and thou, and thou and I,
     Little brother."
     (O Mother, Mary Mother,   *90*
And they and we, between Hell and Heaven!)

"Three days ago, on his marriage-morn,
     Sister Helen,
He sickened, and lies since then forlorn."
"For bridegroom's side is the bride a thorn,
     Little brother?"
     (O Mother, Mary Mother,
Cold bridal cheer, between Hell and Heaven!)

"Three days and nights he has lain abed,
     Sister Helen,   *100*
And he prays in torment to be dead."
"The thing may chance, if he have prayed,
     Little brother!"
     (O Mother, Mary Mother,
If he have prayed, between Hell and Heaven!)

"But he has not ceased to cry to-day,
                    Sister Helen,
That you should take your curse away."
"*My* prayer was heard,—he need but pray,
                    Little brother!"   *110*
                    (*O Mother, Mary Mother,*
Shall God not hear, between Hell and Heaven?)

"But he says, till you take back your ban,
                    Sister Helen,
His soul would pass, yet never can."
"Nay then, shall I slay a living man,
                    Little brother?"
                    (*O Mother, Mary Mother,*
A living soul, between Hell and Heaven!)

"But he calls for ever on your name,   *120*
                    Sister Helen,
And says that he melts before a flame."
"My heart for his pleasure fared the same,
                    Little brother."
                    (*O Mother, Mary Mother,*
Fire at the heart, between Hell and Heaven!)

"Here's Keith of Westholm riding fast,
                    Sister Helen,
For I know the white plume on the blast."
"The hour, the sweet hour I forecast,   *130*
                    Little brother!"
                    (*O Mother, Mary Mother,*
Is the hour sweet, between Hell and Heaven?)

"He stops to speak, and he stills his horse,
                    Sister Helen;
But his words are drowned in the wind's course."
"Nay hear, nay hear, you must hear perforce,
                    Little brother!"
                    (*O Mother, Mary Mother,*
What word now heard, between Hell and Heaven?)

"Oh he says that Keith of Ewern's cry,   *141*
            Sister Helen,
Is ever to see you ere he die."
"In all that his soul sees, there am I,
                Little brother!"
            (*O Mother, Mary Mother,*
The soul's one sight, between Hell and Heaven!)

"He sends a ring and a broken coin,
            Sister Helen,
And bids you mind the banks of Boyne."   *150*
"What else he broke will he ever join,
                Little brother?"
            (*O Mother, Mary Mother,*
No, never joined, between Hell and Heaven!)

"He yields you these and craves full fain,
            Sister Helen,
You pardon him in his mortal pain."
"What else he took will he give again,
                Little brother?"
            (*O Mother, Mary Mother,*   *160*
Not twice to give, between Hell and Heaven!)

"He calls your name in an agony,
            Sister Helen,
That even dead Love must weep to see."
"Hate, born of Love, is blind as he,
                Little brother!"
            (*O Mother, Mary Mother,*
Love turned to hate, between Hell and Heaven!)

"Oh it's Keith of Keith now that rides fast,
                Sister Helen,   *170*
For I know the white hair on the blast."
"The short short hour will soon be past,
                Little brother!"
            (*O Mother, Mary Mother,*
Will soon be past, between Hell and Heaven!)

"He looks at me and he tries to speak,
                    Sister Helen,
But oh! his voice is sad and weak!"
"What here should the mighty Baron seek,
                    Little brother?"   *180*
                    (*O Mother, Mary Mother,*
Is this the end, between Hell and Heaven?)

"Oh his son still cries, if you forgive,
                    Sister Helen,
The body dies but the soul shall live."
"Fire shall forgive me as I forgive,
                    Little brother!"
                    (*O Mother, Mary Mother,*
As she forgives, between Hell and Heaven!)

"Oh he prays you, as his heart would rive,   *190*
                    Sister Helen,
To save his dear son's soul alive."
"Fire cannot slay it, it shall thrive,
                    Little brother!"
                    (*O Mother, Mary Mother,*
Alas, alas, between Hell and Heaven!)

"He cries to you, kneeling in the road,
                    Sister Helen,
To go with him for the love of God!"
"The way is long to his son's abode,   *200*
                    Little brother."
                    (*O Mother, Mary Mother,*
The way is long, between Hell and Heaven!)

"A lady's here, by a dark steed brought,
                    Sister Helen,
So darkly clad, I saw her not."
"See her now or never see aught,
                    Little brother!"
                    (*O Mother, Mary Mother,*
What more to see, between Hell and Heaven?)   *210*

"Her hood falls back, and the moon shines fair,
                    Sister Helen,
On the Lady of Ewern's golden hair."
"Blest hour of my power and her despair,
                    Little brother!"
                    (*O Mother, Mary Mother,*
Hour blest and bann'd, between Hell and Heaven!)

"Pale, pale her cheeks, that in pride did glow,
                    Sister Helen,
'Neath the bridal-wreath three days ago."   220
"One morn for pride and three days for woe,
                    Little brother!"
                    (*O Mother, Mary Mother,*
Three days, three nights, between Hell and Heaven!)

"Her clasped hands stretch from her bending head,
                    Sister Helen;
With the loud wind's wail her sobs are wed."
"What wedding-strains hath her bridal-bed,
                    Little brother?"
                    (*O Mother, Mary Mother,*   230
What strain but death's, between Hell and Heaven!)

"She may not speak, she sinks in a swoon,
                    Sister Helen,—
She lifts her lips and gasps on the moon."
"Oh! might I but hear her soul's blithe tune,
                    Little brother!"
                    (*O Mother, Mary Mother,*
Her woe's dumb cry, between Hell and Heaven!)

"They've caught her to Westholm's saddle-bow,
                    Sister Helen,   240
And her moonlit hair gleams white in its flow."
"Let it turn whiter than winter snow,
                    Little brother!"
                    (*O Mother, Mary Mother,*
Woe-withered gold, between Hell and Heaven!)

"O Sister Helen, you heard the bell,
                   Sister Helen!
More loud than the vesper-chime it fell."
"No vesper-chime, but a dying knell,
                   Little brother!"   250
           (*O Mother, Mary Mother,*
His dying knell, between Hell and Heaven!)

"Alas! but I fear the heavy sound,
                   Sister Helen;
Is it in the sky or in the ground?"
"Say, have they turned their horses round,
                   Little brother?"
           (*O Mother, Mary Mother,*
What would she more, between Hell and Heaven?)

"They have raised the old man from his knee,   260
                   Sister Helen,
And they ride in silence hastily."
"More fast the naked soul doth flee,
                   Little brother!"
           (*O Mother, Mary Mother,*
The naked soul, between Hell and Heaven!)

"Flank to flank are the three steeds gone,
                   Sister Helen,
But the lady's dark steed goes alone."
"And lonely her bridegroom's soul hath flown,   270
                   Little brother."
           (*O Mother, Mary Mother,*
The lonely ghost, between Hell and Heaven!)

"Oh the wind is sad in the iron chill,
                   Sister Helen,
And weary sad they look by the hill."
"But he and I are sadder still,
                   Little brother!"
           (*O Mother, Mary Mother,*
Most sad of all, between Hell and Heaven!)   280

"See, see, the wax has dropped from its place,
                    Sister Helen,
And the flames are winning up apace!"
"Yet here they burn but for a space,
                    Little brother!"
                    (*O Mother, Mary Mother,*
Here for a space, between Hell and Heaven!)

"Ah! what white thing at the door has cross'd,
                    Sister Helen?
Ah! what is this that sighs in the frost?"   290
"A soul that's lost as mine is lost,
                    Little brother!"
                    (*O Mother, Mary Mother,*
Lost, lost, all lost, between Hell and Heaven!)

                                        (1854)

THE BURDEN OF NINEVEH

In our Museum galleries
To-day I lingered o'er the prize
Dead Greece vouchsafes to living eyes,—
Her Art for ever in fresh wise
    From hour to hour rejoicing me.
Sighing I turned at last to win
Once more the London dirt and din;
And as I made the swing-door spin
And issued, they were hoisting in
    A wingèd beast from Nineveh.   10

A human face the creature wore,
And hoofs behind and hoofs before,
And flanks with dark runes fretted o'er
'Twas bull, 'twas mitred Minotaur,
    A dead disbowelled mystery:
The mummy of a buried faith
Stark from the charnel without scathe,

Its wings stood for the light to bathe,—
Such fossil cerements as might swathe
 The very corpse of Nineveh.   *20*

The print of its first rush-wrapping,
Wound ere it dried, still ribbed the thing.
What song did the brown maidens sing,
From purple mouths alternating,
 When that was woven languidly?
What vows, what rites, what prayers preferr'd,
What songs has the strange image heard?
In what blind vigil stood interr'd
For ages, till an English word
 Broke silence first at Nineveh?   *30*

Oh when upon each sculptured court,
Where even the wind might not resort,—
O'er which Time passed, of like import
With the wild Arab boys at sport,—
 A living face looked in to see:—
Oh seemed it not—the spell once broke—
As though the carven warriors woke,
As though the shaft the string forsook,
The cymbals clashed, the chariots shook,
 And there was life in Nineveh?   *40*

On London stones our sun anew
The beast's recovered shadow threw.
(No shade that plague of darkness knew,
No light, no shade, while older grew
 By ages the old earth and sea.)
Lo thou! could all thy priests have shown
Such proof to make thy godhead known?
From their dead Past thou liv'st alone;
And still thy shadow is thine own,
 Even as of yore in Nineveh.   *50*

That day whereof we keep record,
When near thy city-gates the Lord

Sheltered His Jonah with a gourd,
This sun, (I said) here present, pour'd
  Even thus this shadow that I see.
This shadow has been shed the same
From sun and moon,—from lamps which came
For prayer,—from fifteen days of flame,
The last, while smouldered to a name
  Sardanapalus' Nineveh.   60

Within thy shadow, haply, once
Sennacherib has knelt, whose sons
Smote him between the altar-stones:
Or pale Semiramis her zones
  Of gold, her incense brought to thee,
In love for grace, in war for aid: . . . .
Ay, and who else? . . . . till 'neath thy shade
Within his trenches newly made
Last year the Christian knelt and pray'd—
  Not to thy strength—in Nineveh.*   70

Now, thou poor god, within this hall
Where the blank windows blind the wall
From pedestal to pedestal,
The kind of light shall on thee fall
  Which London takes the day to be:
While school-foundations in the act
Of holiday, three files compact,
Shall learn to view thee as a fact
Connected with that zealous tract:
  "Rome,—Babylon and Nineveh."   80

Deemed they of this, those worshipers,
When, in some mythic chain of verse
Which man shall not again rehearse,
The faces of thy ministers

* During the excavations, the Tiyari workmen held their services in
the shadow of the great bulls.—Layard's *Nineveh*, ch. ix.) [Rossetti's
note]

Yearned pale with bitter ecstasy?
Greece, Egypt, Rome,—did any god
Before whose feet men knelt unshod
Deem that in this unblest abode
Another scarce more unknown god
    Should house with him, from Nineveh?   *90*

Ah! in what quarries lay the stone
From which this pillared pile has grown,
Unto man's need how long unknown,
Since those thy temples, court and cone,
    Rose far in desert history?
Ah! what is here that does not lie
All strange to thine awakened eye?
Ah! what is here can testify
(Save that dumb presence of the sky)
    Unto thy day and Nineveh?   *100*

Why, of those mummies in the room
Above, there might indeed have come
One out of Egypt to thy home,
An alien. Nay, but were not some
    Of these thine own "antiquity"?
And now,—they and their gods and thou
All relics here together,—now
Whose profit? whether bull or cow,
Isis or Ibis, who or how,
    Whether of Thebes or Nineveh?   *110*

The consecrated metals found,
And ivory tablets, underground,
Winged teraphim and creatures crown'd,
When air and daylight filled the mound,
    Fell into dust immediately.
And even as these, the images
Of awe and worship,—even as these,—
So, smitten with the sun's increase,
Her glory mouldered and did cease
    From immemorial Nineveh.   *120*

The day her builders made their halt,
Those cities of the lake of salt
Stood firmly 'stablished without fault,
Made proud with pillars of basalt,
  With sardonyx and porphyry.
The day that Jonah bore abroad
To Nineveh the voice of God,
A brackish lake lay in his road,
Where erst Pride fixed her sure abode,
  As then in royal Nineveh.   *130*

The day when he, Pride's lord and Man's,
Showed all the kingdoms at a glance
To Him before whose countenance
The years recede, the years advance,
  And said, Fall down and worship me:—
'Mid all the pomp beneath that look,
Then stirred there, haply, some rebuke,
Where to the wind the Salt Pools shook,
And in those tracts, of life forsook,
  That knew thee not, O Nineveh!   *140*

Delicate harlot! On thy throne
Thou with a world beneath thee prone
In state for ages sat'st alone;
And needs were years and lustres flown
  Ere strength of man could vanquish thee:
Whom even thy victor foes must bring,
Still royal, among maids that sing
As with doves' voices, taboring
Upon their breasts, unto the King,—
  A kingly conquest, Nineveh!   *150*

. . . Here woke my thought. The wind's slow sway
Had waxed; and like the human play
Of scorn that smiling spreads away,
The sunshine shivered off the day:
  The callous wind, it seemed to me,
Swept up the shadow from the ground:

And pale as whom the Fates astound,
The god forlorn stood winged and crown'd:
Within I knew the cry lay bound
  Of the dumb soul of Nineveh.   *160*

And as I turned, my sense half shut
Still saw the crowds of kerb and rut
Go past as marshalled to the strut
Of ranks in gypsum quaintly cut.
  It seemed in one same pageantry
They followed forms which had been erst;
To pass, till on my sight should burst
That future of the best or worst
When some may question which was first,
  Of London or of Nineveh.   *170*

For as that Bull-god once did stand
And watched the burial-clouds of sand,
Till these at last without a hand
Rose o'er his eyes, another land,
  And blinded him with destiny:—
So may he stand again; till now,
In ships of unknown sail and prow,
Some tribe of the Australian plough
Bear him afar,—a relic now
  Of London, not of Nineveh!   *180*

Or it may chance indeed that when
Man's age is hoary among men,—
His centuries threescore and ten,—
His furthest childhood shall seem then
  More clear than later times may be:
Who, finding in this desert place
This form, shall hold us for some race
That walked not in Christ's lowly ways,
But bowed its pride and vowed its praise
  Unto the God of Nineveh.   *190*

The smile rose first,—anon drew nigh
The thought: . . Those heavy wings spread high,

So sure of flight, which do not fly;
That set gaze never on the sky;
   Those scriptured flanks it cannot see;
Its crown, a brow-contracting load;
Its planted feet which trust the sod: . . .
(So grew the image as I trod:)
O Nineveh, was this thy God,—
   Thine also, mighty Nineveh?   200

                                          (1856)

THE WOODSPURGE

The wind flapped loose, the wind was still,
Shaken out dead from tree and hill:
I had walked on at the wind's will,—
I sat now, for the wind was still.

Between my knees my forehead was,—
My lips, drawn in, said not Alas!
My hair was over in the grass,
My naked ears heard the day pass.

My eyes, wide open, had the run
Of some ten weeds to fix upon;   10
Among those few, out of the sun,
The woodspurge flowered, three cups in one.

From perfect grief there need not be
Wisdom or even memory:
One thing then learnt remains to me,—
The woodspurge has a cup of three.

                                          (1856)

JENNY

*Vengeance of Jenny's case! Fie on her! Never name her,
child!*—(Mrs. Quickly)

Lazy laughing languid Jenny,
Fond of a kiss and fond of a guinea,

Whose head upon my knee to-night
Rests for a while, as if grown light
With all our dances and the sound
To which the wild tunes spun you round
Fair Jenny mine, the thoughtless queen
Of kisses which the blush between
Could hardly make much daintier;
Whose eyes are as blue skies, whose hair   10
Is countless gold incomparable:
Fresh flower, scarce touched with signs that tell
Of Love's exuberant hotbed:—Nay,
Poor flower left torn since yesterday
Until to-morrow leave you bare;
Poor handful of bright spring-water
Flung in the whirlpool's shrieking face;
Poor shameful Jenny, full of grace
Thus with your head upon my knee;—
Whose person or whose purse may be   20
The lodestar of your reverie?

    This room of yours, my Jenny, looks
A change from mine so full of books,
Whose serried ranks hold fast, forsooth,
So many captive hours of youth,—
The hours they thieve from day and night
To make one's cherished work come right,
And leave it wrong for all their theft,
Even as to-night my work was left:
Until I vowed that since my brain   30
And eyes of dancing seemed so fain,
My feet should have some dancing too:—
And thus it was I met with you.
Well, I suppose 'twas hard to part,
For here I am. And now, sweetheart,
You seem too tired to get to bed.

    It was a careless life I led
When rooms like this were scarce so strange
Not long ago. What breeds the change,—

The many aims or the few years?   40
Because to-night it all appears
Something I do not know again.

  The cloud's not danced out of my brain,—
The cloud that made it turn and swim
While hour by hour the books grew dim.
Why, Jenny, as I watch you there,—
For all your wealth of loosened hair,
Your silk ungirdled and unlac'd
And warm sweets open to the waist,
All golden in the lamplight's gleam,—   50
You know not what a book you seem,
Half-read by lightning in a dream!
How should you know, my Jenny? Nay,
And I should be ashamed to say:—
Poor beauty, so well worth a kiss!
But while my thought runs on like this
With wasteful whims more than enough,
I wonder what you're thinking of.

  If of myself you think at all,
What is the thought?—conjectural   60
On sorry matters best unsolved?—
Or inly is each grace revolved
To fit me with a lure?—or (sad
To think!) perhaps you're merely glad
That I'm not drunk or ruffianly
And let you rest upon my knee.

  For sometimes, were the truth confess'd,
You're thankful for a little rest,—
Glad from the crush to rest within,
From the heart-sickness and the din   70
Where envy's voice at virtue's pitch
Mocks you because your gown is rich;
And from the pale girl's dumb rebuke,
Whose ill-clad grace and toil-worn look
Proclaim the strength that keeps her weak,

And other nights than yours bespeak;
And from the wise unchildish elf,
To schoolmate lesser than himself
Pointing you out, what thing you are:—
Yes, from the daily jeer and jar,   *80*
From shame and shame's outbraving too,
Is rest not sometimes sweet to you?—
But most from the hatefulness of man,
Who spares not to end what he began,
Whose acts are ill and his speech ill,
Who, having used you at his will,
Thrusts you aside, as when I dine
I serve the dishes and the wine.

Well, handsome Jenny mine, sit up:
I've filled our glasses, let us sup,   *90*
And do not let me think of you,
Lest shame of yours suffice for two.
What, still so tired? Well, well then, keep
Your head there, so you do not sleep;
But that the weariness may pass
And leave you merry, take this glass.
Ah! lazy lily hand, more bless'd
If ne'er in rings it had been dress'd
Nor ever by a glove conceal'd!

Behold the lilies of the field,   *100*
They toil not neither do they spin;
(So doth the ancient text begin,—
Not of such rest as one of these
Can share.) Another rest and ease
Along each summer-sated path
From its new lord the garden hath,
Than that whose spring in blessings ran
Which praised the bounteous husbandman,
Ere yet, in days of hankering breath,
The lilies sickened unto death.   *110*

What, Jenny, are your lilies dead?
Aye, and the snow-white leaves are spread

Like winter on the garden-bed.
But you had roses left in May,—
They were not gone too. Jenny, nay,
But must your roses die, and those
Their purfled buds that should unclose?
Even so; the leaves are curled apart,
Still red as from the broken heart,
And here's the naked stem of thorns.   *120*

  Nay, nay, mere words. Here nothing warns
As yet of winter. Sickness here
Or want alone could waken fear,—
Nothing but passion wrings a tear.
Except when there may rise unsought
Haply at times a passing thought
Of the old days which seem to be
Much older than any history
That is written in any book;   *enjambment*
When she would lie in fields and look   *130*
Along the ground through the blown grass,
And wonder where the city was,
Far out of sight, whose broil and bale
They told her then for a child's tale.

  Jenny, you know the city now.
A child can tell the tale there, how
Some things which are not yet enroll'd
In market-lists are bought and sold
Even till the early Sunday light,
When Saturday night is market-night   *140*
Everywhere, be it dry or wet,
And market-night in the Haymarket.
Our learned London children know,
Poor Jenny, all your pride and woe;
Have seen your lifted silken skirt
Advertise dainties through the dirt;
Have seen your coach-wheels splash rebuke
On virtue; and have learned your look
When, wealth and health slipped past, you stare

Along the streets alone, and there,　　　　　　　*150*
Round the long park, across the bridge,
The cold lamps at the pavement's edge
Wind on together and apart,
A fiery serpent for your heart.

  Let the thoughts pass, an empty cloud!
Suppose I were to think aloud,—
What if to her all this were said?
Why, as a volume seldom read
Being opened halfway shuts again,
So might the pages of her brain　　　　　　　*160*
Be parted at such words, and thence
Close back upon the dusty sense.
For is there hue or shape defin'd
In Jenny's desecrated mind,
Where all contagious currents meet,
A <u>Lethe</u> of the middle street?
Nay, it reflects not any face,
Nor sound is in its sluggish pace,
But as they coil those eddies clot,
And night and day remember not.　　　　　　　*170*

  Why, Jenny, you're asleep at last!—
Asleep, poor Jenny, hard and fast,—
So young and soft and tired; so fair,
With chin thus nestled in your hair,
Mouth quiet, eyelids almost blue
As if some sky of dreams shone through!

  Just as another woman sleeps!
Enough to throw one's thoughts in heaps
Of doubt and horror,—what to say
Or think,—this awful secret sway,　　　　　　　*180*
The potter's power over the clay!
Of the same lump (it has been said)
For honour and dishonour made,
Two sister vessels. Here is one.

My cousin Nell is fond of fun,
And fond of dress, and change, and praise,
So mere a woman in her ways:
And if her sweet eyes rich in youth
Are like her lips that tell the truth,
My cousin Nell is fond of love.   190
And she's the girl I'm proudest of.
Who does not prize her, guard her well?
The love of change, in cousin Nell,
Shall find the best and hold it dear:
The unconquered mirth turn quieter
Not through her own, through others' woe:
The conscious pride of beauty glow
Beside another's pride in her,
One little part of all they share.
For Love himself shall ripen these   200
In a kind soil to just increase
Through years of fertilizing peace.

Of the same lump (as it is said)
For honour and dishonour made,
Two sister vessels. Here is one.

It makes a goblin of the sun.

So pure,—so fall'n! How dare to think
Of the first common kindred link?
Yet, Jenny, till the world shall burn
It seems that all things take their turn;   210
And who shall say but this fair tree
May need, in changes that may be,
Your children's children's charity?
Scorned then, no doubt, as you are scorn'd!
Shall no man hold his pride forewarn'd
Till in the end, the Day of Days,
At Judgment, one of his own race,
As frail and lost as you, shall rise,—
His daughter, with his mother's eyes?

How Jenny's clock ticks on the shelf!   220
Might not the dial scorn itself
That has such hours to register?
Yet as to me, even so to her
Are golden sun and silver moon,
In daily largesse of earth's boon,
Counted for life-coins to one tune.
And if, as blindfold fates are toss'd,
Through some one man this life be lost,
Shall soul not somehow pay for soul?

Fair shines the gilded aureole   230
In which our highest painters place
Some living woman's simple face.
And the stilled features thus descried
As Jenny's long throat droops aside,—
The shadows where the cheeks are thin,
And pure wide curve from ear to chin,—
With Raffael's, Leonardo's hand
To show them to men's souls, might stand,
Whole ages long, the whole world through,
For preachings of what God can do.   240
What has man done here? How atone,
Great God, for this which man has done?
And for the body and soul which by
Man's pitiless doom must now comply
With lifelong hell, what lullaby
Of sweet forgetful second birth
Remains? All dark. No sign on earth
What measure of God's rest endows
The many mansions of his house.

biblical

If but a woman's heart might see   250
Such erring heart unerringly
For once! But that can never be.

Like a rose shut in a book
In which pure women may not look,
For its base pages claim control

To crush the flower within the soul;
Where through each dead rose-leaf that clings,
Pale as transparent Psyche-wings,
To the vile text, are traced such things
As might make lady's cheek indeed   260
More than a living rose to read;
So nought save foolish foulness may
Watch with hard eyes the sure decay;
And so the life-blood of this rose,
Puddled with shameful knowledge, flows
Through leaves no chaste hand may unclose:
Yet still it keeps such faded show
Of when 'twas gathered long ago,
That the crushed petals' lovely grain,
The sweetness of the sanguine stain,   270
Seen of a woman's eyes, must make
Her pitiful heart, so prone to ache,
Love roses better for its sake:—
Only that this can never be:—
Even so unto her sex is she.

    Yet, Jenny, looking long at you,
The woman almost fades from view.
A cipher of man's changeless sum
Of lust, past, present, and to come,
Is left. A riddle that one shrinks   280
To challenge from the scornful sphinx.

    Like a toad within a stone
Seated while Time crumbles on;
Which sits there since the earth was curs'd
For Man's transgression at the first;
Which, living through all centuries,
Not once has seen the sun arise;
Whose life, to its cold circle charmed,
The earth's whole summers have not warmed;
Which always—whitherso the stone   290
Be flung—sits there, deaf, blind, alone;—
Aye, and shall not be driven out

Till that which shuts him round about
Break at the very Master's stroke,
And the dust thereof vanish as smoke,
And the seed of Man vanish as dust:—
Even so within this world is Lust.

    Come, come, what use in thoughts like this?
Poor little Jenny, good to kiss,—
You'd not believe by what strange roads   300
Thought travels, when your beauty goads
A man to-night to think of toads!
Jenny, wake up. . . . Why, there's the dawn!

    And there's an early waggon drawn
To market, and some sheep that jog
Bleating before a barking dog;
And the old streets come peering through
Another night that London knew;
And all as ghostlike as the lamps.

    So on the wings of day decamps   310
My last night's frolic. Glooms begin
To shiver off as lights creep in
Past the gauze curtains half drawn-to,
And the lamp's doubled shade grows blue,—
Your lamp, my Jenny, kept alight,
Like a wise virgin's, all one night!
And in the alcove coolly spread
Glimmers with dawn your empty bed;
And yonder your fair face I see
Reflected lying on my knee,   320
Where teems with first foreshadowings
Your pier-glass scrawled with diamond rings:
And on your bosom all night worn
Yesterday's rose now droops forlorn,
But dies not yet this summer morn.

    And now without, as if some word
Had called upon them that they heard,

The London sparrows far and nigh
Clamour together suddenly;
And Jenny's cage-bird grown awake   330
Here in their song his part must take,
Because here too the day doth break.

   And somehow in myself the dawn
Among stirred clouds and veils withdrawn
Strikes greyly on her. Let her sleep.
But will it wake her if I heap
These cushions thus beneath her head
Where my knee was? No,—there's your bed,
My Jenny, while you dream. And there
I lay among your golden hair   340
Perhaps the subject of your dreams,
These golden coins.
               For still one deems
That Jenny's flattering sleep confers
New magic on the magic purse,—
Grim web, how clogged with shrivelled flies!
Between the threads fine fumes arise
And shape their pictures in the brain.
There roll no streets in glare and rain,
Nor flagrant man-swine whets his tusk;
But delicately sighs in musk   350
The homage of the dim boudoir;
Or like a palpitating star
Thrilled into song, the opera-night
Breathes faint in the quick pulse of light;
Or at the carriage-window shine
Rich wares for choice; or, free to dine,
Whirls through its hour of health (divine
For her) the concourse of the Park.
And though in the discounted dark
Her functions there and here are one,   360
Beneath the lamps and in the sun
There reigns at least the acknowledged belle
Apparelled beyond parallel.
Ah Jenny, yes, we know your dreams.

For even the Paphian Venus seems
A goddess o'er the realms of love,
When silver-shrined in shadowy grove:
Aye, or let offerings nicely plac'd
But hide Priapus to the waist,
And whoso looks on him shall see   370
An eligible deity.

Why, Jenny, waking here alone,
May help you to remember one,
Though all the memory's long outworn
Of many a double-pillowed morn.
I think I see you when you wake,
And rub your eyes for me, and shake
My gold, in rising, from your hair,
A Danaë for a moment there.

Jenny, my love rang true! for still   380
Love at first sight is vague, until
That tinkling makes him audible.

And must I mock you to the last,
Ashamed of my own shame,—aghast
Because some thoughts not born amiss
Rose at a poor fair face like this?
Well, of such thoughts so much I know:
In my life, as in hers, they show,
By a far gleam which I may near,
A dark path I can strive to clear.   390

Only one kiss. Good-bye, my dear.

(*1848, 1858 f.*)

EVEN SO

So it is, my dear.
All such things touch secret strings
For heavy hearts to hear.
So it is, my dear.

Very like indeed:
Sea and sky, afar, on high,
    Sand and strewn seaweed,—
    Very like indeed.

But the sea stands spread
As one wall with the flat skies,   10
Where the lean black craft like flies
    Seem well-nigh stagnated,
    Soon to drop off dead.

Seemed it so to us
When I was thine and thou wast mine,
    And all these things were thus,
    But all our world in us?

Could we be so now?
Not if all beneath heaven's pall
    Lay dead but I and thou,   20
    Could we be so now!

                                        (1859)

THE SONG OF THE BOWER

Say, is it day, is it dusk in thy bower,
    Thou whom I long for, who longest for me?
Oh! be it light, be it night, 'tis Love's hour,
    Love's that is fettered as Love's that is free.
Free Love has leaped to that innermost chamber,
    Oh! the last time, and the hundred before:
Fettered Love, motionless, can but remember,
    Yet something that sighs from him passes the door.

Nay, but my heart when it flies to thy bower,
    What does it find there that knows it again?   10
There it must droop like a shower-beaten flower,
    Red at the rent core and dark with the rain.

Ah! yet what shelter is still shed above it,—
  What waters still image its leaves torn apart?
Thy soul is the shade that clings round it to love it,
  And tears are its mirror deep down in thy heart.

What were my prize, could I enter thy bower,
  This day, to-morrow, at eve or at morn?
Large lovely arms and a neck like a tower,
  Bosom then heaving that now lies forlorn.   20
Kindled with love-breath, (the sun's kiss is colder!)
  Thy sweetness all near me, so distant to-day;
My hand round thy neck and thy hand on my
        shoulder
  My mouth to thy mouth as the world melts away.

What is it keeps me afar from thy bower,—
  My spirit, my body, so fain to be there?
Waters engulfing or fires that devour?—
  Earth heaped against me or death in the air?
Nay, but in day-dreams, for terror, for pity,
  The trees wave their heads with an omen to tell;   30
Nay, but in night-dreams, throughout the dark city,
  The hours, clashed together, lose count in the bell.

Shall I not one day remember thy bower,
  One day when all days are one day to me?—
Thinking, "I stirred not, and yet had the power!"—
  Yearning, "Ah God, if again it might be!"
Peace, peace! such a small lamp illumes, on this
        highway,
  So dimly so few steps in front of my feet,—
Yet shows me that her way is parted from my
        way. . . .
    Out of sight, beyond light, at what goal may we
        meet?   40

                                                          (1860)

ASPECTA MEDUSA

(For a Drawing)

Andromeda, by Perseus saved and wed,
Hankered each day to see the Gorgon's head:
Till o'er a fount he held it, bade her lean,
And mirrored in the wave was safely seen
That death she lived by.

                     Let not thine eyes know
Any forbidden thing itself, although
It once should save as well as kill: but be
Its shadow upon life enough for thee.

                                (1865)

MARY MAGDALENE

AT THE DOOR OF SIMON THE PHARISEE

(For a Drawing) *

"Why wilt thou cast the roses from thine hair?
  Nay, be thou all a rose,—wreath, lips, and cheek.
  Nay, not this house,—that banquet-house we seek;
See how they kiss and enter; come thou there.
This delicate day of love we two will share
  Till at our ear love's whispering night shall speak.
  What, sweet one,—hold'st thou still the foolish
    freak?
Nay, when I kiss thy feet they'll leave the stair."

"Oh loose me! Seest thou not my Bridegroom's face
  That draws me to Him? For His feet my kiss,   *10*
    My hair, my tears He craves to-day:—and oh!

* In the drawing Mary has left a procession of revellers, and is
ascending by a sudden impulse the steps of the house where she sees
Christ. Her lover has followed her, and is trying to turn her back.
[Rossetti's note]

What words can tell what other day and place
   Shall see me clasp those blood-stained feet of His?
     He needs me, calls me, loves me: let me go!"

                              (*1869*)

TROY TOWN

Heavenborn Helen, Sparta's queen,
        (*O Troy Town!*)
Had two breasts of heavenly sheen,
The sun and moon of the heart's desire:
All Love's lordship lay between.
        (*O Troy's down,*
        Tall Troy's on fire!)

Helen knelt at Venus' shrine,
        (*O Troy Town!*)
Saying, "A little gift is mine,   *10*
A little gift for a heart's desire.
Hear me speak and make me a sign!
        (*O Troy's down,*
        Tall Troy's on fire!)

"Look, I bring thee a carven cup;
        (*O Troy Town!*)
See it here as I hold it up,—
Shaped it is to the heart's desire,
Fit to fill when the gods would sup.
        (*O Troy's down,*   *20*
        Tall Troy's on fire!)

"It was moulded like my breast;
        (*O Troy Town!*)
He that sees it may not rest,
Rest at all for his heart's desire.
O give ear to my heart's behest!
        (*O Troy's down,*
        Tall Troy's on fire!)

"See my breast, how like it is;
          (*O Troy Town!*)   *30*
See it bare for the air to kiss!
Is the cup to thy heart's desire?
O for the breast, O make it his!
          (*O Troy's down,*
          Tall Troy's on fire!)

"Yea, for my bosom here I sue;
          (*O Troy Town!*)
Thou must give it where 'tis due,
Give it there to the heart's desire.
Whom do I give my bosom to?   *40*
          (*O Troy's down,*
          Tall Troy's on fire!)

"Each twin breast is an apple sweet.
          (*O Troy Town!*)
Once an apple stirred the beat
Of thy heart with the heart's desire:—
Say, who brought it then to thy feet?
          (*O Troy's down,*
          Tall Troy's on fire!)

"They that claimed it then were three: *50*
          (*O Troy Town!*)
For thy sake two hearts did he
Make forlorn of the heart's desire.
Do for him as he did for thee!
          (*O Troy's down,*
          Tall Troy's on fire!)

"Mine are apples grown to the south,
          (*O Troy Town!*)
Grown to taste in the days of drouth,
Taste and waste to the heart's desire: *60*
Mine are apples meet for his mouth."
          (*O Troy's down,*
          Tall Troy's on fire!)

Venus looked on Helen's gift,
      (O Troy Town!)
Looked and smiled with subtle drift,
Saw the work of her heart's desire:—
"There thou kneel'st for Love to lift!"
      (O Troy's down,
      Tall Troy's on fire!)   70

Venus looked in Helen's face,
      (O Troy Town!)
Knew far off an hour and place,
And fire lit from the heart's desire;
Laughed and said, "Thy gift hath grace!"
      (O Troy's down,
      Tall Troy's on fire!)

Cupid looked on Helen's breast,
      (O Troy Town!)
Saw the heart within its nest,   80
Saw the flame of the heart's desire,—
Marked his arrow's burning crest.
      (O Troy's down,
      Tall Troy's on fire!)

Cupid took another dart,
      (O Troy Town!)
Fledged it for another heart,
Winged the shaft with the heart's desire,
Drew the string and said, "Depart!"
      (O Troy's down,   90
      Tall Troy's on fire!)

Paris turned upon his bed,
      (O Troy Town!)
Turned upon his bed and said,
Dead at heart with the heart's desire—
"Oh to clasp her golden head!"
      (O Troy's down,
      Tall Troy's on fire!)

                        (1869)

FIRST LOVE REMEMBERED

Peace in her chamber, wheresoe'er
    It be, a holy place:
The thought still brings my soul such grace
    As morning meadows wear.

Whether it still be small and light,
    A maid's who dreams alone,
As from her orchard-gate the moon
    Its ceiling showed at night:

Or whether, in a shadow dense
    As nuptial hymns invoke,   *10*
Innocent maidenhood awoke
    To married innocence:

There still the thanks unheard await
    The unconscious gift bequeathed:
For there my soul this hour has breathed
    An air inviolate.

                                        (1869)

AN OLD SONG ENDED

*"How should I your true love know
    From another one?"
"By his cockle-hat and staff
    And his sandal-shoon."*

"And what signs have told you now
    That he hastens home?"
"Lo! the spring is nearly gone,
    He is nearly come."

"For a token is there nought,
    Say, that he should bring?"   *10*
"He will bear a ring I gave
    And another ring."

"How may I, when he shall ask,
    Tell him who lies there?"
"Nay, but leave my face unveiled
    And unbound my hair."

"Can you say to me some word
    I shall say to him?"
"Say I'm looking in his eyes
    Though my eyes are dim."   20

                                    (*1869*)

EDEN BOWER

It was Lilith the wife of Adam:
                (*Sing Eden Bower!*)
Not a drop of her blood was human,
But she was made like a soft sweet woman.

Lilith stood on the skirts of Eden;
                (*Alas the hour!*)
She was the first that thence was driven;
With her was hell and with Eve was heaven.

In the ear of the Snake said Lilith:—
                (*Sing Eden Bower!*)   10
"To thee I come when the rest is over;
A snake was I when thou wast my lover.

"I was the fairest snake in Eden:
                (*Alas the hour!*)
By the earth's will, new form and feature
Made me a wife for the earth's new creature.

"Take me thou as I come from Adam:
                (*Sing Eden Bower!*)
Once again shall my love subdue thee;
The past is past and I am come to thee.   20

"O but Adam was thrall to Lilith!
                    (*Alas the hour!*)
All the threads of my hair are golden,
And there in a net his heart was holden.

"O and Lilith was queen of Adam!
                    (*Sing Eden Bower!*)
All the day and the night together
My breath could shake his soul like a feather.

"What great joys had Adam and Lilith!—
                    (*Alas the hour!*)   30
Sweet close rings of the serpent's twining,
As heart in heart lay sighing and pining.

"What bright babes had Lilith and Adam!—
                    (*Sing Eden Bower!*)
Shapes that coiled in the woods and waters,
Glittering sons and radiant daughters.

"O thou God, the Lord God of Eden!
                    (*Alas the hour!*)
Say, was this fair body for no man,
That of Adam's flesh thou mak'st him a woman?   40

"O thou Snake, the King-snake of Eden!
                    (*Sing Eden Bower!*)
God's strong will our necks are under,
But thou and I may cleave it in sunder.

"Help, sweet Snake, sweet lover of Lilith!
                    (*Alas the hour!*)
And let God learn how I loved and hated
Man in the image of God created.

"Help me once against Eve and Adam!
                    (*Sing Eden Bower!*)   50
Help me once for this one endeavour,
And then my love shall be thine for ever!

"Strong is God, the fell foe of Lilith:
          (*Alas the hour!*)
Nought in heaven or earth may affright Him;
But join thou with me and we will smite Him.

"Strong is God, the great God of Eden:
          (*Sing Eden Bower!*)
Over all He made He hath power;
But lend me thou thy shape for an hour!   60

"Lend thy shape for the love of Lilith!
          (*Alas the hour!*)
Look, my mouth and my cheek are ruddy,
And thou art cold, and fire is my body.

"Lend thy shape for the hate of Adam!
          (*Sing Eden Bower!*)
That he may wail my joy that forsook him,
And curse the day when the bride-sleep took him.

"Lend thy shape for the shame of Eden!
          (*Alas the hour!*)   70
Is not the foe-God weak as the foeman
When love grows hate in the heart of a woman?

"Wouldst thou know the heart's hope of Lilith?
          (*Sing Eden Bower!*)
Then bring thou close thine head till it glisten
Along my breast, and lip me and listen.

"Am I sweet, O sweet Snake of Eden?
          (*Alas the hour!*)
Then ope thine ear to my warm mouth's cooing
And learn what deed remains for our doing.   80

"Thou didst hear when God said to Adam:—
          (*Sing Eden Bower!*)
'Of all this wealth I have made thee warden;
Thou'rt free to eat of the trees of the garden:

" 'Only of one tree eat not in Eden;
    (Alas the hour!)
All save one I give to thy freewill,—
The Tree of the Knowledge of Good and Evil.'

"O my love, come nearer to Lilith!
    (Sing Eden Bower!)   90
In thy sweet folds bind me and bend me,
And let me feel the shape thou shalt lend me

"In thy shape I'll go back to Eden;
    (Alas the hour!)
In these coils that Tree will I grapple,
And stretch this crowned head forth by the apple.

"Lo, Eve bends to the breath of Lilith!
    (Sing Eden Bower!)
O how then shall my heart desire
All her blood as food to its fire!   *100*

"Lo, Eve bends to the words of Lilith!—
    (Alas the hour!)
'Nay, this Tree's fruit,—why should ye hate it,
Or Death be born the day that ye ate it?

" 'Nay, but on that great day in Eden,
    (Sing Eden Bower!)
By the help that in this wise Tree is,
God knows well ye shall be as He is.'

"Then Eve shall eat and give unto Adam;
    (Alas the hour!)   *110*
And then they both shall know they are naked,
And their hearts ache as my heart hath achèd.

"Ay, let them hide 'mid the trees of Eden,
    (Sing Eden Bower!)
As in the cool of the day in the garden
God shall walk without pity or pardon.

"Hear, thou Eve, the man's heart in Adam!
        (*Alas the hour!*)
Of his brave words hark to the bravest:—
'This the woman gave that thou gavest.'   *120*

"Hear Eve speak, yea list to her, Lilith!
            (*Sing Eden Bower!*)
Feast thine heart with words that shall sate it—
'This the serpent gave and I ate it.'

"O proud Eve, cling close to thine Adam,
            (*Alas the hour!*)
Driven forth as the beasts of his naming
By the sword that for ever is flaming.

"Know, thy path is known unto Lilith!
            (*Sing Eden Bower!*)   *130*
While the blithe birds sang at thy wedding,
There her tears grew thorns for thy treading.

"O my love, thou Love-snake of Eden!
            (*Alas the hour!*)
O to-day and the day to come after!
Loose me, love,—give breath to my laughter.

"O bright Snake, the Death-worm of Adam!
            (*Sing Eden Bower!*)
Wreathe thy neck with my hair's bright tether,
And wear my gold and thy gold together!   *140*

"On that day on the skirts of Eden,
            (*Alas the hour!*)
In thy shape shall I glide back to thee,
And in my shape for an instant view thee.

"But when thou'rt thou and Lilith is Lilith,
            (*Sing Eden Bower!*)
In what bliss past hearing or seeing
Shall each one drink of the other's being!

"With cries of 'Eve!' and 'Eden!' and 'Adam!'
            (*Alas the hour!*)   *150*
How shall we mingle our love's caresses,
I in thy coils, and thou in my tresses!

"With those names, ye echoes of Eden,
            (*Sing Eden Bower!*)
Fire shall cry from my heart that burneth,—
'Dust he is and to dust returneth!'

"Yet to-day, thou master of Lilith,—
            (*Alas the hour!*)
Wrap me round in the form I'll borrow
And let me tell thee of sweet to-morrow.   *160*

"In the planted garden eastward in Eden,
            (*Sing Eden Bower!*)
Where the river goes forth to water the garden,
The springs shall dry and the soil shall harden.

"Yea, where the bride-sleep fell upon Adam,
            (*Alas the hour!*)
None shall hear when the storm-wind whistles
Through roses choked among thorns and thistles.

"Yea, beside the east-gate of Eden,
            (*Sing Eden Bower!*)   *170*
Where God joined them and none might sever,
The sword turns this way and that for ever.

"What of Adam cast out of Eden?
            (*Alas the hour!*)
Lo! with care like a shadow shaken,
He tills the hard earth whence he was taken.

"What of Eve too, cast out of Eden?
            (*Sing Eden Bower!*)
Nay, but she, the bride of God's giving,
Must yet be mother of all men living.   *180*

"Lo, God's grace, by the grace of Lilith!
      (*Alas the hour!*)
To Eve's womb, from our sweet to-morrow,
God shall greatly multiply sorrow.

"Fold me fast, O God-snake of Eden!
      (*Sing Eden Bower!*)
What more prize than love to impel thee?
Grip and lip my limbs as I tell thee!

"Lo! two babes for Eve and for Adam!
      (*Alas the hour!*)   *190*
Lo! sweet Snake, the travail and treasure,—
Two men-children born for their pleasure!

"The first is Cain and the second Abel:
      (*Sing Eden Bower!*)
The soul of one shall be made thy brother,
And thy tongue shall lap the blood of the other."
      (*Alas the hour!*)

                (*1869*)

THE BALLAD OF DEAD LADIES

FRANÇOIS VILLON, 1450

Tell me now in what hidden way is
  Lady Flora the lovely Roman?
Where's Hipparchia, and where is Thais,
  Neither of them the fairer woman?
  Where is Echo, beheld of no man,
Only heard on river and mere,—
  She whose beauty was more than human? . . .
But where are the snows of yester-year?

Where's Héloise, the learned nun,
  For whose sake Abeillard, I ween,   *10*
Lost manhood and put priesthood on?
  (From Love he won such dule and teen!)

And where, I pray you, is the Queen
Who willed that Buridan should steer
   Sewed in a sack's mouth down the Seine? . . .
But where are the snows of yester-year?

White Queen Blanche, like a queen of lilies,
   With a voice like any mermaiden,—
Bertha Broadfoot, Beatrice, Alice,
   And Ermengarde the lady of Maine,—   *20*
   And that good Joan whom Englishmen
At Rouen doomed and burned her there,—
   Mother of God, where are they then? . . .
But where are the snows of yester-year?

Nay, never ask this week, fair lord,
   Where they are gone, nor yet this year,
Save with thus much for an overword,—
   But where are the snows of yester-year?

                        (*1869*)

TO DEATH, OF HIS LADY

FRANÇOIS VILLON

Death, of thee do I make my moan,
   Who hadst my lady away from me,
   Nor wilt assuage thine enmity
Till with her life thou hast mine own:
For since that hour my strength has flown.
   Lo! what wrong was her life to thee,
                Death?

Two we were, and the heart was one;
   Which now being dead, dead I must be,
   Or seem alive as lifelessly
As in the choir the painted stone,
                Death!

                        (*1869*)

JOHN OF TOURS

OLD FRENCH

John of Tours is back with peace,
But he comes home ill at ease.

"Good-morrow, mother." "Good-morrow, son;
Your wife has borne you a little one."

"Go now, mother, go before,
Make me a bed upon the floor;

"Very low your foot must fall,
That my wife hear not at all."

As it neared the midnight toll,   *10*
John of Tours gave up his soul.

"Tell me now, my mother my dear,
What's the crying that I hear?"

"Daughter, it's the children wake,
Crying with their teeth that ache."

"Tell me though, my mother my dear,
What's the knocking that I hear?"

"Daughter, it's the carpenter
Mending planks upon the stair."

"Tell me too, my mother my dear,   *20*
What's the singing that I hear?"

"Daughter, it's the priests in rows
Going round about our house."

"Tell me then, my mother my dear,
What's the dress that I should wear?"

"Daughter, any reds or blues,
But the black is most in use."

"Nay, but say, my mother my dear,
Why do you fall weeping here?"

"Oh! the truth must be said,—
It's that John of Tours is dead."   *30*

"Mother, let the sexton know
That the grave must be for two;

"Aye, and still have room to spare,
For you must shut the baby there."

(1869)

MY FATHER'S CLOSE

OLD FRENCH

Inside my father's close,
   (Fly away O my heart away!)
Sweet apple-blossom blows
      So sweet.

Three kings' daughters fair,
   (Fly away O my heart away!)
They lie below it there
      So sweet.

"Ah!" says the eldest one,
   (Fly away O my heart away!)   *10*
"I think the day's begun
      So sweet."

"Ah!" says the second one,
   (Fly away O my heart away!)
"Far off I hear the drum
      So sweet."

"Ah!" says the youngest one,
    (Fly away O my heart away!)
"It's my true love, my own,
        So sweet.   20

"Oh! if he fight and win,"
    (Fly away O my heart away!)
"I keep my love for him,
        So sweet:
Oh! let him lose or win,
        He hath it still complete."

                                    (1869)

The House of Life: A Sonnet-Sequence

Part I • Youth and Change

Part II • Change and Fate

A Sonnet is a moment's monument,—
   Memorial from the Soul's eternity
   To one dead deathless hour. Look that it be,
Whether for lustral rite or dire portent,
Of its own arduous fulness reverent:
   Carve it in ivory or in ebony,
   As Day or Night may rule; and let Time see
Its flowering crest impearled and orient.

A Sonnet is a coin: its face reveals
   The soul,—its converse, to what Power 'tis due:—   10
Whether for tribute to the august appeals
   Of Life, or dower in Love's high retinue,
It serve; or, 'mid the dark wharf's cavernous breath,
In Charon's palm it pay the toll to Death.

Part I • Youth and Change
SONNET I: LOVE ENTHRONED

I marked all kindred Powers the heart finds fair:—
   Truth, with awed lips; and Hope, with eyes upcast;
   And Fame, whose loud wings fan the ashen Past
To signal-fires, Oblivion's flight to scare;
And Youth, with still some single golden hair
   Unto his shoulder clinging, since the last
   Embrace wherein two sweet arms held him fast;
And Life, still wreathing flowers for Death to wear.

Love's throne was not with these; but far above
   All passionate wind of welcome and farewell   *10*
He sat in breathless bowers they dream not of;
   Though Truth foreknow Love's heart, and Hope fore-
      tell,
   And Fame be for Love's sake desirable,
And Youth be dear, and Life be sweet to Love.

SONNET II: BRIDAL BIRTH

As when desire, long darkling, dawns, and first
   The mother looks upon the newborn child,
   Even so my Lady stood at gaze and smiled
When her soul knew at length the Love it nurs'd.
Born with her life, creature of poignant thirst
   And exquisite hunger, at her heart Love lay
   Quickening in darkness, till a voice that day
Cried on him, and the bonds of birth were burst.

Now, shadowed by his wings, our faces yearn
   Together, as his full-grown feet now range   *10*
     The grove, and his warm hands our couch prepare:
Till to his song our bodiless souls in turn
   Be born his children, when Death's nuptial change
     Leaves us for light the halo of his hair.

SONNET III: LOVE'S TESTAMENT

O thou who at Love's hour ecstatically
  Unto my heart dost evermore present,
  Clothed with his fire, thy heart his testament;
Whom I have neared and felt thy breath to be
The inmost incense of his sanctuary;
  Who without speech hast owned him, and, intent
  Upon his will, thy life with mine hast blent,
And murmured, "I am thine, thou'rt one with me!"

O what from thee the grace, to me the prize,
  And what to Love the glory,—when the whole   *10*
  Of the deep stair thou tread'st to the dim shoal
And weary water of the place of sighs,
And there dost work deliverance, as thine eyes
  Draw up my prisoned spirit to thy soul!

SONNET IV: LOVESIGHT

When do I see thee most, beloved one?
  When in the light the spirits of mine eyes
  Before thy face, their altar, solemnize
The worship of that Love through thee made known?
Or when in the dusk hours, (we two alone,)
  Close-kissed and eloquent of still replies
  Thy twilight-hidden glimmering visage lies,
And my soul only sees thy soul its own?

O love, my love! if I no more should see
Thyself, nor on the earth the shadow of thee,   *10*
  Nor image of thine eyes in any spring,—
How then should sound upon Life's darkening slope
The ground-whirl of the perished leaves of Hope,
  The wind of Death's imperishable wing?

SONNET V: HEART'S HOPE

By what word's power, the key of paths untrod,
   Shall I the difficult deeps of Love explore,
   Till parted waves of Song yield up the shore
Even as that sea which Israel crossed dryshod?
For lo! in some poor rhythmic period,
   Lady, I fain would tell how evermore
   Thy soul I know not from thy body, nor
Thee from myself, neither our love from God.

Yea, in God's name, and Love's, and thine, would I
   Draw from one loving heart such evidence   *10*
As to all hearts all things shall signify;
   Tender as dawn's first hill-fire, and intense
   As instantaneous penetrating sense,
In Spring's birth-hour, of other Springs gone by.

SONNET VI: THE KISS

What smouldering senses in death's sick delay
   Or seizure of malign vicissitude
   Can rob this body of honour, or denude
This soul of wedding-raiment worn to-day?
For lo! even now my lady's lips did play
   With these my lips such consonant interlude
   As laurelled Orpheus longed for when he wooed
The half-drawn hungering face with that last lay.

I was a child beneath her touch,—a man
   When breast to breast we clung, even I and she,—   *10*
   A spirit when her spirit looked through me,—
A god when all our life-breath met to fan
Our life-blood, till love's emulous ardours ran,
   Fire within fire, desire in deity.

[SONNET VIa: NUPTIAL SLEEP*

At length their long kiss severed, with sweet smart:
    And as the last slow sudden drops are shed
    From sparkling eaves when all the storm has fled,
So singly flagged the pulses of each heart.
Their bosoms sundered, with the opening start
    Of married flowers to either side outspread
    From the knit stem; yet still their mouths, burnt red,
Fawned on each other where they lay apart.

Sleep sank them lower than the tide of dreams,
    And their dreams watched them sink, and slid away.
Slowly their souls swam up again, through gleams   *11*
    Of watered light and dull drowned waifs of day;
Till from some wonder of new woods and streams
    He woke, and wondered more: for there she lay.]

SONNET VII: SUPREME SURRENDER

To all the spirits of Love that wander by
    Along his love-sown harvest-field of sleep
    My lady lies apparent; and the deep
Calls to the deep; and no man sees but I.
The bliss so long afar, at length so nigh,
    Rests there attained. Methinks proud Love must weep
    When Fate's control doth from his harvest reap
The sacred hour for which the years did sigh.

First touched, the hand now warm around my neck
    Taught memory long to mock desire: and lo!   *10*
    Across my breast the abandoned hair doth flow,
Where one shorn tress long stirred the longing ache:
And next the heart that trembled for its sake
    Lies the queen-heart in sovereign overthrow.

* Published in 1870, attacked by Buchanan as offensively "fleshly,"
and thereafter suppressed.

SONNET VIII: LOVE'S LOVERS

Some ladies love the jewels in Love's zone,
   And gold-tipped darts he hath for painless play
   In idle scornful hours he flings away;
And some that listen to his lute's soft tone
Do love to vaunt the silver praise their own;
   Some prize his blindfold sight; and there be they
   Who kissed his wings which brought him yesterday
And thank his wings to-day that he is flown.

My lady only loves the heart of Love:
   Therefore Love's heart, my lady, hath for thee   *10*
   His bower of unimagined flower and tree:
There kneels he now, and all-anhungered of
Thine eyes grey-lit in shadowing hair above,
   Seals with thy mouth his immortality.

SONNET IX: PASSION AND WORSHIP

One flame-winged brought a white-winged harp-player
   Even where my lady and I lay all alone;
   Saying: "Behold, this minstrel is unknown;
Bid him depart, for I am minstrel here:
Only my strains are to Love's dear ones dear."
   Then said I: "Through thine hautboy's rapturous tone
   Unto my lady still this harp makes moan,
And still she deems the cadence deep and clear."

Then said my lady: "Thou art Passion of Love,
   And this Love's Worship: both he plights to me.   *10*
   Thy mastering music walks the sunlit sea:
But where wan water trembles in the grove
And the wan moon is all the light thereof,
   This harp still makes my name its voluntary."

SONNET X: THE PORTRAIT

O Lord of all compassionate control,
  O Love! let this my lady's picture glow
  Under my hand to praise her name, and show
Even of her inner self the perfect whole:
That he who seeks her beauty's furthest goal,
  Beyond the light that the sweet glances throw
  And refluent wave of the sweet smile, may know
The very sky and sea-line of her soul.

Lo! it is done. Above the enthroning throat
  The mouth's mould testifies of voice and kiss,   *10*
    The shadowed eyes remember and foresee.
Her face is made her shrine. Let all men note
  That in all years (O Love, thy gift is this!)
    They that would look on her must come to me.

SONNET XI: THE LOVE-LETTER

Warmed by her hand and shadowed by her hair
  As close she leaned and poured her heart through thee,
  Whereof the articulate throbs accompany
The smooth black stream that makes thy whiteness fair,—
Sweet fluttering sheet, even of her breath aware,—
  Oh let thy silent song disclose to me
  That soul wherewith her lips and eyes agree
Like married music in Love's answering air.

Fain had I watched her when, at some fond thought,
  Her bosom to the writing closelier press'd,   *10*
  And her breast's secrets peered into her breast;
When, through eyes raised an instant, her soul sought
My soul, and from the sudden confluence caught
  The words that made her love the loveliest.

SONNET XII: THE LOVERS' WALK

Sweet twining hedgeflowers wind-stirred in no wise
    On this June day; and hand that clings in hand:
    Still glades; and meeting faces scarcely fann'd:—
An osier-odoured stream that draws the skies
Deep to its heart; and mirrored eyes in eyes:—
    Fresh hourly wonder o'er the Summer land
    Of light and cloud; and two souls softly spann'd
With one o'erarching heaven of smiles and sighs:—

Even such their path, whose bodies lean unto
    Each other's visible sweetness amorously,—   10
    Whose passionate hearts lean by Love's high decree
Together on his heart for ever true,
As the cloud-foaming firmamental blue
    Rests on the blue line of a foamless sea.

SONNET XIII: YOUTH'S ANTIPHONY

"I love you, sweet: how can you ever learn
    How much I love you?" "You I love even so,
    And so I learn it." "Sweet, you cannot know
How fair you are." "If fair enough to earn
Your love, so much is all my love's concern."
    "My love grows hourly, sweet." "Mine too doth grow,
    Yet love seemed full so many hours ago!"
Thus lovers speak, till kisses claim their turn.

Ah! happy they to whom such words as these
    In youth have served for speech the whole day long,
    Hour after hour, remote from the world's throng,   11
Work, contest, fame, all life's confederate pleas,—
What while Love breathed in sighs and silences
    Through two blent souls one rapturous undersong.

SONNET XIV: YOUTH'S SPRING-TRIBUTE

On this sweet bank your head thrice sweet and dear
  I lay, and spread your hair on either side,
  And see the newborn woodflowers bashful-eyed
Look through the golden tresses here and there.
On these debateable borders of the year
  Spring's foot half falters; scarce she yet may know
  The leafless blackthorn-blossom from the snow;
And through her bowers the wind's way still is clear.

But April's sun strikes down the glades to-day;
  So shut your eyes upturned, and feel my kiss   *10*
Creep, as the Spring now thrills through every spray,
  Up your warm throat to your warm lips: for this
  Is even the hour of Love's sworn suitservice,
With whom cold hearts are counted castaway.

SONNET XV: THE BIRTH-BOND

Have you not noted, in some family
  Where two were born of a first marriage-bed,
  How still they own their gracious bond, though fed
And nursed on the forgotten breast and knee?—
How to their father's children they shall be
  In act and thought of one goodwill; but each
  Shall for the other have, in silence speech,
And in a word complete community?

Even so, when first I saw you, seemed it, love,
  That among souls allied to mine was yet   *10*
One nearer kindred than life hinted of.
  O born with me somewhere that men forget,
  And though in years of sight and sound unmet,
Known for my soul's birth-partner well enough!

SONNET XVI: A DAY OF LOVE

Those envied places which do know her well,
  And are so scornful of this lonely place,
  Even now for once are emptied of her grace:
Nowhere but here she is: and while Love's spell
From his predominant presence doth compel
  All alien hours, an outworn populace,
  The hours of Love fill full the echoing space
With sweet confederate music favourable.

Now many memories make solicitous
  The delicate love-lines of her mouth, till, lit   *10*
  With quivering fire, the words take wing from it;
As here between our kisses we sit thus
  Speaking of things remembered, and so sit
Speechless while things forgotten call to us.

SONNET XVII: BEAUTY'S PAGEANT

What dawn-pulse at the heart of heaven, or last
  Incarnate flower of culminating day,—
  What marshalled marvels on the skirts of May,
Or song full-quired, sweet June's encomiast;
What glory of change by Nature's hand amass'd
  Can vie with all those moods of varying grace
  Which o'er one loveliest woman's form and face
Within this hour, within this room, have pass'd?

Love's very vesture and elect disguise
  Was each fine movement,—wonder new-begot   *10*
  Of lily or swan or swan-stemmed galiot;
Joy to his sight who now the sadlier sighs,
Parted again; and sorrow yet for eyes
  Unborn, that read these words and saw her not.

SONNET XVIII: GENIUS IN BEAUTY

Beauty like hers is genius. Not the call
   Of Homer's or of Dante's heart sublime,—
   Not Michael's hand furrowing the zones of time,—
Is more with compassed mysteries musical;
Nay, not in Spring's or Summer's sweet footfall
   More gathered gifts exuberant Life bequeaths
   Than doth this sovereign face, whose love-spell breathes
Even from its shadowed contour on the wall.

As many men are poets in their youth,
   But for one sweet-strung soul the wires prolong   *10*
   Even through all change the indomitable song;
So in likewise the envenomed years, whose tooth
Rends shallower grace with ruin void of ruth,
   Upon this beauty's power shall wreak no wrong.

SONNET XIX: SILENT NOON

Your hands lie open in the long fresh grass,—
   The finger-points look through like rosy blooms:
   Your eyes smile peace. The pasture gleams and glooms
'Neath billowing skies that scatter and amass.
All round our nest, far as the eye can pass,
   Are golden kingcup-fields with silver edge
   Where the cow-parsley skirts the hawthorn-hedge.
'Tis visible silence, still as the hour-glass.

Deep in the sun-searched growths the dragon-fly
Hangs like a blue thread loosened from the sky:—   *10*
   So this wing'd hour is dropt to us from above.
Oh! clasp we to our hearts, for deathless dower,
This close-companioned inarticulate hour
   When twofold silence was the song of love.

SONNET XX: GRACIOUS MOONLIGHT

Even as the moon grows queenlier in mid-space
  When the sky darkens, and her cloud-rapt car
  Thrills with intenser radiance from afar,—
So lambent, lady, beams thy sovereign grace
When the drear soul desires thee. Of that face
  What shall be said,—which, like a governing star,
  Gathers and garners from all things that are
Their silent penetrative loveliness?

O'er water-daisies and wild waifs of Spring,
  There where the iris rears its gold-crowned sheaf   *10*
  With flowering rush and sceptred arrow-leaf,
So have I marked Queen Dian, in bright ring
Of cloud above and wave below, take wing
  And chase night's gloom, as thou the spirit's grief.

SONNET XXI: LOVE-SWEETNESS

Sweet dimness of her loosened hair's downfall
  About thy face; her sweet hands round thy head
  In gracious fostering union garlanded;
Her tremulous smiles; her glances' sweet recall
Of love; her murmuring sighs memorial;
  Her mouth's culled sweetness by thy kisses shed
  On cheeks and neck and eyelids, and so led
Back to her mouth which answers there for all:—

What sweeter than these things, except the thing
  In lacking which all these would lose their sweet:—
  The confident heart's still fervour: the swift beat   *11*
And soft subsidence of the spirit's wing,
Then when it feels, in cloud-girt wayfaring,
  The breath of kindred plumes against its feet?

SONNET XXII: HEART'S HAVEN

Sometimes she is a child within mine arms,
   Cowering beneath dark wings that love must chase,—
   With still tears showering and averted face,
Inexplicably filled with faint alarms:
And oft from mine own spirit's hurtling harms
   I crave the refuge of her deep embrace,—
   Against all ills the fortified strong place
And sweet reserve of sovereign counter-charms.

And Love, our light at night and shade at noon,
   Lulls us to rest with songs, and turns away   *10*
   All shafts of shelterless tumultuous day.
Like the moon's growth, his face gleams through his tune;
And as soft waters warble to the moon,
   Our answering spirits chime one roundelay.

SONNET XXIII: LOVE'S BAUBLES

I stood where Love in brimming armfuls bore
   Slight wanton flowers and foolish toys of fruit:
   And round him ladies thronged in warm pursuit,
Fingered and lipped and proffered the strange store.
And from one hand the petal and the core
   Savoured of sleep; and cluster and curled shoot
   Seemed from another hand like shame's salute,—
Gifts that I felt my cheek was blushing for.

At last Love bade my Lady give the same:
   And as I looked, the dew was light thereon;   *10*
   And as I took them, at her touch they shone
With inmost heaven-hue of the heart of flame.
And then Love said: "Lo! when the hand is hers,
Follies of love are love's true ministers."

SONNET XXIV: PRIDE OF YOUTH

Even as a child, of sorrow that we give
  The dead, but little in his heart can find,
  Since without need of thought to his clear mind
Their turn it is to die and his to live:—
Even so the winged New Love smiles to receive
  Along his eddying plumes the auroral wind,
  Nor, forward glorying, casts one look behind
Where night-rack shrouds the Old Love fugitive.

There is a change in every hour's recall,
  And the last cowslip in the fields we see
  On the same day with the first corn-poppy.
Alas for hourly change! Alas for all
The loves that from his hand proud Youth lets fall,
  Even as the beads of a told rosary!

10

SONNET XXV: WINGED HOURS

Each hour until we meet is as a bird
  That wings from far his gradual way along
  The rustling covert of my soul,—his song
Still loudlier trilled through leaves more deeply stirr'd:
But at the hour of meeting, a clear word
  Is every note he sings, in Love's own tongue;
  Yet, Love, thou know'st the sweet strain suffers wrong,
Full oft through our contending joys unheard.

What of that hour at last, when for her sake
  No wing may fly to me nor song may flow;
  When, wandering round my life unleaved, I know
The bloodied feathers scattered in the brake,
And think how she, far from me, with like eyes
Sees through the untuneful bough the wingless skies?

10

SONNET XXVI: MID-RAPTURE

Thou lovely and beloved, thou my love;
   Whose kiss seems still the first; whose summoning eyes,
   Even now, as for our love-world's new sunrise,
Shed very dawn; whose voice, attuned above
All modulation of the deep-bowered dove,
   Is like a hand laid softly on the soul;
   Whose hand is like a sweet voice to control
Those worn tired brows it hath the keeping of:—

What word can answer to thy word,—what gaze
   To thine, which now absorbs within its sphere   *10*
   My worshiping face, till I am mirrored there
Light-circled in a heaven of deep-drawn rays?
What clasp, what kiss mine inmost heart can prove,
O lovely and beloved, O my love?

SONNET XXVII: HEART'S COMPASS

Sometimes thou seem'st not as thyself alone,
   But as the meaning of all things that are;
   A breathless wonder, shadowing forth afar
Some heavenly solstice hushed and halcyon;
Whose unstirred lips are music's visible tone;
   Whose eyes the sun-gate of the soul unbar,
   Being of its furthest fires oracular;—
The evident heart of all life sown and mown.

Even such Love is; and is not thy name Love?
   Yea, by thy hand the Love-god rends apart   *10*
   All gathering clouds of Night's ambiguous art;
Flings them far down, and sets thine eyes above;
And simply, as some gage of flower or glove,
   Stakes with a smile the world against thy heart.

SONNET XXVIII: SOUL-LIGHT

What other woman could be loved like you,
    Or how of you should love possess his fill?
    After the fulness of all rapture, still,—
As at the end of some deep avenue
A tender glamour of day,—there comes to view
    Far in your eyes a yet more hungering thrill,—
    Such fire as Love's soul-winnowing hands distil
Even from his inmost ark of light and dew.

And as the traveller triumphs with the sun,
    Glorying in heat's mid-height, yet startide brings   *10*
    Wonder new-born, and still fresh transport springs
From limpid lambent hours of day begun;—
Even so, through eyes and voice, your soul doth move
My soul with changeful light of infinite love.

SONNET XXIX: THE MOONSTAR

Lady, I thank thee for thy loveliness,
    Because my lady is more lovely still.
    Glorying I gaze, and yield with glad goodwill
To thee thy tribute; by whose sweet-spun dress
Of delicate life Love labours to assess
    My lady's absolute queendom; saying, "Lo!
    How high this beauty is, which yet doth show
But as that beauty's sovereign votaress."

Lady, I saw thee with her, side by side;
    And as, when night's fair fires their queen surround,
An emulous star too near the moon will ride,—   *11*
    Even so thy rays within her luminous bound
    Were traced no more; and by the light so drown'd,
Lady, not thou but she was glorified.

SONNET XXX: LAST FIRE

Love, through your spirit and mine what summer eve
  Now glows with glory of all things possess'd,
  Since this day's sun of rapture filled the west
And the light sweetened as the fire took leave?
Awhile now softlier let your bosom heave,
  As in Love's harbour, even that loving breast,
  All care takes refuge while we sink to rest,
And mutual dreams the bygone bliss retrieve.

Many the days that Winter keeps in store,
  Sunless throughout, or whose brief sun-glimpses   *10*
  Scarce shed the heaped snow through the naked trees.
This day at least was Summer's paramour,
Sun-coloured to the imperishable core
  With sweet well-being of love and full heart's ease.

SONNET XXXI: HER GIFTS

High grace, the dower of queens; and therewithal
  Some wood-born wonder's sweet simplicity;
  A glance like water brimming with the sky
Or hyacinth-light where forest-shadows fall;
Such thrilling pallor of cheek as doth enthral
  The heart; a mouth whose passionate forms imply
  All music and all silence held thereby;
Deep golden locks, her sovereign coronal;
A round reared neck, meet column of Love's shrine
  To cling to when the heart takes sanctuary;   *10*
  Hands which for ever at Love's bidding be,
And soft-stirred feet still answering to his sign:—
These are her gifts, as tongue may tell them o'er.
Breathe low her name, my soul; for that means more.

SONNET XXXII: EQUAL TROTH

Not by one measure mayst thou mete our love;
  For how should I be loved as I love thee?—
  I, graceless, joyless, lacking absolutely
All gifts that with thy queenship best behove;—
Thou, throned in every heart's elect alcove,
  And crowned with garlands culled from every tree,
  Which for no head but thine, by Love's decree,
All beauties and all mysteries interwove.

But here thine eyes and lips yield soft rebuke:—
  "Then only" (say'st thou) "could I love thee less,   *10*
    When thou couldst doubt my love's equality."
Peace, sweet! If not to sum but worth we look,—
  Thy heart's transcendence, not my heart's excess,—
    Then more a thousandfold thou lov'st than I.

SONNET XXXIII: VENUS VICTRIX

Could Juno's self more sovereign presence wear
  Than thou, 'mid other ladies throned in grace?—
  Or Pallas, when thou bend'st with soul-stilled face
O'er poet's page gold-shadowed in thy hair?
Dost thou than Venus seem less heavenly fair
  When o'er the sea of love's tumultuous trance
  Hovers thy smile, and mingles with thy glance
That sweet voice like the last wave murmuring there?

Before such triune loveliness divine
  Awestruck I ask, which goddess here most claims   *10*
The prize that, howsoe'er adjudged, is thine?
  Then Love breathes low the sweetest of thy names;
And Venus Victrix to my heart doth bring
Herself, the Helen of her guerdoning.

SONNET XXXIV: THE DARK GLASS

Not I myself know all my love for thee:
 How should I reach so far, who cannot weigh
 To-morrow's dower by gage of yesterday?
Shall birth and death, and all dark names that be
As doors and windows bared to some loud sea,
 Lash deaf mine ears and blind my face with spray;
 And shall my sense pierce love,—the last relay
And ultimate outpost of eternity?

Lo! what am I to Love, the lord of all?
 One murmuring shell he gathers from the sand,—   *10*
 One little heart-flame sheltered in his hand.
Yet through thine eyes he grants me clearest call
And veriest touch of powers primordial
 That any hour-girt life may understand.

SONNET XXXV: THE LAMP'S SHRINE

Sometimes I fain would find in thee some fault,
 That I might love thee still in spite of it:
 Yet how should our Lord Love curtail one whit
Thy perfect praise whom most he would exalt?
Alas! he can but make my heart's low vault
 Even in men's sight unworthier, being lit
 By thee, who thereby show'st more exquisite
Like fiery chrysoprase in deep basalt.

Yet will I nowise shrink; but at Love's shrine
 Myself within the beams his brow doth dart   *10*
 Will set the flashing jewel of thy heart
In that dull chamber where it deigns to shine:
For lo! in honour of thine excellencies
My heart takes pride to show how poor it is.

SONNET XXXVI: LIFE-IN-LOVE

Not in thy body is thy life at all,
   But in this lady's lips and hands and eyes;
   Through these she yields thee life that vivifies
What else were sorrow's servant and death's thrall.
Look on thyself without her, and recall
   The waste remembrance and forlorn surmise
   That lived but in a dead-drawn breath of sighs
O'er vanished hours and hours eventual.

Even so much life hath the poor tress of hair
   Which, stored apart, is all love hath to show   *10*
   For heart-beats and for fire-heats long ago;
Even so much life endures unknown, even where,
'Mid change the changeless night environeth,
Lies all that golden hair undimmed in death.

SONNET XXXVII: THE LOVE-MOON

"When that dead face, bowered in the furthest years,
   Which once was all the life years held for thee,
   Can now scarce bid the tides of memory
Cast on thy soul a little spray of tears,—
How canst thou gaze into these eyes of hers
   Whom now thy heart delights in, and not see
   Within each orb Love's philtred euphrasy
Make them of buried troth remembrancers?"

"Nay, pitiful Love, nay, loving Pity! Well
   Thou knowest that in these twain I have confess'd   *10*
Two very voices of thy summoning bell.
   Nay, Master, shall not Death make manifest
In these the culminant changes which approve
The love-moon that must light my soul to Love?"

SONNET XXXVIII: THE MORROW'S MESSAGE

"Thou Ghost," I said, "and is thy name To-day?—
   Yesterday's son, with such an abject brow!—
   And can To-morrow be more pale than thou?"
While yet I spoke, the silence answered: "Yea,
Henceforth our issue is all grieved and grey,
   And each beforehand makes such poor avow
   As of old leaves beneath the budding bough
Or night-drift that the sundawn shreds away."

Then cried I: "Mother of many malisons,
   O Earth, receive me to thy dusty bed!"   *10*
   But therewithal the tremulous silence said:
"Lo! Love yet bids thy lady greet thee once:—
Yea, twice,—whereby thy life is still the sun's,
   And thrice,—whereby the shadow of death is dead."

SONNET XXXIX: SLEEPLESS DREAMS

Girt in dark growths, yet glimmering with one star,
   O night desirous as the nights of youth!
   Why should my heart within thy spell, forsooth,
Now beat, as the bride's finger-pulses are
Quickened within the girdling golden bar?
   What wings are these that fan my pillow smooth?
   And why does Sleep, waved back by Joy and Ruth,
Tread softly round and gaze at me from far?

Nay, night deep-leaved! And would Love feign in thee
   Some shadowy palpitating grove that bears   *10*
   Rest for man's eyes and music for his ears?
O lonely night! art thou not known to me,
A thicket hung with masks of mockery
   And watered with the wasteful warmth of tears?

SONNET XL: SEVERED SELVES

Two separate divided silences,
   Which, brought together, would find loving voice;
   Two glances which together would rejoice
In love, now lost like stars beyond dark trees;
Two hands apart whose touch alone gives ease;
   Two bosoms which, heart-shrined with mutual flame,
   Would, meeting in one clasp, be made the same;
Two souls, the shores wave-mocked of sundering seas:—

Such are we now. Ah! may our hope forecast
   Indeed one hour again, when on this stream   *10*
   Of darkened love once more the light shall gleam?—
An hour how slow to come, how quickly past,—
Which blooms and fades, and only leaves at last,
   Faint as shed flowers, the attenuated dream.

SONNET XLI: THROUGH DEATH TO LOVE

Like labour-laden moonclouds faint to flee
   From winds that sweep the winter-bitten wold,—
   Like multiform circumfluence manifold
Of night's flood-tide,—like terrors that agree
Of hoarse-tongued fire and inarticulate sea,—
   Even such, within some glass dimmed by our breath,
   Our hearts discern wild images of Death,
Shadows and shoals that edge eternity.

Howbeit athwart Death's imminent shade doth soar
   One Power, than flow of stream or flight of dove   *10*
   Sweeter to glide around, to brood above.
Tell me, my heart,—what angel-greeted door
Or threshold of wing-winnowed threshing-floor
   Hath guest fire-fledged as thine, whose lord is Love?

SONNET XLII: HOPE OVERTAKEN

I deemed thy garments, O my Hope, were grey,
  So far I viewed thee. Now the space between
  Is passed at length; and garmented in green
Even as in days of yore thou stand'st to-day.
Ah God! and but for lingering dull dismay,
  On all that road our footsteps erst had been
  Even thus commingled, and our shadows seen
Blent on the hedgerows and the water-way.

O Hope of mine whose eyes are living love,
  No eyes but hers,—O Love and Hope the same!—   *10*
    Lean close to me, for now the sinking sun
That warmed our feet scarce gilds our hair above.
  O hers thy voice and very hers thy name!
    Alas, cling round me, for the day is done!

SONNET XLIII: LOVE AND HOPE

Bless love and hope. Full many a withered year
  Whirled past us, eddying to its chill doomsday;
  And clasped together where the blown leaves lay
We long have knelt and wept full many a tear.
Yet lo! one hour at last, the Spring's compeer,
  Flutes softly to us from some green byeway:
  Those years, those tears are dead, but only they:—
Bless love and hope, true soul; for we are here.

Cling heart to heart; nor of this hour demand
  Whether in very truth, when we are dead,   *10*
  Our hearts shall wake to know Love's golden head
Sole sunshine of the imperishable land;
Or but discern, through night's unfeatured scope,
Scorn-fired at length the illusive eyes of Hope.

SONNET XLIV: CLOUD AND WIND

Love, should I fear death most for you or me?
    Yet if you die, can I not follow you,
    Forcing the straits of change? Alas! but who
Shall wrest a bond from night's inveteracy,
Ere yet my hazardous soul put forth, to be
    Her warrant against all her haste might rue?—
    Ah! in your eyes so reached what dumb adieu,
What unsunned gyres of waste eternity?

And if I die the first, shall death be then
    A lampless watchtower whence I see you weep?—   *10*
    Or (woe is me!) a bed wherein my sleep
Ne'er notes (as death's dear cup at last you drain)
The hour when you too learn that all is vain
    And that Hope sows what Love shall never reap?

SONNET XLV: SECRET PARTING

Because our talk was of the cloud-control
    And moon-track of the journeying face of Fate,
    Her tremulous kisses faltered at love's gate
And her eyes dreamed against a distant goal:
But soon, remembering her how brief the whole
    Of joy, which its own hours annihilate,
    Her set gaze gathered, thirstier than of late,
And as she kissed, her mouth became her soul.

Thence in what ways we wandered, and how strove
    To build with fire-tried vows the piteous home   *10*
    Which memory haunts and whither sleep may roam,—
They only know for whom the roof of Love
Is the still-seated secret of the grove,
    Nor spire may rise nor bell be heard therefrom.

SONNET XLVI: PARTED LOVE

What shall be said of this embattled day
   And armèd occupation of this night
   By all thy foes beleaguered,—now when sight
Nor sound denotes the loved one far away?
Of these thy vanquished hours what shalt thou say,—
   As every sense to which she dealt delight
   Now labours lonely o'er the stark noon-height
To reach the sunset's desolate disarray?

Stand still, fond fettered wretch! while Memory's art
   Parades the Past before thy face, and lures   *10*
   Thy spirit to her passionate portraitures:
Till the tempestuous tide-gates flung apart
Flood with wild will the hollows of thy heart,
   And thy heart rends thee, and thy body endures.

SONNET XLVII: BROKEN MUSIC

The mother will not turn, who thinks she hears
   Her nursling's speech first grow articulate;
   But breathless with averted eyes elate
She sits, with open lips and open ears,
That it may call her twice. 'Mid doubts and fears
   Thus oft my soul has hearkened; till the song,
   A central moan for days, at length found tongue,
And the sweet music welled and the sweet tears.

But now, whatever while the soul is fain
   To list that wonted murmur, as it were   *10*
The speech-bound sea-shell's low importunate strain,—
   No breath of song, thy voice alone is there,
O bitterly beloved! and all her gain
   Is but the pang of unpermitted prayer.

SONNET XLVIII: DEATH-IN-LOVE

There came an image in Life's retinue
   That had Love's wings and bore his gonfalon:
   Fair was the web, and nobly wrought thereon,
O soul-sequestered face, thy form and hue!
Bewildering sounds, such as Spring wakens to,
   Shook in its folds; and through my heart its power
   Sped trackless as the immemorable hour
When birth's dark portal groaned and all was new.

But a veiled woman followed, and she caught
   The banner round its staff, to furl and cling,   *10*
   Then plucked a feather from the bearer's wing,
And held it to his lips that stirred it not,
And said to me, "Behold, there is no breath:
I and this Love are one, and I am Death."

SONNETS XLIX, L, LI, LII:
WILLOWWOOD

I

I sat with Love upon a woodside well,
   Leaning across the water, I and he;
   Nor ever did he speak nor looked at me,
But touched his lute wherein was audible
The certain secret thing he had to tell:
   Only our mirrored eyes met silently
   In the low wave; and that sound came to be
The passionate voice I knew; and my tears fell.

And at their fall, his eyes beneath grew hers;
And with his foot and with his wing-feathers   *10*
   He swept the spring that watered my heart's drouth.
Then the dark ripples spread to waving hair,
And as I stooped, her own lips rising there
   Bubbled with brimming kisses at my mouth.

I I

And now Love sang: but his was such a song
    So meshed with half-remembrance hard to free,
    As souls disused in death's sterility
May sing when the new birthday tarries long.
And I was made aware of a dumb throng
    That stood aloof, one form by every tree,
    All mournful forms, for each was I or she,
The shades of those our days that had no tongue.

They looked on us, and knew us and were known;
    While fast together, alive from the abyss,   10
    Clung the soul-wrung implacable close kiss;
And pity of self through all made broken moan
Which said, "For once, for once, for once alone!"
    And still Love sang, and what he sang was this:—

I I I

"O ye, all ye that walk in Willowwood,
    That walk with hollow faces burning white;
What fathom-depth of soul-struck widowhood,
    What long, what longer hours, one lifelong night,
Ere ye again, who so in vain have wooed
    Your last hope lost, who so in vain invite
Your lips to that their unforgotten food,
    Ere ye, ere ye again shall see the light!

Alas! the bitter banks in Willowwood,
    With tear-spurge wan, with blood-wort burning red:
Alas! if ever such a pillow could   11
    Steep deep the soul in sleep till she were dead,—
Better all life forget her than this thing,
That Willowwood should hold her wandering!"

I V

So sang he: and as meeting rose and rose
    Together cling through the wind's wellaway
    Nor change at once, yet near the end of day

The leaves drop loosened where the heart-stain glows,—
So when the song died did the kiss unclose;
   And her face fell back drowned, and was as grey
   As its grey eyes; and if it ever may
Meet mine again I know not if Love knows.

Only I know that I leaned low and drank
A long draught from the water where she sank,   *10*
   Her breath and all her tears and all her soul:
And as I leaned, I know I felt Love's face
Pressed on my neck with moan of pity and grace,
   Till both our heads were in his aureole.

SONNET LIII: WITHOUT HER

What of her glass without her? The blank grey
   There where the pool is blind of the moon's face.
   Her dress without her? The tossed empty space
Of cloud-rack whence the moon has passed away.
Her paths without her? Day's appointed sway
   Usurped by desolate night. Her pillowed place
   Without her? Tears, ah me! for love's good grace,
And cold forgetfulness of night or day.

What of the heart without her? Nay, poor heart,
   Of thee what word remains ere speech be still?   *10*
   A wayfarer by barren ways and chill,
Steep ways and weary, without her thou art,
Where the long cloud, the long wood's counterpart,
   Sheds doubled darkness up the labouring hill.

SONNET LIV: LOVE'S FATALITY

Sweet Love,—but oh! most dread Desire of Love
   Life-thwarted. Linked in gyves I saw them stand,
   Love shackled with Vain-longing, hand to hand:
And one was eyed as the blue vault above:

But hope tempestuous like a fire-cloud hove
   I' the other's gaze, even as in his whose wand
   Vainly all night with spell-wrought power has spann'd
The unyielding caves of some deep treasure-trove.

Also his lips, two writhen flakes of flame,
   Made moan: "Alas O Love, thus leashed with me!   *10*
   Wing-footed thou, wing-shouldered, once born free:
And I, thy cowering self, in chains grown tame,—
Bound to thy body and soul, named with thy name,—
   Life's iron heart, even Love's Fatality."

SONNET LV: STILLBORN LOVE

The hour which might have been yet might not be,
   Which man's and woman's heart conceived and bore
   Yet whereof life was barren,—on what shore
Bides it the breaking of Time's weary sea?
Bondchild of all consummate joys set free,
   It somewhere sighs and serves, and mute before
   The house of Love, hears through the echoing door
His hours elect in choral consonancy.

But lo! what wedded souls now hand in hand
Together tread at last the immortal strand   *10*
   With eyes where burning memory lights love home?
Lo! how the little outcast hour has turned
And leaped to them and in their faces yearned:—
   "I am your child: O parents, ye have come!"

SONNETS LVI, LVII, LVIII: TRUE WOMAN

I HERSELF

To be a sweetness more desired than Spring;
   A bodily beauty more acceptable
   Than the wild rose-tree's arch that crowns the fell;
To be an essence more environing

Than wine's drained juice; a music ravishing
   More than the passionate pulse of Philomel;—
   To be all this 'neath one soft bosom's swell
That is the flower of life:—how strange a thing!

How strange a thing to be what Man can know
   But as a sacred secret! Heaven's own screen   *10*
Hides her soul's purest depth and loveliest glow;
   Closely withheld, as all things most unseen,—
   The wave-bowered pearl,—the heart-shaped seal of green
That flecks the snowdrop underneath the snow.

II HER LOVE

She loves him; for her infinite soul is Love,
   And he her lodestar. Passion in her is
   A glass facing his fire, where the bright bliss
Is mirrored, and the heat returned. Yet move
That glass, a stranger's amorous flame to prove,
   And it shall turn, by instant contraries,
   Ice to the moon; while her pure fire to his
For whom it burns, clings close i' the heart's alcove.

Lo! they are one. With wifely breast to breast
   And circling arms, she welcomes all command   *10*
   Of love,—her soul to answering ardours fann'd:
Yet as morn springs or twilight sinks to rest,
Ah! who shall say she deems not loveliest
   The hour of sisterly sweet hand-in-hand?

III HER HEAVEN

If to grow old in Heaven is to grow young,
   (As the Seer saw and said,) then blest were he
   With youth for evermore, whose heaven should be
True Woman, she whom these weak notes have sung.
Here and hereafter,—choir-strains of her tongue,—
   Sky-spaces of her eyes,—sweet signs that flee
   About her soul's immediate sanctuary,—
Were Paradise all uttermost worlds among.

The sunrise blooms and withers on the hill
   Like any hillflower; and the noblest troth   *10*
   Dies here to dust. Yet shall Heaven's promise clothe
Even yet those lovers who have cherished still
This test for love:—in every kiss sealed fast
To feel the first kiss and forebode the last.

SONNET LIX: LOVE'S LAST GIFT

Love to his singer held a glistening leaf,
   And said: "The rose-tree and the apple-tree
   Have fruits to vaunt or flowers to lure the bee;
And golden shafts are in the feathered sheaf
Of the great harvest-marshal, the year's chief,
   Victorious Summer; aye, and 'neath warm sea
   Strange secret grasses lurk inviolably
Between the filtering channels of sunk reef.

All are my blooms; and all sweet blooms of love
   To thee I gave while Spring and Summer sang;   *10*
   But Autumn stops to listen, with some pang
From those worse things the wind is moaning of.
Only this laurel dreads no winter days:
Take my last gift; thy heart hath sung my praise.

Part II • Change and Fate

SONNET LX: TRANSFIGURED LIFE

As growth of form or momentary glance
   In a child's features will recall to mind
   The father's with the mother's face combin'd,—
Sweet interchange that memories still enhance:
And yet, as childhood's years and youth's advance,
   The gradual mouldings leave one stamp behind,
   Till in the blended likeness now we find
A separate man's or woman's countenance:—

So in the Song, the singer's Joy and Pain,
　Its very parents, evermore expand　　　　　　　　*10*
To bid the passion's fullgrown birth remain,
　By Art's transfiguring essence subtly spann'd;
　And from that song-cloud shaped as a man's hand
There comes the sound as of abundant rain.

SONNET LXI: THE SONG-THROE

By thine own tears thy song must tears beget,
　O Singer! Magic mirror thou hast none
　Except thy manifest heart; and save thine own
Anguish or ardour, else no amulet.
Cisterned in Pride, verse is the feathery jet
　Of soulless air-flung fountains; nay, more dry
　Than the Dead Sea for throats that thirst and sigh,
That song o'er which no singer's lids grew wet.

The Song-god—He the Sun-god—is no slave
　Of thine: thy Hunter he, who for thy soul　　　　*10*
　Fledges his shaft: to no august control
Of thy skilled hand his quivered store he gave:
But if thy lips' loud cry leap to his smart,
The inspir'd recoil shall pierce thy brother's heart.

SONNET LXII: THE SOUL'S SPHERE

Some prisoned moon in steep cloud-fastnesses,—
　Throned queen and thralled; some dying sun whose
　　　pyre
　Blazed with momentous memorable fire;—
Who hath not yearned and fed his heart with these?
Who, sleepless, hath not anguished to appease
　Tragical shadow's realm of sound and sight
　Conjectured in the lamentable night? . . . . .
Lo! the soul's sphere of infinite images!

What sense shall count them? Whether it forecast
  The rose-winged hours that flutter in the van   *10*
  Of Love's unquestioning unrevealèd span,—
Visions of golden futures: or that last
Wild pageant of the accumulated past
  That clangs and flashes for a drowning man.

SONNET LXIII: INCLUSIVENESS

The changing guests, each in a different mood,
  Sit at the roadside table and arise:
  And every life among them in likewise
Is a soul's board set daily with new food.
What man has bent o'er his son's sleep, to brood
  How that face shall watch his when cold it lies—
  Or thought, as his own mother kissed his eyes,
Of what her kiss was when his father wooed?

May not this ancient room thou sitt'st in dwell
  In separate living souls for joy or pain?   *10*
  Nay, all its corners may be painted plain
Where Heaven shows pictures of some life spent well,
  And may be stamped, a memory all in vain,
Upon the sight of lidless eyes in Hell.

SONNET LXIV: ARDOUR AND MEMORY

The cuckoo-throb, the heartbeat of the Spring;
  The rosebud's blush that leaves it as it grows
  Into the full-eyed fair unblushing rose;
The summer clouds that visit every wing
With fires of sunrise and of sunsetting;
  The furtive flickering streams to light re-born
  'Mid airs new-fledged and valorous lusts of morn,
While all the daughters of the daybreak sing:—

These ardour loves, and memory: and when flown
  All joys, and through dark forest-boughs in flight   *10*
  The wind swoops onward brandishing the light,
Even yet the rose-tree's verdure left alone
Will flush all ruddy though the rose be gone;
  With ditties and with dirges infinite.

SONNET LXV: KNOWN IN VAIN

As two whose love, first foolish, widening scope,
  Knows suddenly, to music high and soft,
  The Holy of holies; who because they scoff'd
Are now amazed with shame, nor dare to cope
With the whole truth aloud, lest heaven should ope;
  Yet, at their meetings, laugh not as they laugh'd
  In speech; nor speak, at length; but sitting oft
Together, within hopeless sight of hope
For hours are silent:—So it happeneth
  When Work and Will awake too late, to gaze   *10*
After their life sailed by, and hold their breath.
  Ah! who shall dare to search through what sad maze
  Thenceforth their incommunicable ways
Follow the desultory feet of Death?

SONNET LXVI: THE HEART OF THE NIGHT

From child to youth; from youth to arduous man;
  From lethargy to fever of the heart;
  From faithful life to dream-dowered days apart;
From trust to doubt; from doubt to brink of ban;—
Thus much of change in one swift cycle ran
  Till now. Alas, the soul!—how soon must she
  Accept her primal immortality,—
The flesh resume its dust whence it began?

O Lord of work and peace! O Lord of life!
  O Lord, the awful Lord of will! though late,   *10*
    Even yet renew this soul with duteous breath:
That when the peace is garnered in from strife,
  The work retrieved, the will regenerate,
    This soul may see thy face, O Lord of death!

SONNET LXVII: THE LANDMARK

Was *that* the landmark? What,—the foolish well
  Whose wave, low down, I did not stoop to drink
  But sat and flung the pebbles from its brink
In sport to send its imaged skies pell-mell,
(And mine own image, had I noted well!)—
  Was that my point of turning?—I had thought
  The stations of my course should rise unsought,
As altar-stone or ensigned citadel.

But lo! the path is missed, I must go back,
  And thirst to drink when next I reach the spring   *10*
  Which once I stained, which since may have grown
    black.
  Yet though no light be left nor bird now sing
  As here I turn, I'll thank God, hastening,
That the same goal is still on the same track.

SONNET LXVIII: A DARK DAY

The gloom that breathes upon me with these airs
  Is like the drops which strike the traveller's brow
  Who knows not, darkling, if they bring him now
Fresh storm, or be old rain the covert bears.
Ah! bodes this hour some harvest of new tares,
  Or hath but memory of the day whose plough
  Sowed hunger once,—the night at length when thou,
O prayer found vain, didst fall from out my prayers?

How prickly were the growths which yet how smooth,
   Along the hedgerows of this journey shed,   *10*
Lie by Time's grace till night and sleep may soothe!
   Even as the thistledown from pathsides dead
Gleaned by a girl in autumns of her youth,
   Which one new year makes soft her marriage-bed.

SONNET LXIX: AUTUMN IDLENESS

This sunlight shames November where he grieves
   In dead red leaves, and will not let him shun
   The day, though bough with bough be over-run.
But with a blessing every glade receives
High salutation; while from hillock-eaves
   The deer gaze calling, dappled white and dun,
   As if, being foresters of old, the sun
Had marked them with the shade of forest-leaves.

Here dawn to-day unveiled her magic glass;
   Here noon now gives the thirst and takes the dew;
Till eve bring rest when other good things pass.   *11*
   And here the lost hours the lost hours renew
While I still lead my shadow o'er the grass,
   Nor know, for longing, that which I should do.

SONNET LXX: THE HILL SUMMIT

This feast-day of the sun, his altar there
   In the broad west has blazed for vesper-song;
   And I have loitered in the vale too long
And gaze now a belated worshiper.
Yet may I not forget that I was 'ware,
   So journeying, of his face at intervals
   Transfigured where the fringed horizon falls,—
A fiery bush with coruscating hair.

And now that I have climbed and won this height,
   I must tread downward through the sloping shade   *10*
And travel the bewildered tracks till night.
    Yet for this hour I still may here be stayed
    And see the gold air and the silver fade
And the last bird fly into the last light.

SONNETS LXXI, LXXII, LXXIII: THE CHOICE

I

Eat thou and drink; to-morrow thou shalt die.
    Surely the earth, that's wise being very old,
    Needs not our help. Then loose me, love, and hold
Thy sultry hair up from my face; that I
May pour for thee this golden wine, brim-high,
    Till round the glass thy fingers glow like gold.
    We'll drown all hours: thy song, while hours are
        toll'd,
Shall leap, as fountains veil the changing sky.

Now kiss, and think that there are really those,
    My own high-bosomed beauty, who increase   *10*
      Vain gold, vain lore, and yet might choose our
        way!
      Through many years they toil; then on a day
    They die not,—for their life was death,—but cease;
And round their narrow lips the mould falls close.

II

Watch thou and fear; to-morrow thou shalt die.
    Or art thou sure thou shalt have time for death?
    Is not the day which God's word promiseth
To come man knows not when? In yonder sky,
Now while we speak, the sun speeds forth: can I
    Or thou assure him of his goal? God's breath
    Even at this moment haply quickeneth
The air to a flame; till spirits, always nigh

Though screened and hid, shall walk the daylight
    here.
  And dost thou prate of all that man shall do?   *10*
    Canst thou, who hast but plagues, presume to be
    Glad in his gladness that comes after thee?
  Will *his* strength slay *thy* worm in Hell? Go to:
Cover thy countenance, and watch, and fear.

III

Think thou and act; to-morrow thou shalt die.
  Outstretched in the sun's warmth upon the shore,
  Thou say'st: "Man's measured path is all gone o'er:
Up all his years, steeply, with strain and sigh,
Man clomb until he touched the truth; and I,
  Even I, am he whom it was destined for."
  How should this be? Art thou then so much more
Than they who sowed, that thou shouldst reap thereby?

Nay, come up hither. From this wave-washed mound
  Unto the furthest flood-brim look with me;   *10*
Then reach on with thy thought till it be drown'd.
  Miles and miles distant though the last line be,
And though thy soul sail leagues and leagues
    beyond,—
  Still, leagues beyond those leagues, there is more
    sea.

SONNETS LXXIV, LXXV, LXXVI: OLD AND NEW ART

I ST. LUKE THE PAINTER

Give honour unto Luke Evangelist;
  For he it was (the aged legends say)
  Who first taught Art to fold her hands and pray.
Scarcely at once she dared to rend the mist
Of devious symbols: but soon having wist
  How sky-breadth and field-silence and this day
  Are symbols also in some deeper way,
She looked through these to God and was God's priest.

And if, past noon, her toil began to irk,
  And she sought talismans, and turned in vain   *10*
    To soulless self-reflections of man's skill,—
    Yet now, in this the twilight, she might still
  Kneel in the latter grass to pray again,
Ere the night cometh and she may not work.

II NOT AS THESE

"I am not as these are," the poet saith
  In youth's pride, and the painter, among men
    At bay, where never pencil comes nor pen,
And shut about with his own frozen breath.
To others, for whom only rhyme wins faith
  As poets,—only paint as painters,—then
    He turns in the cold silence; and again
Shrinking, "I am not as these are," he saith.

And say that this is so, what follows it?
  For were thine eyes set backwards in thine head,   *10*
    Such words were well; but they see on, and far.
Unto the lights of the great Past, new-lit
  Fair for the Future's track, look thou instead,—
    Say thou instead, "I am not as *these* are."

III THE HUSBANDMEN

Though God, as one that is an householder,
  Called these to labour in His vineyard first,
  Before the husk of darkness was well burst
Bidding them grope their way out and bestir,
(Who, questioned of their wages, answered, "Sir,
  Unto each man a penny":) though the worst
  Burthen of heat was theirs and the dry thirst:
Though God has since found none such as these were
To do their work like them:—Because of this
  Stand not ye idle in the market-place.   *10*
    Which of ye knoweth *he* is not that last
Who may be first by faith and will?—yea, his
  The hand which after the appointed days
    And hours shall give a Future to their Past?

SONNET LXXVII: SOUL'S BEAUTY

Under the arch of Life, where love and death,
 Terror and mystery, guard her shrine, I saw
 Beauty enthroned; and though her gaze struck awe,
I drew it in as simply as my breath.
Hers are the eyes which, over and beneath,
 The sky and sea bend on thee,—which can draw,
 By sea or sky or woman, to one law,
The allotted bondman of her palm and wreath.

This is that Lady Beauty, in whose praise
 Thy voice and hand shake still,—long known to thee
  By flying hair and fluttering hem,—the beat   *11*
  Following her daily of thy heart and feet,
 How passionately and irretrievably,
In what fond flight, how many ways and days!

SONNET LXXVIII: BODY'S BEAUTY

Of Adam's first wife, Lilith, it is told
 (The witch he loved before the gift of Eve,)
 That, ere the snake's, her sweet tongue could deceive,
And her enchanted hair was the first gold.
And still she sits, young while the earth is old,
 And, subtly of herself contemplative,
 Draws men to watch the bright web she can weave,
Till heart and body and life are in its hold.

The rose and poppy are her flowers; for where
 Is he not found, O Lilith, whom shed scent   *10*
And soft-shed kisses and soft sleep shall snare?
 Lo! as that youth's eyes burned at thine, so went
 Thy spell through him, and left his straight neck bent
And round his heart one strangling golden hair.

SONNET LXXIX: THE MONOCHORD

Is it this sky's vast vault or ocean's sound
   That is Life's self and draws my life from me,
   And by instinct ineffable decree
Holds my breath quailing on the bitter bound?
Nay, is it Life or Death, thus thunder-crown'd,
   That 'mid the tide of all emergency
   Now notes my separate wave, and to what sea
Its difficult eddies labour in the ground?

Oh! what is this that knows the road I came,
The flame turned cloud, the cloud returned to flame,   *10*
   The lifted shifted steeps and all the way?—
That draws round me at last this wind-warm space,
And in regenerate rapture turns my face
   Upon the devious coverts of dismay?

SONNET LXXX: FROM DAWN TO NOON

As the child knows not if his mother's face
   Be fair; nor of his elders yet can deem
   What each most is; but as of hill or stream
At dawn, all glimmering life surrounds his place:
Who yet, tow'rd noon of his half-weary race,
   Pausing awhile beneath the high sun-beam
   And gazing steadily back,—as through a dream,
In things long past new features now can trace:—

Even so the thought that is at length fullgrown
   Turns back to note the sun-smit paths, all grey   *10*
And marvellous once, where first it walked alone;
   And haply doubts, amid the unblenching day,
   Which most or least impelled its onward way,—
Those unknown things or these things overknown.

SONNET LXXXI: MEMORIAL THRESHOLDS

What place so strange,—though unrevealèd snow
   With unimaginable fires arise
   At the earth's end,—what passion of surprise
Like frost-bound fire-girt scenes of long ago?
Lo! this is none but I this hour; and lo!
   This is the very place which to mine eyes
   Those mortal hours in vain immortalize,
'Mid hurrying crowds, with what alone I know.

City, of thine a single simple door,
   By some new Power reduplicate, must be   *10*
   Even yet my life-porch in eternity,
Even with one presence filled, as once of yore:
Or mocking winds whirl round a chaff-strown floor
   Thee and thy years and these my words and me.

SONNET LXXXII: HOARDED JOY

I said: "Nay, pluck not,—let the first fruit be:
   Even as thou sayest, it is sweet and red,
   But let it ripen still. The tree's bent head
Sees in the stream its own fecundity
And bides the day of fulness. Shall not we
   At the sun's hour that day possess the shade,
   And claim our fruit before its ripeness fade,
And eat it from the branch and praise the tree?"

I say: "Alas! our fruit hath wooed the sun
   Too long,—'tis fallen and floats adown the stream.
Lo, the last clusters! Pluck them every one,   *11*
   And let us sup with summer; ere the gleam
Of autumn set the year's pent sorrow free,
And the woods wail like echoes from the sea."

SONNET LXXXIII: BARREN SPRING

Once more the changed year's turning wheel returns:
   And as a girl sails balanced in the wind,
   And now before and now again behind
Stoops as it swoops, with cheek that laughs and
      burns,—
So Spring comes merry towards me here, but earns
   No answering smile from me, whose life is twin'd
   With the dead boughs that winter still must bind,
And whom to-day the Spring no more concerns.

Behold, this crocus is a withering flame;
   This snowdrop, snow; this apple-blossom's part   *10*
   To breed the fruit that breeds the serpent's art.
Nay, for these Spring-flowers, turn thy face from them,
Nor stay till on the year's last lily-stem
   The white cup shrivels round the golden heart.

SONNET LXXXIV: FAREWELL
TO THE GLEN

Sweet stream-fed glen, why say "farewell" to thee
   Who far'st so well and find'st for ever smooth
   The brow of Time where man may read no ruth?
Nay, do thou rather say "farewell" to me,
Who now fare forth in bitterer fantasy
   Than erst was mine where other shade might soothe
   By other streams, what while in fragrant youth
The bliss of being sad made melancholy.

And yet, farewell! For better shalt thou fare
   When children bathe sweet faces in thy flow   *10*
And happy lovers blend sweet shadows there
   In hours to come, than when an hour ago
Thine echoes had but one man's sighs to bear
   And thy trees whispered what he feared to know.

SONNET LXXXV: VAIN VIRTUES

What is the sorriest thing that enters Hell?
  None of the sins,—but this and that fair deed
  Which a soul's sin at length could supersede.
These yet are virgins, whom death's timely knell
Might once have sainted; whom the fiends compel
    Together now, in snake-bound shuddering sheaves
    Of anguish, while the pit's pollution leaves
Their refuse maidenhood abominable.

Night sucks them down, the tribute of the pit,
  Whose names, half entered in the book of Life,   *10*
    Were God's desire at noon. And as their hair
And eyes sink last, the Torturer deigns no whit
  To gaze, but, yearning, waits his destined wife,
    The Sin still blithe on earth that sent them there.

SONNET LXXXVI: LOST DAYS

The lost days of my life until to-day,
  What were they, could I see them on the street
  Lie as they fell? Would they be ears of wheat
Sown once for food but trodden into clay?
Or golden coins squandered and still to pay?
  Or drops of blood dabbling the guilty feet?
  Or such spilt water as in dreams must cheat
The undying throats of Hell, athirst alway?

I do not see them here; but after death
  God knows I know the faces I shall see,   *10*
Each one a murdered self, with low last breath.
  "I am thyself,—what hast thou done to me?"
"And I—and I—thyself," (lo! each one saith,)
  "And thou thyself to all eternity!"

SONNET LXXXVII: DEATH'S SONGSTERS

When first that horse, within whose populous womb
  The birth was death, o'ershadowed Troy with fate,
  Her elders, dubious of its Grecian freight,
Brought Helen there to sing the songs of home;
She whispered, "Friends, I am alone; come, come!"
  Then, crouched within, Ulysses waxed afraid,
  And on his comrades' quivering mouths he laid
His hands, and held them till the voice was dumb.

The same was he who, lashed to his own mast,
  There where the sea-flowers screen the charnel-caves,
Beside the sirens' singing island pass'd,   *11*
  Till sweetness failed along the inveterate waves. . . .
Say, soul,—are songs of Death no heaven to thee,
Nor shames her lip the cheek of Victory?

SONNET LXXXVIII: HERO'S LAMP*

That lamp thou fill'st in Eros' name to-night,
  O Hero, shall the Sestian augurs take
  To-morrow, and for drowned Leander's sake
To Anteros its fireless lip shall plight.
Aye, waft the unspoken vow: yet dawn's first light
  On ebbing storm and life twice ebb'd must break;
  While 'neath no sunrise, by the Avernian Lake,
Lo where Love walks, Death's pallid neophyte.

That lamp within Anteros' shadowy shrine
  Shall stand unlit (for so the gods decree)   *10*
  Till some one man the happy issue see
Of a life's love, and bid its flame to shine:
Which still may rest unfir'd; for, theirs or thine,
  O brother, what brought love to them or thee?

  * After the deaths of Leander and of Hero, the signal-lamp was dedi-
cated to Anteros, with the edict that no man should light it unless his
love had proved fortunate. [Rossetti's note]

SONNET LXXXIX: THE TREES OF THE GARDEN

Ye who have passed Death's haggard hills; and ye
  Whom trees that knew your sires shall cease to know
  And still stand silent:—is it all a show,—
A wisp that laughs upon the wall?—decree
Of some inexorable supremacy
  Which ever, as man strains his blind surmise
  From depth to ominous depth, looks past his eyes,
Sphinx-faced with unabashèd augury?

Nay, rather question the Earth's self. Invoke
  The storm-felled forest-trees moss-grown to-day   *10*
  Whose roots are hillocks where the children play;
Or ask the silver sapling 'neath what yoke
Those stars, his spray-crown's clustering gems, shall wage
Their journey still when his boughs shrink with age.

SONNET XC: "RETRO ME, SATHANA!"

Get thee behind me. Even as, heavy-curled,
  Stooping against the wind, a charioteer
  Is snatched from out his chariot by the hair,
So shall Time be; and as the void car, hurled
Abroad by reinless steeds, even so the world:
  Yea, even as chariot-dust upon the air,
  It shall be sought and not found anywhere.
Get thee behind me, Satan. Oft unfurled,
Thy perilous wings can beat and break like lath
  Much mightiness of men to win thee praise.   *10*
  Leave these weak feet to tread in narrow ways.
Thou still, upon the broad vine-sheltered path,
Mayst wait the turning of the phials of wrath
  For certain years, for certain months and days.

SONNET XCI: LOST ON BOTH SIDES

As when two men have loved a woman well,
  Each hating each, through Love's and Death's deceit;
  Since not for either this stark marriage-sheet
And the long pauses of this wedding-bell;
  Yet o'er her grave the night and day dispel
  At last their feud forlorn, with cold and heat;
  Nor other than dear friends to death may fleet
The two lives left that most of her can tell:—

So separate hopes, which in a soul had wooed
  The one same Peace, strove with each other long,   *10*
    And Peace before their faces perished since:
So through that soul, in restless brotherhood,
  They roam together now, and wind among
    Its bye-streets, knocking at the dusty inns.

SONNETS XCII, XCIII: THE SUN'S SHAME

I

Beholding youth and hope in mockery caught
  From life; and mocking pulses that remain
  When the soul's death of bodily death is fain;
Honour unknown, and honour known unsought;
And penury's sedulous self-torturing thought
  On gold, whose master therewith buys his bane;
  And longed-for woman longing all in vain
For lonely man with love's desire distraught;
And wealth, and strength, and power, and pleasantness,
  Given unto bodies of whose souls men say,   *10*
  None poor and weak, slavish and foul, as they:—
Beholding these things, I behold no less
The blushing morn and blushing eve confess
  The shame that loads the intolerable day.

11

As some true chief of men, bowed down with stress
    Of life's disastrous eld, on blossoming youth
    May gaze, and murmur with self-pity and ruth,—
"Might I thy fruitless treasure but possess,
Such blessing of mine all coming years should bless;"—
    Then sends one sigh forth to the unknown goal,
    And bitterly feels breathe against his soul
The hour swift-winged of nearer nothingness:—

Even so the World's grey Soul to the green World
    Perchance one hour must cry: "Woe's me, for whom
    Inveteracy of ill portends the doom,—   *11*
Whose heart's old fire in shadow of shame is furl'd:
While thou even as of yore art journeying,
All soulless now, yet merry with the Spring!"

SONNET XCIV: MICHELANGELO'S KISS

Great Michelangelo, with age grown bleak
    And uttermost labours, having once o'ersaid
    All grievous memories on his long life shed,
This worst regret to one true heart could speak:—
That when, with sorrowing love and reverence meek,
    He stooped o'er sweet Colonna's dying bed,
    His Muse and dominant Lady, spirit-wed,—
Her hand he kissed, but not her brow or cheek.

O Buonarruoti,—good at Art's fire-wheels
    To urge her chariot!—even thus the Soul,   *10*
    Touching at length some sorely-chastened goal,
Earns oftenest but a little: her appeals
Were deep and mute,—lowly her claim. Let be:
What holds for her Death's garner? And for thee?

SONNET XCV: THE VASE OF LIFE

Around the vase of Life at your slow pace
  He has not crept, but turned it with his hands,
  And all its sides already understands.
There, girt, one breathes alert for some great race;
Whose road runs far by sands and fruitful space;
  Who laughs, yet through the jolly throng has pass'd;
  Who weeps, nor stays for weeping; who at last,
A youth, stands somewhere crowned, with silent face.

And he has filled this vase with wine for blood,
  With blood for tears, with spice for burning vow,   *10*
    With watered flowers for buried love most fit;
And would have cast it shattered to the flood,
  Yet in Fate's name has kept it whole; which now
    Stands empty till his ashes fall in it.

SONNET XCVI: LIFE THE BELOVED

As thy friend's face, with shadow of soul o'erspread,
  Somewhile unto thy sight perchance hath been
  Ghastly and strange, yet never so is seen
In thought, but to all fortunate favour wed;
As thy love's death-bound features never dead
  To memory's glass return, but contravene
  Frail fugitive days, and alway keep, I ween,
Than all new life a livelier lovelihead:—

So Life herself, thy spirit's friend and love,
  Even still as Spring's authentic harbinger   *10*
    Glows with fresh hours for hope to glorify;
Though pale she lay when in the winter grove
  Her funeral flowers were snow-flakes shed on her
    And the red wings of frost-fire rent the sky.

SONNET XCVII: A SUPERSCRIPTION

Look in my face; my name is Might-have-been;
  I am also called No-more, Too-late, Farewell;
  Unto thine ear I hold the dead-sea shell
Cast up thy Life's foam-fretted feet between;
Unto thine eyes the glass where that is seen
  Which had Life's form and Love's, but by my spell
  Is now a shaken shadow intolerable,
Of ultimate things unuttered the frail screen.

Mark me, how still I am! But should there dart
  One moment through thy soul the soft surprise   *10*
  Of that winged Peace which lulls the breath of sighs,—
Then shalt thou see me smile, and turn apart
Thy visage to mine ambush at thy heart
  Sleepless with cold commemorative eyes.

SONNET XCVIII: HE AND I

Whence came his feet into my field, and why?
  How is it that he sees it all so drear?
  How do I see his seeing, and how hear
The name his bitter silence knows it by?
This was the little fold of separate sky
  Whose pasturing clouds in the soul's atmosphere
  Drew living light from one continual year:
How should he find it lifeless? He, or I?

Lo! this new Self now wanders round my field,
  With plaints for every flower, and for each tree   *10*
  A moan, the sighing wind's auxiliary:
And o'er sweet waters of my life, that yield
Unto his lips no draught but tears unseal'd,
  Even in my place he weeps. Even I, not he.

SONNETS XCIX, C: NEWBORN DEATH

I

To-day Death seems to me an infant child
   Which her worn mother Life upon my knee
   Has set to grow my friend and play with me;
If haply so my heart might be beguil'd
To find no terrors in a face so mild,—
   If haply so my weary heart might be
   Unto the newborn milky eyes of thee,
O Death, before resentment reconcil'd.

How long, O Death? And shall thy feet depart
   Still a young child's with mine, or wilt thou stand   *10*
Fullgrown the helpful daughter of my heart,
   What time with thee indeed I reach the strand
Of the pale wave which knows thee what thou art,
   And drink it in the hollow of thy hand?

I I

And thou, O Life, the lady of all bliss,
   With whom, when our first heart beat full and fast,
   I wandered till the haunts of men were pass'd,
And in fair places found all bowers amiss
Till only woods and waves might hear our kiss,
   While to the winds all thought of Death we cast:—
   Ah, Life! and must I have from thee at last
No smile to greet me and no babe but this?

Lo! Love, the child once ours; and Song, whose hair
   Blew like a flame and blossomed like a wreath;   *10*
And Art, whose eyes were worlds by God found fair:
   These o'er the book of Nature mixed their breath
With neck-twined arms, as oft we watched them there;
   And did these die that thou mightst bear me Death?

SONNET CI: THE ONE HOPE

When vain desire at last and vain regret
  Go hand in hand to death, and all is vain,
  What shall assuage the unforgotten pain
And teach the unforgetful to forget?
Shall Peace be still a sunk stream long unmet,—
  Or may the soul at once in a green plain
  Stoop through the spray of some sweet life-fountain
And cull the dew-drenched flowering amulet?

Ah! when the wan soul in that golden air
  Between the scriptured petals softly blown   *10*
  Peers breathless for the gift of grace unknown,—
Ah! let none other alien spell soe'er
But only the one Hope's one name be there,—
  Not less nor more, but even that word alone.

                                 (1848–1881)

THE CLOUD CONFINES

The day is dark and the night
  To him that would search their heart;
  No lips of cloud that will part
Nor morning song in the light:
  Only, gazing alone,
  To him wild shadows are shown,
  Deep under deep unknown
And height above unknown height.
      Still we say as we go,—
        "Strange to think by the way,   *10*
      Whatever there is to know,
        That shall we know one day."

The Past is over and fled;
  Named new, we name it the old;
  Thereof some tale hath been told,

But no word comes from the dead;
  Whether at all they be,
  Or whether as bond or free,
  Or whether they too were we,
Or by what spell they have sped.   *20*
      Still we say as we go,—
        "Strange to think by the way,
        Whatever there is to know,
          That shall we know one day."

What of the heart of hate
  That beats in thy breast, O Time?—
  Red strife from the furthest prime,
And anguish of fierce debate;
  War that shatters her slain,
  And peace that grinds them as grain,   *30*
  And eyes fixed ever in vain
On the pitiless eyes of Fate.
      Still we say as we go,—
        "Strange to think by the way,
        Whatever there is to know,
          That shall we know one day."

What of the heart of love
  That bleeds in thy breast, O Man?—
  Thy kisses snatched 'neath the ban
Of fangs that mock them above;   *40*
  Thy bells prolonged unto knells,
  Thy hope that a breath dispels,
  Thy bitter forlorn farewells
And the empty echoes thereof?
      Still we say as we go,—
        "Strange to think by the way,
        Whatever there is to know,
          That shall we know one day."

The sky leans dumb on the sea,
  Aweary with all its wings;   *50*
  And oh! the song the sea sings

Is dark everlastingly.
  Our past is clean forgot,
  Our present is and is not,
  Our future's a sealed seedplot,
And what betwixt them are we?—
     We who say as we go,—
      "Strange to think by the way,
     Whatever there is to know,
      That shall we know one day."

(1871)

SOOTHSAY

Let no man ask thee of anything
Not yearborn between Spring and Spring.
More of all worlds than he can know,
Each day the single sun doth show.
A trustier gloss than thou canst give
From all wise scrolls demonstrative,
The sea doth sigh and the wind sing.

Let no man awe thee on any height
Of earthly kingship's mouldering might.
The dust his heel holds meet for thy brow   *10*
Hath all of it been what both are now;
And thou and he may plague together
A beggar's eyes in some dusty weather
When none that is now knows sound or sight.

Crave thou no dower of earthly things
Unworthy Hope's imaginings.
To have brought true birth of Song to be
And to have won hearts to Poesy,
Or anywhere in the sun or rain
To have loved and been beloved again,   *20*
Is loftiest reach of Hope's bright wings.

The wild waifs cast up by the sea
Are diverse ever seasonably.
Even so the soul-tides still may land
A different drift upon the sand.
But one the sea is evermore:
And one be still, 'twixt shore and shore,
As the sea's life, thy soul in thee.

Say, hast thou pride? How then may fit
Thy mood with flatterers' silk-spun wit?   30
Haply the sweet voice lifts thy crest,
A breeze of fame made manifest.
Nay, but then chaf'st at flattery? Pause:
Be sure thy wrath is not because
It makes thee feel thou lovest it.

Let thy soul strive that still the same
Be early friendship's sacred flame.
The affinities have strongest part
In youth, and draw men heart to heart:
As life wears on and finds no rest,   40
The individual in each breast
Is tyrannous to sunder them.

In the life-drama's stern cue-call,
A friend's a part well-prized by all:
And if thou meet an enemy,
What art thou that none such should be?
Even so: but if the two parts run
Into each other and grow one,
Then comes the curtain's cue to fall.

Whate'er by other's need is claimed   50
More than by thine,—to him unblamed
Resign it: and if he should hold
What more than he thou lack'st, bread, gold,
Or any good whereby we live,—
To thee such substance let him give
Freely: nor he nor thou be shamed.

Strive that thy works prove equal: lest
That work which thou hast done the best
Should come to be to thee at length
(Even as to envy seems the strength   60
Of others) hateful and abhorr'd,—
Thine own above thyself made lord,—
Of self-rebuke the bitterest.

Unto the man of yearning thought
And aspiration, to do nought
Is in itself almost an act,—
Being chasm-fire and cataract
Of the soul's utter depths unseal'd.
Yet woe to thee if once thou yield
Unto the act of doing nought!   70

How callous seems beyond revoke
The clock with its last listless stroke!
How much too late at length!—to trace
The hour on its forewarning face,
The thing thou hast not dared to do! . . .
Behold, this *may* be thus! Ere true
It prove, arise and bear thy yoke.

Let lore of all Theology
Be to thy soul what it *can* be:
But know,—the Power that fashions man   80
Measured not out thy little span
For thee to take the meting-rod
In turn, and so approve on God
Thy science of Theometry.

To God at best, to Chance at worst,
Give thanks for good things, last as first.
But windstrown blossom is that good
Whose apple is not gratitude.
Even if no prayer uplift thy face,
Let the sweet right to render grace   90
As thy soul's cherished child be nurs'd.

Didst ever say, "Lo, I forget?"
Such thought was to remember yet.
As in a gravegarth, count to see
The monuments of memory.
Be this thy soul's appointed scope:—
Gaze onward without claim to hope,
Nor, gazing backward, court regret.

(1871–1880)

THREE SHADOWS

I looked and saw your eyes
  In the shadow of your hair
As a traveller sees the stream
  In the shadow of the wood;
And I said, "My faint heart sighs
  Ah me! to linger there,
To drink deep and to dream
  In that sweet solitude."

I looked and saw your heart
  In the shadow of your eyes,   *10*
As a seeker sees the gold
  In the shadow of the stream;
And I said, "Ah me! what art
  Should win the immortal prize,
Whose want must make life cold
  And Heaven a hollow dream?"

I looked and saw your love
  In the shadow of your heart,
As a diver sees the pearl
  In the shadow of the sea;   *20*
And I murmured, not above
  My breath, but all apart,—
"Ah! you can love, true girl,
  And is your love for me?"

(1876)

ASTARTE SYRIACA

(For a Picture)

Mystery: lo! betwixt the sun and moon
   Astarte of the Syrians: Venus Queen
   Ere Aphrodite was. In silver sheen
Her twofold girdle clasps the infinite boon
Of bliss whereof the heaven and earth commune:
   And from her neck's inclining flower-stem lean
   Love-freighted lips and absolute eyes that wean
The pulse of hearts to the spheres' dominant tune.

Torch-bearing, her sweet ministers compel
   All thrones of light beyond the sky and sea   *10*
   The witnesses of Beauty's face to be:
That face, of Love's all-penetrative spell
Amulet, talisman, and oracle,—
   Betwixt the sun and moon a mystery.

                                  (1877)

INSOMNIA

Thin are the night-skirts left behind
   By daybreak hours that onward creep,
   And thin, alas! the shred of sleep
That wavers with the spirit's wind:
But in half-dreams that shift and roll
   And still remember and forget,
My soul this hour has drawn your soul
      A little nearer yet.

Our lives, most dear, are never near,
   Our thoughts are never far apart,   *10*
   Though all that draws us heart to heart
Seems fainter now and now more clear.
To-night Love claims his full control,
   And with desire and with regret

My soul this hour has drawn your soul
    A little nearer yet.

Is there a home where heavy earth
    Melts to bright air that breathes no pain,
    Where water leaves no thirst again
And springing fire is Love's new birth?   20
If faith long bound to one true goal
    May there at length its hope beget,
My soul that hour shall draw your soul
      For ever nearer yet.

                        (1881)

THE KING'S TRAGEDY

JAMES I OF SCOTS—20TH FEBRUARY 1437*

I Catherine am a Douglas born,
    A name to all Scots dear;
And Kate Barlass they've called me now
    Through many a waning year.

This old arm's withered now. 'Twas once
    Most deft 'mong maidens all
To rein the steed, to wing the shaft,
    To smite the palm-play ball.

In hall adown the close-linked dance
    It has shone most white and fair;   10

* Tradition says that Catherine Douglas, in honour of her heroic act when she barred the door with her arm against the murderers of James the First of Scots, received popularly the name of "Barlass." This name remains to her descendants, the Barlas family, in Scotland, who bear for their crest a broken arm. She married Alexander Lovell of Bolunnie.

A few stanzas from King James's lovely poem, known as *The King's Quair*, are quoted in the course of this ballad. The writer must express regret for the necessity which has compelled him to shorten the ten-syllabled lines to eight syllables, in order that they might harmonize with the ballad metre. [Rossetti's note]

It has been the rest for a true lord's head,
And many a sweet babe's nursing-bed,
   And the bar to a King's chan_bère.

Aye, lasses, draw round Kate Barlass,
   And hark with bated breath
How good King James, King Robert's son,
   Was foully done to death.

Through all the days of his gallant youth
   The princely James was pent,
By his friends at first and then by his foes,   20
   In long imprisonment.

For the elder Prince, the kingdom's heir,
   By treason's murderous brood
Was slain; and the father quaked for the child
   With the royal mortal blood.

I' the Bass Rock fort, by his father's care,
   Was his childhood's life assured;
And Henry the subtle Bolingbroke,
Proud England's King, 'neath the southron yoke
   His youth for long years immured.   30

Yet in all things meet for a kingly man
   Himself did he approve;
And the nightingale through his prison-wall
   Taught him both lore and love.

For once, when the bird's song drew him close
   To the opened window-pane,
In her bower beneath a lady stood,
A light of life to his sorrowful mood,
   Like a lily amid the rain.

And for her sake, to the sweet bird's note,   40
   He framed a sweeter Song,
More sweet than ever a poet's heart
   Gave yet to the English tongue.

She was a lady of royal blood;
   And when, past sorrow and teen,
He stood where still through his crownless years
   His Scotish realm had been,
At Scone were the happy lovers crowned,
   A heart-wed King and Queen.

But the bird may fall from the bough of youth,   *50*
   And song be turned to moan,
And Love's storm-cloud be the shadow of Hate,
When the tempest-waves of a troubled State
   Are beating against a throne.

Yet well they loved; and the god of Love,
   Whom well the King had sung,
Might find on the earth no truer hearts
   His lowliest swains among.

From the days when first she rode abroad
   With Scotish maids in her train,   *60*
I Catherine Douglas won the trust
   Of my mistress sweet Queen Jane.

And oft she sighed, "To be born a King!"
   And oft along the way
When she saw the homely lovers pass
   She has said, "Alack the day!"

Years waned,—the loving and toiling years:
   Till England's wrong renewed
Drove James, by outrage cast on his crown,
   To the open field of feud.   *70*

'Twas when the King and his host were met
   At the leaguer of Roxbro' hold,
The Queen o' the sudden sought his camp
   With a tale of dread to be told.

And she showed him a secret letter writ
  That spoke of treasonous strife,
And how a band of his noblest lords
  Were sworn to take his life.

"And it may be here or it may be there,
  In the camp or the court," she said: 80
"But for my sake come to your people's arms
  And guard your royal head."

Quoth he, " 'Tis the fifteenth day of the siege,
  And the castle's nigh to yield."
"O face your foes on your throne," she cried,
  "And show the power you wield;
And under your Scotish people's love
  You shall sit as under your shield."

At the fair Queen's side I stood that day
  When he bade them raise the siege,   90
And back to his Court he sped to know
  How the lords would meet their Liege.

But when he summoned his Parliament,
  The louring brows hung round,
Like clouds that circle the mountain-head
  Ere the first low thunders sound.

For he had tamed the nobles' lust
  And curbed their power and pride,
And reached out an arm to right the poor
  Through Scotland far and wide;   100
And many a lordly wrong-doer
  By the headsman's axe had died.

'Twas then upspoke Sir Robert Græme,
  The bold o'ermastering man:—
"O King, in the name of your Three Estates
  I set you under their ban!

"For, as your lords made oath to you
    Of service and fealty,
Even in like wise you pledged your oath
    Their faithful sire to be:—   110

"Yet all we here that are nobly sprung
    Have mourned dear kith and kin
Since first for the Scotish Barons' curse
    Did your bloody rule begin."

With that he laid his hands on his King:—
    "Is this not so, my lords?"
But of all who had sworn to league with him
    Not one spake back to his words.

Quoth the King:—"Thou speak'st but for one Estate,
    Nor doth it avow thy gage.   120
Let my liege lords hale this traitor hence!"
    The Græme fired dark with rage:—
"Who works for lesser men than himself,
    He earns but a witless wage!"

But soon from the dungeon where he lay
    He won by privy plots,
And forth he fled with a price on his head
    To the country of the Wild Scots.

And word there came from Sir Robert Græme
    To the King at Edinbro':—   130
"No Liege of mine thou art; but I see
From this day forth alone in thee
    God's creature, my mortal foe.

"Through thee are my wife and children lost,
    My heritage and lands;
And when my God shall show me a way,
Thyself my mortal foe will I slay
    With these my proper hands."

Against the coming of Christmastide
   That year the King bade call   *140*
I' the Black Friars' Charterhouse of Perth
   A solemn festival.

And we of his household rode with him
   In a close-ranked company;
But not till the sun had sunk from his throne
   Did we reach the Scotish Sea.

That eve was clenched for a boding storm,
   'Neath a toilsome moon half seen;
The cloud stooped low and the surf rose high;
And where there was a line of the sky,   *150*
   Wild wings loomed dark between.

And on a rock of the black beach-side,
   By the veiled moon dimly lit,
There was something seemed to heave with life
   As the King drew nigh to it.

And was it only the tossing furze
   Or brake of the waste sea-wold?
Or was it an eagle bent to the blast?
When near we came, we knew it at last
   For a woman tattered and old.   *160*

But it seemed as though by a fire within
   Her writhen limbs were wrung;
And as soon as the King was close to her,
   She stood up gaunt and strong.

'Twas then the moon sailed clear of the rack
   On high in her hollow dome;
And still as aloft with hoary crest
   Each clamorous wave rang home,
Like fire in snow the moonlight blazed
   Amid the champing foam.   *170*

And the woman held his eyes with her eyes:—
   "O King, thou art come at last;
But thy wraith has haunted the Scotish Sea
   To my sight for four years past.

"Four years it is since first I met,
   'Twixt the Duchray and the Dhu,
A shape whose feet clung close in a shroud,
   And that shape for thine I knew.

"A year again, and on Inchkeith Isle
   I saw thee pass in the breeze,   *180*
With the cerecloth risen above thy feet
   And wound about thy knees.

"And yet a year, in the Links of Forth,
   As a wanderer without rest,
Thou cam'st with both thine arms i' the shroud
   That clung high up thy breast.

"And in this hour I find thee here,
   And well mine eyes may note
That the winding-sheet hath passed thy breast
   And risen around thy throat.   *190*

"And when I meet thee again, O King,
   That of death hast such sore drouth,—
Except thou turn again on this shore,—
The winding-sheet shall have moved once more
   And covered thine eyes and mouth.

"O King, whom poor men bless for their King,
   Of thy fate be not so fain;
But these my words for God's message take,
And turn thy steed, O King, for her sake
   Who rides beside thy rein!"   *200*

While the woman spoke, the King's horse reared
   As if it would breast the sea,

And the Queen turned pale as she heard on the gale
   The voice die dolorously.

When the woman ceased, the steed was still,
   But the King gazed on her yet,
And in silence save for the wail of the sea
   His eyes and her eyes met.

At last he said:—"God's ways are His own;
   Man is but shadow and dust.   210
Last night I prayed by His altar-stone;
To-night I wend to the Feast of His Son;
   And in Him I set my trust.

"I have held my people in sacred charge,
   And have not feared the sting
Of proud men's hate,—to His will resign'd
Who has but one same death for a hind
   And one same death for a King.

"And if God in His wisdom have brought close
   The day when I must die,   220
That day by water or fire or air
My feet shall fall in the destined snare
   Wherever my road may lie.

"What man can say but the Fiend hath set
   Thy sorcery on my path,
My heart with the fear of death to fill,
And turn me against God's very will
   To sink in His burning wrath?"

The woman stood as the train rode past,
   And moved nor limb nor eye;   230
And when we were shipped, we saw her there
   Still standing against the sky.

As the ship made way, the moon once more
   Sank slow in her rising pall;

And I thought of the shrouded wraith of the King,
   And I said, "The Heavens know all."

And now, ye lasses, must ye hear
   How my name is Kate Barlass:—
But a little thing, when all the tale
   Is told of the weary mass   *240*
Of crime and woe which in Scotland's realm
   God's will let come to pass.

'Twas in the Charterhouse of Perth
   That the King and all his Court
Were met, the Christmas Feast being done,
   For solace and disport.

'Twas a wind-wild eve in February,
   And against the casement-pane
The branches smote like summoning hands,
   And muttered the driving rain.   *250*

And when the wind swooped over the lift
   And made the whole heaven frown,
It seemed a grip was laid on the walls
   To tug the housetop down.

And the Queen was there, more stately fair
   Than a lily in garden set;
And the King was loth to stir from her side;
For as on the day when she was his bride,
   Even so he loved her yet.

And the Earl of Athole, the King's false friend,   *260*
   Sat with him at the board;
And Robert Stuart the chamberlain
   Who had sold his sovereign Lord.

Yet the traitor Christopher Chaumber there
   Would fain have told him all,
And vainly four times that night he strove
   To reach the King through the hall.

But the wine is bright at the goblet's brim
   Though the poison lurk beneath;
And the apples still are red on the tree   *270*
Within whose shade may the adder be
   That shall turn thy life to death.

There was a knight of the King's fast friends
   Whom he called the King of Love;
And to such bright cheer and courtesy
   That name might best behove.

And the King and Queen both loved him well
   For his gentle knightliness;
And with him the King, as that eve wore on,
   Was playing at the chess.   *280*

And the King said, (for he thought to jest
   And soothe the Queen thereby;)—
"In a book 'tis writ that this same year
   A King shall in Scotland die.

"And I have pondered the matter o'er,
   And this have I found, Sir Hugh,—
There are but two Kings on Scotish ground,
   And those Kings are I and you.

"And I have a wife and a newborn heir,
   And you are yourself alone;   *290*
So stand you stark at my side with me
   To guard our double throne.

"For here sit I and my wife and child,
   As well your heart shall approve,
In full surrender and soothfastness,
   Beneath your Kingdom of Love."

And the Knight laughed, and the Queen too smiled;
   But I knew her heavy thought,
And I strove to find in the good King's jest
   What cheer might thence be wrought.   *300*

And I said, "My Liege, for the Queen's dear love
  Now sing the song that of old
You made, when a captive Prince you lay,
And the nightingale sang sweet on the spray,
  In Windsor's castle-hold."

Then he smiled the smile I knew so well
  When he thought to please the Queen;
The smile which under all bitter frowns
  Of fate that rose between
For ever dwelt at the poet's heart   *310*
  Like the bird of love unseen.

And he kissed her hand and took his harp,
  And the music sweetly rang;
And when the song burst forth, it seemed
  'Twas the nightingale that sang.

"Worship, ye lovers, on this May:
  Of bliss your kalends are begun:
Sing with us, Away, Winter, away!
  Come, Summer, the sweet season and sun!
  Awake for shame,—your heaven is won,—   *320*
And amorously your heads lift all:
Thank Love, that you to his grace doth call!"

But when he bent to the Queen, and sang
  The speech whose praise was hers,
It seemed his voice was the voice of the Spring
  And the voice of the bygone years.

"The fairest and the freshest flower
That ever I saw before that hour,
The which o' the sudden made to start
The blood of my body to my heart.   *330*
    *   *   *   *   *   *

Ah sweet, are ye a worldly creature
Or heavenly thing in form of nature?"

And the song was long, and richly stored
  With wonder and beauteous things;
And the harp was tuned to every change
  Of minstrel ministerings;
But when he spoke of the Queen at the last,
  Its strings were his own heart-strings.

"Unworthy but only of her grace,
  Upon Love's rock that's easy and sure,   340
In guerdon of all my love's space
  She took me her humble creäture.
Thus fell my blissful aventure
In youth of love that from day to day
Flowereth aye new, and further I say.

"To reckon all the circumstance
  As it happed when lessen gan my sore,
Of my rancour and woful chance,
  It were too long,—I have done therefor.
  And of this flower I say no more,   350
But unto my help her heart hath tended
And even from death her man defended."

"Aye, even from death," to myself I said;
  For I thought of the day when she
Had borne him the news, at Roxbro' siege,
  Of the fell confederacy.

But Death even then took aim as he sang
  With an arrow deadly bright;
And the grinning skull lurked grimly aloof,
And the wings were spread far over the roof   360
  More dark than the winter night.

Yet truly along the amorous song
  Of Love's high pomp and state,
There were words of Fortune's trackless doom
  And the dreadful face of Fate.

And oft have I heard again in dreams
    The voice of dire appeal
In which the King then sang of the pit
    That is under Fortune's wheel.

"And under the wheel beheld I there   370
    An ugly Pit as deep as hell,
That to behold I quaked for fear:
    And this I heard, that who therein fell
    Came no more up, tidings to tell:
Whereat, astound of the fearful sight,
I wist not what to do for fright."

And oft has my thought called up again
    These words of the changeful song:—
"Wist thou thy pain and thy travàil
To come, well might'st thou weep and wail!"   380
    And our wail, O God! is long.

But the song's end was all of his love;
    And well his heart was grac'd
With her smiling lips and her tear-bright eyes
    As his arm went round her waist.

And on the swell of her long fair throat
    Close clung the necklet-chain
As he bent her pearl-tir'd head aside,
And in the warmth of his love and pride
    He kissed her lips full fain.   390

And her true face was a rosy red,
    The very red of the rose
That, couched on the happy garden-bed,
    In the summer sunlight glows.

And all the wondrous things of love
    That sang so sweet through the song
Were in the look that met in their eyes,
    And the look was deep and long.

'Twas then a knock came at the outer gate,
   And the usher sought the King.
"The woman you met by the Scotish Sea,   400
   My Liege, would tell you a thing;
And she says that her present need for speech
   Will bear no gainsaying."

And the King said: "The hour is late
   To-morrow will serve, I ween."
Then he charged the usher strictly, and said:
   "No word of this to the Queen."

But the usher came again to the King.
   "Shall I call her back?" quoth he: 410
"For as she went on her way, she cried,
   'Woe! Woe! then the thing must be!'"

And the King paused, but he did not speak.
   Then he called for the Voidee-cup:
And as we heard the twelfth hour strike,
There by true lips and false lips alike
   Was the draught of trust drained up.

So with reverence meet to King and Queen,
   To bed went all from the board;
And the last to leave of the courtly train   420
Was Robert Stuart the chamberlain
   Who had sold his sovereign lord.

And all the locks of the chamber-door
   Had the traitor riven and brast;
And that Fate might win sure way from afar,
He had drawn out every bolt and bar
   That made the entrance fast.

And now at midnight he stole his way
   To the moat of the outer wall,
And laid strong hurdles closely across   430
   Where the traitors' tread should fall.

But we that were the Queen's bower-maids
  Alone were left behind;
And with heed we drew the curtains close
  Against the winter wind.

And now that all was still through the hall,
  More clearly we heard the rain
That clamoured ever against the glass
  And the boughs that beat on the pane.

But the fire was bright in the ingle-nook,   440
  And through empty space around
The shadows cast on the arras'd wall
'Mid the pictured kings stood sudden and tall
  Like spectres sprung from the ground.

And the bed was dight in a deep alcove;
  And as he stood by the fire
The King was still in talk with the Queen
  While he doffed his goodly attire.

And the song had brought the image back
  Of many a bygone year;   450
And many a loving word they said
With hand in hand and head laid to head;
  And none of us went anear.

But Love was weeping outside the house,
  A child in the piteous rain;
And as he watched the arrow of Death,
He wailed for his own shafts close in the sheath
  That never should fly again.

And now beneath the window arose
  A wild voice suddenly: 460
And the King reared straight, but the Queen fell back
  As for bitter dule to dree;
And all of us knew the woman's voice
  Who spoke by the Scotish Sea.

"O King," she cried, "in an evil hour
   They drove me from thy gate;
And yet my voice must rise to thine ears;
   But alas! it comes too late!

'Last night at mid-watch, by Aberdour,
   When the moon was dead in the skies,   *470*
O King, in a death-light of thine own
   I saw thy shape arise.

"And in full season, as erst I said,
   The doom had gained its growth;
And the shroud had risen above thy neck
   And covered thine eyes and mouth.

"And no moon woke, but the pale dawn broke,
   And still thy soul stood there;
And I thought its silence cried to my soul
   As the first rays crowned its hair.   *480*

"Since then have I journeyed fast and fain
   In very despite of Fate,
Lest Hope might still be found in God's will:
   But they drove me from thy gate.

"For every man on God's ground, O King,
   His death grows up from his birth
In a shadow-plant perpetually;
And thine towers high, a black yew-tree,
   O'er the Charterhouse of Perth!"

That room was built far out from the house;   *490*
   And none but we in the room
Might hear the voice that rose beneath,
   Nor the tread of the coming doom.

For now there came a torchlight-glare,
   And a clang of arms there came;
And not a soul in that space but thought
   Of the foe Sir Robert Græme.

Yea, from the country of the Wild Scots,
   O'er mountain, valley, and glen,
He had brought with him in murderous league   *500*
   Three hundred armèd men.

The King knew all in an instant's flash;
   And like a King did he stand;
But there was no armour in all the room,
   Nor weapon lay to his hand.

And all we women flew to the door
   And thought to have made it fast;
But the bolts were gone and the bars were gone
   And the locks were riven and brast.

And he caught the pale pale Queen in his arms   *510*
   As the iron footsteps fell,—
Then loosed her, standing alone, and said,
   "Our bliss was our farewell!"

And 'twixt his lips he murmured a prayer,
   And he crossed his brow and breast;
And proudly in royal hardihood
Even so with folded arms he stood,—
   The prize of the bloody quest.

Then on me leaped the Queen like a deer:—
   "O Catherine, help!" she cried.   *520*
And low at his feet we clasped his knees
   Together side by side.
"Oh! even a King, for his people's sake,
   From treasonous death must hide!"

"For *her* sake most!" I cried, and I marked
   The pang that my words could wring.
And the iron tongs from the chimney-nook
   I snatched and held to the king:—
"Wrench up the plank! and the vault beneath
   Shall yield safe harbouring."   *530*

With brows low-bent, from my eager hand
   The heavy heft did he take;
And the plank at his feet he wrenched and tore;
And as he frowned through the open floor,
   Again I said, "For her sake!"

Then he cried to the Queen, "God's will be done!"
   For her hands were clasped in prayer.
And down he sprang to the inner crypt;
And straight we closed the plank he had ripp'd
   And toiled to smooth it fair.   *540*

(Alas! in that vault a gap once was
   Wherethro' the King might have fled:
But three days since close-walled had it been
By his will; for the ball would roll therein
   When without at the palm he play'd.)

Then the Queen cried, "Catherine, keep the door,
   And I to this will suffice!"
At her word I rose all dazed to my feet,
   And my heart was fire and ice.

And louder ever the voices grew,   *550*
   And the tramp of men in mail;
Until to my brain it seemed to be
As though I tossed on a ship at sea
   In the teeth of a crashing gale.

Then back I flew to the rest; and hard
   We strove with sinews knit
To force the table against the door;
   But we might not compass it.

Then my wild gaze sped far down the hall
   To the place of the hearthstone-sill;   *560*
And the Queen bent ever above the floor,
   For the plank was rising still.

And now the rush was heard on the stair,
   And "God, what help?" was our cry:
And was I frenzied or was I bold?
I looked at each empty stanchion-hold,
   And no bar but my arm had I!

Like iron felt my arm, as through
   The staple I made it pass:—
Alack! it was flesh and bone—no more!   570
'Twas Catherine Douglas sprang to the door,
   But I fell back Kate Barlass.

With that they all thronged into the hall,
   Half dim to my failing ken;
And the space that was but a void before
   Was a crowd of wrathful men.

Behind the door I had fall'n and lay,
   Yet my sense was wildly aware,
And for all the pain of my shattered arm
   I never fainted there.   580

Even as I fell, my eyes were cast
   Where the King leaped down to the pit;
And lo! the plank was smooth in its place,
   And the Queen stood far from it.

And under the litters and through the bed
   And within the presses all
The traitors sought for the King, and pierced
   The arras around the wall.

And through the chamber they ramped and stormed
   Like lions loose in the lair,   590
And scarce could trust to their very eyes,—
   For behold! no King was there.

Then one of them seized the Queen, and cried,—
    "Now tell us, where is thy lord?"
And he held the sharp point over her heart:
She drooped not her eyes nor did she start,
    But she answered never a word.

Then the sword half pierced the true true breast:
    But it was the Græme's own son
Cried, "This is a woman,—we seek a man!"   600
    And away from her girdle zone
He struck the point of the murderous steel;
    And that foul deed was not done.

And forth flowed all the throng like a sea
    And 'twas empty space once more;
And my eyes sought out the wounded Queen
    As I lay behind the door.

And I said: "Dear Lady, leave me here,
    For I cannot help you now;
But fly while you may, and none shall reck   610
    Of my place here lying low."

And she said, "My Catherine, God help thee!"
    Then she looked to the distant floor,
And clasping her hands, "O God help *him*,"
    She sobbed, "for we can no more!"

But God He knows what help may mean,
    If it mean to live or to die;
And what sore sorrow and mighty moan
On earth it may cost ere yet a throne
    Be filled in His house on high.   620

And now the ladies fled with the Queen;
    And through the open door
The night-wind wailed round the empty room
    And the rushes shook on the floor.

And the bed drooped low in the dark recess
   Whence the arras was rent away;
And the firelight still shone over the space
   Where our hidden secret lay.

And the rain had ceased, and the moonbeams lit
   The window high in the wall,—   630
Bright beams that on the plank that I knew
   Through the painted pane did fall,
And gleamed with the splendour of Scotland's crown
   And shield armorial.

But then a great wind swept up the skies
   And the climbing moon fell back;
And the royal blazon fled from the floor,
   And nought remained on its track;
And high in the darkened window-pane
   The shield and the crown were black.   640

And what I say next I partly saw
   And partly I heard in sooth,
And partly since from the murderers' lips
   The torture wrung the truth.

For now again came the armèd tread,
   And fast through the hall it fell;
But the throng was less; and ere I saw,
   By the voice without I could tell
That Robert Stuart had come with them
   Who knew that chamber well.   650

And over the space the Græme strode dark
   With his mantle round him flung;
And in his eye was a flaming light
   But not a word on his tongue.

And Stuart held a torch to the floor,
   And he found the thing he sought;
And they slashed the plank away with their swords;
   And O God! I fainted not!

And the traitor held his torch in the gap,
  All smoking and smouldering;   660
And through the vapour and fire, beneath
  In the dark crypt's narrow ring,
With a shout that pealed to the room's high roof
  They saw their naked King.

Half naked he stood, but stood as one
  Who yet could do and dare:
With the crown, the King was stript away,—
The Knight was 'reft of his battle-array,—
  But still the Man was there.

From the rout then stepped a villain forth,—   670
  Sir John Hall was his name;
With a knife unsheathed he leapt to the vault
  Beneath the torchlight-flame.

Of his person and stature was the King
  A man right manly strong,
And mightily by the shoulder-blades
  His foe to his feet he flung.

Then the traitor's brother, Sir Thomas Hall,
  Sprang down to work his worst;
And the King caught the second man by the neck   680
  And flung him above the first.

And he smote and trampled them under him;
  And a long month thence they bare
All black their throats with the grip of his hands
  When the hangman's hand came there.

And sore he strove to have had their knives,
  But the sharp blades gashed his hands.
Oh James! so armed, thou hadst battled there
  Till help had come of thy bands;
And oh! once more thou hadst held our throne   690
  And ruled thy Scotish lands!

But while the King o'er his foes still raged
  With a heart that nought could tame,
Another man sprang down to the crypt;
And with his sword in his hand hard-gripp'd,
  There stood Sir Robert Græme.

(Now shame on the recreant traitor's heart
  Who durst not face his King
Till the body unarmed was wearied out
  With two-fold combating!   700

Ah! well might the people sing and say,
  As oft ye have heard aright:—
"O Robert Græme, O Robert Græme,
Who slew our King, God give thee shame!"
  For he slew him not as a knight.)

And the naked King turned round at bay,
  But his strength had passed the goal,
And he could but gasp:—"Mine hour is come;
But oh! to succour thine own soul's doom,
  Let a priest now shrive my soul!"   710

And the traitor looked on the King's spent strength,
  And said:—"Have I kept my word?—
Yea, King, the mortal pledge that I gave?
No black friar's shrift thy soul shall have,
  But the shrift of this red sword!"

With that he smote his King through the breast;
  And all they three in that pen
Fell on him and stabbed and stabbed him there
  Like merciless murderous men.

Yet seemed it now that Sir Robert Græme,   720
  Ere the King's last breath was o'er,
Turned sick at heart with the deadly sight
  And would have done no more.

But a cry came from the troop above:—
  "If him thou do not slay,
The price of his life that thou dost spare
  Thy forfeit life shall pay!"

O God! what more did I hear or see,
  Or how should I tell the rest?
But there at length our King lay slain   730
  With sixteen wounds in his breast.

O God! and now did a bell boom forth,
  And the murderers turned and fled;—
Too late, too late, O God, did it sound!—
And I heard the true men mustering round,
  And the cries and the coming tread.

But ere they came, to the black death-gap
  Somewise did I creep and steal;
And lo! or ever I swooned away,
Through the dusk I saw where the white face lay   740
  In the Pit of Fortune's Wheel.

And now, ye Scotish maids who have heard
  Dread things of the days grown old,—
Even at the last, of true Queen Jane
  May somewhat yet be told,
And how she dealt for her dear lord's sake
  Dire vengeance manifold.

'Twas in the Charterhouse of Perth,
  In the fair-lit Death-chapelle,
That the slain King's corpse on bier was laid   750
  With chaunt and requiem-knell.

And all with royal wealth of balm
  Was the body purified;
And none could trace on the brow and lips
  The death that he had died.

In his robes of state he lay asleep
   With orb and sceptre in hand;
And by the crown he wore on his throne
   Was his kingly forehead spann'd.

And, girls, 'twas a sweet sad thing to see   760
   How the curling golden hair,
As in the day of the poet's youth,
   From the King's crown clustered there.

And if all had come to pass in the brain
   That throbbed beneath those curls,
Then Scots had said in the days to come
That this their soil was a different home
   And a different Scotland, girls!

And the Queen sat by him night and day,
   And oft she knelt in prayer,   770
All wan and pale in the widow's veil
   That shrouded her shining hair.

And I had got good help of my hurt:
   And only to me some sign
She made; and save the priests that were there,
   No face would she see but mine.

And the month of March wore on apace;
   And now fresh couriers fared
Still from the country of the Wild Scots
   With news of the traitors snared.   780

And still as I told her day by day,
   Her pallor changed to sight,
And the frost grew to a furnace-flame
   That burnt her visage white.

And evermore as I brought her word,
   She bent to her dead King James,
And in the cold ear with fire-drawn breath
   She spoke the traitors' names.

But when the name of Sir Robert Græme
  Was the one she had to give,   790
I ran to hold her up from the floor;
For the froth was on her lips, and sore
  I feared that she could not live.

And the month of March wore nigh to its end,
  And still was the death-pall spread;
For she would not bury her slaughtered lord
  Till his slayers all were dead.

And now of their dooms dread tidings came,
  And of torments fierce and dire;
And nought she spake,—she had ceased to speak,—   800
  But her eyes were a soul on fire.

But when I told her the bitter end
  Of the stern and just award,
She leaned o'er the bier, and thrice three times
  She kissed the lips of her lord.

And then she said,—"My King, they are dead!"
  And she knelt on the chapel-floor,
And whispered low with a strange proud smile,—
  "James, James, they suffered more!"

Last she stood up to her queenly height,   810
  But she shook like an autumn leaf,
As though the fire wherein she burned
Then left her body, and all were turned
  To winter of life-long grief.

And "O James!" she said,—"My James!" she said,—
  "Alas for the woful thing,
That a poet true and a friend of man,
In desperate days of bale and ban,
  Should needs be born a King!"

                         (1881)

PROSE SENTENCES AND VERSE
FRAGMENTS FROM ROSSETTI'S PAPERS

Picture and poem bear the same relation to each other as beauty does in man and woman: the point of meeting where the two are most identical is the supreme perfection.

❧

Poetry should seem to the hearer to have been always present to his thought, but never heard before.

❧

The true artist will first perceive in another's work the beauties, and in his own the defects.

❧

TO ART

I loved thee ere I loved a woman, Love.

❧

I shut myself in with my soul,
And the shapes come eddying forth.

❧

Invention absolute is slow of acceptance, and must be so. This Coleridge and others have found. Why make a place for what is neither adaptation nor reproduction? Let it hew its way if it can.

❧

The sense of the *momentous* is strongest in Coleridge; not the weird and ominous only, but the value of monumental moments.

❧

Could Keats but have a day or two on earth
Once every year!

❧

It is bad enough when there is a gifted and powerful opposition to the teachings of the best minds in any period: but when the best minds themselves are on a false tack, who shall stem the tide?

❧

For the garlands of heaven were all laid by,
And the Daylight sucked at the breasts of a Lie.

❧

Where is the man whose soul has never waked
To sudden pity of the poor torn past?

❧

As the waifs cast up by the sea change with the changing season, so the tides of the soul throw up their changing drift on the sand, but the sea beyond is one for ever.

❧

He belonged to that extraordinary class of persons whom no amount of intellect can prevent from being fools.

❧

I was one of those whose little is their own.

HAND AND SOUL

Rivolsimi in quel lato
Là onde venìa la voce,
E parvemi una luce
Che lucea quanto stella:
La mia menta era quella.
　　　　Bonaggiunta Urbiciani (1250)*

　* Rossetti later rendered these lines as follows:

　　　I turn to where I heard
　　　That whisper in the night;
　　　And there a breath of light
　　　Shines like a silver star.
　　　The same is mine own soul.

Before any knowledge of painting was brought to Florence, there were already painters in Lucca, and Pisa, and Arezzo, who feared God and loved the art. The workmen from Greece, whose trade it was to sell their own works in Italy and teach Italians to imitate them, had already found in rivals of the soil a skill that could forestall their lessons and cheapen their labours, more years than is supposed before the art came at all into Florence. The pre-eminence to which Cimabue was raised at once by his contemporaries, and which he still retains to a wide extent even in the modern mind, is to be accounted for, partly by the circumstances under which he arose, and partly by that extraordinary *purpose of fortune* born with the lives of some few, and through which it is not a little thing for any who went before, if they are even remembered as the shadows of the coming of such an one, and the voices which prepared his way in the wilderness. It is thus, almost exclusively, that the painters of whom I speak are now known. They have left little, and but little heed is taken of that which men hold to have been surpassed; it is gone like time gone,—a track of dust and dead leaves that merely led to the fountain.

Nevertheless, of very late years and in very rare instances, some signs of a better understanding have become manifest. A case in point is that of the triptych and two cruciform pictures at Dresden, by Chiaro di Messer Bello dell' Erma, to which the eloquent pamphlet of Dr. Aemmster has at length succeeded in attracting the students. There is another still more solemn and beautiful work, now proved to be by the same hand, in the Pitti gallery at Florence. It is the one to which my narrative will relate.

This Chiaro dell' Erma was a young man of very honourable family in Arezzo; where, conceiving art almost for himself, and loving it deeply, he endeavoured from early boyhood towards the imitation of any objects offered in nature. The extreme longing after a visible embodiment of his thoughts strengthened as his years increased, more even than his sinews or the blood of his life; until he would feel faint in sunsets and at the sight of stately persons. When he had lived nineteen years, he heard of the famous Giunta Pisano; and, feeling much of admiration, with perhaps a little of that envy which youth always feels until it has learned to measure success by time and opportunity, he determined that he would seek out Giunta, and, if possible, become his pupil.

Having arrived in Pisa, he clothed himself in humble apparel, being unwilling that any other thing than the desire he had for knowledge should be his plea with the great painter; and then, leaving his baggage at a house of entertainment, he took his way along the street, asking whom he met for the lodging of Giunta. It soon chanced that one of that city, conceiving him to be a stranger and poor, took him into his house and refreshed him; afterwards directing him on his way.

When he was brought to speech of Giunta, he said merely that he was a student, and that nothing in the world was so much at his heart as to become that which he had heard told of him with whom he was speaking. He was received with courtesy and consideration, and soon stood among the works of the famous artist. But the forms he saw there were lifeless and incomplete; and a sudden exultation possessed him as he said within himself, "I am the master of this man." The blood came at first into his face, but the next moment he was quite pale and fell to trembling. He was able, however, to conceal his emotion; speaking very little to Giunta, but when he took his leave, thanking him respectfully.

After this, Chiaro's first resolve was, that he would work out thoroughly some one of his thoughts, and let the world know him. But the lesson which he had now learned, of how small a greatness might win fame, and how little there was to strive against, served to make him torpid, and rendered his exertions less continual. Also Pisa was a larger and more luxurious city than Arezzo; and when, in his walks, he saw the great gardens laid out for pleasure, and the beautiful women who passed to and fro, and heard the music that was in the groves of the city at evening, he was taken with wonder that he had never claimed his share of the inheritance of those years in which his youth was cast. And women loved Chiaro; for, in despite of the burthen of study, he was well-favoured and very manly in his walking; and, seeing his face in front, there was a glory upon it, as upon the face of one who feels a light round his hair.

So he put thought from him, and partook of his life. But, one night, being in a certain company of ladies, a gentleman that was there with him began to speak of the paintings of a youth named Bonaventura, which he had seen in Lucca; adding that Giunta Pisano might now look for a rival. When Chiaro heard this, the lamps shook before him and the music beat in his ears. He rose up, alleging a sudden sickness, and went out of that house with his teeth set. And, being again within his room, he wrote up over the door the name of Bonaventura, that it might stop him when he would go out.

He now took to work diligently, not returning to Arezzo, but remaining in Pisa, that no day more might be lost; only living entirely to himself. Sometimes, after nightfall, he would walk abroad in the most solitary places he could find; hardly feeling the ground under him, because of the thoughts of the day which held him in fever.

The lodging Chiaro had chosen was in a house that looked upon gardens fast by the Church of San Petronio. It was here, and at this time, that he painted the Dresden pictures; as also, in all likelihood, the one—inferior in merit, but certainly his—which is now at Munich. For the most part he was calm and regular in his manner of study; though often he would remain at work through the whole of a day, not resting once so long as the light lasted; flushed, and with the hair from his face. Or, at times, when he could not paint, he would sit for hours in thought of all the greatness the world had known from of old; until he was weak with yearning, like one who gazes upon a path of stars.

He continued in this patient endeavour for about three

years, at the end of which his name was spoken throughout all Tuscany. As his fame waxed, he began to be employed, besides easel-pictures, upon wall-paintings; but I believe that no traces remain to us of any of these latter. He is said to have painted in the Duomo; and D'Agincourt mentions having seen some portions of a picture by him which originally had its place above the high altar in the Church of the Certosa; but which, at the time he saw it, being very dilapidated, had been hewn out of the wall, and was preserved in the stores of the convent. Before the period of Dr. Aemmster's researches, however, it had been entirely destroyed.

Chiaro was now famous. It was for the race of fame that he had girded up his loins; and he had not paused until fame was reached; yet now, in taking breath, he found that the weight was still at his heart. The years of his labour had fallen from him, and his life was still in its first painful desire.

With all that Chiaro had done during these three years, and even before with the studies of his early youth, there had always been a feeling of worship and service. It was the peace-offering that he made to God and to his own soul for the eager selfishness of his aim. There was earth, indeed, upon the hem of his raiment; but *this* was of the heaven, heavenly. He had seasons when he could endure to think of no other feature of his hope than this. Sometimes it had even seemed to him to behold that day when his mistress—his mystical lady (now hardly in her ninth year, but whose smile at meeting had already lighted on his soul,)—even she, his own gracious Italian Art—should pass, through the sun that never sets, into the shadow of the tree of life, and be seen of God and found good: and then it had seemed to him that he, with many who, since his coming, had joined the band of whom he was one (for, in his dream, the body he had worn on earth had been dead an hundred years), were permitted to gather round the blessed maiden, and to worship with her through all ages and ages of ages, saying, Holy, holy, holy. This thing he had seen with the eyes of his spirit;

and in this thing had trusted, believing that it would surely come to pass.

But now, (being at length led to inquire closely into himself,) even as, in the pursuit of fame, the unrest abiding after attainment had proved to him that he had misinterpreted the craving of his own spirit—so also, now that he would willingly have fallen back on devotion, he became aware that much of that reverence which he had mistaken for faith had been no more than the worship of beauty. Therefore, after certain days passed in perplexity, Chiaro said within himself, "My life and my will are yet before me: I will take another aim to my life."

From that moment Chiaro set a watch on his soul, and put his hand to no other works but only to such as had for their end the presentment of some moral greatness that should influence the beholder: and to this end, he multiplied abstractions, and forgot the beauty and passion of the world. So the people ceased to throng about his pictures as heretofore; and, when they were carried through town and town to their destination, they were no longer delayed by the crowds eager to gaze and admire; and no prayers or offerings were brought to them on their path, as to his Madonnas, and his Saints, and his Holy Children, wrought for the sake of the life he saw in the faces that he loved. Only the critical audience remained to him; and these, in default of more worthy matter, would have turned their scrutiny on a puppet or a mantle. Meanwhile, he had no more of fever upon him; but was calm and pale each day in all that he did and in his goings in and out. The works he produced at this time have perished—in all likelihood, not unjustly. It is said (and we may easily believe it), that, though more laboured than his former pictures, they were cold and unemphatic; bearing marked out upon them the measure of that boundary to which they were made to conform.

And the weight was still close at Chiaro's heart: but he held in his breath, never resting (for he was afraid), and would not know it.

Now it happened, within these days, that there fell a

great feast in Pisa, for holy matters: and each man left
his occupation; and all the guilds and companies of the
city were got together for games and rejoicings. And
there were scarcely any that stayed in the houses, except
ladies who lay or sat along their balconies between open
windows which let the breeze beat through the rooms
and over the spread tables from end to end. And the
golden cloths that their arms lay upon drew all eyes up-
ward to see their beauty; and the day was long; and
every hour of the day was bright with the sun.

So Chiaro's model, when he awoke that morning on
the hot pavement of the Piazza Nunziata, and saw the
hurry of people that passed him, got up and went along
with them; and Chiaro waited for him in vain.

For the whole of that morning, the music was in
Chiaro's room from the Church close at hand; and he
could hear the sounds that the crowd made in the streets;
hushed only at long intervals while the processions for
the feast-day chanted in going under his windows. Also,
more than once, there was a high clamour from the meet-
ing of factious persons: for the ladies of both leagues were
looking down; and he who encountered his enemy could
not choose but draw upon him. Chiaro waited a long time
idle; and then knew that his model was gone elsewhere.
When at his work, he was blind and deaf to all else; but
he feared sloth: for then his stealthy thoughts would be-
gin to beat round and round him, seeking a point for
attack. He now rose, therefore, and went to the window.
It was within a short space of noon; and underneath him
a throng of people was coming out through the porch of
San Petronio.

The two greatest houses of the feud in Pisa had filled
the church for that mass. The first to leave had been the
Gherghiotti; who, stopping on the threshold, had fallen
back in ranks along each side of the archway: so that now,
in passing outward, the Marotoli had to walk between
two files of men whom they hated, and whose fathers
had hated theirs. All the chiefs were there and their whole
adherence; and each knew the name of each. Every man

of the Marotoli, as he came forth and saw his foes, laid back his hood and gazed about him, to show the badge upon the close cap that held his hair. And of the Gherghiotti there were some who tightened their girdles; and some shrilled and threw up their wrists scornfully, as who flies a falcon; for that was the crest of their house.

On the walls within the entry were a number of tall narrow pictures, presenting a moral allegory of Peace, which Chiaro had painted that year for the Church. The Gherghiotti stood with their backs to these frescoes; and among them Golzo Ninuccio, the youngest noble of the faction, called by the people Golaghiotta, for his debased life. This youth had remained for some while talking listlessly to his fellows, though with his sleepy sunken eyes fixed on them who passed: but now, seeing that no man jostled another, he drew the long silver shoe off his foot and struck the dust out of it on the cloak of him who was going by, asking him how far the tides rose at Viderza. And he said so because it was three months since, at that place, the Gherghiotti had beaten the Marotoli to the sands, and held them there while the sea came in; whereby many had been drowned. And, when he had spoken, at once the whole archway was dazzling with the light of confused swords; and they who had left turned back; and they who were still behind made haste to come forth; and there was so much blood cast up the walls on a sudden, that it ran in long streams down Chiaro's paintings.

Chiaro turned himself from the window; for the light felt dry between his lids, and he could not look. He sat down, and heard the noise of contention driven out of the church-porch and a great way through the streets; and soon there was a deep murmur that heaved and waxed from the other side of the city, where those of both parties were gathering to join in the tumult.

Chiaro sat with his face in his open hands. Once again he had wished to set his foot on a place that looked green and fertile; and once again it seemed to him that the thin rank mask was about to spread away, and that this

time the chill of the water must leave leprosy in his flesh.
The light still swam in his head, and bewildered him at
first; but when he knew his thoughts, they were these:—

"Fame failed me: faith failed me: and now this also,
—the hope that I nourished in this my generation of men,
—shall pass from me, and leave my feet and my hands
groping. Yet because of this are my feet become slow and
my hands thin. I am as one who, through the whole
night, holding his way diligently, hath smitten the steel
unto the flint, to lead some whom he knew darkling;
who hath kept his eyes always on the sparks that himself
made, lest they should fail; and who, towards dawn, turn-
ing to bid them that he had guided God speed, sees the
wet grass untrodden except of his own feet. I am as the
last hour of the day, whose chimes are a perfect number;
whom the next followeth not, nor light ensueth from him;
but in the same darkness is the old order begun afresh.
Men say, 'This is not God nor man; he is not as we are,
neither above us: let him sit beneath us, for we are many.'
Where I write Peace, in that spot is the drawing of swords,
and there men's footprints are red. When I would sow,
another harvest is ripe. Nay, it is much worse with me
than thus much. Am I not as a cloth drawn before the
light, that the looker may not be blinded? but which
sheweth thereby the grain of its own coarseness, so that
the light seems defiled, and men say, 'We will not walk
by it.' Wherefore through me they shall be doubly ac-
cursed, seeing that through me they reject the light. May
one be a devil and not know it?"

As Chiaro was in these thoughts, the fever encroached
slowly on his veins, till he could sit no longer and would
have risen; but suddenly he found awe within him, and
held his head bowed, without stirring. The warmth of
the air was not shaken; but there seemed a pulse in the
light, and a living freshness, like rain. The silence was a
painful music, that made the blood ache in his temples;
and he lifted his face and his deep eyes.

A woman was present in his room, clad to the hands
and feet with a green and grey raiment, fashioned to that

time. It seemed that the first thoughts he had ever known were given him as at first from her eyes, and he knew her hair to be the golden veil through which he beheld his dreams. Though her hands were joined, her face was not lifted, but set forward; and though the gaze was austere, yet her mouth was supreme in gentleness. And as he looked, Chiaro's spirit appeared abashed of its own intimate presence, and his lips shook with the thrill of tears; it seemed such a bitter while till the spirit might be indeed alone.

She did not move closer towards him, but he felt her to be as much with him as his breath. He was like one who, scaling a great steepness, hears his own voice echoed in some place much higher than he can see, and the name of which is not known to him. As the woman stood, her speech was with Chiaro: not, as it were, from her mouth or in his ears; but distinctly between them.

"I am an image, Chiaro, of thine own soul within thee. See me, and know me as I am. Thou sayest that fame has failed thee, and faith failed thee; but because at least thou hast not laid thy life unto riches, therefore, though thus late, I am suffered to come into thy knowledge. Fame sufficed not, for that thou didst seek fame: seek thine own conscience (not thy mind's conscience, but thine heart's), and all shall approve and suffice. For Fame, in noble soils, is a fruit of the Spring: but not therefore should it be said: 'Lo! my garden that I planted is barren: the crocus is here, but the lily is dead in the dry ground, and shall not lift the earth that covers it: therefore I will fling my garden together, and give it unto the builders.' Take heed rather that thou trouble not the wise secret earth; for in the mould that thou throwest up shall the first tender growth lie to waste; which else had been made strong in its season. Yea, and even if the year fall past in all its months, and the soil be indeed, to thee, peevish and incapable, and though thou indeed gather all thy harvest, and it suffice for others, and thou remain vexed with emptiness; and others drink of thy streams, and the drouth rasp thy throat;—let it be enough that these have found the feast good, and thanked the giver: remembering that, when the winter is striven through, there is another year, whose wind is meek, and whose sun fulfilleth all."

While he heard, Chiaro went slowly on his knees. It was not to her that spoke, for the speech seemed within him and his own. The air brooded in sunshine, and though the turmoil was great outside, the air within was at peace. But when he looked in her eyes, he wept. And she came to him, and cast her hair over him, and took her hands about his forehead, and spoke again:—

"Thou hast said," she continued, gently, "that faith failed thee. This cannot be. Either thou hadst it not, or thou hast it. But who bade thee strike the point betwixt love and faith? Wouldst thou sift the warm breeze from the sun that quickens it? Who bade thee turn upon God and say: 'Behold, my offering is of earth, and not worthy: Thy fire comes not upon it; therefore, though I slay not my brother whom Thou acceptest, I will depart before Thou smite me.' Why shouldst thou rise up and tell God He is not content? Had He, of His warrant, certified so to thee? Be not nice to seek out division; but possess thy love in sufficiency: assuredly this is faith, for the heart must believe first. What He hath set in thine heart to do, that do thou; and even though thou do it without thought of Him, it shall be well done; it is this sacrifice that He asketh of thee, and His flame is upon it for a sign. Think not of Him; but of His love and thy love. For God is no morbid exactor: He hath no hand to bow beneath, nor a foot, that thou shouldst kiss it."

And Chiaro held silence, and wept into her hair which covered his face; and the salt tears that he shed ran through her hair upon his lips; and he tasted the bitterness of shame.

Then the fair woman, that was his soul, spoke again to him, saying:

"And for this thy last purpose, and for those unprofitable truths of thy teaching,—thine heart hath already put them away, and it needs not that I lay my bidding upon thee. How is it that thou, a man, wouldst say coldly to

the mind what God hath said to the heart warmly? Thy
will was honest and wholesome; but look well lest this
also be folly,—to say, 'I, in doing this, do strengthen God
among men.' When at any time hath He cried unto thee,
saying, 'My son, lend Me thy shoulder, for I fall'? Deem-
est thou that the men who enter God's temple in malice,
to the provoking of blood, and neither for His love nor
for His wrath will abate their purpose,—shall afterwards
stand, with thee in the porch midway between Him and
themselves, to give ear unto thy thin voice, which merely
the fall of their visors can drown, and to see thy hands,
stretched feebly, tremble among their swords? Give thou
to God no more than He asketh of thee; but to man also,
that which is man's. In all that thou doest, work from
thine own heart, simply; for his heart is as thine, when
thine is wise and humble; and he shall have understand-
ing of thee. One drop of rain is as another, and the sun's
prism in all: and shalt thou not be as he, whose lives
are the breath of One? Only by making thyself his equal
can he learn to hold communion with thee, and at last
own thee above him. Not till thou lean over the water
shalt thou see thine image therein: stand erect, and it
shall slope from thy feet and be lost. Know that there is
but this means whereby thou mayst serve God with man:
—Set thine hand and thy soul to serve man with God."

And when she that spoke had said these words within
Chiaro's spirit, she left his side quietly, and stood up as
he had first seen her: with her fingers laid together, and
her eyes steadfast, and with the breadth of her long dress
covering her feet on the floor. And, speaking again, she
said:—

"Chiaro, servant of God, take now thine Art unto thee,
and paint me thus, as I am, to know me: weak, as I am,
and in the weeds of this time; only with eyes which seek
out labour, and with a faith, not learned, yet jealous of
prayer. Do this; so shall thy soul stand before thee always,
and perplex thee no more."

And Chiaro did as she bade him. While he worked,
his face grew solemn with knowledge: and before the

shadows had turned, his work was done. Having finished, he lay back where he sat, and was asleep immediately: for the growth of that strong sunset was heavy about him, and he felt weak and haggard; like one just come out of a dusk, hollow country, bewildered with echoes, where he had lost himself, and who has not slept for many days and nights. And when she saw him lie back, the beautiful woman came to him, and sat at his head, gazing, and quieted his sleep with her voice.

The tumult of the factions had endured all that day through all Pisa, though Chiaro had not heard it: and the last service of that feast was a mass sung at midnight from the windows of all the churches for the many dead who lay about the city, and who had to be buried before morning, because of the extreme heat.

———

In the spring of 1847, I was at Florence. Such as were there at the same time with myself—those, at least, to whom Art is something,—will certainly recollect how many rooms of the Pitti Gallery were closed through that season, in order that some of the pictures they contained might be examined and repaired without the necessity of removal. The hall, the staircases, and the vast central suite of apartments, were the only accessible portions; and in these such paintings as they could admit from the sealed *penetralia* were profanely huddled together, without respect of dates, schools, or persons.

I fear that, through this interdict, I may have missed seeing many of the best pictures. I do not mean *only* the most talked of: for these, as they were restored, generally found their way somehow into the open rooms, owing to the clamours raised by the students; and I remember how old Ercoli's, the curator's, spectacles used to be mirrored in the reclaimed surface, as he leaned mysteriously over these works with some of the visitors, to scrutinize and elucidate.

One picture that I saw that spring, I shall not easily

forget. It was among those, I believe, brought from the other rooms, and had been hung, obviously out of all chronology, immediately beneath that head by Raphael so long known as the *Berrettino,* and now said to be the portrait of Cecco Ciulli.

The picture I speak of is a small one, and represents merely the figure of a woman, clad to the hands and feet with a green and grey raiment, chaste and early in its fashion, but exceedingly simple. She is standing: her hands are held together lightly, and her eyes set earnestly open.

The face and hands in this picture, though wrought with great delicacy, have the appearance of being painted at once, in a single sitting: the drapery is unfinished. As soon as I saw the figure, it drew an awe upon me, like water in shadow: I shall not attempt to describe it more than I have already done; for the most absorbing wonder of it was its literality. You knew that figure, when painted, had been seen; yet it was not a thing to be seen of men. This language will appear ridiculous to such as have never looked on the work; and it may be even to some among those who have. On examining it closely, I perceived in one corner of the canvas the words *Manus Animam pinxit,* and the date 1239.

I turned to my Catalogue, but that was useless, for the pictures were all displaced. I then stepped up to the Cavaliere Ercoli, who was in the room at the moment, and asked him regarding the subject and authorship of the painting. He treated the matter, I thought, somewhat slightingly, and said that he could show me the reference in the Catalogue, which he had compiled. This, when found, was not of much value, as it merely said, "Schizzo d'autore incerto," adding the inscription.* I could willingly

* I should here say, that in the latest catalogues (owing, as in cases before mentioned, to the zeal and enthusiasm of Dr. Aemmster), this, and several other pictures, have been more competently entered. The work in question is now placed in the *Sala Sessagona,* a room I did not see—under the number 161. It is described as "Figura mistica di Chiaro dell' Erma," and there is a brief notice of the author appended. [Rossetti's note]

have prolonged my inquiry, in the hope that it might somehow lead to some result; but I had disturbed the curator from certain yards of Guido, and he was not communicative. I went back, therefore, and stood before the picture till it grew dusk.

The next day I was there again; but this time a circle of students was round the spot, all copying the *Berrettino*. I contrived, however, to find a place whence I could see *my* picture, and where I seemed to be in nobody's way. For some minutes I remained undisturbed; and then I heard, in an English voice: "Might I beg of you, sir, to stand a little more to this side, as you interrupt my view?"

I felt vexed, for, standing where he asked me, a glare struck on the picture from the windows, and I could not see it. However, the request was reasonably made, and from a countryman; so I complied, and turning away, stood by his easel. I knew it was not worth while; yet I referred in some way to the work underneath the one he was copying. He did not laugh, but he smiled as we do in England. "*Very* odd, is it not?" said he.

The other students near us were all continental; and seeing an Englishman select an Englishman to speak with, conceived, I suppose, that he could understand no language but his own. They had evidently been noticing the interest which the little picture appeared to excite in me.

One of them, an Italian, said something to another who stood next to him. He spoke with a Genoese accent, and I lost the sense in the villainous dialect. "Che so?" * replied the other, lifting his eyebrows towards the figure; "roba mistica: 'st' Inglesi son matti sul misticismo: somiglia alle nebbie di là. Li fa pensare alla patria,

'e intenerisce il core
Lo dì ch' han detto ai dolci amici adio.' "

* The Italian may be translated: "Who knows? . . . mystical stuff: these Englishmen are mad about mysticism: as if in the clouds beyond. It makes them think of heaven, 'and the heart grows tender on the day when one has said farewell to a dear friend.'" "The night, you mean."

"La notte, vuoi dire," said a third.

There was a general laugh. My compatriot was evidently a novice in the language, and did not take in what was said. I remained silent, being amused.

"Et toi donc?" said he who had quoted Dante, turning to a student, whose birthplace was unmistakable, even had he been addressed in any other language: "que dis-tu de ce genre-là?"

"Moi?" returned the Frenchman, standing back from his easel, and looking at me and at the figure, quite politely, though with an evident reservation: "Je dis, mon cher, que c'est une spécialité dont je me fiche pas mal. Je tiens que quand on ne comprend pas une chose, c'est qu' elle ne signifie rien."

My reader thinks possibly that the French student was right.

(*1849*)

CHRISTINA ROSSETTI

(1830–1894)

Model for her brother's early paintings "The Girlhood of
Mary Virgin" and "The Annunciation," Christina Rossetti
was from the beginning both close to the center of the
Pre-Raphaelite movement and at the same time, in her
quiet asceticism, aloof from its bohemian exuberance. Any
perceptive reader of *The Germ* (there were, alas, very
few) might have observed that her contributions surpassed
all others in sureness of diction and finish of form. In
1862 her *Goblin Market,* the first Pre-Raphaelite volume
to enjoy a fairly wide reception, did succeed in convincing
a critical public that the Pre-Raphaelites could not be
summarily dismissed. Meanwhile, she had seen the original
group disband (as she notes in "The P. R. B."), Elizabeth
Siddal come to dominate Dante Gabriel's imagination (see
"In an Artist's Studio"), and a new and more literary
circle gather. As many of her lyrics testify, her own life
was marked by unhappiness in love, broken engagements,
and renunciations, but also by a steadfast, sustaining re-
ligious faith. Her secular poems, though generally less
elaborately wrought and less ornate than Rossetti's, reflect
a Pre-Raphaelite response to sharp outline and vivid color
and a delight in detail that takes on a symbolic force. Her
devotional pieces, some of them among the best of the
Victorian period, less troubled than the metaphysical prob-

ings of Dante Gabriel's *House of Life,* approximate the original Pre-Raphaelite ideal in their naive literal vision, the assumption—beyond her brother's reach—that spiritual mysteries were real entities which she might one day "see . . . with my very sight/ And touch and handle and attain." Though plagued with serious illness (a distressing glandular disease and ultimately a painful cancer), from the age of forty till her death at sixty-four she continued to write with courage, good humor, and unbroken clarity of line and emotion. Edith Sitwell once said of "Goblin Market" that it was "the most perfect poem in English written by a woman." Other readers, considering all the poems, have found reason to regard Christina Rossetti as the most distinguished English woman poet.

SONG

When I am dead, my dearest,
  Sing no sad songs for me;
Plant thou no roses at my head,
  Nor shady cypress tree:
Be the green grass above me
  With showers and dewdrops wet;
And if thou wilt, remember,
  And if thou wilt, forget.

I shall not see the shadows,
  I shall not feel the rain;   *10*
I shall not hear the nightingale
  Sing on, as if in pain:
And dreaming through the twilight
  That doth not rise nor set,
Haply I may remember,
  And haply may forget.

                    (1848)

DREAM LAND

Where sunless rivers weep
Their waves into the deep,
She sleeps a charmèd sleep:
   Awake her not.
Led by a single star,
She came from very far
To seek where shadows are
   Her pleasant lot.

She left the rosy morn,
She left the fields of corn,   *10*
For twilight cold and lorn
   And water springs.
Through sleep, as through a veil,
She sees the sky look pale,
And hears the nightingale
   That sadly sings.

Rest, rest, a perfect rest
Shed over brow and breast;
Her face is toward the west
   The purple land.   *20*
She cannot see the grain
Ripening on hill and plain;
She cannot feel the rain
   Upon her hand.

Rest, rest, for evermore
Upon a mossy shore;
Rest, rest at the heart's core
   Till time shall cease:
Sleep that no pain shall wake;
Night that no morn shall break   *30*
Till joy shall overtake
   Her perfect peace.

                             (1849)

REST

O earth, lie heavily upon her eyes;
   Seal her sweet eyes weary of watching, Earth;
   Lie close around her; leave no room for mirth
With its harsh laughter, nor for sound of sighs.
She hath no questions, she hath no replies,
   Hushed in and curtained with a blessed dearth
   Of all that irked her from the hour of birth;
With stillness that is almost Paradise.
Darkness more clear than noonday holdeth her,
   Silence more musical than any song;   *10*
Even her very heart has ceased to stir:
Until the morning of Eternity
Her rest shall not begin nor end, but be;
   And when she wakes she will not think it long.

                                   (1849)

AFTER DEATH

The curtains were half drawn, the floor was swept
   And strewn with rushes, rosemary and may
   Lay thick upon the bed on which I lay,
Where through the lattice ivy-shadows crept.
He leaned above me, thinking that I slept
   And could not hear him; but I heard him say:
   "Poor child, poor child:" and as he turned away
Came a deep silence, and I knew he wept.
He did not touch the shroud, or raise the fold
   That hid my face, or take my hand in his,   *10*
      Or ruffle the smooth pillows for my head:
      He did not love me living; but once dead
   He pitied me; and very sweet it is
To know he still is warm though I am cold.

                                   (1849)

REMEMBER

Remember me when I am gone away,
 Gone far away into the silent land;
 When you can no more hold me by the hand,
Nor I half turn to go yet turning stay.
Remember me when no more, day by day,
 You tell me of our future that you plann'd:
 Only remember me; you understand
It will be late to counsel then or pray.
Yet if you should forget me for a while
 And afterwards remember, do not grieve: *10*
 For if the darkness and corruption leave
 A vestige of the thoughts that once I had,
Better by far you should forget and smile
 Than that you should remember and be sad.

             (1849)

THE THREE ENEMIES

THE FLESH

"Sweet, thou art pale."
       "More pale to see,
Christ hung upon the cruel tree
And bore His Father's wrath for me."

"Sweet, thou art sad."
       "Beneath a rod
More heavy, Christ for my sake trod
The winepress of the wrath of God."

"Sweet, thou art weary."
       "Not so Christ:
Whose mighty love of me sufficed
For Strength, Salvation, Eucharist."

"Sweet, thou art footsore."
       "If I bleed,   *10*

His feet have bled; yea in my need.
His Heart once bled for mine indeed."

THE WORLD

"Sweet, thou art young."
                                    "So He was young
Who for my sake in silence hung
Upon the Cross with Passion wrung."

"Look, thou art fair.
                                    "He was more fair
Than men, Who deigned for me to wear
A visage marred beyond compare."

"And thou hast riches."
                                    "Daily bread:
All else is His: Who, living, dead,   20
For me lacked where to lay His Head."

"And life is sweet."
                                    "It was not so
To Him, Whose Cup did overflow
With mine unutterable woe."

THE DEVIL

"Thou drinkest deep."
                                    "When Christ would sup
He drained the dregs from out my cup:
So how should I be lifted up?"

"Thou shalt win Glory."
                                    "In the skies.
Lord Jesus, cover up mine eyes
Lest they should look on vanities."   30

"Thou shalt have Knowledge."
                                    "Helpless dust!
In Thee, O Lord, I put my trust:
Answer Thou for me, Wise and Just."

"And Might."
            "Get thee behind me. Lord,
Who has redeemed and not abhorred
My soul, O keep it by Thy Word."

(*1851*)

THE P. R. B.

The P. R. B. is in its decadence:
    For Woolner in Australia cooks his chops,
    And Hunt is yearning for the land of Cheops;
        D. G. Rossetti shuns the vulgar optic;
    While William M. Rossetti merely lops
        His B's in English disesteemed as Coptic;
    Calm Stephens in the twilight smokes his pipe,
        But long the dawning of his public day;
        And he at last the champion great Millais,
Attaining academic opulence,   *10*
        Winds up his signature with A. R. A.
So rivers merge in the perpetual sea;
So luscious fruit must fall when overripe;
And so the consummated P. R. B.

(*1853*)

SLEEP AT SEA

Sound the deep waters:—
    Who shall sound that deep?—
Too short the plummet,
    And the watchmen sleep.
Some dream of effort
    Up a toilsome steep;
Some dream of pasture grounds
    For harmless sheep.

White shapes flit to and fro
    From mast to mast;   *10*

They feel the distant tempest
   That nears them fast:
Great rocks are straight ahead,
   Great shoals not past;
They shout to one another
   Upon the blast.

Oh, soft the streams drop music
   Between the hills,
And musical the birds' nests
   Beside those rills   20
The nests are types of home
   Love-hidden from ills,
The nests are types of spirits
   Love-music fills.

So dream the sleepers,
   Each man in his place;
The lightning shows the smile
   Upon each face:
The ship is driving,—driving,—
   It drives apace: 30
And sleepers smile, and spirits
   Bewail their case.

The lightning glares and reddens
   Across the skies;
It seems but sunset
   To those sleeping eyes.
When did the sun go down
   On such a wise?
From such a sunset
   When shall day arise?   40

"Wake," call the spirits:
   But to heedless ears:
They have forgotten sorrows
   And hopes and fears;

They have forgotten perils
   And smiles and tears;
Their dream has held them long,
   Long years and years.

"Wake," call the spirits again:
   But it would take   50
A louder summons
   To bid them awake.
Some dream of pleasure
   For another's sake;
Some dream, forgetful
   Of a lifelong ache.

One by one slowly,
   Ah, how sad and slow!
Wailing and praying,
   The spirits rise and go: 60
Clear stainless spirits
   White, as white as snow;
Pale spirits, wailing
   For an overthrow,

One by one flitting,
   Like a mournful bird
Whose song is tired at last
   For no mate heard.
The loving voice is silent,
   The useless word;   70
One by one flitting,
   Sick with hope deferred.

Driving and driving,
   The ship drives amain:
While swift from mast to mast
   Shapes flit again,
Flit silent as the silence
   Where men lie slain;

Their shadow cast upon the sails
   Is like a stain.   *80*

No voice to call the sleepers,
   No hand to raise:
They sleep to death in dreaming
   Of length of days.
Vanity of vanities,
   The Preacher says:
Vanity is the end
   Of all their ways.

                              (1853)

THE BOURNE

Underneath the growing grass,
   Underneath the living flowers,
   Deeper than the sound of showers:
   There we shall not count the hours
By the shadows as they pass.

Youth and health will be but vain,
   Beauty reckoned of no worth:
   There a very little girth
   Can hold round what once the earth
Seemed too narrow to contain.   *10*

                              (1854)

ECHO

Come to me in the silence of the night;
   Come in the speaking silence of a dream;
Come with soft rounded cheeks and eyes as bright
   As sunlight on a stream;
     Come back in tears,
O memory, hope, love of finished years.

O dream how sweet, too sweet, too bitter sweet,
   Whose wakening should have been in Paradise,
Where souls brimfull of love abide and meet;
    Where thirsting longing eyes   *10*
      Watch the slow door
That opening, letting in, lets out no more.

Yet come to me in dreams, that I may live
   My very life again though cold in death:
Come back to me in dreams, that I may give
    Pulse for pulse, breath for breath:
      Speak low, lean low,
As long ago, my love, how long ago.

                               (1854)

PARADISE

Once in a dream I saw the flowers
   That bud and bloom in Paradise;
   More fair they are than waking eyes
Have seen in all this world of ours.
And faint the perfume-bearing rose,
   And faint the lily on its stem,
And faint the perfect violet
    Compared with them.

I heard the songs of Paradise:
   Each bird sat singing in his place;   *10*
   A tender song so full of grace
It soared like incense to the skies.
Each bird sat singing to his mate
   Soft cooing notes among the trees:
The nightingale herself were cold
    To such as these.

I saw the fourfold River flow,
   And deep it was, with golden sand;
   It flowed between a mossy land

With murmured music grave and low.   20
It hath refreshment for all thirst,
    For fainting spirits strength and rest;
Earth holds not such a draught as this
        From east to west.

The Tree of Life stood budding there,
    Abundant with its twelvefold fruits;
    Eternal sap sustains its roots,
Its shadowing branches fill the air.
Its leaves are healing for the world,
    Its fruit the hungry world can feed.   30
Sweeter than honey to the taste
        And balm indeed.

I saw the gate called Beautiful;
    And looked, but scarce could look, within;
    I saw the golden streets begin,
And outskirts of the glassy pool.
Oh harps, oh crowns of plenteous stars,
    Oh green palm-branches many-leaved—
Eye hath not seen, nor ear hath heard,
        Nor heart conceived.   40

I hope to see these things again,
    But not as once in dreams by night;
    To see them with my very sight,
And touch, and handle, and attain:
To have all Heaven beneath my feet
    For narrow way that once they trod;
To have my part with all the saints,
        And with my God.

                                        (1854)

MAY

I cannot tell you how it was;
But this I know: it came to pass

Upon a bright and breezy day
When May was young; ah, pleasant May!
As yet the poppies were not born
Between the blades of tender corn;
The last eggs had not hatched as yet,
Nor any bird forgone its mate.

I cannot tell you what it was;
But this I know: it did but pass.   10
It passed away with sunny May,
With all sweet things it passed away,
And left me old, and cold, and grey.

(1855)

IN AN ARTIST'S STUDIO

One face looks out from all his canvases,
    One selfsame figure sits or walks or leans:
    We found her hidden just behind those screens,
That mirror gave back all her loveliness.
A queen in opal or in ruby dress,
    A nameless girl in freshest summer-greens,
    A saint, an angel—every canvas means
The same one meaning, neither more or less.
He feeds upon her face by day and night,
    And she with true kind eyes looks back on him,   10
Fair as the moon and joyful as the light:
    Not wan with waiting, not with sorrow dim;
Not as she is, but was when hope shone bright;
    Not as she is, but as she fills his dream.

(1856)

SHUT OUT

The door was shut. I looked between
    Its iron bars; and saw it lie,
    My garden, mine, beneath the sky,
Pied with all flowers bedewed and green:

From bough to bough the song-birds crossed,
　　From flower to flower the moths and bees:
　　With all its nests and stately trees
It had been mine, and it was lost.

A shadowless spirit kept the gate,
　　Blank and unchanging like the grave.　　　　　　　　*10*
　　I, peering through, said; "Let me have
Some buds to cheer my outcast state."

He answered not. "Or give me, then,
　　But one small twig from shrub or tree;
　　And bid my home remember me
Until I come to it again."

The spirit was silent; but he took
　　Mortar and stone to build a wall;
　　He left no loophole great or small
Through which my straining eyes might look:　　　　　　　20

So now I sit here quite alone
　　Blinded with tears; nor grieve for that,
　　For nought is left worth looking at
Since my delightful land is gone.

A violet bed is budding near,
　　Wherein a lark has made her nest:
　　And good they are, but not the best;
And dear they are, but not so dear.

　　　　　　　　　　　　　　　　　　　　　　(*1856*)

A BIRTHDAY

My heart is like a singing bird
　　Whose nest is in a watered shoot;
My heart is like an apple-tree
　　Whose boughs are bent with thickset fruit;

My heart is like a rainbow shell
   That paddles in a halcyon sea;
My heart is gladder than all these
   Because my love is come to me.

Raise me a dais of silk and down;
   Hang it with vair and purple dyes;   *10*
Carve it in doves and pomegranates,
   And peacocks with a hundred eyes;
Work it in gold and silver grapes,
   In leaves and silver fleurs-de-lys;
Because the birthday of my life
   Is come, my love is come to me.

                    (1857)

A BETTER RESURRECTION

I have no wit, no words, no tears;
   My heart within me like a stone
Is numbed too much for hopes or fears.
   Look right, look left, I dwell alone;
I lift mine eyes, but dimmed with grief
   No everlasting hills I see;
My life is in the falling leaf:
     O Jesus, quicken me.

My life is like a faded leaf,
   My harvest dwindled to a husk: *10*
Truly my life is void and brief
   And tedious in the barren dusk;
My life is like a frozen thing,
   No bud nor greenness can I see:
Yet rise it shall—the sap of Spring;
     O Jesus, rise in me.

My life is like a broken bowl,
   A broken bowl that cannot hold

One drop of water for my soul
  Or cordial in the searching cold;   20
Cast in the fire the perished thing;
  Melt and remould it, till it be
A royal cup for Him, my King:
  O Jesus, drink of me.

                      (*1857*)

AN APPLE GATHERING

I plucked pink blossoms from mine apple-tree
  And wore them all that evening in my hair;
Then in due season when I went to see,
    I found no apples there.

With dangling basket all along the grass
  As I had come I went the self-same track;
My neighbors mocked me while they saw me pass
    So empty-handed back.

Lilian and Lilias smiled in trudging by,
  Their heaped-up basket teased me like a jeer;   10
Sweet-voiced they sang beneath the sunset sky,
    Their mother's home was near.

Plump Gertrude passed me with her basket full,
  A stronger hand than hers helped it along;
A voice talked with her through the shadows cool
    More sweet to me than song.

Ah Willie, Willie, was my love less worth
  Than apples with their green leaves piled above?
I counted rosiest apples on the earth
    Of far less worth than love.   20

So once it was with me you stooped to talk,
  Laughing and listening in this very lane;
To think that by this way we used to walk
    We shall not walk again!

I let my neighbors pass me, ones and twos
   And groups; the latest said the night grew chill,
And hastened. But I loitered; while the dews
     Fell fast I loitered still.

                             (*1857*)

THE CONVENT THRESHOLD

There's blood between us, love, my love,
There's father's blood, there's brother's blood,
And blood's a bar I cannot pass.
I choose the stairs that mount above,
Stair after golden sky-ward stair,
To city and to sea of glass.
My lily feet are soiled with mud,
With scarlet mud which tells a tale
Of hope that was, of guilt that was,
Of love that shall not yet avail;   *10*
Alas, my heart, if I could bare
My heart, this selfsame stain is there:
I seek the sea of glass and fire
To wash the spot, to burn the snare;
Lo, stairs are meant to lift us higher—
Mount with me, mount the kindled stair.

Your eyes look earthward, mine look up.
I see the far-off city grand,
Beyond the hills a watered land,
Beyond the gulf a gleaming strand   *20*
Of mansions where the righteous sup;
Who sleep at ease among their trees,
Or wake to sing a cadenced hymn
With Cherubim and Seraphim;
They bore the Cross, they drained the cup,
Racked, roasted, crushed, wrenched limb from limb,
They the offscouring of the world.
The heaven of starry heavens unfurled,
The sun before their face is dim.

You looking earthward, what see you?   *30*
Milk-white, wine-flushed among the vines,
Up and down leaping, to and fro,
Most glad, most full, made strong with wines,
Blooming as peaches pearled with dew,
Their golden windy hair afloat,
Love-music warbling in their throat,
Young men and women come and go.

You linger, yet the time is short:
Flee for your life, gird up your strength
To flee; the shadows stretched at length   *40*
Show that day wanes, that night draws nigh;
Flee to the mountain, tarry not.
Is this a time for smile and sigh,
For songs among the secret trees
Where sudden blue birds nest and sport?
The time is short and yet you stay:
To-day, while it is called to-day,
Kneel, wrestle, knock, do violence, pray;
To-day is short, to-morrow nigh:
Why will you die? why will you die?   *50*

You sinned with me a pleasant sin:
Repent with me, for I repent.
Woe's me the lore I must unlearn!
Woe's me that easy way we went,
So rugged when I would return!
How long until my sleep begin,
How long shall stretch these nights and days?
Surely, clean Angels cry, she prays;
She laves her soul with tedious tears:
How long must stretch these years and years?   *60*

I turn from you my cheeks and eyes,
My hair which you shall see no more—
Alas for joy that went before,
For joy that dies, for love that dies.

Only my lips still turn to you,
My livid lips that cry, Repent.
O weary life, O weary Lent,
O weary time whose stars are few.

How should I rest in Paradise,
Or sit on steps of heaven alone   70
If Saints and Angels spoke of love
Should I not answer from my throne:
Have pity upon me, ye my friends,
For I have heard the sound thereof:
Should I not turn with yearning eyes,
Turn earthwards with a pitiful pang?
Oh save me from a pang in heaven.
By all the gifts we took and gave,
Repent, repent, and be forgiven:
This life is long, but yet it ends;   80
Repent and purge your soul and save:
No gladder song the morning stars
Upon their birthday morning sang
Than Angels sing when one repents.

I tell you what I dreamed last night:
A spirit with transfigured face
Fire-footed clomb an infinite space.
I heard his hundred pinions clang,
Heaven-bells rejoicing rang and rang,
Heaven-air was thrilled with subtle scents,   90
Worlds spun upon their rushing cars.
He mounted, shrieking, "Give me light!"
Still light was poured on him, more light;
Angels, Archangels he outstripped,
Exulting in exceeding might,
And trod the skirts of Cherubim.
Still "Give me light," he shrieked; and dipped
His thirsty face, and drank a sea,
Athirst with thirst it could not slake.
I saw him, drunk with knowledge, take   100

From aching brows the aureole crown—
His locks writhe like a cloven snake—
He left his throne to grovel down
And lick the dust of Seraphs' feet;
For what is knowledge duly weighed?
Knowledge is strong, but love is sweet;
Yea, all the progress he had made
Was but to learn that all is small
Save love, for love is all in all.

I tell you what I dreamed last night: 110
It was not dark, it was not light,
Cold dews had drenched my plenteous hair
Through clay; you came to seek me there.
And "Do you dream of me?" you said.
My heart was dust that used to leap
To you; I answered half asleep:
"My pillow is damp, my sheets are red,
There's a leaden tester to my bed;
Find you a warmer playfellow,
A warmer pillow for your head,   120
A kinder love to love than mine."
You wrung your hands, while I, like lead,
Crushed downwards through the sodden earth;
You smote your hands but not in mirth,
And reeled but were not drunk with wine.

For all night long I dreamed of you;
I woke and prayed against my will,
Then slept to dream of you again.
At length I rose and knelt and prayed.
I cannot write the words I said,   130
My words were slow, my tears were few;
But through the dark my silence spoke
Like thunder. When this morning broke,
My face was pinched, my hair was grey,
And frozen blood was on the sill
Where stifling in my struggle I lay.

If now you saw me you would say:
Where is the face I used to love?
And I would answer: Gone before;
It tarries veiled in paradise.   *140*
When once the morning star shall rise,
When earth with shadow flees away
And we stand safe within the door,
Then you shall lift the veil thereof.
Look up, rise up: for far above
Our palms are grown, our place is set;
There we shall meet as once we met,
And love with old familiar love.

                                                    (1858)

AT HOME

When I was dead, my spirit turned
    To seek the much-frequented house:
I passed the door, and saw my friends
    Feasting beneath green orange boughs;
From hand to hand they pushed the wine,
    They sucked the pulp of plum and peach;
They sang, they jested, and they laughed,
    For each was loved of each.

I listened to their honest chat:
    Said one: "To-morrow we shall be   *10*
Plod plod along the featureless sands,
    And coasting miles and miles of sea."
Said one: "Before the turn of tide
    We will achieve the eyrie-seat."
Said one: "To-morrow shall be like
    To-day, but much more sweet."

"To-morrow," said they, strong with hope,
    And dwelt upon the pleasant way:
"To-morrow," cried they, one and all,
    While no one spoke of yesterday.   *20*

Their life stood full at blessed noon;
   I, only I, had passed away:
"To-morrow and to-day," they cried;
   I was of yesterday.

I shivered comfortless, but cast
   No chill across the table-cloth;
I, all-forgotten, shivered, sad
   To stay, and yet to part how loth:
I passed from the familiar room,
   I who from love had passed away,   30
Like the remembrance of a guest
   That tarrieth but a day.

                                (1858)

UP-HILL

Does the road wind up-hill all the way?
   Yes, to the very end.
Will the day's journey take the whole long day?
   From morn to night, my friend.

But is there for the night a resting-place?
   A roof for when the slow dark hours begin.
May not the darkness hide it from my face?
   You cannot miss that inn.

Shall I meet other wayfarers at night?
   Those who have gone before.   10
Then must I knock, or call when just in sight?
   They will not keep you standing at that door.

Shall I find comfort, travel-sore and weak?
   Of labour you shall find the sum.
Will there be beds for me and all who seek?
   Yea, beds for all who come.

                                (1858)

ADVENT

This Advent moon shines cold and clear,
   These Advent nights are long;
Our lamps have burned year after year,
   And still their flame is strong.
"Watchman, what of the night?" we cry,
   Heart-sick with hope deferred:
"No speaking signs are in the sky,"
   Is still the watchman's word.

The Porter watches at the gate,
   The servants watch within;   *10*
The watch is long betimes and late,
   The prize is slow to win.
"Watchman, what of the night?" But still
   His answer sounds the same:
"No daybreak tops the utmost hill,
   Nor pale our lamps of flame."

One to another hear them speak,
   The patient virgins wise:
"Surely He is not far to seek,"—
   "All night we watch and rise."   *20*
"The days are evil looking back,
   The coming days are dim;
Yet count we not His promise slack,
   But watch and wait for Him."

One with another, soul with soul,
   They kindle fire from fire:
"Friends watch us who have touched the goal."
   "They urge us, come up higher."
"With them shall rest our waysore feet,
   With them is built our home,   *30*
With Christ."—"They sweet, but He most sweet,
   Sweeter than honeycomb."

There no more parting, no more pain,
　　The distant ones brought near,
The lost so long are found again,
　　Long lost but longer dear:
Eye hath not seen, ear hath not heard,
　　Nor heart conceived that rest,
With them our good things long deferred,
　　With Jesus Christ our Best.   40

We weep because the night is long,
　　We laugh, for day shall rise,
We sing a slow contented song
　　And knock at Paradise.
Weeping we hold Him fast Who wept
　　For us, we hold Him fast;
And will not let Him go except
　　He bless us first or last.

Weeping we hold Him fast to-night;
　　We will not let Him go   50
Till daybreak smite our wearied sight,
　　And summer smite the snow:
Then figs shall bud, and dove with dove
　　Shall coo the livelong day;
Then He shall say, "Arise, My love,
　　My fair one, come away."

　　　　　　　　　　　　　　　　　(1858)

GOBLIN MARKET

Morning and evening
Maids heard the goblins cry:
"Come buy our orchard fruits,
Come buy, come buy:
Apples and quinces,
Lemons and oranges,
Plump unpecked cherries,
Melons and raspberries,

Bloom-down-cheeked peaches,
Swart-headed mulberries,   *10*
Wild free-born cranberries,
Crab-apples, dewberries,
Pine-apples, blackberries,
Apricots, strawberries;—
All ripe together
In summer weather,—-
Morns that pass by,
Fair eves that fly;
Come buy, come buy:
Our grapes fresh from the vine,   *20*
Pomegranates full and fine,
Dates and sharp bullaces,
Rare pears and greengages,
Damsons and bilberries,
Taste them and try:
Currants and gooseberries,
Bright-fire-like barberries,
Figs to fill your mouth,
Citrons from the South,
Sweet to tongue and sound to eye;   *30*
Come buy, come buy."

    Evening by evening
Among the brookside rushes,
Laura bowed her head to hear,
Lizzie veiled her blushes:
Crouching close together
In the cooling weather,
With clasping arms and cautioning lips,
With tingling cheeks and finger-tips.
"Lie close," Laura said,   *40*
Pricking up her golden head:
"We must not look at goblin men,
We must not buy their fruits:
Who knows upon what soil they fed
Their hungry thirsty roots?"

"Come buy," call the goblins
Hobbling down the glen.
"O," cried Lizzie, "Laura, Laura,
You should not peep at goblin men."
Lizzie covered up her eyes,   *50*
Covered close lest they should look;
Laura reared her glossy head,
And whispered like the restless brook:
"Look, Lizzie, look, Lizzie,
Down the glen tramp little men.
One hauls a basket,
One bears a plate,
One lugs a golden dish
Of many pounds' weight.
How fair the vine must grow   *60*
Whose grapes are so luscious;
How warm the wind must blow
Through those fruit bushes."
"No," said Lizzie: "No, no, no;
Their offers should not charm us,
Their evil gifts would harm us."
She thrust a dimpled finger
In each ear, shut eyes and ran:
Curious Laura chose to linger
Wondering at each merchant man.   *70*
One had a cat's face,
One whisked a tail,
One tramped at a rat's pace,
One crawled like a snail,
One like a wombat prowled obtuse and furry,
One like a ratel tumbled hurry skurry.
She heard a voice like voice of doves
Cooing all together:
They sounded kind and full of loves
In the pleasant weather.   *80*

   Laura stretched her gleaming neck
Like a rush-imbedded swan,

Like a lily from the beck,
Like a moonlit poplar branch,
Like a vessel at the launch
When its last restraint is gone.

Backwards up the mossy glen
Turned and trooped the goblin men,
With their shrill repeated cry,
"Come buy, come buy."   90
When they reached where Laura was
They stood stock still upon the moss,
Leering at each other,
Brother with queer brother;
Signalling each other,
Brother with sly brother.
One set his basket down,
One reared his plate;
One began to weave a crown
Of tendrils, leaves, and rough nuts brown   100
(Men sell not such in any town);
One heaved the golden weight
Of dish and fruit to offer her:
"Come buy, come buy," was still their cry.
Laura stared but did not stir,
Longed but had no money:
The whisk-tailed merchant bade her taste
In tones as smooth as honey,
The cat-faced purr'd,
The rat-paced spoke a word   110
Of welcome, and the snail-paced even was heard;
One parrot-voiced and jolly
Cried "Pretty Goblin" still for "Pretty Polly";—
One whistled like a bird.

But sweet-tooth Laura spoke in haste:
"Good folk, I have no coin;
To take were to purloin:
I have no copper in my purse,

I have no silver either,
And all my gold is on the furze   120
That shakes in windy weather
Above the rusty heather."
"You have much gold upon your head,"
They answered altogether:
"Buy from us with a golden curl."
She clipped a precious golden lock,
She dropped a tear more rare than pearl,
Then sucked their fruit globes fair or red:
Sweeter than honey from the rock,
Stronger than man-rejoicing wine,   130
Clearer than water flowed that juice;
She never tasted such before,
How should it cloy with length of use?
She sucked and sucked and sucked the more
Fruits which that unknown orchard bore;
She sucked until her lips were sore;
Then flung the emptied rinds away,
But gathered up one kernel stone,
And knew not was it night or day
As she turned home alone.   140

    Lizzie met her at the gate
Full of wise upbraidings:
"Dear, you should not stay so late,
Twilight is not good for maidens;
Should not loiter in the glen
In the haunts of goblin men.
Do you not remember Jeanie,
How she met them in the moonlight,
Took their gifts both choice and many,
Ate their fruits and wore their flowers   150
Plucked from bowers
Where summer ripens at all hours?
But ever in the noonlight
She pined and pined away;
Sought them by night and day,

Leaning
grave

Found them no more, but dwindled and grew grey;
Then fell with the first snow,
While to this day no grass will grow
Where she lies low:
I planted daisies there a year ago   160
That never blow.
You should not loiter so."
"Nay, hush," said Laura:
"Nay, hush, my sister:
I ate and ate my fill,
Yet my mouth waters still;
To-morrow night I will
Buy more,"—and kissed her.
"Have done with sorrow;
I'll bring you plums to-morrow   170
Fresh on their mother twigs,
Cherries worth getting;
You cannot think what figs
My teeth have met in,
What melons icy-cold
Piled on a dish of gold
Too huge for me to hold,
What peaches with a velvet nap,
Pellucid grapes without one seed:
Odorous indeed must be the mead   180
Whereon they grow, and pure the wave they drink,
With lilies at the brink,
And sugar-sweet their sap."

Golden head by golden head,
Like two pigeons in one nest
Folded in each other's wings,
They lay down in their curtained bed:
Like two blossoms on one stem,
Like two flakes of new-fall'n snow,
Like two wands of ivory   190
Tipped with gold for awful kings.
Moon and stars gazed in at them,

*Illustrations by Dante Gabriel Rossetti for
Christina Rossetti's "Goblin Market"*

Wind sang to them lullaby,
Lumbering owls forbore to fly,
Not a bat flapped to and fro
Round their rest:
Cheek to cheek and breast to breast
Locked together in one nest.

   Early in the morning
When the first cock crowed his warning,   *200*
Neat like bees, as sweet and busy,
Laura rose with Lizzie:
Fetched in honey, milked the cows,
Aired and set to rights the house,
Kneaded cakes of whitest wheat,
Cakes for dainty mouths to eat,
Next churned butter, whipped up cream,
Fed their poultry, sat and sewed;
Talked as modest maidens should:
Lizzie with an open heart,   *210*
Laura in an absent dream,
One content, one sick in part;
One warbling for the mere bright day's delight,
One longing for the night.

   At length slow evening came:
They went with pitchers to the reedy brook;
Lizzie most placid in her look,
Laura most like a leaping flame.
They drew the gurgling water from its deep;
Lizzie plucked purple and rich golden flags,   *220*
Then turning homeward said: "The sunset flushes
Those furthest loftiest crags;
Come, Laura, not another maiden lags,
No wilful squirrel wags,
The beasts and birds are fast asleep."
But Laura loitered still among the rushes
And said the bank was steep.

And said the hour was early still,
The dew not fall'n, the wind not chill:
Listening ever, but not catching   230
The customary cry,
"Come buy, come buy,"
With its iterated jingle
Of sugar-baited words:
Not for all her watching
Once discerning even one goblin
Racing, whisking, tumbling, hobbling;
Let alone the herds
That used to tramp along the glen,
In groups or single,   240
Of brisk fruit-merchant men.

    Till Lizzie urged: "O Laura, come;
I hear the fruit-call, but I dare not look:
You should not loiter longer at this brook:
Come with me home.
The stars rise, the moon bends her arc,
Each glow-worm winks her spark,
Let us get home before the night grows dark:
For clouds may gather
Though this is summer weather,   250
Put out the lights and drench us through;
Then if we lost our way what should we do?"

    Laura turned cold as stone
To find her sister heard that cry alone,
That goblin cry,
"Come buy our fruits, come buy."
Must she then buy no more such dainty fruit?
Must she no more such succous pasture find,
Gone deaf and blind?
Her tree of life drooped from the root: 260
She said not one word in her heart's sore ache;
But peering thro' the dimness, nought discerning,
Trudged home, her pitcher dripping all the way;

So crept to bed, and lay
Silent till Lizzie slept;
Then sat up in a passionate yearning,
And gnashed her teeth for baulked desire, and wept
As if her heart would break.

    Day after day, night after night,
Laura kept watch in vain,   270
In sullen silence of exceeding pain.
She never caught again the goblin cry:
"Come buy, come buy";—
She never spied the goblin men
Hawking their fruits along the glen:
But when the noon waxed bright
Her hair grew thin and grey;
She dwindled, as the fair full moon doth turn
To swift decay, and burn
Her fire away.   280

    One day remembering her kernel-stone
She set it by a wall that faced the south;
Dewed it with tears, hoped for a root,
Watched for a waxing shoot,
But there came none;
It never saw the sun,
It never felt the trickling moisture run:
While with sunk eyes and faded mouth
She dreamed of melons, as a traveller sees
False waves in desert drouth   290
With shade of leaf-crowned trees,
And burns the thirstier in the sandful breeze.

    She no more swept the house,
Tended the fowls or cows,
Fetched honey, kneaded cakes of wheat,
Brought water from the brook:
But sat down listless in the chimney-nook
And would not eat.

Tender Lizzie could not bear
To watch her sister's cankerous care,   *300*
Yet not to share.
She night and morning
Caught the goblins' cry:
"Come buy our orchard fruits,
Come buy, come buy":—
Beside the brook, along the glen,
She heard the tramp of goblin men,
The voice and stir
Poor Laura could not hear;
Longed to buy fruit to comfort her,   *310*
But feared to pay too dear.
She thought of Jeanie in her grave,
Who should have been a bride;
But who for joys brides hope to have
Fell sick and died
In her gay prime,
In earliest Winter time,
With the first glazing rime,
With the first snow-fall of crisp Winter time.

Till Laura, dwindling,   *320*
Seemed knocking at Death's door:
Then Lizzie weighed no more
Better and worse,
But put a silver penny in her purse,
Kissed Laura, crossed the heath with clumps of furze
At twilight, halted by the brook;
And for the first time in her life
Began to listen and look.

Laughed every goblin
When they spied her peeping: *330*
Came towards her hobbling,
Flying, running, leaping,
Puffing and blowing,
Chuckling, clapping, crowing,
Clucking and gobbling,

Mopping and mowing,
Full of airs and graces,
Pulling wry faces,
Demure grimaces,
Cat-like and rat-like,   340
Ratel and wombat-like,
Snail-paced in a hurry,
Parrot-voiced and whistler,
Helter-skelter, hurry skurry,
Chattering like magpies,
Fluttering like pigeons,
Gliding like fishes,—
Hugged her and kissed her;
Squeezed and caressed her;
Stretched up their dishes,   350
Panniers and plates:
"Look at our apples
Russet and dun,
Bob at our cherries,
Bite at our peaches,
Citrons and dates,
Grapes for the asking,
Pears red with basking
Out in the sun,
Plums on their twigs;   360
Pluck them and suck them,
Pomegranates, figs."

   "Good folk," said Lizzie,
Mindful of Jeanie, ——➔ *first to die at the*
"Give me much and many":— *hands of the*
Held out her apron,   *goblins*
Tossed them her penny.
"Nay, take a seat with us,
Honour and eat with us,"
They answered grinning: 370
"Our feast is but beginning.
Night yet is early,

Warm and dew-pearly,
Wakeful and starry:
Such fruits as these
No man can carry;
Half their bloom would fly,
Half their dew would dry,
Half their flavour would pass by.
Sit down and feast with us,   380
Be welcome guest with us,
Cheer you and rest with us."
"Thank you," said Lizzie; "but one waits
At home alone for me:
So, without further parleying,
If you will not sell me any
Of your fruits though much and many,
Give me back my silver penny
I tossed you for a fee."—
They began to scratch their pates,   390
No longer wagging, purring,
But visibly demurring,
Grunting and snarling.
One called her proud,
Cross-grained, uncivil;
Their tones waxed loud,
Their looks were evil.
Lashing their tails
They trod and hustled her,
Elbowed and jostled her,   400
Clawed with their nails,
Barking, mewing, hissing, mocking,
Tore her gown and soiled her stocking,
Twitched her hair out by the roots,
Stamped upon her tender feet,
Held her hands and squeezed their fruits
Against her mouth to make her eat.

    White and golden Lizzie stood,
    Like a lily in a flood,—

[handwritten marginal note: Violent attack of Lizzie by all the goblins.]

Like a rock of blue-veined stone   *410*
Lashed by tides obstreperously,—
Like a beacon left alone
In a hoary roaring sea,
Sending up a golden fire,—
Like a fruit-crowned orange-tree
White with blossoms honey-sweet
Sore beset by wasp and bee,—
Like a royal virgin town
Topped with gilded dome and spire
Close beleaguered by a fleet   *420*
Mad to tug her standard down.

One may lead a horse to water,
Twenty cannot make him drink.
Though the goblins cuffed and caught her,
Coaxed and fought her,
Bullied and besought her,
Scratched her, pinched her black as ink,
Kicked and knocked her,
Mauled and mocked her,
Lizzie uttered not a word;   *430*
Would not open lip from lip
Lest they should cram a mouthful in;
But laughed in heart to feel the drip
Of juice that syrupped all her face
And lodged in dimples of her chin,
And streaked her neck which quaked like curd.
At last the evil people,
Worn out by her resistance,
Flung back her penny, kicked their fruit
Along whichever road they took,   *440*
Not leaving root or stone or shoot;
Some writhed into the ground,
Some dived into the brook
With ring and ripple,
Some scudded on the gale without a sound,
Some vanished in the distance.

In a smart, ache, tingle,
Lizzie went her way;
Knew not was it night or day;
Sprang up the bank, tore through the furze,   450
Threaded copse and dingle,
And heard her penny jingle
Bouncing in her purse,—
Its bounce was music to her ear.
She ran and ran
As if she feared some goblin man
Dogged her with gibe or curse
Or something worse:
But not one goblin skurried after,
Nor was she pricked by fear;   460
The kind heart made her windy-paced
That urged her home quite out of breath with haste
And inward laughter.

   She cried "Laura," up the garden,
"Did you miss me?
Come and kiss me.
Never mind my bruises,
Hug me, kiss me, suck my juices
Squeezed from goblin fruits for you,
Goblin pulp and goblin dew.   470
Eat me, drink me, love me;
Laura, make much of me;
For your sake I have braved the glen
And had to do with goblin merchant men."

   Laura started from her chair,
Flung her arms up in the air,
Clutched her hair:
"Lizzie, Lizzie, have you tasted
For my sake the fruit forbidden?
Must your light like mine be hidden,   480
Your young life like mine be wasted,
Undone in mine undoing

And ruined in my ruin,
Thirsty, cankered, goblin-ridden?"
She clung about her sister,
Kissed and kissed and kissed her:
Tears once again
Refreshed her shrunken eyes,
Dropping like rain
After long sultry drouth;   490
Shaking with aguish fear, and pain,
She kissed and kissed her with a hungry mouth.

    Her lips began to scorch,
That juice was wormwood to her tongue,
She loathed the feast:
Writhing as one possessed she leaped and sung,
Rent all her robe, and wrung
Her hands in lamentable haste,
And beat her breast.
Her locks streamed like the torch   500
Borne by a racer at full speed,
Or like the mane of horses in their flight,
Or like an eagle when she stems the light
Straight toward the sun,
Or like a caged thing freed,
Or like a flying flag when armies run.

    Swift fire spread through her veins, knocked at her heart,
Met the fire smouldering there
And overbore its lesser flame;
She gorged on bitterness without a name: 510
Ah! fool, to choose such part
Of soul-consuming care!
Sense failed in the mortal strife:
Like the watch-tower of a town
Which an earthquake shatters down,
Like a lightning-stricken mast,
Like a wind-uprooted tree
Spun about,

Like a foam-topped waterspout
Cast down headlong in the sea,   520
She fell at last;
Pleasure past and anguish past,
Is it death or is it life?

    Life out of death.
That night long Lizzie watched by her,
Counted her pulse's flagging stir,
Felt for her breath,
Held water to her lips, and cooled her face
With tears and fanning leaves:
But when the first birds chirped about their eaves,   530
And early reapers plodded to the place
Of golden sheaves,
And dew-wet grass
Bowed in the morning winds so brisk to pass,
And new buds with new day
Opened of cup-like lilies on the stream,
Laura awoke as from a dream,
Laughed in the innocent old way,
Hugged Lizzie but not twice or thrice;
Her gleaming locks showed not one thread of grey,   540
Her breath was sweet as May,
And light danced in her eyes.

    Days, weeks, months, years
Afterwards, when both were wives
With children of their own;
Their mother-hearts beset with fears,
Their lives bound up in tender lives;
Laura would call the little ones
And tell them of her early prime,
Those pleasant days long gone   550
Of not-returning time:
Would talk about the haunted glen,
The wicked, quaint fruit-merchant men,
Their fruits like honey to the throat,

But poison in the blood;
(Men sell not such in any town):
Would tell them how her sister stood
In deadly peril to do her good,
And win the fiery antidote:
Then joining hands to little hands   560
Would bid them cling together,
"For there is no friend like a sister,
In calm or stormy weather,
To cheer one on the tedious way,
To fetch one if one goes astray,
To lift one if one totters down,
To strengthen whilst one stands."

                                                        (1859)

MIRAGE

The hope I dreamed of was a dream,
    Was but a dream; and now I wake
Exceeding comfortless, and worn, and old,
    For a dream's sake.

I hang my harp upon a tree,
    A weeping willow in a lake;
I hang my silenced harp there, wrung and snapt
    For a dream's sake.

Lie still, lie still, my breaking heart;
    My silent heart, lie still and break: 10
Life, and the world, and mine own self, are changed
    For a dream's sake.

                                                        (1860)

THE LOWEST PLACE

Give me the lowest place: not that I dare
    Ask for that lowest place, but Thou hast died

That I might live and share
  Thy glory by Thy side.

Give me the lowest place: or if for me
  That lowest place too high, make one more low
Where I may sit and see
  My God and love Thee so.

                                        (1863)

WEARY IN WELL-DOING

I would have gone; God bade me stay:
  I would have worked; God bade me rest.
He broke my will from day to day,
  He read my yearnings unexpressed
            And said them nay.

Now I would stay; God bids me go:
  Now I would rest; God bids me work.
He breaks my heart tossed to and fro,
  My soul is wrung with doubts that lurk
            And vex it so.   *10*

I go, Lord, where Thou sendest me;
  Day after day I plod and moil:
But, Christ my God, when will it be
  That I may let alone my toil
            And rest with Thee?

                                        (1864)

A DIRGE

Why were you born when the snow was falling?
You should have come to the cuckoo's calling,
Or when grapes are green in the cluster,
Or, at least, when lithe swallows muster
    For their far off flying
    From summer dying.

Why did you die when the lambs were cropping?
You should have died at the apples' dropping,
When the grasshopper comes to trouble,
And the wheat-fields are sodden stubble,   10
    And all winds go sighing
    For sweet things dying.

                            (1865)

EVE

'While I sit at the door,
Sick to gaze within,
Mine eye weepeth sore
For sorrow and sin:
As a tree my sin stands
To darken all lands;
Death is the fruit it bore.

'How have Eden bowers grown
Without Adam to bend them?
How have Eden flowers blown,   10
Squandering their sweet breath,
Without me to tend them?
The Tree of Life was ours,
Tree twelvefold-fruited,
Most lofty tree that flowers,
Most deeply rooted:
I chose the Tree of Death.

'Hadst thou but said me nay,
   Adam my brother,
I might have pined away—   20
   I, but none other:
God might have let thee stay
Safe in our garden,
By putting me away
Beyond all pardon.

'I, Eve, sad mother
Of all who must live,
I, not another,
Plucked bitterest fruit to give
My friend, husband, lover.   30
O wanton eyes, run over!
Who but I should grieve?
Cain hath slain his brother:
Of all who must die mother,
Miserable Eve!'

Thus she sat weeping,
Thus Eve our mother,
Where one lay sleeping
Slain by his brother.
Greatest and least   40
Each piteous beast
To hear her voice
Forgot his joys
And set aside his feast.

The mouse paused in his walk
And dropped his wheaten stalk;
Grave cattle wagged their heads
In rumination;
The eagle gave a cry
From his cloud station: 50
Larks on thyme beds
Forbore to mount or sing;
Bees drooped upon the wing;
The raven perched on high
Forgot his ration;
The conies in their rock,
A feeble nation,
Quaked sympathetical;
The mocking-bird left off to mock;
Huge camels knelt as if   60
In deprecation;
The kind hart's tears were falling;

Chattered the wistful stork;
Dove-voices with a dying fall
Cooed desolation,
Answering grief by grief.

Only the serpent in the dust,
Wriggling and crawling,
Grinned an evil grin and thrust
His tongue out with its fork.   70

(1865)

AMOR MUNDI

"O where are you going with your love-locks flowing
    On the west wind blowing along this valley track?"
"The downhill path is easy, come with me an' it please ye,
    We shall escape the uphill by never turning back."

So they two went together in glowing August weather,
    The honey-breathing heather lay to their left and right;
And dear she was to doat on, her swift feet seemed to float
        on
    The air like soft twin pigeons too sportive to alight.

"Oh, what is that in heaven where grey cloud-flakes are
        seven,
    Where blackest clouds hang riven just at the rainy
        skirt?"   10
"Oh, that 's a meteor sent us, a message dumb, porten-
        tous,—
    An undecipher'd solemn signal of help or hurt."

"Oh, what is that glides quickly where velvet flowers grow
        thickly,
    Their scent comes rich and sickly?"—"A scaled and
        hooded worm."
"Oh, what 's that in the hollow, so pale I quake to fol-
        low?"

"Oh, that 's a thin dead body which waits th' eternal
    term."

"Turn again, O my sweetest,—turn again, false and fleet-
    est:
  This beaten way thou beatest, I fear, is hell's own track."
"Nay, too steep for hill-mounting; nay, too late for cost-
    counting: *19*
  This downhill path is easy, but there's no turning back."

                                        (*1865*)

"ITALIA, IO TI SALUTO"

To come back from the sweet South, to the North
  Where I was born, bred, look to die;
Come back to do my day's work in its day,
    Play out my play—
Amen, amen, say I.

To see no more the country half my own,
  Nor hear the half familiar speech,
Amen, I say; I turn to that bleak North
    Whence I came forth—
  The South lies out of reach.   *10*

But when our swallows fly back to the South,
  To the sweet South, to the sweet South,
The tears may come again into my eyes
    On the old wise,
  And the sweet name to my mouth.

                                        (*1865*)

"TO-DAY FOR ME"

She sitteth still who used to dance,
She weepeth sore and more and more:—

Let us sit with thee weeping sore,
    O fair France.

  She trembleth as the days advance
Who used to be so light of heart:—
We in thy trembling bear a part,
    Sister France.

  Her eyes shine tearful as they glance:
"Who shall give back my slaughtered sons?   *10*
"Bind up," she saith, "my wounded ones."—
    Alas, France!

  She struggles in a deathly trance,
As in a dream her pulses stir,
She hears the nations calling her,
    "France, France, France."

  Thou people of the lifted lance,
Forbear her tears, forbear her blood:
Roll back, roll back, thy whelming flood,
    Back from France.   *20*

  Eye not her loveliness askance,
Forge not for her a galling chain;
Leave her at peace to bloom again,
    Vine-clad France.

  A time there is for change and chance,
A time for passing of the cup:
And One abides can yet bind up
    Broken France.

  A time there is for change and chance:
Who next shall drink the trembling cup,   *30*
Wring out its dregs and suck them up
    After France?

                                  (1871)

BIRD RAPTURES

The sunrise wakes the lark to sing,
   The moonrise wakes the nightingale.
Come darkness, moonrise, everything
   That is so silent, sweet, and pale,
   Come, so ye wake the nightingale.

Make haste to mount, thou wistful moon,
   Make haste to wake the nightingale:
Let silence set the world in tune
   To hearken to that wordless tale
   Which warbles from the nightingale.   10

O herald skylark, stay thy flight
   One moment, for a nightingale
Floods us with sorrow and delight.
   To-morrow thou shalt hoist the sail;
   Leave us to-night the nightingale.

                                          (c. 1876)

Monna Innominata

A Sonnet of Sonnets

I

"Lo dì che han detto a' dolci amici addio."—Dante
"Amor, con quanto sforzo oggi mi vinci!"—Petrarca*

Come back to me, who wait and watch for you:—
   Or come not yet, for it is over then,
   And long it is before you come again,
So far between my pleasures are and few.

---

   * W. M. Rossetti, when editing the poems, supplied the following
translations of the epigraphs from Dante and Petrarch.
   Sonnet I: "The day that they have said adieu to their sweet friends."
"Love, with how great a stress dost thou vanquish me today!"

While, when you come not, what I do I do
   Thinking, 'Now when he comes,' my sweetest 'when':
   For one man is my world of all the men
This wide world holds; O love, my world is you.
Howbeit, to meet you grows almost a pang
   Because the pang of parting comes so soon;   *10*
   My hope hangs waning, waxing, like a moon
   Between the heavenly days on which we meet:
Ah me, but where are now the songs I sang
   When life was sweet because you called them sweet?

II

"Era già l'ora che volge il desio."—Dante
"Ricorro al tempo ch' io vi vidi prima."—Petrarca*

I wish I could remember that first day,
   First hour, first moment of your meeting me,
   If bright or dim the season, it might be
Summer or Winter for aught I can say;
So unrecorded did it slip away,
   So blind was I to see and to foresee,
   So dull to mark the budding of my tree
That would not blossom yet for many a May.
If only I could recollect it, such
   A day of days! I let it come and go   *10*
   As traceless as a thaw of bygone snow;
It seemed to mean so little, meant so much;
If only now I could recall that touch,
   First touch of hand in hand—Did one but know!

III

"O ombre vane, fuor che ne l'aspetto!"—Dante
"Immaginata guida la conduce."—Petrarca†

   * Sonnet II: "It was already the hour which turns back the desire."
"I recur to the time when I first saw thee."
   † Sonnet III: "Oh shades, empty save in semblance!" "An imaginary
guide conducts her."

I dream of you to wake: would that I might
   Dream of you and not wake but slumber on;
   Nor find with dreams the dear companion gone,
As Summer ended Summer birds take flight.
In happy dreams I hold you full in sight,
   I blush again who waking look so wan;
   Brighter than sunniest day that ever shone,
In happy dreams your smile makes day of night.
Thus only in a dream we are at one,
   Thus only in a dream we give and take   *10*
      The faith that maketh rich who take or give:
If thus to sleep is sweeter than to wake,
      To die were surely sweeter than to live,
Though there be nothing new beneath the sun.

IV

"Poca favilla gran fiamma seconda."—Dante
"Ogni altra cosa, ogni pensier va fore,
E sol ivi con voi rimansi amore."—Petrarca*

I loved you first: but afterwards your love,
   Outsoaring mine, sang such a loftier song
As drowned the friendly cooings of my dove.
   Which owes the other most? My love was long,
   And yours one moment seemed to wax more strong;
I loved and guessed at you, you construed me
And loved me for what might or might not be—
   Nay, weights and measures do us both a wrong.
For verily love knows not "mine" or "thine";
   With separate "I" and "thou" free love has done,   *10*
      For one is both and both are one in love:
Rich love knows nought of "thine that is not mine";
      Both have the strength and both the length thereof,
Both of us, of the love which makes us one.

   * Sonnet IV: "A small spark fosters a great flame." "Every other thing,
every thought, goes off, and love alone remains there with you."

V

"Amor che a nullo amato amar perdona."—Dante
"Amor m'addusse in sì gioiosa spene."—Petrarca*

O my heart's heart, and you who are to me
  More than myself myself, God be with you,
  Keep you in strong obedience leal and true
To Him whose noble service setteth free,
Give you all good we see or can foresee,
  Make your joys many and your sorrows few,
  Bless you in what you bear and what you do,
Yea, perfect you as He would have you be.
So much for you; but what for me, dear friend?
  To love you without stint and all I can   *10*
To-day, to-morrow, world without an end;
    To love you much and yet to love you more,
    As Jordan at his flood sweeps either shore;
Since woman is the helpmeet made for man.

VI

        "Or puoi la quantitate
Comprender de l'amor che a te mi scalda."—Dante
"Non vo' che da tal nodo amor mi scioglia."—Petrarca†

Trust me, I have not earned your dear rebuke,
  I love, as you would have me, God the most;
  Would lose not Him, but you, must one be lost,
Nor with Lot's wife cast back a faithless look
Unready to forego what I forsook;
  This say I, having counted up the cost,
  This, though I be the feeblest of God's host,
The sorriest sheep Christ shepherds with His crook.

  * Sonnet V: "Love, who exempts no loved one from loving." "Love led me into such joyous hope."
  † Sonnet VI: "Now canst thou comprehend the quantity of the love which glows in me towards thee." "I do not choose that Love should release me from such a tie."

Yet while I love my God the most, I deem
   That I can never love you overmuch;   *10*
      I love Him more so let me love you too;
   Yea, as I apprehend it, love is such
I cannot love you if I love not Him,
   I cannot love Him if I love not you.

VII

"Qui primavera sempre ed ogni frutto."—Dante
"Ragionando con meco ed io con lui."—Petrarca*

"Love me, for I love you"—and answer me,
   "Love me, for I love you": so shall we stand
   As happy equals in the flowering land
Of love, that knows not a dividing sea.
Love builds the house on rock and not on sand,
   Love laughs what while the winds rave desperately;
And who hath found love's citadel unmanned?
   And who hath held in bonds love's liberty?—
My heart's a coward though my words are brave—
   We meet so seldom, yet we surely part   *10*
   So often; there's a problem for your art!
   Still I find comfort in his Book who saith,
Though jealousy be cruel as the grave,
   And death be strong, yet love is strong as death.

VIII

"Come dicesse a Dio: D'altro non calme."—Dante
"Spero trovar pietà non che perdono."—Petrarca†

"I, if I perish, perish"—Esther spake:
   And bride of life or death she made her fair
   In all the lustre of her perfumed hair

   * Sonnet VII: "Here always Spring and every fruit." "Conversing with me, and I with him."
   † Sonnet VIII: "As if he were to say to God, 'I care for nought else.' " "I hope to find pity, and not only pardon."

And smiles that kindle longing but to slake.
She put on pomp of loveliness, to take
   Her husband through his eyes at unaware;
   She spread abroad her beauty for a snare,
Harmless as doves and subtle as a snake.
She trapped him with one mesh of silken hair,
   She vanquished him by wisdom of her wit,   *10*
      And built her people's house that it should stand: —
      If I might take my life so in my hand,
And for my love to Love put up my prayer,
   And for love's sake by Love be granted it!

IX

"O dignitosa coscienza e netta!"—Dante
"Spirto più acceso di virtuti ardenti."—Petrarca*

Thinking of you, and all that was, and all
   That might have been and now can never be,
   I feel your honoured excellence, and see
Myself unworthy of the happier call:
For woe is me who walk so apt to fall,
   So apt to shrink afraid, so apt to flee,
   Apt to lie down and die (ah, woe is me!)
Faithless and hopeless turning to the wall.
And yet not hopeless quite nor faithless quite,
Because not loveless; love may toil all night,   *10*
   But take at morning; wrestle till the break
      Of day, but then wield power with God and man:—
      So take I heart of grace as best I can,
   Ready to spend and be spent for your sake.

   * Sonnet IX: "O dignified and pure conscience!" "Spirit more lit with burning virtues."

X

"Con miglior corso e con migliore stella."—Dante
"La vita fugge e non s'arresta un' ora."—Petrarca*

Time flies, hope flags, life plies a wearied wing;
   Death following hard on life gains ground apace;
   Faith runs with each and rears an eager face,
Outruns the rest, makes light of everything,
Spurns earth, and still finds breath to pray and sing;
   While love ahead of all uplifts his praise,
   Still asks for grace and still gives thanks for grace,
Content with all day brings and night will bring.
Life wanes; and when love folds his wings above
   Tired hope, and less we feel his conscious pulse,   *10*
      Let us go fall asleep, dear friend, in peace:
      A little while, and age and sorrow cease;
   A little while, and life reborn annuls
Loss and decay and death, and all is love.

XI

"Vien dietro a me e lascia dir le genti."—Dante
"Contando i casi della vita nostra."—Petrarca†

Many in aftertimes will say of you
   "He loved her"—while of me what will they say?
   Not that I loved you more than just in play,
For fashion's sake as idle women do.
Even let them prate; who know not what we knew
   Of love and parting in exceeding pain,
   Of parting hopeless here to meet again,
Hopeless on earth, and heaven is out of view.
But by my heart of love laid bare to you,
   My love that you can make not void nor vain,   *10*

   * Sonnet X: "With better course and with better star." "Life flees and stays not an hour."

   † Sonnet XI: "Come after me, and leave folk to talk." "Relating the casualties of our life."

Love that foregoes you but to claim anew
Beyond this passage of the gate of death,
 I charge you at the Judgment make it plain
My love of you was life and not a breath.

XII

"Amor che ne la mente mi ragiona."—Dante
"Amor vien nel bel viso di costei."—Petrarca*

If there be any one can take my place
 And make you happy whom I grieve to grieve,
 Think not that I can grudge it, but believe
I do commend you to that nobler grace,
That readier wit than mine, that sweeter face;
 Yea, since your riches make me rich, conceive
 I too am crowned, while bridal crowns I weave,
And thread the bridal dance with jocund pace.
For if I did not love you, it might be
 That I should grudge you some one dear delight;   *10*
  But since the heart is yours that was mine own,
 Your pleasure is my pleasure, right my right,
Your honourable freedom makes me free,
  And you companioned I am not alone.

XIII

"E drizzeremo gli occhi al Primo Amore."—Dante
"Ma trovo peso non da le mie braccia."—Petrarca†

If I could trust mine own self with your fate,
 Shall I not rather trust it in God's hand?
 Without Whose Will one lily doth not stand,

 * Sonnet XII: "Love, who speaks within my mind." "Love comes in the beautiful face of this lady."
 † Sonnet XIII: "And we will direct our eyes to the Primal Love." "But I find a burden to which my arms suffice not."

Nor sparrow fall at his appointed date;
   Who numbereth the innumerable sand,
Who weighs the wind and water with a weight,
To Whom the world is neither small nor great,
   Whose knowledge foreknew every plan we planned.
Searching my heart for all that touches you,
   I find there only love and love's goodwill   *10*
   Helpless to help and impotent to do,
      Of understanding dull, of sight most dim;
      And therefore I commend you back to Him
     Whose love your love's capacity can fill.

XIV

"E la Sua Voluntade è nostra pace."—Dante
"Sol con questi pensier, con altre chiome."—Petrarca*

Youth gone, and beauty gone if ever there
   Dwelt beauty in so poor a face as this;
   Youth gone and beauty, what remains of bliss?
I will not bind fresh roses in my hair,
To shame a cheek at best but little fair,—
   Leave youth his roses, who can bear a thorn,—
I will not seek for blossoms anywhere,
   Except such common flowers as blow with corn.
Youth gone and beauty gone, what doth remain?
The longing of a heart pent up forlorn,   *10*
   A silent heart whose silence loves and longs;
   The silence of a heart which sang its songs
While youth and beauty made a summer morn,
Silence of love that cannot sing again.

                   (before *1882*)

  * Sonnet XIV: "And His Will is our peace." "Only with these thoughts, with different locks."

THE THREAD OF LIFE

I

The irresponsive silence of the land,
  The irresponsive sounding of the sea,
  Speak both one message of one sense to me:—
Aloof, aloof, we stand aloof, so stand
Thou too aloof bound with the flawless band
  Of inner solitude; we bind not thee;
  But who from thy self-chain shall set thee free?
What heart shall touch thy heart? what hand thy hand?—
And I am sometimes proud and sometimes meek,
  And sometimes I remember days of old   *10*
When fellowship seemed not so far to seek
  And all the world and I seemed much less cold,
  And at the rainbow's foot lay surely gold,
And hope felt strong and life itself not weak.

II

Thus am I mine own prison. Everything
  Around me free and sunny and at ease:
  Or if in shadow, in a shade of trees
Which the sun kisses, where the gay birds sing
And where all winds make various murmuring;
  Where bees are found, with honey for the bees;
  Where sounds are music, and where silences
Are music of an unlike fashioning.
Then gaze I at the merrymaking crew,
  And smile a moment and a moment sigh   *10*
Thinking: Why can I not rejoice with you?
  But soon I put the foolish fancy by:
I am not what I have nor what I do;
  But what I was I am, I am even I.

III

Therefore myself is that one only thing
  I hold to use or waste, to keep or give;
  My sole possession every day I live,

And still mine own despite Time's winnowing.
Ever mine own, while moons and seasons bring
    From crudeness ripeness mellow and sanative;
    Ever mine own, till Death shall ply his sieve;
And still mine own, when saints break grave and sing.
And this myself as king unto my King
    I give, to Him Who gave Himself for me;   *10*
Who gives Himself to me, and bids me sing
    A sweet new song of His redeemed set free;
He bids me sing: O death, where is thy sting?
    And sing: O grave, where is thy victory?

                                        (before *1882*)

HE AND SHE

"Should one of us remember,
    And one of us forget,
I wish I knew what each will do—
    But who can tell as yet?"

"Should one of us remember,
    And one of us forget,
I promise you what I will do—
And I'm content to wait for you,
    And not be sure as yet."

                                        (before *1882*)

DE PROFUNDIS

Oh why is heaven built so far,
    Oh why is earth set so remote?
I cannot reach the nearest star
    That hangs afloat.

I would not care to reach the moon,
    One round monotonous of change;
Yet even she repeats her tune
    Beyond my range.

I never watch the scattered fire
   Of stars, or sun's far-trailing train,   *10*
But all my heart is one desire,
   And all in vain:

For I am bound with fleshly bands,
   Joy, beauty, lie beyond my scope;
I strain my heart, I stretch my hands,
   And catch at hope.

                        (before *1882*)

ONE SEA-SIDE GRAVE

Unmindful of the roses,
   Unmindful of the thorn,
A reaper tired reposes
   Among his gathered corn:
   So might I, till the morn!

Cold as the cold Decembers,
   Past as the days that set,
While only one remembers
   And all the rest forget,—
   But one remembers yet.   *10*

                        (*1884*)

SLEEPING AT LAST

Sleeping at last, the trouble and tumult over,
   Sleeping at last, the struggle and horror past,
Cold and white, out of sight of friend and of lover,
           Sleeping at last.

   No more a tired heart downcast or overcast,
No more pangs that wring or shifting fears that hover,
   Sleeping at last in a dreamless sleep locked fast.

Fast asleep. Singing birds in their leafy cover
   Cannot wake her, nor shake her the gusty blast.
Under the purple thyme and the purple clover   *10*
    Sleeping at last.

                  (c. *1893*)

WILLIAM MORRIS

(1834–1896)

William Morris did his reputation as poet more harm
than good by his remark, "If a chap can't compose an
epic poem while he's weaving a tapestry he had better shut
up." For his best verse was in fact more than a casual
by-product or incidental pastime; he took the art of poetry
at least as seriously as the skill of weaving—and he was
indeed an excellent weaver of intricate designs. Master of
many crafts, Morris was the most versatile of the Pre-
Raphaelites and in some respects the most consistent. At
Oxford in 1856 he made the *Oxford and Cambridge
Magazine* in effect a successor to *The Germ,* and he
joined enthusiastically in Rossetti's "jovial campaign" in
1857 to provide Arthurian murals for the Oxford Union.
Ever afterwards the medieval aspect of Pre-Raphaelitism
remained central to his work and thought. In 1858 he
dedicated to "Dante Gabriel Rossetti, Painter," his *De-
fence of Guenevere and Other Poems,* the first and most
thoroughly Pre-Raphaelite of all volumes and the very
prototype (or so it seemed to Walter Pater) of "aesthetic
poetry." These solidly objective narratives and mono-
logues, poems of psychic bewilderment, raised no moral
issue beyond the sensuous gesture, the intensely realized
physical detail.

In 1859 Morris married Jane Burden, who, as Rossetti

later idealized her, became the quintessential Pre-Raphaelite beauty. In the 1860s as director of Morris and Company, he strove to bring interior decoration under the standards of creative craftsmanship and "truth to nature" that had prevailed, he believed, in medieval culture. The long poetic narratives of his middle period, *The Life and Death of Jason* (1867) and the tales of *The Earthly Paradise* (1868–1870), though less strikingly Pre-Raphaelite in style, made no less a refusal to compromise with the harsh realities of his own time. His protest against the ugliness of the modern world led to strenuous socialist activities in the 1880s and animated his utopian romance *News from Nowhere* (1890), which depicts an England of the future, a land of lovely shapes and colors where all men can experience the joys of creative work. Part of the setting of the novel was inspired by Kelmscott Manor, up the Thames from Oxford, which Morris had first leased in 1871 with Rossetti as co-tenant. In his last years he frequently returned to the Kelmscott ideal, and much of his prodigious energy went into the productions of the Kelmscott Press in Hammersmith, beautifully wrought books, the visible culmination of the ornate element in Pre-Raphaelitism.

THE DEFENCE OF GUENEVERE

But, knowing now that they would have her speak,
She threw her wet hair backward from her brow,
Her hand close to her mouth touching her cheek,

As though she had had there a shameful blow,
And feeling it shameful to feel ought but shame
All through her heart, yet felt her cheek burned so,

She must a little touch it; like one lame
She walked away from Gauwaine, with her head
Still lifted up; and on her cheek of flame

THE ARGUMENT OF THE DEFENCE OF GUENEVERE.

BUT, KNOW-
ING NOW
THAT THEY
WOULD
HAVE HER
SPEAK,
SHE THREW
HER WET
HAIR BACK-
WARD FROM
HER BROW,
HER HAND CLOSE TO HER
MOUTH TOUCHING HER
CHEEK,
AS THOUGH SHE HAD HAD
THERE A SHAMEFUL BLOW,
AND FEELING IT SHAMEFUL
TO FEEL OUGHT BUT SHAME
ALL THROUGH HER HEART,
YET FELT HER CHEEK BURN-
ED SO,
SHE MUST A LITTLE TOUCH
IT; LIKE ONE LAME
SHE WALKED AWAY FROM
GAUWAINE, WITH HER HEAD

The first page of "The Defence of Guenevere"
by William Morris as printed by his Kelmscott Press
in 1892

The tears dried quick; she stopped at last and said:　　*10*
"O knights and lords, it seems but little skill
To talk of well-known things past now and dead.

"God wot I ought to say, I have done ill,
And pray you all forgiveness heartily!
Because you must be right, such great lords; still

"Listen, suppose your time were come to die,
And you were quite alone and very weak;
Yea, laid a-dying while very mightily

"The wind was ruffling up the narrow streak
Of river through your broad lands running well:　　*20*
Suppose a hush should come, then some one speak:

" 'One of these cloths is heaven, and one is hell,
Now choose one cloth for ever; which they be,
I will not tell you, you must somehow tell

" 'Of your own strength and mightiness; here, see!'
Yea, yea, my lord, and you to ope your eyes,
At foot of your familiar bed to see

"A great God's angel standing, with such dyes,
Not known on earth, on his great wings, and hands,
Held out two ways, light from the inner skies　　*30*

"Showing him well, and making his commands
Seem to be God's commands, moreover, too,
Holding within his hands the cloths on wands;

"And one of these strange choosing cloths was blue,
Wavy and long, and one cut short and red;
No man could tell the better of the two.

"After a shivering half-hour you said,
'God help! heaven's colour, the blue;' and he said, 'Hell.'
Perhaps you then would roll upon your bed,

"And cry to all good men that loved you well,   40
'Ah Christ! if only I had known, known, known;'
Launcelot went away, then I could tell,

"Like wisest man how all things would be, moan,
And roll and hurt myself, and long to die,
And yet fear much to die for what was sown.

"Nevertheless you, O Sir Gauwaine, lie;
Whatever may have happened through these years,
God knows I speak truth, saying that you lie."

Her voice was low at first, being full of tears,
But as it cleared, it grew full loud and shrill,   50
Growing a windy shriek in all men's ears,

A ringing in their startled brains, until
She said that Gauwaine lied, then her voice sunk,
And her great eyes began again to fill,

Though still she stood right up, and never shrunk,
But spoke on bravely, glorious lady fair!
Whatever tears her full lips may have drunk,

She stood, and seemed to think, and wrung her hair,
Spoke out at last with no more trace of shame,
With passionate twisting of her body there: 60

"It chanced upon a day that Launcelot came
To dwell at Arthur's court: at Christmas-time
This happened; when the heralds sung his name,

" 'Son of King Ban of Benwick,' seemed to chime
Along with all the bells that rang that day,
O'er the white roofs, with little change of rhyme.

"Christmas and whitened Winter passed away,
And over me the April sunshine came,
Made very awful with black hail-clouds, yea,

"And in the Summer I grew white with flame,   70
And bowed my head down—Autumn, and the sick
Sure knowledge things would never be the same,

"However often Spring might be most thick
Of blossoms and buds, smote on me, and I grew
Careless of most things, let the clock tick, tick,

"To my unhappy pulse, that beat right through
My eager body; while I laughed out loud,
And let my lips curl up at false or true,

"Seemed cold and shallow without any cloud.
Behold, my judges, then the cloths were brought: 80
While I was dizzied thus, old thoughts would crowd,

"Belonging to the time ere I was bought
By Arthur's great name and his little love;
Must I give up for ever then, I thought,

"That which I deemed would ever round me move
Glorifying all things; for a little word,
Scarce ever meant at all, must I now prove

"Stone-cold for ever? Pray you, does the Lord
Will that all folks should be quite happy and good?
I love God now a little, if this cord   90

"Were broken, once for all what striving could
Make me love anything in earth or heaven?
So day by day it grew, as if one should

"Slip slowly down some path worn smooth and even,
Down to a cool sea on a summer day;
Yet still in slipping there was some small leaven

"Of stretched hands catching small stones by the way,
Until one surely reached the sea at last,
And felt strange new joy as the worn head lay

"Back, with the hair like sea-weed; yea, all past   *100*
Sweat of the forehead, dryness of the lips,
Washed utterly out by the dear waves o'ercast,

"In the lone sea, far off from any ships!
Do I not know now of a day in Spring?
No minute of that wild day ever slips

"From out my memory; I hear thrushes sing,
And wheresoever I may be, straightway
Thoughts of it all come up with most fresh sting:

"I was half mad with beauty on that day,
And went without my ladies all alone,   *110*
In a quiet garden walled round every way;

"I was right joyful of that wall of stone,
That shut the flowers and trees up with the sky,
And trebled all the beauty: to the bone,

"Yea, right through to my heart, grown very shy
With weary thoughts, it pierced, and made me glad;
Exceedingly glad, and I knew verily,

"A little thing just then had made me mad;
I dared not think, as I was wont to do,
Sometimes, upon my beauty; if I had   *120*

"Held out my long hand up against the blue,
And, looking on the tenderly darken'd fingers,
Thought that by rights one ought to see quite through,

"There, see you, where the soft still light yet lingers,
Round by the edges; what should I have done,
If this had joined with yellow spotted singers,

"And startling green drawn upward by the sun?
But shouting, loosed out, see now! all my hair,
And trancedly stood watching the west wind run

"With faintest half-heard breathing sound—why there   *130*
I lose my head e'en now in doing this;
But shortly listen—In that garden fair

"Came Launcelot walking; this is true, the kiss
Wherewith we kissed in meeting that spring day,
I scarce dare talk of the remember'd bliss,

"When both our mouths went wandering in one way,
And aching sorely, met among the leaves;
Our hands being left behind strained far away.

"Never within a yard of my bright sleeves
Had Launcelot come before—and now, so nigh!   *140*
After that day why is it Guenevere grieves?

"Nevertheless you, O Sir Gauwaine, lie,
Whatever happened on through all those years,
God knows I speak truth, saying that you lie.

"Being such a lady could I weep these tears
If this were true? A great queen such as I
Having sinn'd this way, straight her conscience sears;

"And afterwards she liveth hatefully,
Slaying and poisoning, certes never weeps,—
Gauwaine be friends now, speak me lovingly.   *150*

"Do I not see how God's dear pity creeps
All through your frame, and trembles in your mouth?
Remember in what grave your mother sleeps,

"Buried in some place far down in the south,
Men are forgetting as I speak to you;
By her head sever'd in that awful drouth

"Of pity that drew Agravaine's fell blow,
I pray your pity! let me not scream out
For ever after, when the shrill winds blow

"Through half your castle-locks! let me not shout   *160*
For ever after in the winter night
When you ride out alone! in battle-rout

"Let not my rusting tears make your sword light!
Ah! God of mercy, how he turns away!
So, ever must I dress me to the fight,

"So—let God's justice work! Gauwaine, I say,
See me hew down your proofs: yea, all men know
Even as you said how Mellyagraunce one day,

"One bitter day in *la Fausse Garde,* for so
All good knights held it after, saw—   *170*
Yea, sirs, by cursed unknightly outrage; though

"You, Gauwaine, held his word without a flaw,
This Mellyagraunce saw blood upon my bed—
Whose blood then pray you? is there any law

"To make a queen say why some spots of red
Lie on her coverlet? or will you say,
'Your hands are white, lady, as when you wed,

" 'Where did you bleed?' and must I stammer out, 'Nay,
I blush indeed, fair lord, only to rend
My sleeve up to my shoulder, where there lay   *180*

" 'A knife-point last night:' so must I defend
The honour of the Lady Guenevere?
Not so, fair lords, even if the world should end

"This very day, and you were judges here
Instead of God. Did you see Mellyagraunce
When Launcelot stood by him? what white fear

"Curdled his blood, and how his teeth did dance,
His side sink in? as my knight cried and said,
'Slayer of unarm'd men, here is a chance!

" 'Setter of traps, I pray you guard your head,   *190*
By God, I am so glad to fight with you,
Stripper of ladies, that my hand feels lead

" 'For driving weight; hurrah now! draw and do,
For all my wounds are moving in my breast,
And I am getting mad with waiting so.'

"He struck his hands together o'er the beast,
Who fell down flat, and grovell'd at his feet,
And groan'd at being slain so young. 'At least,'

"My knight said, 'Rise you, sir, who are so fleet
At catching ladies, half-arm'd will I fight,   *200*
My left side all uncovered!' then I weet,

"Up sprang Sir Mellyagraunce with great delight
Upon his knave's face; not until just then
Did I quite hate him, as I saw my knight

"Along the lists look to my stake and pen
With such a joyous smile, it made me sigh
From agony beneath my waist-chain, when

"The fight began, and to me they drew nigh;
Ever Sir Launcelot kept him on the right,
And traversed warily, and ever high   *210*

"And fast leapt caitiff's sword, until my knight
Sudden threw up his sword to his left hand,
Caught it, and swung it; that was all the fight,

"Except a spout of blood on the hot land;
For it was hottest summer; and I know
I wonder'd how the fire, while I should stand,

"And burn, against the heat, would quiver so,
Yards above my head; thus these matters went:
Which things were only warnings of the woe

"That fell on me. Yet Mellyagraunce was shent, 220
For Mellyagraunce had fought against the Lord;
Therefore, my lords, take heed lest you be blent

"With all this wickedness; say no rash word
Against me, being so beautiful; my eyes,
Wept all away the grey, may bring some sword

"To drown you in your blood; see my breast rise,
Like waves of purple sea, as here I stand;
And how my arms are moved in wonderful wise,

"Yea, also at my full heart's strong command,
See through my long throat how the words go up 230
In ripples to my mouth; how in my hand

"The shadow lies like wine within a cup
Of marvellously colour'd gold; yea, now
This little wind is rising, look you up,

"And wonder how the light is falling so
Within my moving tresses: will you dare,
When you have looked a little on my brow,

"To say this thing is vile? or will you care
For any plausible lies of cunning woof,
When you can see my face with no lie there 240

"For ever? am I not a gracious proof—
'But in your chamber Launcelot was found'—
Is there a good knight then would stand aloof,

"When a queen says with gentle queenly sound:
'O true as steel, come now and talk with me,
I love to see your step upon the ground

" 'Unwavering, also well I love to see
That gracious smile light up your face, and hear
Your wonderful words, that all mean verily

" 'The thing they seem to mean: good friend, so dear
To me in everything, come here to-night,   251
Or else the hours will pass most dull and drear;

" 'If you come not, I fear this time I might
Get thinking over much of times gone by,
When I was young, and green hope was in sight:

" 'For no man cares now to know why I sigh;
And no man comes to sing me pleasant songs,
Nor any brings me the sweet flowers that lie

" 'So thick in the gardens; therefore one so longs
To see you, Launcelot; that we may be   260
Like children once again, free from all wrongs

" 'Just for one night.' Did he not come to me?
What thing could keep true Launcelot away
If I said, 'Come'? there was one less than three

"In my quiet room that night, and we were gay;
Till sudden I rose up, weak, pale, and sick,
Because a bawling broke our dream up, yea,

"I looked at Launcelot's face and could not speak,
For he looked helpless too, for a little while;
Then I remember how I tried to shriek,   270

"And could not, but fell down; from tile to tile
The stones they threw up rattled o'er my head
And made me dizzier; till within a while

"My maids were all about me, and my head
On Launcelot's breast was being soothed away
From its white chattering, until Launcelot said—

"By God! I will not tell you more to-day,
Judge any way you will—what matters it?
You know quite well the story of that fray,

"How Launcelot still'd their bawling, the mad fit   *280*
That caught up Gauwaine—all, all, verily,
But just that which would save me; these things flit.

"Nevertheless you, O Sir Gauwaine, lie;
Whatever may have happen'd these long years,
God knows I speak truth, saying that you lie!

"All I have said is truth, by Christ's dear tears."
She would not speak another word, but stood
Turn'd sideways; listening, like a man who hears

His brother's trumpet sounding through the wood
Of his foes' lances. She lean'd eagerly,   *290*
And gave a slight spring sometimes, as she could

At last hear something really; joyfully
Her cheek grew crimson, as the headlong speed
Of the roan charger drew all men to see,
The knight who came was Launcelot at good need.

                                        (1858)

SHAMEFUL DEATH

There were four of us about that bed;
    The mass-priest knelt at the side,
I and his mother stood at the head,
    Over his feet lay the bride;
We were quite sure that he was dead,
    Though his eyes were open wide.

He did not die in the night,
    He did not die in the day,
But in the morning twilight
    His spirit pass'd away,   *10*
When neither sun nor moon was bright,
    And the trees were merely grey.

He was not slain with the sword,
    Knight's axe, or the knightly spear,
Yet spoke he never a word
    After he came in here;
I cut away the cord
    From the neck of my brother dear.

He did not strike one blow,
    For the recreants came behind,   20
In a place where the hornbeams grow,
    A path right hard to find,
For the hornbeam boughs swing so,
    That the twilight makes it blind.

They lighted a great torch then,
    When his arms were pinion'd fast,
Sir John the knight of the Fen,
    Sir Guy of the Dolorous Blast,
With knights threescore and ten,
    Hung brave Lord Hugh at last.   30

I am threescore and ten,
    And my hair is all turn'd grey,
But I met Sir John of the Fen
    Long ago on a summer day,
And am glad to think of the moment when
    I took his life away.

I am threescore and ten,
    And my strength is mostly pass'd,
But long ago I and my men,
    When the sky was overcast,   40
And the smoke roll'd over the reeds of the fen,
    Slew Guy of the Dolorous Blast.

And now, knights all of you,
    I pray you pray for Sir Hugh,
A good knight and a true,
    And for Alice, his wife, pray too.

                                                    (1858)

SUMMER DAWN

Pray but one prayer for me 'twixt thy closed lips,
　　Think but one thought of me up in the stars.
The summer night waneth, the morning light slips,
　　Faint and grey 'twixt the leaves of the aspen, betwixt the
　　　　cloud-bars,
That are patiently waiting there for the dawn,—
　　Patient and colourless, though Heaven's gold
Waits to float through them along with the sun.
Far out in the meadows, above the young corn,
　　The heavy elms wait, and restless and cold,
The uneasy wind rises; the roses are dun;　　　　　　　　　*10*
Through the long twilight they pray for the dawn,
Round the lone house in the midst of the corn.
　　Speak but one word to me over the corn,
　　Over the tender, bow'd locks of the corn.

(1858)

THE GILLIFLOWER OF GOLD

A golden gilliflower to-day
I wore upon my helm alway,
And won the prize of this tourney.
　　Hah! hah! la belle jaune giroflée.

However well Sir Giles might sit,
His sun was weak to wither it,
Lord Miles's blood was dew on it:
　　Hah! hah! la belle jaune giroflée.

Although my spear in splinters flew,
From John's steel-coat, my eye was true;　　　　　　*10*
I wheel'd about, and cried for you,
　　Hah! hah! la belle jaune giroflée.

Yea, do not doubt my heart was good,
Though my sword flew like rotten wood,
To shout, although I scarcely stood,
    Hah! hah! la belle jaune giroflée.

My hand was steady too, to take
My axe from round my neck, and break
John's steel-coat up for my love's sake.
    Hah! hah! la belle jaune giroflée.   *20*

When I stood in my tent again,
Arming afresh, I felt a pain
Take hold of me, I was so fain—
    Hah! hah! la belle jaune giroflée.

To hear: *"Honneur aux fils des preux!"*
Right in my ears again, and shew
The gilliflower blossom'd new.
    Hah! hah! la belle jaune giroflée.

The Sieur Guillaume against me came,
His tabard bore three points of flame   *30*
From a red heart: with little blame—
    Hah! hah! la belle jaune giroflée—

Our tough spears crackled up like straw;
He was the first to turn and draw
His sword, that had nor speck nor flaw;—
    Hah! hah! la belle jaune giroflée.

But I felt weaker than a maid,
And my brain, dizzied and afraid,
Within my helm a fierce tune play'd,
    Hah! hah! la belle jaune giroflée,   *40*

Until I thought of your dear head,
Bow'd to the gilliflower bed,
The yellow flowers stain'd with red;—
    Hah! hah! la belle jaune giroflée.

Crash! how the swords met, *giroflée!*
The fierce tune in my helm would play,
La belle! la belle! jaune giroflée!
  Hah! hah! la belle jaune giroflée.

Once more the great swords met again,
La belle! la belle! but who fell then?   50
Le Sieur Guillaume, who struck down ten;—
  Hah! hah! la belle jaune giroflée.

And as with mazed and unarm'd face,
Toward my own crown and the Queen's place,
They led me at a gentle pace—
  Hah! hah! la belle jaune giroflée.

I almost saw your quiet head
Bow'd o'er the gilliflower bed,
The yellow flowers stain'd with red.—
  Hah! hah! la belle jaune giroflée.   60

                                            (1858)

IN PRISON

Wearily, drearily,
Half the day long,
Flap the great banners
High over the stone;
Strangely and eerily
Sounds the wind's song,
Bending the banner-poles.

While, all alone,
Watching the loophole's spark,
Lie I, with life all dark,   10
Feet tether'd, hands fetter'd
Fast to the stone,
The grim wall, square letter'd
With prisoned men's groan.

Still strain the banner-poles
Through the wind's song
Westward the banner rolls
Over my wrong.

(1858)

THE SAILING OF THE SWORD

Across the empty garden-beds,
   When the Sword went out to sea,
I scarcely saw my sisters' heads
   Bowed each beside a tree.
I could not see the castle-leads,
   When the Sword went out to sea.

Alicia wore a scarlet gown,
   When the Sword went out to sea,
But Ursula's was russet brown:
   For the mist we could not see   *10*
The scarlet roofs of the good town,
   When the Sword went out to sea.

Green holly in Alicia's hand,
   When the Sword went out to sea;
With sere oak-leaves did Ursula stand;
   O! yet alas for me!
I did but bear a peel'd white wand,
   When the Sword went out to sea.

O, russet brown and scarlet bright,
   When the Sword went out to sea,   *20*
My sisters wore; I wore but white:
   Red, brown, and white are three;
Three damozels; each had a knight,
   When the Sword went out to sea.

Sir Robert shouted loud, and said,
   When the Sword went out to sea,

"Alicia, while I see thy head,
    What shall I bring for thee?"
"O, my sweet Lord, a ruby red"—
    The Sword went out to sea.   30

Sir Miles said, while the sails hung down,
    When the Sword went out to sea,
"O, Ursula! while I see the town,
    What shall I bring for thee?"
"Dear knight, bring back a falcon brown"—
    The Sword went out to sea.

But my Roland, no word he said
    When the Sword went out to sea,
But only turn'd away his head;
    A quick shriek came from me: 40
"Come back, dear lord, to your white maid!"—
    The Sword went out to sea.

The hot sun bit the garden-beds,
    When the Sword came back from sea;
Beneath an apple-tree our heads
    Stretched out toward the sea;
Grey gleamed the thirsty castle-leads,
    When the Sword came back from sea.

Lord Robert brought a ruby red,
    When the Sword came back from sea,   50
He kissed Alicia on the head—
    "I am come back to thee;
'T is time, sweet love, that we were wed,
    Now the Sword is back from sea!"

Sir Miles he bore a falcon brown,
    When the Sword came back from sea;
His arms went round tall Ursula's gown—
    "What joy, O love, but thee?
Let us be wed in the good town,
    Now the Sword is back from sea!"   60

My heart grew sick, no more afraid,
   When the Sword came back from sea;
Upon the deck a tall white maid
   Sat on Lord Roland's knee;
His chin was press'd upon her head,
   When the Sword came back from sea!

                                        (1858)

THE BLUE CLOSET

THE DAMOZELS

Lady Alice, Lady Louise,
   Between the wash of the tumbling seas
We are ready to sing, if so ye please;
So lay your long hands on the keys;
                  Sing, *"Laudate pueri."*

And ever the great bell overhead
Boom'd in the wind a knell for the dead,
Though no one toll'd it, a knell for the dead.

LADY LOUISE

Sister, let the measure swell
Not too loud; for you sing not well   *10*
If you drown the faint boom of the bell;
                  He is weary, so am I.

And ever the chevron overhead
Flapp'd on the banner of the dead;
(Was he asleep, or was he dead?)

LADY ALICE

Alice the Queen, and Louise the Queen,
Two damozels wearing purple and green,
Four lone ladies dwelling here
From day to day and year to year;
And there is none to let us go;   *20*
To break the locks of the doors below,

Or shovel away the heaped-up snow;
And when we die no man will know
That we are dead; but they give us leave,
Once every year on Christmas-eve,
To sing in the Closet Blue one song;
And we should be so long, so long,
If we dared, in singing; for dream on dream,
They float on in a happy stream;
Float from the gold strings, float from the keys,   30
Float from the open'd lips of Louise;
But, alas! the sea-salt oozes through
The chinks of the tiles of the Closet Blue;

And ever the great bell overhead
Booms in the wind a knell for the dead,
The wind plays on it a knell for the dead.

　　[They sing all together]

How long ago was it, how long ago,
He came to this tower with hands full of snow?

"Kneel down, O love Louise, kneel down," he said,
And sprinkled the dusty snow over my head.   40

He watch'd the snow melting, it ran through my hair,
Ran over my shoulders, white shoulders and bare.

"I cannot weep for thee, poor love Louise,
For my tears are all hidden deep under the seas;

"In a gold and blue casket she keeps all my tears,
But my eyes are no longer blue, as in old years;

"Yea, they grow grey with time, grow small and dry,
I am so feeble now, would I might die."

And in truth the great bell overhead
Left off his pealing for the dead,   50
Perchance, because the wind was dead.

Will he come back again, or is he dead?
O! is he sleeping, my scarf round his head?

Or did they strangle him as he lay there,
With the long scarlet scarf I used to wear?

Only I pray thee, Lord, let him come here!
Both his soul and his body to me are most dear.

Dear Lord, that loves me, I wait to receive
Either body or spirit this wild Christmas-eve.

Through the floor shot up a lily red,   60
With a patch of earth from the land of the dead,
For he was strong in the land of the dead.

What matter that his cheeks were pale,
    His kind kiss'd lips all grey?
"O, love Louise, have you waited long?"
    "O, my lord Arthur, yea."

What if his hair that brush'd her cheek
    Was stiff with frozen rime?
His eyes were grown quite blue again,
    As in the happy time.   70

"O, love Louise, this is the key
    Of the happy golden land!
O, sisters, cross the bridge with me,
    My eyes are full of sand.
What matter that I cannot see,
    If ye take me by the hand?"

And ever the great bell overhead,
And the tumbling seas mourn'd for the dead;
For their song ceased, and they were dead.

(1858)

THE HAYSTACK IN THE FLOODS

Had she come all the way for this,
To part at last without a kiss?
Yea, had she borne the dirt and rain
That her own eyes might see him slain
Beside the haystack in the floods?

Along the dripping leafless woods,
The stirrup touching either shoe,
She rode astride as troopers do;
With kirtle kilted to her knee,
To which the mud splash'd wretchedly;   10
And the wet dripp'd from every tree
Upon her head and heavy hair,
And on her eyelids broad and fair;
The tears and rain ran down her face.

By fits and starts they rode apace,
And very often was his place
Far off from her; he had to ride
Ahead, to see what might betide
When the roads cross'd; and sometimes, when
There rose a murmuring from his men,   20
Had to turn back with promises;
Ah me! she had but little ease;
And often for pure doubt and dread
She sobb'd, made giddy in the head
By the swift riding; while, for cold,
Her slender fingers scarce could hold
The wet reins; yea, and scarcely, too,
She felt the foot within her shoe
Against the stirrup: all for this,
To part at last without a kiss   30
Beside the haystack in the floods.

For when they near'd that old soak'd hay,
They saw across the only way

That Judas, Godmar, and the three
Red running lions dismally
Grinn'd from his pennon, under which
In one straight line along the ditch,
They counted thirty heads.

                    So then,
While Robert turn'd round to his men,
She saw at once the wretched end,   40
And, stooping down, tried hard to rend
Her coif the wrong way from her head,
And hid her eyes; while Robert said:
"Nay, love, 't is scarcely two to one;
At Poictiers where we made them run
So fast—why, sweet my love, good cheer,
The Gascon frontier is so near,
Nought after this."

                   But, "O," she said,
"My God! my God! I have to tread
The long way back without you; then   50
The court at Paris; those six men;
The gratings of the Chatelet;
The swift Seine on some rainy day
Like this, and people standing by,
And laughing, while my weak hands try
To recollect how strong men swim.
All this, or else a life with him,
For which I should be damned at last;
Would God that this next hour were past!"

He answer'd not, but cried his cry,   60
"St. George for Marny!" cheerily;
And laid his hand upon her rein.
Alas! no man of all his train
Gave back that cheery cry again;
And, while for rage his thumb beat fast
Upon his sword-hilt, some one cast

About his neck a kerchief long,
And bound him.

            Then they went along
To Godmar; who said: "Now, Jehane,
Your lover's life is on the wane   70
So fast, that, if this very hour
You yield not as my paramour,
He will not see the rain leave off—
Nay, keep your tongue from gibe and scoff,
Sir Robert, or I slay you now."

She laid her hand upon her brow,
Then gazed upon the palm, as though
She thought her forehead bled, and "No,"
She said, and turn'd her head away,
As there were nothing else to say,   80
And everything were settled: red
Grew Godmar's face from chin to head:
"Jehane, on yonder hill there stands
My castle, guarding well my lands:
What hinders me from taking you,
And doing that I list to do
To your fair wilful body, while
Your knight lies dead?"

            A wicked smile
Wrinkled her face, her lips grew thin,
A long way out she thrust her chin: 90
"You know that I should strangle you
While you were sleeping; or bite through
Your throat, by God's help—ah!" she said,
"Lord Jesus, pity your poor maid!
For in such wise they hem me in,
I cannot choose but sin and sin,
Whatever happens: yet I think
They could not make me eat or drink,
And so should I just reach my rest."
"Nay, if you do not my behest,   100

O Jehane! though I love you well,"
Said Godmar, "would I fail to tell
All that I know?" "Foul lies," she said.
"Eh! lies, my Jehane? by God's head,
At Paris folks would deem them true!
Do you know, Jehane, they cry for you,
'Jehane the brown! Jehane the brown!
Give us Jehane to burn or drown!'—
Eh—gag me, Robert!—sweet my friend,
This were indeed a piteous end   110
For those long fingers, and long feet,
And long neck, and smooth shoulders sweet;
An end that few men would forget
That saw it—So, an hour yet:
Consider, Jehane, which to take
Of life or death!"

           So, scarce awake,
Dismounting, did she leave that place,
And totter some yards: with her face
Turn'd upward to the sky she lay,
Her head on a wet heap of hay,   120
And fell asleep: and while she slept,
And did not dream, the minutes crept
Round to the twelve again; but she,
Being waked at last, sigh'd quietly,
And strangely childlike came, and said:
"I will not." Straightway Godmar's head,
As though it hung on strong wires turn'd
Most sharply round, and his face burn'd.

For Robert—both his eyes were dry,
He could not weep, but gloomily   130
He seem'd to watch the rain; yea, too,
His lips were firm; he tried once more
To touch her lips; she reach'd out, sore
And vain desire so tortured them,
The poor grey lips, and now the hem
Of his sleeve brush'd them.

With a start
Up Godmar rose, thrust them apart;
From Robert's throat he loosed the bands
Of silk and mail; with empty hands
Held out, she stood and gazed, and saw   *140*
The long bright blade without a flaw
Glide out from Godmar's sheath, his hand
In Robert's hair; she saw him bend
Back Robert's head; she saw him send
The thin steel down; the blow told well,
Right backward the knight Robert fell,
And moan'd as dogs do, being half dead,
Unwitting, as I deem: so then
Godmar turn'd grinning to his men,
Who ran, some five or six, and beat   *150*
His head to pieces at their feet.

Then Godmar turn'd again and said:
"So Jehane, the first fitte is read!
Take note, my lady, that your way
Lies backward to the Chatelet!"
She shook her head and gazed awhile
At her cold hands with a rueful smile,
As though this thing had made her mad.

This was the parting that they had
Beside the haystack in the floods.   *160*

(1858)

PRAISE OF MY LADY

My lady seems of ivory,
Forehead, straight nose, and cheeks that be
Hollow'd a little mournfully.
              Beata mea Domina!

Her forehead, overshadow'd much
By bows of hair, has a wave such

As God was good to make for me.
            Beata mea Domina!

Not greatly long my lady's hair,
Nor yet with yellow colour fair,   *10*
But thick and crispèd wonderfully:
            Beata mea Domina!

Heavy to make the pale face sad,
And dark, but dead as though it had
Been forged by God most wonderfully
            —Beata mea Domina!—

Of some strange metal, thread by thread,
To stand out from my lady's head,
Not moving much to tangle me.
            Beata mea Domina!   *20*

Beneath her brows the lids fall slow,
The lashes a clear shadow throw
Where I would wish my lips to be.
            Beata mea Domina!

Her great eyes, standing far apart,
Draw up some memory from her heart,
And gaze out very mournfully;
            —Beata mea Domina!—

So beautiful and kind they are,
But most times looking out afar,   *30*
Waiting for something, not for me.
            Beata mea Domina!

I wonder if the lashes long
Are those that do her bright eyes wrong,
For always half tears seem to be
            —Beata mea Domina!—

Lurking below the underlid,
Darkening the place where they lie hid—
If they should rise and flow for me!
        Beata mea Domina!   *40*

Her full lips being made to kiss,
Curl'd up and pensive each one is;
This makes me faint to stand and see.
        Beata mea Domina!

Her lips are not contented now,
Because the hours pass so slow
Towards a sweet time: (pray for me),
        —Beata mea Domina!—

Nay, hold thy peace! for who can tell;
But this at least I know full well,   *50*
Her lips are parted longingly,
        —Beata mea Domina!—

So passionate and swift to move,
To pluck at any flying love,
That I grow faint to stand and see.
        Beata mea Domina!

Yea! there beneath them is her chin,
So fine and round, it were a sin
To feel no weaker when I see
        —Beata mea Domina!—   *60*

God's dealings; for with so much care
And troublous, faint lines wrought in there,
He finishes her face for me.
        Beata mea Domina!

Of her long neck what shall I say?
What things about her body's sway,
Like a knight's pennon or slim tree
        —Beata mea Domina!—

"*Aurea Catena (The Lady of the Golden Chain)*,"
drawing by Dante Gabriel Rossetti, 1868, an unfinished
portrait of Mrs. William Morris. Courtesy of the Fogg
Art Museum, Harvard University, Grenville L. Winthrop
Bequest

Set gently waving in the wind;
Or her long hands that I may find
On some day sweet to move o'er me?
        Beata mea Domina!

God pity me though, if I miss'd
The telling, how along her wrist
The veins creep, dying languidly
        —Beata mea Domina!—

Inside her tender palm and thin.
Now give me pardon, dear, wherein
My voice is weak and vexes thee.
        Beata mea Domina!

All men that see her any time,
I charge you straightly in this rhyme,
What, and wherever you may be,
        —Beata mea Domina!—

To kneel before her; as for me,
I choke and grow quite faint to see
My lady moving graciously.
        Beata mea Domina!

        (1858)

FOR THE BED AT KELMSCOTT

The wind's on the wold
And the night is a-cold,
And Thames runs chill
Twixt mead and hill;
But kind and dear
Is the old house here,
And my heart is warm
Midst winter's harm.
Rest, then, and rest,
And think of the best

'Twixt summer and spring,
When all birds sing
In the town of the tree,
And ye lie in me
And scarce dare move,
Lest the earth and its love
Should fade away
Ere the full of the day.

I am old and have seen
Many things that have been—   20
Both grief and peace
And wane and increase.
No tale I tell
Of ill or well,
But this I say:
Night treadeth on day,
And for worst or best
Right good is rest.

                                        (1893)

ALGERNON CHARLES SWINBURNE

(1837–1909)

Algernon Charles Swinburne denied that he was really
a Pre-Raphaelite at all after his exuberant undergraduate
days at Oxford, when he had joined Morris and Burne-
Jones in worshipful tribute to Rossetti. But the more
direct Pre-Raphaelite influence actually began with Swin-
burne's abrupt departure in 1860—without a degree—for
London. Rossetti's charmed circle, much impressed by his
metrical virtuosity and personal high spirits, received him
gladly. For his part, his admiration for Rossetti at close
range approached reverence. Moreover, he deeply respected
the disciplined character and art of Christina Rossetti and
soon came to regard the beautiful, sad Elizabeth Siddal
"with little less than a brother's affection." When Eliza-
beth died in 1862 he lived for about a year as joint tenant
of Tudor House with Rossetti, and during that period,
despite many distractions, he wrote a number of poems
mingling Pre-Raphaelite mannerism with his own in-
creasingly individual idiom. In 1865 he published *Atalanta
in Calydon*, which Ruskin greeted as "the grandest thing
ever done by a youth—though he is a demoniac youth."
Poems and Ballads followed in 1866—a brilliant book, in
its pulsing rhythms quite unlike the poetry of Rossetti or

Morris, yet often Pre-Raphaelite in its themes and imagery and something more than Pre-Raphaelite in its boisterous defiance of middle-class respectabilities. Later volumes diverted the lyrical energies toward political ends, as in *Songs before Sunrise* (1871), or repeated the aesthetic protest in milder terms of nostalgia and escape, as in the second series of *Poems and Ballads* (1878). *Tristram of Lyonesse,* published in 1882, retained strong traces of Pre-Raphaelite coloring, but the surging music of the poem was incontestably the poet's own. By 1880, if not long before, Swinburne had succeeded, as his amusing "Sonnet for a Picture" suggests, in viewing even Rossetti—whom he never ceased to admire—in ironic perspective. Though he rightly refused to be bound by the Pre-Raphaelite label, the fact remains that he produced some of his best work (as the following pieces bear witness) in close relation to Pre-Raphaelite practice.

A BALLAD OF LIFE

I found in dreams a place of wind and flowers,
　　Full of sweet trees and colour of glad grass,
　　In midst whereof there was
A lady clothed like summer with sweet hours.
Her beauty, fervent as a fiery moon,
　　Made my blood burn and swoon
　　　Like a flame rained upon.
Sorrow had filled her shaken eyelids' blue,
And her mouth's sad red heavy rose all through
　　Seemed sad with glad things gone.　　　　　*10*

She held a little cithern by the strings,
　　Shaped heartwise, strung with subtle-coloured hair
　　Of some dead lute-player
That in dead years had done delicious things.
The seven strings were named accordingly;
　　The first string charity,
　　　The second tenderness,

The rest were pleasure, sorrow, sleep, and sin,
And loving-kindness, that is pity's kin
    And is most pitiless.   *20*

There were three men with her, each garmented
  With gold and shod with gold upon the feet;
    And with plucked ears of wheat
The first man's hair was wound upon his head:
His face was red, and his mouth curled and sad;
  All his gold garment had
    Pale stains of dust and rust.
A riven hood was pulled across his eyes;
The token of him being upon this wise
    Made for a sign of Lust.   *30*

The next was Shame, with hollow heavy face
  Coloured like green wood when flame kindles it.
  He hath such feeble feet
They may not well endure in any place.
His face was full of grey old miseries,
  And all his blood's increase
    Was even increase of pain.
The last was Fear, that is akin to Death;
He is Shame's friend, and always as Shame saith
    Fear answers him again.   *40*

My soul said in me: This is marvellous,
  Seeing the air's face is not so delicate
  Nor the sun's grace so great,
If sin and she be kin or amorous.
And seeing where maidens served her on their knees,
  I bade one crave of these
    To know the cause thereof.
Then Fear said: I am Pity that was dead.
And Shame said: I am Sorrow comforted.
    And Lust said: I am Love.   *50*

Thereat her hands began a lute-playing
   And her sweet mouth a song in a strange tongue;
   And all the while she sung
There was no sound but long tears following
Long tears upon men's faces, waxen white
    With extreme sad delight.
     But those three following men
Became as men raised up among the dead;
Great glad mouths open, and fair cheeks made red
    With child's blood come again.   *60*

Then I said: Now assuredly I see
   My lady is perfect, and transfigureth
   All sin and sorrow and death,
Making them fair as her own eyelids be,
Or lips wherein my whole soul's life abides;
    Or as her sweet white sides
     And bosom carved to kiss.
Now therefore, if her pity further me,
Doubtless for her sake all my days shall be
    As righteous as she is.   *70*

Forth, ballad, and take roses in both arms,
   Even till the top rose touch thee in the throat
Where the least thornprick harms;
   And girdled in thy golden singing-coat,
Come thou before my lady and say this:
   Borgia, thy gold hair's colour burns in me,
    Thy mouth makes beat my blood in feverish rhymes;
   Therefore so many as these roses be,
    Kiss me so many times.
Then it may be, seeing how sweet she is,   *80*
   That she will stoop herself none otherwise
    Than a blown vine-branch doth,
And kiss thee with soft laughter on thine eyes,
    Ballad, and on thy mouth.

                (1866)

A BALLAD OF DEATH

Kneel down, fair Love, and fill thyself with tears,
Girdle thyself with sighing for a girth
Upon the sides of mirth,
Cover thy lips and eyelids, let thine ears
Be filled with rumour of people sorrowing;
Make thee soft raiment out of woven sighs
Upon the flesh to cleave,
Set pains therein and many a grievous thing,
And many sorrows after each his wise
For armlet and for gorget and for sleeve.   *10*

O Love's lute heard about the lands of death,
Left hanged upon the trees that were therein;
O Love and Time and Sin,
Three singing mouths that mourn now under breath,
Three lovers, each one evil spoken of;
O smitten lips wherethrough this voice of mine
Came softer with her praise;
Abide a little for our lady's love.
The kisses of her mouth were more than wine,
And more than peace the passage of her days.   *20*

O love, thou knowest if she were good to see.
O Time, thou shalt not find in any land
Till, cast out of thine hand,
The sunlight and the moonlight fail from thee,
Another woman fashioned like as this.
O Sin, thou knowest that all thy shame in her
Was made a goodly thing;
Yea, she caught Shame and shamed him with her kiss,
With her fair kiss, and lips much lovelier
Than lips of amorous roses in late spring.   *30*

By night there stood over against my bed
Queen Venus with a hood striped gold and black,
Both sides drawn fully back

From brows wherein the sad blood failed of red,
And temples drained of purple and full of death.
Her curled hair had the wave of sea-water
And the sea's gold in it.
Her eyes were as a dove's that sickeneth.
Strewn dust of gold she had shed over her,
And pearl and purple and amber on her feet.   40

Upon her raiment of dyed sendaline
Were painted all the secret ways of love
And covered things thereof,
That hold delight as grape-flowers hold their wine;
Red mouths of maidens and red feet of doves,
And brides that kept within the bride-chamber
Their garment of soft shame,
And weeping faces of the wearied loves
That swoon in sleep and awake wearier,
With heat of lips and hair shed out like flame.   50

The tears that through her eyelids fell on me
Made my own bitter where they ran between
As blood had fallen therein,
She saying: Arise, lift up thine eyes and see
If any glad thing be or any good
Now the best thing is taken forth of us;
Even she to whom all praise
Was as one flower in a great multitude,
One glorious flower of many and glorious,
One day found gracious among many days: 60

Even she whose handmaiden was Love—to whom
At kissing times across her stateliest bed
Kings bowed themselves and shed
Pale wine, and honey with the honeycomb,
And spikenard bruised for a burnt-offering;
Even she between whose lips the kiss became
As fire and frankincense;
Whose hair was as gold raiment on a king,

Whose eyes were as the morning purged with flame,
Whose eyelids as sweet savour issuing thence.   70

Then I beheld, and lo on the other side
My lady's likeness crowned and robed and dead.
Sweet still, but now not red,
Was the shut mouth whereby men lived and died,
And sweet, but emptied of the blood's blue shade,
The great curled eyelids that withheld her eyes.
And sweet, but like spoilt gold,
The weight of colour in her tresses weighed,
And sweet, but as a vesture with new dyes,
The body that was clothed with love of old.   80

Ah! that my tears filled all her woven hair
And all the hollow bosom of her gown—
Ah! that my tears ran down
Even to the place where many kisses were,
Even where her parted breast-flowers have place,
Even where they are cloven apart—who knows not this?
Ah! the flowers cleave apart
And their sweet fills the tender interspace;
Ah! the leaves grown thereof were things to kiss
Ere their fine gold was tarnished at the heart.   90

Ah! in the days when God did good to me,
Each part about her was a righteous thing;
Her mouth an almsgiving,
The glory of her garments charity,
The beauty of her bosom a good deed,
In the good days when God kept sight of us;
Love lay upon her eyes,
And on that hair whereof the world takes heed:
And all her body was more virtuous
Than souls of women fashioned otherwise.   100

Now, ballad, gather poppies in thine hands
And sheaves of brier and many rusted sheaves
Rain-rotten in rank lands,

Waste marigold and late unhappy leaves
And grass that fades ere any of it be mown;
And when thy bosom is filled full thereof
Seek out Death's face ere the light altereth,
And say "My master that was thrall to Love
Is become thrall to Death."
Bow down before him, ballad, sigh and groan,   110
But make no sojourn in thy outgoing;
For haply it may be
That when thy feet return at evening
Death shall come in with thee.

                                                    (1866)

LAUS VENERIS

Asleep or waking is it? for her neck,
Kissed over close, wears yet a purple speck,
    Wherein the pained blood falters and goes out;
Soft, and stung softly—fairer for a fleck.

But though my lips shut sucking on the place,
There is no vein at work upon her face;
    Her eyelids are so peaceable, no doubt
Deep sleep has warmed her blood through all its ways.

Lo, this is she that was the world's delight;
The old grey years were parcels of her might;   10
    The strewings of the ways wherein she trod
Were the twain seasons of the day and night.

Lo, she was thus when her clear limbs enticed
All lips that now grow sad with kissing Christ,
    Stained with blood fallen from the feet of God,
The feet and hands whereat our souls were priced.

Alas, Lord, surely thou art great and fair.
But lo her wonderfully woven hair!
    And thou didst heal us with thy piteous kiss;
But see now, Lord; her mouth is lovelier.   20

She is right fair; what hath she done to thee?
Nay, fair Lord Christ, lift up thine eyes and see;
    Had now thy mother such a lip—like this?
Thou knowest how sweet a thing it is to me.

Inside the Horsel here the air is hot;
Right little peace one hath for it, God wot;
    The scented dusty daylight burns the air,
And my heart chokes me till I hear it not.

Behold, my Venus, my soul's body, lies
With my love laid upon her garment-wise,   *30*
    Feeling my love in all her limbs and hair
And shed between her eyelids through her eyes.

She holds my heart in her sweet open hands
Hanging asleep; hard by her head there stands,
    Crowned with gilt thorns and clothed with flesh like
        fire,
Love, wan as foam blown up the salt burnt sands—

Hot as the brackish waifs of yellow spume
That shift and steam—loose clots of arid fume
    From the sea's panting mouth of dry desire;
There stands he, like one labouring at a loom.   *40*

The warp holds fast across; and every thread
That makes the woof up has dry specks of red;
    Always the shuttle cleaves clean through, and he
Weaves with the hair of many a ruined head.

Love is not glad nor sorry, as I deem;
Labouring he dreams, and labours in the dream,
    Till when the spool is finished, lo, I see
His web, reeled off, curls and goes out like steam.

Night falls like fire; the heavy lights run low,
And as they drop, my blood and body so   *50*
    Shake as the flame shakes, full of days and hours
That sleep not neither weep they as they go.

Ah yet would God this flesh of mine might be
Where air might wash and long leaves cover me,
 Where tides of grass break into foam of flowers,
Or where the wind's feet shine along the sea.

Ah yet would God that stems and roots were bred
Out of my weary body and my head,
 That sleep were sealed upon me with a seal,
And I were as the least of all his dead.   60

Would God my blood were dew to feed the grass,
Mine ears made deaf and mine eyes blind as glass,
 My body broken as a turning wheel,
And my mouth stricken ere it saith Alas!

Ah God, that love were as a flower or flame,
That life were as the naming of a name,
 That death were not more pitiful than desire,
That these things were not one thing and the same!

Behold now, surely somewhere there is death:
For each man hath some space of years, he saith.   70
 A little space of time ere time expire,
A little day, a little way of breath.

And lo, between the sundawn and the sun,
His day's work and his night's work are undone;
 And lo, between the nightfall and the light,
He is not, and none knoweth of such an one.

Ah God, that I were as all souls that be,
As any herb or leaf of any tree,
 As men that toil through hours of labouring night,
As bones of men under the deep sharp sea.   80

Outside it must be winter among men;
For at the gold bars of the gates again
 I heard all night and all the hours of it,
The wind's wet wings and fingers drip with rain.

Knights gather, riding sharp for cold; I know
The ways and woods are strangled with the snow;
   And with short song the maidens spin and sit
Until Christ's birthnight, lily-like, arow.

The scent and shadow shed about me make
The very soul in all my senses ache;   90
   The hot hard night is fed upon my breath,
And sleep beholds me from afar awake.

Alas, but surely where the hills grow deep,
Or where the wild ways of the sea are steep,
   Or in strange places somewhere there is death,
And on death's face the scattered hair of sleep.

There lover-like with lips and limbs that meet
They lie, they pluck sweet fruit of life and eat;
   But me the hot and hungry days devour,
And in my mouth no fruit of theirs is sweet.   100

No fruit of theirs, but fruit of my desire,
For her love's sake whose lips through mine respire;
   Her eyelids on her eyes like flower on flower,
Mine eyelids on mine eyes like fire on fire.

So lie we, not as sleep that lies by death,
With heavy kisses and with happy breath;
   Not as man lies by woman, when the bride
Laughs low for love's sake and the words he saith.

For she lies, laughing low with love; she lies
And turns his kisses on her lips to sighs,   110
   To sighing sound of lips unsatisfied,
And the sweet tears are tender with her eyes.

Ah, not as they, but as the souls that were
Slain in the old time, having found her fair;
   Who, sleeping with her lips upon their eyes,
Heard sudden serpents hiss across her hair.

Their blood runs round the roots of time like rain:
She casts them forth and gathers them again;
    With nerve and bone she weaves and multiplies
Exceeding pleasure out of extreme pain.   *120*

Her little chambers drip with flower-like red,
Her girdles, and the chaplets of her head,
    Her armlets and her anklets; with her feet,
She tramples all that winepress of the dead.

Her gateways smoke with fume of flowers and fires,
With loves burnt out and unassuaged desires;
    Between her lips the steam of them is sweet,
The languor in her ears of many lyres.

Her beds are full of perfume and sad sound,
Her doors are made with music and barred round   *130*
    With sighing and with laughter and with tears,
With tears whereby strong souls of men are bound.

There is the knight Adonis that was slain;
With flesh and blood she chains him for a chain;
    The body and the spirit in her ears
Cry, for her lips divide him vein by vein.

Yea, all she slayeth; yea, every man save me;
Me, love, thy lover that must cleave to thee
    Till the ending of the days and ways of earth,
The shaking of the sources of the sea.   *140*

Me, most forsaken of all souls that fell;
Me, satiated with things insatiable;
    Me, for whose sake the extreme hell makes mirth,
Yea, laughter kindles at the heart of hell.

Alas thy beauty! for thy mouth's sweet sake
My soul is bitter to me, my limbs quake
    As water, as the flesh of men that weep,
As their heart's vein whose heart goes nigh to break.

Ah God, that sleep with flower-sweet fingertips
Would crush the fruit of death upon my lips;   *150*
   Ah God, that death would tread the grapes of sleep
And wring their juice upon me as it drips.

There is no change of cheer for many days,
But change of chimes high up in the air, that sways
   Rung by the running fingers of the wind;
And singing sorrows heard on hidden ways.

Day smiteth day in twain, night sundereth night,
And on mine eyes the dark sits as the light;
   Yea, Lord, thou knowest I know not, having sinned,
If heaven be clean or unclean in thy sight.   *160*

Yea, as if earth were sprinkled over me,
Such chafed harsh earth as chokes a sandy sea,
   Each pore doth yearn, and the dried blood thereof
Gasps by sick fits, my heart swims heavily,

There is a feverish famine in my veins;
Below her bosom, where a crushed grape stains
   The white and blue, there my lips caught and clove
An hour since, and what mark of me remains?

I dare not always touch her, lest the kiss
Leave my lips charred. Yea, Lord, a little bliss,   *170*
   Brief bitter bliss, one hath for a great sin;
Nathless thou knowest how sweet a thing it is.

Sin, is it sin whereby men's souls are thrust
Into the pit? yet had I a good trust
   To save my soul before it slipped therein,
Trod under by the fire-shod feet of lust.

For if mine eyes fail and my soul takes breath,
I look between the iron sides of death
   Into sad hell where all sweet love hath end,
All but the pain that never finisheth.   *180*

There are the naked faces of great kings,
The singing folk with all their lute-playings;
   There when one cometh he shall have to friend
The grave that covets and the worm that clings.

There sit the knights that were so great of hand,
The ladies that were queens of fair green land,
   Grown grey and black now, brought unto the dust,
Soiled, without raiment, clad about with sand.

There is one end for all of them; they sit
Naked and sad, they drink the dregs of it,   *190*
   Trodden as grapes in the wine-press of lust,
Trampled and trodden by the fiery feet.

I see the marvellous mouth whereby there fell
Cities and people whom the gods loved well,
   Yet for her sake on them the fire gat hold,
And for their sakes on her the fire of hell.

And softer than the Egyptian lote-leaf is,
The queen whose face was worth the world to kiss,
   Wearing at breast a suckling snake of gold;
And large pale lips of strong Semiramis,   *200*

Curled like a tiger's that curl back to feed;
Red only where the last kiss made them bleed;
   Her hair most thick with many a carven gem,
Deep in the mane, great-chested, like a steed.

Yea, with red sin the faces of them shine;
But in all these there was no sin like mine;
   No, not in all the strange great sins of them
That made the wine-press froth and foam with wine.

For I was of Christ's choosing, I God's knight,
No blinkard heathen stumbling for scant light;   *210*
   I can well see, for all the dusty days
Gone past, the clean great time of goodly fight.

I smell the breathing battle sharp with blows,
With shriek of shafts and snapping short of bows;
   The fair pure sword smites out in subtle ways,
Sounds and long lights are shed between the rows

Of beautiful mailed men; the edged light slips,
Most like a snake that takes short breath and dips
   Sharp from the beautifully bending head,
With all its gracious body lithe as lips   220

That curl in touching you; right in this wise
My sword doth, seeming fire in mine own eyes,
   Leaving all colours in them brown and red
And flecked with death; then the keen breaths like
    sighs,

The caught-up choked dry laughters following them,
When all the fighting face is grown a flame
   For pleasure, and the pulse that stuns the ears,
And the heart's gladness of the goodly game.

Let me think yet a little; I do know
These things were sweet, but sweet such years ago,   230
   Their savour is all turned now into tears;
Yea, ten years since, where the blue ripples blow,

The blue curled eddies of the blowing Rhine,
I felt the sharp wind shaking grass and vine
   Touch my blood, too, and sting me with delight
Through all this waste and weary body of mine

That never feels clear air; right gladly then
I rode alone, a great way off my men,
   And heard the chiming bridle smite and smite.
And gave each rhyme thereof some rhyme again,   240

Till my song shifted to that iron one;
Seeing there rode up between me and the sun

Some certain of my foe's men, for his three
White wolves across their painted coats did run.

The first red-bearded, with square cheeks—alack,
I made my knave's blood turn his beard to black;
    The slaying of him was a joy to see:
Perchance, too, when at night he came not back,

Some woman fell a-weeping, whom this thief
Would beat when he had drunken; yet small grief   250
    Hath any for the ridding of such knaves;
Yea, if one wept, I doubt her teen was brief.

This bitter love is sorrow in all lands,
Draining of eyelids, wringing of drenched hands,
    Sighing of hearts and filling up of graves;
A sign across the head of the world he stands,

As one that hath a plague-mark on his brows;
Dust and spilt blood do track him to his house
    Down under earth; sweet smells of lip and cheek,
Like a sweet snake's breath made more poisonous   260

With chewing of some perfumed deadly grass,
Are shed all round his passage if he pass,
    And their quenched savour leaves the whole soul
        weak,
Sick with keen guessing whence the perfume was.

As one who hidden in deep sedge and reeds
Smells the rare scent made where a panther feeds,
    And tracking ever slotwise the warm smell
Is snapped upon by the sweet mouth and bleeds,

His head far down the hot sweet throat of her—
So one tracks love, whose breath is deadlier,   270
    And lo, one springe and you are fast in hell,
Fast as the gin's grip of a wayfarer.

I think now, as the heavy hours decease
One after one, and bitter thoughts increase
   One upon one, of all sweet finished things;
The breaking of the battle; the long peace

Wherein we sat clothed softly, each man's hair
Crowned with green leaves beneath white hoods of
      vair;
   The sounds of sharp spears at great tourneyings,
And noise of singing in the late sweet air.   *280*

I sang of love, too, knowing nought thereof;
"Sweeter," I said, "the little laugh of love
   Than tears out of the eyes of Magdalen,
Or any fallen feather of the Dove.

"The broken little laugh that spoils a kiss,
The ache of purple pulses, and the bliss
   Of blinded eyelids that expand again—
Love draws them open with those lips of his,

"Lips that cling hard till the kissed face has grown
Of one same fire and colour with their own;   *290*
   Then ere one sleep, appeased with sacrifice,
Where his lips wounded, there his lips atone."

I sang these things long since and knew them not;
"Lo, here is love, or there is love, God wot,
   This man and that finds favour in his eyes,"
I said, "but I, what guerdon have I got?

"The dust of praise that is blown everywhere
In all men's faces with the common air;
   The bay-leaf that wants chafing to be sweet
Before they wind it in a singer's hair."   *300*

So that one dawn I rode forth sorrowing;
I had no hope but of some evil thing,
   And so rode slowly past the windy wheat,
And past the vineyard and the water-spring,

Up to the Horsel. A great elder-tree
Held back its heaps of flowers to let me see
   The ripe tall grass, and one that walked therein,
Naked, with hair shed over to the knee.

She walked between the blossom and the grass;
I knew the beauty of her, what she was,   *310*
   The beauty of her body and her sin,
And in my flesh the sin of hers, alas!

Alas! for sorrow is all the end of this.
O sad kissed mouth, how sorrowful it is!
   O breast whereat some suckling sorrow clings,
Red with the bitter blossom of a kiss!

Ah, with blind lips I felt for you, and found
About my neck your hands and hair enwound,
   The hands that stifle and the hair that stings,
I felt them fasten sharply without sound.   *320*

Yea, for my sin I had great store of bliss:
Rise up, make answer for me, let thy kiss
   Seal my lips hard from speaking of my sin,
Lest one go mad to hear how sweet it is.

Yet I waxed faint with fume of barren bowers,
And murmuring of the heavy-headed hours;
   And let the dove's beak fret and peck within
My lips in vain, and Love shed fruitless flowers,

So that God looked upon me when your hands
Were hot about me; yea, God brake my bands   *330*
   To save my soul alive, and I came forth
Like a man blind and naked in strange lands

That hears men laugh and weep, and knows not
      whence
Nor wherefore, but is broken in his sense;
   Howbeit I met folk riding from the north
Towards Rome, to purge them of their souls' offence,

And rode with them, and spake to none; the day
Stunned me like lights upon some wizard way,
   And ate like fire mine eyes and mine eyesight;
So rode I, hearing all these chant and pray,   *340*

And marvelled; till before us rose and fell
White cursed hills, like outer skirts of hell
   Seen where men's eyes look through the day to
      night,
Like a jagged shell's lips, harsh, untunable,

Blown in between by devils' wrangling breath;
Nathless we won well past that hell and death,
   Down to the sweet land where all airs are good,
Even unto Rome where God's grace tarrieth.

Then came each man and worshipped at his knees
Who in the Lord God's likeness bears the keys   *350*
   To bind or loose, and called on Christ's shed blood,
And so the sweet-souled father gave him ease.

But when I came I fell down at his feet,
Saying, "Father, though the Lord's blood be right
      sweet,
   The spot it takes not off the panther's skin,
Nor shall an Ethiop's stain be bleached with it.

"Lo, I have sinned and have spat out at God,
Wherefore his hand is heavier and his rod
   More sharp because of mine exceeding sin,
And all his raiment redder than bright blood   *360*

"Before mine eyes; yea, for my sake I wot
The heat of hell is waxen seven times hot
   Through my great sin." Then spake he some sweet
      word,
Giving me cheer; which thing availed me not;

Yea, scarce I wist if such indeed were said;
For when I ceased—lo, as one newly dead
  Who hears a great cry out of hell, I heard
The crying of his voice across my head.

"Until this dry shred staff, that hath no whit
Of leaf nor bark, bear blossom and smell sweet,   370
  Seek thou not any mercy in God's sight,
For so long shalt thou be cast out from it."

Yea, what if dried-up stems wax red and green,
Shall that thing be which is not nor has been?
  Yea, what if sapless bark wax green and white,
Shall any good fruit grow upon my sin?

Nay, though sweet fruit were plucked of a dry tree,
And though men drew sweet waters of the sea,
    There should not grow sweet leaves on this dead
      stem,
This waste wan body and shaken soul of me.   380

Yea, though God search it warily enough,
There is not one sound thing in all thereof;
    Though he search all my veins through, searching
      them
He shall find nothing whole therein but love.

For I came home right heavy, with small cheer,
And lo my love, mine own soul's heart, more dear
  Than mine own soul, more beautiful than God,
Who hath my being between the hands of her—

Fair still, but fair for no man saving me,
As when she came out of the naked sea   390
  Making the foam as fire whereon she trod,
And as the inner flower of fire was she.

Yea, she laid hold upon me, and her mouth
Clove unto mine as soul to body doth,
   And, laughing, made her lips luxurious;
Her hair had smells of all the sunburnt south,

Strange spice and flower, strange savour of crushed
     fruit,
And perfume the swart kings tread underfoot
   For pleasure when their minds wax amorous,
Charred frankincense and grated sandal-root.   *400*

And I forgot fear and all weary things,
All ended prayers and perished thanksgivings,
   Feeling her face with all her eager hair
Cleave to me, clinging as a fire that clings

To the body and to the raiment, burning them;
As after death I know that such-like flame
   Shall cleave to me for ever; yea, what care,
Albeit I burn then, having felt the same?

Ah love, there is no better life than this;
To have known love, how bitter a thing it is,   *410*
   And afterward be cast out of God's sight;
Yea, these that know not, shall they have such bliss

High up in barren heaven before his face
As we twain in the heavy-hearted place,
   Remembering love and all the dead delight,
And all that time was sweet with for a space?

For till the thunder in the trumpet be,
Soul may divide from body, but not we
   One from another; I hold thee with my hand,
I let mine eyes have all their will of thee,   *420*

I seal myself upon thee with my might,
Abiding alway out of all men's sight
   Until God loosen over sea and land
The thunder of the trumpets of the night.

       EXPLICIT LAUS VENERIS.

                    (1866)

THE TRIUMPH OF TIME

Before our lives divide for ever,
   While time is with us and hands are free,
(Time, swift to fasten and swift to sever
   Hand from hand, as we stand by the sea)
I will say no word that a man might say
Whose whole life's love goes down in a day;
For this could never have been; and never,
   Though the gods and the years relent, shall be.

Is it worth a tear, is it worth an hour,
   To think of things that are well outworn?   *10*
Of fruitless husk and fugitive flower,
   The dream foregone and the deed forborne?
Though joy be done with and grief be vain,
Time shall not sever us wholly in twain;
Earth is not spoilt for a single shower;
   But the rain has ruined the ungrown corn.

It will grow not again, this fruit of my heart,
   Smitten with sunbeams, ruined with rain.
The singing seasons divide and depart,
   Winter and summer depart in twain.   *20*
It will grow not again, it is ruined at root,
The bloodlike blossom, the dull red fruit;
Though the heart yet sickens, the lips yet smart,
   With sullen savour of poisonous pain.

I have given no man of my fruit to eat;
   I trod the grapes, I have drunken the wine.
Had you eaten and drunken and found it sweet,
   This wild new growth of the corn and vine,
This wine and bread without lees or leaven,
We had grown as gods, as the gods in heaven,   *30*
Souls fair to look upon, goodly to greet,
   One splendid spirit, your soul and mine.

In the change of years, in the coil of things,
   In the clamour and rumour of life to be,
We, drinking love at the furthest springs,
   Covered with love as a covering tree,
We had grown as gods, as the gods above,
Filled from the heart to the lips with love,
Held fast in his hands, clothed warm with his wings,
   O love, my love, had you loved but me!   *40*

We had stood as the sure stars stand, and moved
   As the moon moves, loving the world; and seen
Grief collapse as a thing disproved,
   Death consume as a thing unclean.
Twain halves of a perfect heart, made fast,
Soul to soul while the years fell past;
Had you loved me once, as you have not loved;
   Had the chance been with us that has not been.

I have put my days and dreams out of mind,
   Days that are over, dreams that are done.   *50*
Though we seek life through, we shall surely find
   There is none of them clear to us now, not one.
But clear are these things: the grass and the sand,
Where, sure as the eyes reach, ever at hand,
With lips wide open and face burnt blind,
   The strong sea-daisies feast on the sun.

The low downs lean to the sea; the stream,
   One loose thin pulseless tremulous vein,

Rapid and vivid and dumb as a dream,
  Works downward, sick of the sun and the rain;   *60*
No wind is rough with the rank rare flowers;
The sweet sea, mother of loves and hours,
Shudders and shines as the grey winds gleam,
  Turning her smile to a fugitive pain.

Mother of loves that are swift to fade,
  Mother of mutable winds and hours.
A barren mother, a mother-maid,
  Cold and clean as her faint salt flowers.
I would we twain were even as she,
Lost in the night and the light of the sea,   *70*
Where faint sounds falter and wan beams wade,
  Break, and are broken, and shed into showers.

The loves and hours of the life of a man,
  They are swift and sad, being born of the sea.
Hours that rejoice and regret for a span,
  Born with a man's breath, mortal as he;
Loves that are lost ere they come to birth,
Weeds of the wave, without fruit upon earth,
I lose what I long for, save what I can,
  My love, my love, and no love for me!   *80*

It is not much that a man can save
  On the sands of life, in the straits of time,
Who swims in sight of the great third wave
  That never a swimmer shall cross or climb.
Some waif washed up with the strays and spars
That ebb-tide shows to the shore and the stars;
Weed from the water, grass from a grave,
  A broken blossom, a ruined rhyme.

There will no man do for your sake, I think,
  What I would have done for the least word said.   *90*
I had wrung life dry for your lips to drink,
  Broken it up for your daily bread:
Body for body and blood for blood,

As the flow of the full sea risen to flood
That yearns and trembles before it sink,
   I had given, and lain down for you, glad and dead.

Yea, hope at highest and all her fruit,
   And time at fullest and all his dower,
I had given you surely, and life to boot,
   Were we once made one for a single hour.   *100*
But now, you are twain, you are cloven apart,
Flesh of his flesh, but heart of my heart;
And deep in one is the bitter root,
   And sweet for one is the lifelong flower.

To have died if you cared I should die for you, clung
   To my life if you bade me, played my part
As it pleased you—these were the thoughts that stung,
   The dreams that smote with a keener dart
Than shafts of love or arrows of death;
These were but as fire is, dust or breath,   *110*
Or poisonous foam on the tender tongue
   Of the little snakes that eat my heart.

I wish we were dead together to-day,
   Lost sight of, hidden away out of sight,
Clasped and clothed in the cloven clay,
   Out of the world's way, out of the light,
Out of the ages of worldly weather,
Forgotten of all men altogether,
As the world's first dead, taken wholly away,
   Made one with death, filled full of the night.   *120*

How we should slumber, how we should sleep,
   Far in the dark with the dreams and the dews!
And dreaming, grow to each other, and weep,
   Laugh low, live softly, murmur and muse;
Yea, and it may be, struck through by the dream,
Feel the dust quicken and quiver, and seem
Alive as of old to the lips, and leap
   Spirit to spirit as lovers use.

Sick dreams and sad of a dull delight;
  For what shall it profit when men are dead   *130*
To have dreamed, to have loved with the whole soul's
      might,
  To have looked for day when the day was fled?
Let come what will, there is one thing worth,
To have had fair love in the life upon earth:
To have held love safe till the day grew night,
  While skies had colour and lips were red.

Would I lose you now? would I take you then,
  If I lose you now that my heart has need?
And come what may after death to men,
  What thing worth this will the dead years breed?   *140*
Lose life, lose all; but at least I know,
O sweet life's love, having loved you so,
Had I reached you on earth, I should lose not again,
  In death nor life, nor in dream or deed.

Yea, I know this well: were you once sealed mine,
  Mine in the blood's beat, mine in the breath,
Mixed into me as honey in wine,
  Not time that sayeth and gainsayeth,
Nor all strong things had severed us then;
Not wrath of gods, nor wisdom of men,   *150*
Nor all things earthly, nor all divine,
  Nor joy nor sorrow, nor life nor death.

I had grown pure as the dawn and the dew,
  You had grown strong as the sun or the sea.
But none shall triumph a whole life through:
  For death is one, and the fates are three.
At the door of life, by the gate of breath,
There are worse things waiting for men than death;
Death could not sever my soul and you,
  As these have severed your soul from me.   *160*

  You have chosen and clung to the chance they sent you,
    Life sweet as perfume and pure as prayer.

But will it not one day in heaven repent you?
   Will they solace you wholly, the days that were?
Will you lift up your eyes between sadness and bliss,
Meet mine, and see where the great love is,
And tremble and turn and be changed? Content you;
   The gate is strait; I shall not be there.

But you, had you chosen, had you stretched hand,
   Had you seen good such a thing were done,   *170*
I too might have stood with the souls that stand
   In the sun's sight, clothed with the light of the sun;
But who now on earth need care how I live?
Have the high gods anything left to give,
Save dust and laurels and gold and sand?
   Which gifts are goodly; but I will none.

O all fair lovers about the world,
   There is none of you, none, that shall comfort me.
My thoughts are as dead things, wrecked and whirled
   Round and round in a gulf of the sea;   *180*
And still, through the sound and the straining stream,
Through the coil and chafe, they gleam in a dream,
The bright fine lips so cruelly curled,
   And strange swift eyes where the soul sits free.

Free, without pity, withheld from woe,
   Ignorant; fair as the eyes are fair.
Would I have you change now, change at a blow,
   Startled and stricken, awake and aware?
Yea, if I could, would I have you see
My very love of you filling me,   *190*
And know my soul to the quick, as I know
   The likeness and look of your throat and hair?

I shall not change you. Nay, though I might,
   Would I change my sweet one love with a word?
I had rather your hair should change in a night,
   Clear now as the plume of a black bright bird;

Your face fail suddenly, cease, turn grey,
Die as a leaf that dies in a day.
I will keep my soul in a place out of sight,
    Far off, where the pulse of it is not heard.   200

Far off it walks, in a bleak blown space,
    Full of the sound of the sorrow of years.
I have woven a veil for the weeping face,
    Whose lips have drunken the wine of tears;
I have found a way for the failing feet,
A place for slumber and sorrow to meet;
There is no rumour about the placc,
    Nor light, nor any that sees or hears.

I have hidden my soul out of sight, and said
    "Let none take pity upon thee, none   210
Comfort thy crying: for lo, thou art dead,
    Lie still now, safe out of sight of the sun.
Have I not built thee a grave, and wrought
Thy grave-clothes on thee of grievous thought,
With soft spun verses and tears unshed,
    And sweet light visions of things undone?

"I have given thee garments and balm and myrrh,
    And gold, and beautiful burial things.
But thou, be at peace now, make no stir;
    Is not thy grave as a royal king's?   220
Fret not thyself though the end were sore;
Sleep, be patient, vex me no more.
Sleep; what hast thou to do with her?
    The eyes that weep, with the mouth that sings?"

Where the dead red leaves of the years lie rotten,
    The cold old crimes and the deeds thrown by,
The misconceived and the misbegotten,
    I would find a sin to do ere I die,
Sure to dissolve and destroy me all through,
That would set you higher in heaven, serve you   230

And leave you happy, when clean forgotten,
   As a dead man out of mind, am I.

Your lithe hands draw me, your face burns through me,
   I am swift to follow you, keen to see;
But love lacks might to redeem or undo me;
   As I have been, I know I shall surely be;
"What should such fellows as I do?" Nay,
My part were worse if I chose to play;
For the worst is this after all; if they knew me,
   Not a soul upon earth would pity me.   240

And I play not for pity of these; but you,
   If you saw with your soul what man am I,
You would praise me at least that my soul all through
   Clove to you, loathing the lives that lie;
The souls and lips that are bought and sold,
The smiles of silver and kisses of gold,
The lapdog loves that whine as they chew,
   The little lovers that curse and cry.

There are fairer women, I hear; that may be;
   But I, that I love you and find you fair,   250
Who are more than fair in my eyes if they be,
   Do the high gods know or the great gods care?
Though the swords in my heart for one were seven,
Would the iron hollow of doubtful heaven,
That knows not itself whether night-time or day be,
   Reverberate words and a foolish prayer?

I will go back to the great sweet mother,
   Mother and lover of men, the sea.
I will go down to her, I and none other,
   Close with her, kiss her and mix her with me;   260
Cling to her, strive with her, hold her fast;
O fair white mother, in days long past
Born without sister, born without brother,
   Set free my soul as thy soul is free.

O fair green-girdled mother of mine,
   Sea, that art clothed with the sun and the rain,
Thy sweet hard kisses are strong like wine,
   Thy large embraces are keen like pain.
Save me and hide me with all thy waves,
Find me one grave of thy thousand graves,   270
Those pure cold populous graves of thine,
   Wrought without hand in a world without stain.

I shall sleep, and move with the moving ships,
   Change as the winds change, veer in the tide;
My lips will feast on the foam of thy lips,
   I shall rise with thy rising, with thee subside;
Sleep, and not know if she be, if she were,
Filled full with life to the eyes and hair,
As a rose is fulfilled to the roseleaf tips
   With splendid summer and perfume and pride.   280

This woven raiment of nights and days,
   Were it once cast off and unwound from me,
Naked and glad would I walk in thy ways,
   Alive and aware of thy ways and thee;
Clear of the whole world, hidden at home,
Clothed with the green and crowned with the foam,
A pulse of the life of thy straits and bays,
   A vein in the heart of the streams of the sea.

Fair mother, fed with the lives of men,
   Thou art subtle and cruel of heart, men say.   290
Thou hast taken, and shalt not render again;
   Thou art full of thy dead, and cold as they.
But death is the worst that comes of thee;
Thou art fed with our dead, O mother, O sea,
But when hast thou fed on our hearts? or when,
   Having given us love, hast thou taken away?

O tender-hearted, O perfect lover,
   Thy lips are bitter, and sweet thine heart.

The hopes that hurt and the dreams that hover,
   Shall they not vanish away and apart?   *300*
But thou, thou art sure, thou art older than earth;
Thou art strong for death and fruitful of birth;
Thy depths conceal and thy gulfs discover;
   From the first thou wert; in the end thou art.

And grief shall endure not for ever, I know.
   As things that are not shall these things be;
We shall live through seasons of sun and of snow,
   And none be grievous as this to me.
We shall hear, as one in a trance that hears,
The sound of time, the rhyme of the years;   *310*
Wrecked hope and passionate pain will grow
   As tender things of a spring-tide sea,

Sea-fruit that swings in the waves that hiss,
   Drowned gold and purple and royal rings.
And all time past, was it all for this?
   Times unforgotten, and treasures of things?
Swift years of liking, and sweet long laughter,
That wist not well of the years thereafter
Till love woke, smitten at heart by a kiss,
   With lips that trembled and trailing wings?   *320*

There lived a singer in France of old,
   By the tideless dolorous midland sea.
In a land of sand and ruin and gold
   There shone one woman, and none but she.
And finding life for her love's sake fail,
Being fain to see her, he bade set sail,
Touched land, and saw her as life grew cold,
   And praised God, seeing; and so died he.

Died, praising God for his gift and grace:
   For she bowed down to him weeping, and said   *330*
"Live;" and her tears were shed on his face
   Or ever the life in his face was shed.

The sharp tears fell through her hair, and stung
Once, and her close lips touched him and clung
Once, and grew one with his lips for a space;
   And so drew back, and the man was dead.

O brother, the gods were good to you.
   Sleep, and be glad while the world endures.
Be well content as the years wear through;
   Give thanks for life, and the loves and lures;   *340*
Give thanks for life, O brother, and death,
For the sweet last sound of her feet, her breath,
For gifts she gave you, gracious and few,
   Tears and kisses, that lady of yours.

Rest and be glad of the gods; but I,
   How shall I praise them, or how take rest?
There is not room under all the sky
   For me that know not of worst or best,
Dream or desire of the days before,
Sweet things or bitterness, any more.   *350*
Love will not come to me now though I die,
   As love came close to you, breast to breast.

I shall never be friends again with roses;
   I shall loathe sweet tunes, where a note grown strong
Relents and recoils, and climbs and closes,
   As a wave of the sea turned back by song.
There are sounds where the soul's delight takes fire,
Face to face with its own desire;
A delight that rebels, a desire that reposes,
   I shall hate sweet music my whole life long.   *360*

The pulse of war and passion of wonder,
   The heavens that murmur, the sounds that shine,
The stars that sing and the loves that thunder,
   The music burning at heart like wine,
An armed archangel whose hands raise up
All senses mixed in the spirit's cup

Till flesh and spirit are molten in sunder—
  These things are over, and no more mine.

These were a part of the playing I heard
  Once, ere my love and my heart were at strife;   *370*
Love that sings and hath wings as a bird,
  Balm of the wound and heft of the knife.
Fairer than earth is the sea, and sleep
Than overwatching of eyes that weep,
Now time has done with his one sweet word,
  The wine and leaven of lovely life.

I shall go my ways, tread out my measure,
  Fill the days of my daily breath
With fugitive things not good to treasure,
  Do as the world doth, say as it saith;   *380*
But if we had loved each other—O sweet,
Had you felt, lying under the palms of your feet,
The heart of my heart, beating harder with pleasure
  To feel you tread it to dust and death—

Ah, had I not taken my life up and given
  All that life gives and the years let go,
The wine and honey, the balm and leaven,
  The dreams reared high and the hopes brought low?
Come life, come death, not a word be said;
Should I lose you living, and vex you dead?   *390*
I never shall tell you on earth; and in heaven
  If I cry to you then, will you hear or know?

(1866)

THE LEPER

Nothing is better, I well think,
  Than love; the hidden well-water
Is not so delicate to drink:
  This was well seen of me and her.

I served her in a royal house;
  I served her wine and curious meat.
For will to kiss between her brows,
  I had no heart to sleep or eat.

Mere scorn God knows she had of me,
  A poor scribe, nowise great or fair,   10
Who plucked his clerk's hood back to see
  Her curled-up lips and amorous hair.

I vex my head with thinking this.
  Yea, though God always hated me,
And hates me now that I can kiss
  Her eyes, plait up her hair to see

How she then wore it on the brows,
  Yet am I glad to have her dead
Here in this wretched wattled house
  Where I can kiss her eyes and head.   20

Nothing is better, I well know,
  Than love; no amber in cold sea
Or gathered berries under snow:
  That is well seen of her and me.

Three thoughts I make my pleasure of:
  First I take heart and think of this:
That knight's gold hair she chose to love,
  His mouth she had such will to kiss.

Then I remember that sundawn
  I brought him by a privy way   30
Out at her lattice, and thereon
  What gracious words she found to say.

(Cold rushes for such little feet—
  Both feet could lie into my hand.
A marvel was it of my sweet
  Her upright body could so stand.)

"Sweet friend, God give you thank and grace;
  Now am I clean and whole of shame,
Nor shall men burn me in the face
  For my sweet fault that scandals them."   40

I tell you over word by word.
  She, sitting edgewise on her bed,
Holding her feet, said thus. The third,
  A sweeter thing than these, I said.

God, that makes time and ruins it,
  And alters not, abiding God,
Changed with disease her body sweet,
  The body of love wherein she abode.

Love is more sweet and comelier
  Than a dove's throat strained out to sing.   50
All they spat out and cursed at her
  And cast her forth for a base thing.

They cursed her, seeing how God had wrought
  This curse to plague her, a curse of his.
Fools were they surely, seeing not
  How sweeter than all sweet she is.

He that had held her by the hair,
  With kissing lips blinding her eyes,
Felt her bright bosom, strained and bare,
  Sigh under him, with short mad cries   60

Out of her throat and sobbing mouth
  And body broken up with love,
With sweet hot tears his lips were loth
  Her own should taste the savour of,

Yea, he inside whose grasp all night
  Her fervent body leapt or lay,
Stained with sharp kisses red and white,
  Found her a plague to spurn away.

I hid her in this wattled house,
   I served her water and poor bread.   70
For joy to kiss between her brows
   Time upon time I was nigh dead.

Bread failed; we got but well-water
   And gathered grass with dropping seed.
I had such joy of kissing her,
   I had small care to sleep or feed.

Sometimes when service made me glad
   The sharp tears leapt between my lids,
Falling on her, such joy I had
   To do the service God forbids.   80

"I pray you let me be at peace,
   Get hence, make room for me to die."
She said that: her poor lip would cease,
   Put up to mine, and turn to cry.

I said, "Bethink yourself how love
   Fared in us twain, what either did;
Shall I unclothe my soul thereof?
   That I should do this, God forbid."

Yea, though God hateth us, he knows
   That hardly in a little thing   90
Love faileth of the work it does
   Till it grow ripe for gathering.

Six months, and now my sweet is dead
   A trouble takes me; I know not
If all were done well, all well said,
   No word or tender deed forgot.

Too sweet, for the least part in her,
   To have shed life out by fragments; yet,
Could the close mouth catch breath and stir,
   I might see something I forget.   100

Six months, and I sit still and hold
   In two cold palms her cold two feet.
Her hair, half grey half ruined gold,
   Thrills me and burns me in kissing it.

Love bites and stings me through, to see
   Her keen face made of sunken bones.
Her worn-off eyelids madden me,
   That were shot through with purple once.

She said, "Be good with me; I grow
   So tired for shame's sake, I shall die   110
If you say nothing": even so.
   And she is dead now, and shame put by.

Yea, and the scorn she had of me
   In the old time, doubtless vexed her then.
I never should have kissed her. See
   What fools God's anger makes of men!

She might have loved me a little too,
   Had I been humbler for her sake.
But that new shame could make love new
   She saw not—yet her shame did make.   120

I took too much upon my love,
   Having for such mean service done
Her beauty and all the ways thereof,
   Her face and all the sweet thereon.

Yea, all this while I tended her,
   I know the old love held fast his part:
I know the old scorn waxed heavier,
   Mixed with sad wonder, in her heart.

It may be all my love went wrong—
   A scribe's work writ awry and blurred,   130
Scrawled after the blind evensong—
   Spoilt music with no perfect word.

But surely I would fain have done
   All things the best I could. Perchance
Because I failed, came short of one,
   She kept at heart that other man's.

I am grown blind with all these things:
   It may be now she hath in sight
Some better knowledge; still there clings
   The old question. Will not God do right?   *140*

                      (1866)

A CAMEO

There was a graven image of Desire
    Painted with red blood on a ground of gold
    Passing between the young men and the old,
And by him Pain, whose body shone like fire,
And Pleasure with gaunt hands that grasped their hire.
    Of his left wrist, with fingers clenched and cold,
    The insatiable Satiety kept hold,
Walking with feet unshod that pashed the mire;
The senses and the sorrows and the sins,   9
    And the strange loves that suck the breasts of Hate
    Till lips and teeth bite in their sharp indenture,
Followed like beasts with flap of wings and fins.
    Death stood aloof behind a gaping grate,
    Upon whose lock was written *Peradventure*.

                      (1866)

THE GARDEN OF PROSERPINE

Here, where the world is quiet,
   Here, where all trouble seems
Dead winds' and spent waves' riot
   In doubtful dreams of dreams;
I watch the green field growing

For reaping folk and sowing,
For harvest-time and mowing,
    A sleepy world of streams.

I am tired of tears and laughter,
    And men that laugh and weep;
Of what may come hereafter
    For men that sow to reap:
I am weary of days and hours,
Blown buds of barren flowers,
Desires and dreams and powers
    And everything but sleep.

Here life has death for neighbour,
    And far from eye or ear
Wan waves and wet winds labour,
    Weak ships and spirits steer;
They drive adrift, and whither
They wot not who make thither;
But no such winds blow hither,
    And no such things grow here.

No growth of moor or coppice,
    No heather-flower or vine,
But bloomless buds of poppies,
    Green grapes of Proserpine,
Pale beds of blowing rushes
Where no leaf blooms or blushes,
Save this whereout she crushes
    For dead men deadly wine.

Pale, without name or number,
    In fruitless fields of corn,
They bow themselves and slumber
    All night till light is born;
And like a soul belated,
In hell and heaven unmated,
By cloud and mist abated
    Comes out of darkness morn.

Though one were strong as seven,
  He too with death shall dwell,
Nor wake with wings in heaven,
  Nor weep for pains in hell;
Though one were fair as roses,
His beauty clouds and closes;
And well though love reposes,
  In the end it is not well.

Pale, beyond porch and portal,
  Crowned with calm leaves, she stands   50
Who gathers all things mortal
  With cold immortal hands;
Her languid lips are sweeter
Than love's who fears to greet her
To men that mix and meet her
  From many times and lands.

She waits for each and other,
  She waits for all men born;
Forgets the earth her mother,
  The life of fruits and corn;   60
And spring and seed and swallow
Take wing for her and follow
Where summer song rings hollow
  And flowers are put to scorn.

There go the loves that wither,
  The old loves with wearier wings;
And all dead years draw thither,
  And all disastrous things;
Dead dreams of days forsaken,
Blind buds that snows have shaken,   70
Wild leaves that winds have taken,
  Red strays of ruined springs.

We are not sure of sorrow,
  And joy was never sure;

To-day will die to-morrow;
  Time stoops to no man's lure;
And love, grown faint and fretful,
With lips but half regretful
Sighs, and with eyes forgetful
  Weeps that no loves endure.   80

From too much love of living,
  From hope and fear set free,
We thank with brief thanksgiving
  Whatever gods may be
That no life lives for ever;
That dead men rise up never;
That even the weariest river
  Winds somewhere safe to sea.

Then star nor sun shall waken,
  Nor any change of light: 90
Nor sound of waters shaken,
  Nor any sound or sight:
Nor wintry leaves nor vernal,
Nor days nor things diurnal;
Only the sleep eternal
  In an eternal night.

                (1866)

MADONNA MIA

Under green apple-boughs
That never a storm will rouse,
My lady hath her house
  Between two bowers;
In either of the twain
Red roses full of rain;
She hath for bondwomen
  All kind of flowers.

She hath no handmaid fair
To draw her curled gold hair   *10*
Through rings of gold that bear
   Her whole hair's weight;
She hath no maids to stand
Gold-clothed on either hand;
In all the great green land
   None is so great.

She hath no more to wear
But one white hood of vair
Drawn over eyes and hair,
   Wrought with strange gold,   *20*
Made for some great queen's head,
Some fair great queen since dead;
And one strait gown of red
   Against the cold.

Beneath her eyelids deep
Love lying seems asleep,
Love, swift to wake, to weep,
   To laugh, to gaze;
Her breasts are like white birds,
And all her gracious words   *30*
As water-grass to herds
   In the June-days.

To her all dews that fall
And rains are musical;
Her flowers are fed from all,
   Her joy from these;
In the deep-feathered firs
Their gift of joy is hers,
In the least breath that stirs
   Across the trees.   *40*

She grows with greenest leaves,
Ripens with reddest sheaves,

Forgets, remembers, grieves,
   And is not sad;
The quiet lands and skies
Leave light upon her eyes;
None knows her, weak or wise,
   Or tired or glad.

None knows, none understands,
What flowers are like her hands;   *50*
Though you should search all lands
   Wherein time grows,
What snows are like her feet,
Though his eyes burn with heat
Through gazing on my sweet,
   Yet no man knows.

Only this thing is said;
That white and gold and red,
God's three chief words, man's bread
   And oil and wine,   *60*
Were given her for dowers,
And kingdom of all hours,
And grace of goodly flowers
   And various vine.

This is my lady's praise:
God after many days
Wrought her in unknown ways,
   In sunset lands;
This was my lady's birth;
God gave her might and mirth   *70*
And laid his whole sweet earth
   Between her hands.

Under deep apple-boughs
My lady hath her house;
She wears upon her brows
   The flower thereof;

All saying but what God saith
To her is as vain breath;
She is more strong than death,
  Being strong as love.   *80*

                    (1866)

BEFORE THE MIRROR

(VERSES WRITTEN UNDER A PICTURE)

Inscribed to J. A. Whistler

I

White rose in red rose-garden
  Is not so white;
Snowdrops that plead for pardon
  And pine for fright
Because the hard East blows
Over their maiden rows
  Grow not as this face grows from pale to bright.

Behind the veil, forbidden
  Shut up from sight,
Love, is there sorrow hidden,   *10*
  Is there delight?
Is joy thy dower of grief,
White rose of weary leaf,
  Late rose whose life is brief, whose loves are light?

Soft snows that hard winds harden
  Till each flake bite
Fill all the flowerless garden
  Whose flowers took flight
Long since when summer ceased,
And men rose up from feast,   *20*
  And warm west wind grew east, and warm day night.

II

"Come snow, come wind or thunder
  High up in air,

I watch my face, and wonder
  At my bright hair;
Nought else exalts or grieves
The rose at heart, that heaves
  With love of her own leaves and lips that pair.

"She knows not loves that kissed her
  She knows not where,   *30*
Art thou the ghost, my sister,
  White sister there,
Am I the ghost, who knows?
My hand, a fallen rose,
  Lies snow-white on white snows, and takes no care.

"I cannot see what pleasures
  Or what pains were;
What pale new loves and treasures
  New years will bear;
What beam will fall, what shower,   *40*
What grief or joy for dower;
  But one thing knows the flower; the flower is fair."

III

Glad, but not flushed with gladness,
  Since joys go by;
Sad, but not bent with sadness,
  Since sorrows die;
Deep in the gleaming glass
She sees all past things pass,
  And all sweet life that was lie down and lie.

There glowing ghosts of flowers   *50*
  Draw down, draw nigh;
And wings of swift spent hours
  Take flight and fly;
She sees by formless gleams,
She hears across cold streams,
  Dead mouths of many dreams that sing and sigh.

Face fallen and white throat lifted,
   With sleepless eye
She sees old loves that drifted,
   She knew not why,   60
Old loves and faded fears
Float down a stream that hears
   The flowing of all men's tears beneath the sky.

                           (1866)

AFTER DEATH

The four boards of the coffin lid
Heard all the dead man did.

The first curse was in his mouth,
Made of grave's mould and deadly drouth.

The next curse was in his head,
Made of God's work discomfited.

The next curse was in his hands,
Made out of two grave-bands.

The next curse was in his feet,
Made out of a grave-sheet.   10

"I had fair coins red and white,
And my name was as great light;

"I had fair clothes green and red,
And strong gold bound round my head.

"But no meat comes in my mouth,
Now I fare as the worm doth;

"And no gold binds in my hair,
Now I fare as the blind fare.

"My live thews were of great strength,
Now I am waxen a span's length;   20

"My live sides were full of lust,
Now are they dried with dust."

The first board spake and said:
"Is it best eating flesh or bread?"

The second answered it:
"Is wine or honey the more sweet?"

The third board spake and said:
"Is red gold worth a girl's gold head?"

The fourth made answer thus:
"All these things are as one with us."   30

The dead man asked of them:
"Is the green land stained brown with flame?

"Have they hewn my son for beasts to eat,
And my wife's body for beasts' meat?

"Have they boiled my maid in a brass pan,
And built a gallows to hang my man?"

The boards said to him:
"This is a lewd thing that ye deem.

"Your wife has gotten a golden bed,
All the sheets are sewn with red.   40

"Your son has gotten a coat of silk,
The sleeves are soft as curded milk.

"Your maid has gotten a kirtle new,
All the skirt has braids of blue.

"Your man has gotten both ring and glove,
Wrought well for eyes to love."

The dead man answered thus:
"What good gift shall God give us?"

The boards answered him anon:
"Flesh to feed hell's worm upon."   50

(1866)

A CHRISTMAS CAROL

Suggested by a drawing of Mr. D. G. Rossetti's

Three damsels in the queen's chamber,
    The queen's mouth was most fair;
She spake a word of God's mother
    As the combs went in her hair.
        Mary that is of might,
        Bring us to thy Son's sight.

They held the gold combs out from her,
    A span's length off her head;
She sang this song of God's mother
    And of her bearing-bed.   10
        Mary most full of grace,
        Bring us to thy Son's face.

When she sat at Joseph's hand,
    She looked against her side;
And either way from the short silk band
    Her girdle was all wried.
        Mary that all good may,
        Bring us to thy Son's way.

Mary had three women for her bed,
    The twain were maidens clean;   20

The first of them had white and red,
    The third had riven green.
        Mary that is so sweet,
        Bring us to thy Son's feet.

She had three women for her hair,
    Two were gloved soft and shod;
The third had feet and fingers bare,
    She was the likest God.
        Mary that wieldeth land,
        Bring us to thy Son's hand.   *30*

She had three women for her ease,
    The twain were good women:
The first two were the two Maries,
    The third was Magdalen.
        Mary that perfect is,
        Bring us to thy Son's kiss.

Joseph had three workmen in his stall,
    To serve him well upon;
The first of them were Peter and Paul,
    The third of them was John.   *40*
        Mary, God's handmaiden,
        Bring us to thy Son's ken.

"If your child be none other man's,
    But if it be very mine,
The bedstead shall be gold two spans,
    The bedfoot silver fine."
        Mary that made God mirth,
        Bring us to thy Son's birth.

"If the child be some other man's
    And if it be none of mine,   *50*
The manger shall bestraw two spans,
    Betwixen kine and kine."
        Mary that made sin cease,
        Bring us to thy Son's peace.

"*A Christmas Carol*," *water color by Dante Gabriel Rossetti, 1857, which suggested Swinburne's poem of the same title. Courtesy of the Fogg Art Museum, Harvard University, Grenville L. Winthrop Bequest*

Christ was born upon this wise,
    It fell on such a night,
Neither with sounds of psalteries,
    Nor with fire for light.
        Mary that is God's spouse,
        Bring us to thy Son's house.   60

The star came out upon the east
    With a great sound and sweet:
Kings gave gold to make him feast
    And myrrh for him to eat.
        Mary, of thy sweet mood,
        Bring us to thy Son's good.

He had two handmaids at his head,
    One handmaid at his feet;
The twain of them were fair and red,
    The third one was right sweet.   70
        Mary that is most wise,
        Bring us to thy Son's eyes. Amen.

                (1866)

THE SUNDEW

A little marsh-plant, yellow green,
And pricked at lip with tender red.
Tread close, and either way you tread
Some faint black water jets between
Lest you should bruise the curious head.

A live thing maybe; who shall know?
The summer knows and suffers it;
For the cool moss is thick and sweet
Each side, and saves the blossom so
That it lives out the long June heat.   10

The deep scent of the heather burns
About it; breathless though it be,

Bow down and worship; more than we
Is the least flower whose life returns,
Least weed renascent in the sea.

We are vexed and cumbered in earth's sight
With wants, with many memories;
These see their mother what she is,
Glad-growing, till August leave more bright
The apple-coloured cranberries.   20

Wind blows and bleaches the strong grass,
Blown all one way to shelter it
From trample of strayed kine, with feet
Felt heavier than the moorhen was,
Strayed up past patches of wild wheat.

You call it sundew: how it grows,
If with its colour it have breath,
If life taste sweet to it, if death
Pain its soft petal, no man knows:
Man has no sight or sense that saith.   30

My sundew, grown of gentle days,
In these green miles the spring begun
Thy growth ere April had half done
With the soft secret of her ways
Or June made ready for the sun.

O red-lipped mouth of marsh-flower,
I have a secret halved with thee.
The name that is love's name to me
Thou knowest, and the face of her
Who is my festival to see.   40

The hard sun, as thy petals knew,
Coloured the heavy moss-water:
Thou wert not worth green midsummer

Nor fit to live to August blue,
O sundew, not remembering her.

(1866)

A FORSAKEN GARDEN

In a coign of the cliff between lowland and highland,
   At the sea-down's edge between windward and lee,
Walled round with rocks as an inland island,
   The ghost of a garden fronts the sea.
A girdle of brushwood and thorn encloses
   The steep square slope of the blossomless bed
Where the weeds that grew green from the graves of its
     roses
   Now lie dead.

The fields fall southward, abrupt and broken,
   To the low last edge of the long lone land.   *10*
If a step should sound or a word be spoken,
   Would a ghost not rise at the strange guest's hand?
So long have the grey bare walks lain guestless,
   Through branches and briers if a man make way,
He shall find no life but the sea-wind's, restless
   Night and day.

The dense hard passage is blind and stifled
   That crawls by a track none turn to climb
To the strait waste place that the years have rifled
   Of all but the thorns that are touched not of time.   *20*
The thorns he spares when the rose is taken;
   The rocks are left when he wastes the plain.
The wind that wanders, the weeds windshaken,
   These remain.

Not a flower to be pressed of the foot that falls not;
   As the heart of a dead man the seed-plots are dry;
From the thicket of thorns whence the nightingale calls
     not,

Could she call, there were never a rose to reply.
Over the meadows that blossom and wither
  Rings but the note of a sea-bird's song;   *30*
Only the sun and the rain come hither
    All year long.

The sun burns sere and the rain dishevels
  One gaunt bleak blossom of scentless breath.
Only the wind here hovers and revels
  In a round where life seems barren as death.
Here there was laughing of old, there was weeping,
  Haply, of lovers none ever will know,
Whose eyes went seaward a hundred sleeping
    Years ago.   *40*

Heart handfast in heart as they stood, "Look thither,"
  Did he whisper? "look forth from the flowers to the sea;
For the foam-flowers endure when the rose-blossoms
    wither,
  And men that love lightly may die—but we?"
And the same wind sang and the same waves whitened,
  And or ever the garden's last petals were shed,
In the lips that had whispered, the eyes that had lightened,
    Love was dead.

Or they loved their life through, and then went whither?
  And were one to the end—but what end who knows?
Love deep as the sea as a rose must wither,   *51*
  As the rose-red seaweed that mocks the rose.
Shall the dead take thought for the dead to love them?
  What love was ever as deep as a grave?
They are loveless now as the grass above them
    Or the wave.

All are at one now, roses and lovers,
  Not known of the cliffs and the fields and the sea.
Not a breath of the time that has been hovers
  In the air now soft with a summer to be.   *60*

Not a breath shall there sweeten the seasons hereafter
  Of the flowers or the lovers that laugh now or weep,
When as they that are free now of weeping and laughter
    We shall sleep.

Here death may deal not again for ever;
  Here change may come not till all change end.
From the graves they have made they shall rise up never,
  Who have left nought living to ravage and rend.
Earth, stones, and thorns of the wild ground growing,
  While the sun and the rain live, these shall be;
Till a last wind's breath upon all these blowing   *71*
    Roll the sea.

Till the slow sea rise and the sheer cliff crumble,
  Till terrace and meadow the deep gulfs drink,
Till the strength of the waves of the high tides humble
  The fields that lessen, the rocks that shrink,
Here now in his triumph where all things falter,
  Stretched out on the spoils that his own hand spread,
As a god self-slain on his own strange altar,
    Death lies dead.   *80*

(1876)

A BALLAD OF DREAMLAND

I hid my heart in a nest of roses,
  Out of the sun's way, hidden apart;
In a softer bed than the soft white snow's is,
  Under the roses I hid my heart.
  Why would it sleep not? why should it start,
When never a leaf of the rose-tree stirred?
  What made sleep flutter his wings and part?
Only the song of a secret bird.

Lie still, I said, for the wind's wing closes,
  And mild leaves muffle the keen sun's dart;   *10*

Lie still, for the wind on the warm sea dozes,
   And the wind is unquieter yet than thou art.
   Does a thought in thee still as a thorn's wound smart?
Does the fang still fret thee of hope deferred?
   What bids the lids of thy sleep dispart?
Only the song of a secret bird.

The green land's name that a charm encloses,
   It never was writ in the traveller's chart,
And sweet on its trees as the fruit that grows is,
   It never was sold in the merchant's mart.   20
   The swallows of dreams through its dim fields dart,
And sleep's are the tunes in its tree-tops heard;
   No hound's note wakens the wildwood hart,
Only the song of a secret bird.

ENVOI

In the world of dreams I have chosen my part,
   To sleep for a season and hear no word
Of true love's truth or of light love's art,
   Only the song of a secret bird.

                     (1878)

A BALLAD OF FRANCOIS VILLON

PRINCE OF ALL BALLAD-MAKERS

Bird of the bitter bright grey golden morn
   Scarce risen upon the dusk of dolorous years,
First of us all and sweetest singer born
   Whose far shrill note the world of new men hears
   Cleave the cold shuddering shade as twilight clears;
When song new-born put off the old world's attire
And felt its tune on her changed lips expire,
   Writ foremost on the roll of them that came
Fresh girt for service of the latter lyre,
   Villon, our sad bad glad mad brother's name!   *10*

Alas the joy, the sorrow, and the scorn,
  That clothed thy life with hopes and sins and fears,
And gave thee stones for bread and tares for corn
    And plume-plucked gaol-birds for thy starveling peers
    Till death clipt close their flight with shameful shears;
Till shifts came short and loves were hard to hire,
When lilt of song nor twitch of twangling wire
  Could buy thee bread or kisses; when light fame
Spurned like a ball and haled through brake and brier,
    Villon, our sad bad glad mad brother's name!   20

Poor splendid wings so frayed and soiled and torn!
  Poor kind wild eyes so dashed with light quick tears!
Poor perfect voice, most blithe when most forlorn,
    That rings athwart the sea whence no man steers
    Like joy-bells crossed with death-bells in our ears!
What far delight has cooled the fierce desire
That like some ravenous bird was strong to tire
  On that frail flesh and soul consumed with flame,
But left more sweet than roses to respire,
    Villon, our sad bad glad mad brother's name?   30

ENVOI

Prince of sweet songs made out of tears and fire,
A harlot was thy nurse, a God thy sire;
  Shame soiled thy song, and song assoiled thy shame.
But from thy feet now death has washed the mire,
Love reads out first at head of all our quire,
  Villon, our sad bad glad mad brother's name.

                                          (1878)

SONNET FOR A PICTURE

That nose is out of drawing. With a gasp,
  She pants upon the passionate lips that ache
  With the red drain of her own mouth, and make
A monochord of colour. Like an asp,

One lithe lock wriggles in his rutilant grasp.
   Her bosom is an oven of myrrh, to bake
   Love's white warm shewbread to a browner cake.
The lock his fingers clench has burst its hasp.
The legs are absolutely abominable.
   Ah! what keen overgust of wild-eyed woes   *10*
   Flags in that bosom, flushes in that nose?
Nay! Death sets riddles for desire to spell,
   Responsive. What red hem earth's passion sews,
But may be ravenously unripped in hell?

                                (1880)

GEORGE MEREDITH

(1828–1909)

George Meredith was both poet and novelist—in some-
times disconcerting proportions: his prose fiction is heav-
ily metaphoric and given to elaborate poetic description;
his verse is often prosaically discursive, weighted with
argument and doctrine. *Modern Love* (1862), his poetical
masterpiece, a kind of novel in the form of a sequence of
fifty sixteen-line sonnets, compounds his strengths and es-
capes most of his more trying idiosyncrasies. Written and
published during the time of Meredith's close friendship
with Rossetti, whom he met about 1860 and at whose
residence, Tudor House in Chelsea, he lived at intervals
for some months two years later, the poem shares some
characteristics in common with the work of the literary
Pre-Raphaelites: a probing analysis of the inner life, a con-
centration on specific moments of insight and crisis, a pre-
cise use of graphic detail, a mingling of archaic and collo-
quial diction, and a highly allusive imagery. In subject
matter *Modern Love*—like the novel that preceded it, *The
Ordeal of Richard Feveral* (1859)—bears directly on Mere-
dith's unhappy marriage to Mary Ellen Nicoll, the daugh-
ter of Thomas Love Peacock, a union that ended in sepa-
ration and misery. But, as great art must, it transcends its
personal origin to achieve a self-subsistent drama; and in
such objective delineation it realizes yet another Pre-
Raphaelite ideal.

Modern Love

I

By this he knew she wept with waking eyes:
That, at his hand's light quiver by her head,
The strange low sobs that shook their common bed
Were called into her with a sharp surprise,
And strangled mute, like little gaping snakes,
Dreadfully venomous to him. She lay
Stone-still, and the long darkness flowed away
With muffled pulses. Then, as midnight makes
Her giant heart of Memory and Tears
Drink the pale drug of silence, and so beat   10
Sleep's heavy measure, they from head to feet
Were moveless, looking through their dead black years.
By vain regret scrawled over the blank wall.
Like sculptured effigies they might be seen
Upon their marriage-tomb, the sword between;
Each wishing for the sword that severs all.

II

It ended, and the morrow brought the task.
Her eyes were guilty gates, that let him in
By shutting all too zealous for their sin:
Each sucked a secret, and each wore a mask.
But, oh, the bitter taste her beauty had!
He sickened as at breath of poison-flowers:
A languid humour stole among the hours,
And if their smiles encountered, he went mad,
And raged deep inward, till the light was brown
Before his vision, and the world, forgot,   10
Looked wicked as some old dull murder-spot.
A star with lurid beams, she seemed to crown
The pit of infamy: and then again
He fainted on his vengefulness, and strove
To ape the magnanimity of love,
And smote himself, a shuddering heap of pain.

III

This was the woman; what now of the man?
But pass him. If he comes beneath a heel,
He shall be crushed until he cannot feel,
Or, being callous, haply till he can.
But he is nothing:—nothing? Only mark
The rich light striking out from her on him!
Ha! what a sense it is when her eyes swim
Across the man she singles, leaving dark
All else! Lord God, who mad'st the thing so fair,
See that I am drawn to her even now!   10
It cannot be such harm on her cool brow
To put a kiss? Yet if I meet him there!
But she is mine! Ah, no! I know too well
I claim a star whose light is overcast:
I claim a phantom-woman in the Past.
The hour has struck, though I heard not the bell!

IV

All other joys of life he strove to warm,
And magnify, and catch them to his lip:
But they had suffered shipwreck with the ship,
And gazed upon him sallow from the storm.
Or if Delusion came, 'twas but to show
The coming minute mock the one that went.
Cold as a mountain in its star-pitched tent,
Stood high Philosophy, less friend than foe:
Whom self-caged Passion, from its prison-bars,
Is always watching with a wondering hate.   10
Not till the fire is dying in the grate,
Look we for any kinship with the stars.
Oh, wisdom never comes when it is gold,
And the great price we pay for it full worth:
We have it only when we are half earth.
Little avails that coinage to the old!

V

A message from her set his brain aflame.
A world of household matters filled her mind,
Wherein he saw hypocrisy designed:
She treated him as something that is tame,
And but at other provocation bites.
Familiar was her shoulder in the glass,
Through that dark rain: yet it may come to pass
That a changed eye finds such familiar sights
More keenly tempting than new loveliness.
The 'What has been' a moment seemed his own: *10*
The splendours, mysteries, dearer because known,
Nor less divine: Love's inmost sacredness
Called to him, 'Come!'—In his restraining start,
Eyes nurtured to be looked at scarce could see
A wave of the great waves of Destiny
Convulsed at a checked impulse of the heart.

VI

It chanced his lips did meet her forehead cool.
She had no blush, but slanted down her eye.
Shamed nature, then, confesses love can die:
And most she punishes the tender fool
Who will believe what honours her the most!
Dead! is it dead? She has a pulse, and flow
Of tears, the price of blood-drops, as I know,
For whom the midnight sobs around Love's ghost,
Since then I heard her, and so will sob on.
The love is here; it has but changed its aim.   *10*
O bitter barren woman! what 's the name?
The name, the name, the new name thou hast won?
Behold me striking the world's coward stroke!
That will I not do, though the sting is dire.
—Beneath the surface this, while by the fire
They sat, she laughing at a quiet joke.

VII

She issues radiant from her dressing-room,
Like one prepared to scale an upper sphere:
—By stirring up a lower, much I fear!
How deftly that oiled barber lays his bloom!
That long-shanked dapper Cupid with frisked curls
Can make known women torturingly fair;
The gold-eyed serpent dwelling in rich hair
Awakes beneath his magic whisks and twirls.
His art can take the eyes from out my head,
Until I see with eyes of other men;   *10*
While deeper knowledge crouches in its den,
And sends a spark up:—is it true we are wed?
Yea! filthiness of body is most vile,
But faithlessness of heart I do hold worse.
The former, it were not so great a curse
To read on the steel-mirror of her smile.

VIII

Yet it was plain she struggled, and that salt
Of righteous feeling made her pitiful.
Poor twisting worm, so queenly beautiful!
Where came the cleft between us? whose the fault?
My tears are on thee, that have rarely dropped
As balm for any bitter wound of mine:
My breast will open for thee at a sign!
But, no: we are two reed-pipes, coarsely stopped:
The God once filled them with his mellow breath;
And they were music till he flung them down,   *10*
Used! used! Hear now the discord-loving clown
Puff his gross spirit in them, worse than death!
I do not know myself without thee more:
In this unholy battle I grow base:
If the same soul be under the same face,
Speak, and a taste of that old time restore!

IX

He felt the wild beast in him betweenwhiles
So masterfully rude, that he would grieve
To see the helpless delicate thing receive
His guardianship through certain dark defiles.
Had he not teeth to rend, and hunger too?
But still he spared her. Once: 'Have you no fear?'
He said: 'twas dusk; she in his grasp; none near.
She laughed: 'No, surely; am I not with you?'
And uttering that soft starry 'you,' she leaned
Her gentle body near him, looking up;   10
And from her eyes, as from a poison-cup,
He drank until the flittering eyelids screened.
Devilish malignant witch! and oh, young beam
Of heaven's circle-glory! Here thy shape
To squeeze like an intoxicating grape—
I might, and yet thou goest safe, supreme.

X

But where began the change; and what 's my crime?
The wretch condemned, who has not been arraigned,
Chafes at his sentence. Shall I, unsustained,
Drag on Love's nerveless body thro' all time?
I must have slept, since now I wake. Prepare,
You lovers, to know Love a thing of moods:
Not, like hard life, of laws. In Love's deep woods,
I dreamt of loyal Life:—the offence is there!
Love's jealous woods about the sun are curled;
At least, the sun far brighter there did beam.—   10
My crime is, that the puppet of a dream,
I plotted to be worthy of the world.
Oh, had I with my darling helped to mince
The facts of life, you still had seen me go
With hindward feather and with forward toe,
Her much-adored delightful Fairy Prince!

XI

Out in the yellow meadows, where the bee
Hums by us with the honey of the Spring,
And showers of sweet notes from the larks on wing
Are dropping like a noon-dew, wander we.
Or is it now? or was it then? for now,
As then, the larks from running rings pour showers:
The golden foot of May is on the flowers,
And friendly shadows dance upon her brow.
What 's this, when Nature swears there is no change
To challenge eyesight? Now, as then, the grace   *10*
Of heaven seems holding earth in its embrace.
Nor eyes, nor heart, has she to feel it strange?
Look, woman, in the West. There wilt thou see
An amber cradle near the sun's decline:
Within it, featured even in death divine,
Is lying a dead infant, slain by thee.

XII

Not solely that the Future she destroys,
And the fair life which in the distance lies
For all men, beckoning out from dim rich skies:
Nor that the passing hour's supporting joys
Have lost the keen-edged flavour, which begat
Distinction in old times, and still should breed
Sweet Memory, and Hope,—earth's modest seed,
And heaven's high-prompting: not that the world is flat
Since that soft-luring creature I embraced
Among the children of Illusion went: *10*
Methinks with all this loss I were content,
If the mad Past, on which my foot is based,
Were firm, or might be blotted: but the whole
Of life is mixed: the mocking Past will stay:
And if I drink oblivion of a day,
So shorten I the stature of my soul.

XIII

'I play for Seasons; not Eternities!'
Says Nature, laughing on her way. 'So must
All those whose stake is nothing more than dust!'
And lo, she wins, and of her harmonies
She is full sure! Upon her dying rose
She drops a look of fondness, and goes by,
Scarce any retrospection in her eye;
For she the laws of growth most deeply knows,
Whose hands bear, here, a seed-bag—there, an urn.
Pledged she herself to aught, 'twould mark her end!   *10*
This lesson of our only visible friend
Can we not teach our foolish hearts to learn?
Yes! yes!—but, oh, our human rose is fair
Surpassingly! Lose calmly Love's great bliss,
When the renewed for ever of a kiss
Whirls life within the shower of loosened hair!

XIV

What soul would bargain for a cure that brings
Contempt the nobler agony to kill?
Rather let me bear on the bitter ill,
And strike this rusty bosom with new stings!
It seems there is another veering fit,
Since on a gold-haired lady's eyeballs pure
I looked with little prospect of a cure,
The while her mouth's red bow loosed shafts of wit.
Just heaven! can it be true that jealousy
Has decked the woman thus? and does her head   *10*
Swim somewhat for possessions forfeited?
Madam, you teach me many things that be.
I open an old book, and there I find
That 'Women still may love whom they deceive.'
Such love I prize not, madam: by your leave,
The game you play at is not to my mind.

XV

I think she sleeps: it must be sleep, when low
Hangs that abandoned arm toward the floor;
The face turned with it. Now make fast the door.
Sleep on: it is your husband, not your foe.
The Poet's black stage-lion of wronged love
Frights not our modern dames:—well if he did!
Now will I pour new light upon that lid,
Full-sloping like the breasts beneath. 'Sweet dove,
Your sleep is pure. Nay, pardon: I disturb.
I do not? good!' Her waking infant-stare   *10*
Grows woman to the burden my hands bear:
Her own handwriting to me when no curb
Was left on Passion's tongue. She trembles through;
A woman's tremble—the whole instrument:—
I show another letter lately sent.
The words are very like: the name is new.

XVI

In our old shipwrecked days there was an hour,
When in the firelight steadily aglow,
Joined slackly, we beheld the red chasm grow
Among the clicking coals. Our library-bower
That eve was left to us: and hushed we sat
As lovers to whom Time is whispering.
From sudden-opened doors we heard them sing:
The nodding elders mixed good wine with chat.
Well knew we that Life's greatest treasure lay
With us, and of it was our talk. 'Ah, yes!   *10*
Love dies!' I said: I never thought it less.
She yearned to me that sentence to unsay.
Then when the fire domed blackening, I found
Her cheek was salt against my kiss, and swift
Up the sharp scale of sobs her breast did lift:—
Now am I haunted by that taste! that sound!

XVII

At dinner, she is hostess, I am host.
Went the feast ever cheerfuller? She keeps
The Topic over intellectual deeps
In buoyancy afloat. They see no ghost.
With sparkling surface-eyes we ply the ball:
It is in truth a most contagious game:
HIDING THE SKELETON, shall be its name.
Such play as this the devils might appal!
But here 's the greater wonder; in that we,
Enamoured of an acting nought can tire,   *10*
Each other, like true hypocrites, admire;
Warm-lighted looks, Love's ephemerioe,
Shoot gaily o'er the dishes and the wine.
We waken envy of our happy lot.
Fast, sweet, and golden, shows the marriage-knot.
Dear guests, you now have seen Love's corpse-light shine.

XVIII

Here Jack and Tom are paired with Moll and Meg.
Curved open to the river-reach is seen
A country merry-making on the green.
Fair space for signal shakings of the leg.
That little screwy fiddler from his booth,
Whence flows one nut-brown stream, commands the joints
Of all who caper here at various points.
I have known rustic revels in my youth:
The May-fly pleasures of a mind at ease.
An early goddess was a country lass: *10*
A charmed Amphion-oak she tripped the grass.
What life was that I lived? The life of these?
Heaven keep them happy! Nature they seem near.
They must, I think, be wiser than I am;
They have the secret of the bull and lamb.
'Tis true that when we trace its source, 'tis beer.

XIX

No state is enviable. To the luck alone
Of some few favoured men I would put claim.
I bleed, but her who wounds I will not blame.
Have I not felt her heart as 'twere my own
Beat thro' me? could I hurt her? heaven and hell!
But I could hurt her cruelly! Can I let
My Love's old time-piece to another set,
Swear it can't stop, and must for ever swell?
Sure, that 's one way Love drifts into the mart
Where goat-legged buyers throng. I see not plain:—   *10*
My meaning is, it must not be again.
Great God! the maddest gambler throws his heart.
If any state be enviable on earth,
'Tis yon born idiot's, who, as days go by,
Still rubs his hands before him, like a fly,
In a queer sort of meditative mirth.

XX

I am not of those miserable males
Who sniff at vice and, daring not to snap,
Do therefore hope for heaven. I take the hap
Of all my deeds. The wind that fills my sails
Propels; but I am helmsman. Am I wrecked,
I know the devil has sufficient weight
To bear: I lay it not on him, or fate.
Besides, he 's damned. That man I do suspect
A coward, who would burden the poor deuce
With what ensues from his own slipperiness.   *10*
I have just found a wanton-scented tress
In an old desk, dusty for lack of use.
Of days and nights it is demonstrative,
That, like some aged star, gleam luridly.
If for those times I must ask charity,
Have I not any charity to give?

XXI

We three are on the cedar-shadowed lawn;
My friend being third. He who at love once laughed
Is in the weak rib by a fatal shaft
Struck through, and tells his passion's bashful dawn
And radiant culmination, glorious crown,
When 'this' she said: went 'thus': most wondrous she,
Our eyes grow white, encountering: that we are three,
Forgetful; then together we look down.
But he demands our blessing; is convinced
That words of wedded lovers must bring good.   *10*
We question; if we dare! or if we should!
And pat him, with light laugh. We have not winced
Next, she has fallen. Fainting points the sign
To happy things in wedlock. When she wakes,
She looks the star that thro' the cedar shakes:
Her lost moist hand clings mortally to mine.

XXII

What may the woman labour to confess?
There is about her mouth a nervous twitch.
'Tis something to be told, or hidden:—which?
I get a glimpse of hell in this mild guess.
She has desires of touch, as if to feel
That all the household things are things she knew.
She stops before the glass. What sight in view?
A face that seems the latest to reveal!
For she turns from it hastily, and tossed
Irresolute steals shadow-like to where   *10*
I stand; and wavering pale before me there,
Her tears fall still as oak-leaves after frost.
She will not speak. I will not ask. We are
League-sundered by the silent gulf between.
You burly lovers on the village green,
Yours is a lower, and a happier star!

XXIII

'Tis Christmas weather, and a country house
Receives us: rooms are full: we can but get
An attic-crib. Such lovers will not fret
At that, it is half-said. The great carouse
Knocks hard upon the midnight's hollow door,
But when I knock at hers, I see the pit.
Why did I come here in that dullard fit?
I enter, and lie couched upon the floor.
Passing, I caught the coverlet's quick beat:—
Come, Shame, burn to my soul! and Pride, and Pain—
Foul demons that have tortured me, enchain!   *11*
Out in the freezing darkness the lambs bleat.
The small bird stiffens in the low starlight.
I know not how, but shuddering as I slept,
I dreamed a banished angel to me crept:
My feet were nourished on her breasts all night.

XXIV

The misery is greater, as I live!
To know her flesh so pure, so keen her sense,
That she does penance now for no offence,
Save against Love. The less can I forgive!
The less can I forgive, though I adore
That cruel lovely pallor which surrounds
Her footsteps; and the low vibrating sounds
That come on me, as from a magic shore.
Low are they, but most subtle to find out
The shrinking soul. Madam, 'tis understood   *10*
When women play upon their womanhood,
It means, a Season gone. And yet I doubt
But I am duped. That nun-like look waylays
My fancy. Oh! I do but wait a sign!
Pluck out the eyes of pride! thy mouth to mine!
Never! though I die thirsting. Go thy ways!

XXV

You like not that French novel? Tell me why.
You think it quite unnatural. Let us see.
The actors are, it seems, the usual three:
Husband, and wife, and lover. She—but fie!
In England we 'll not hear of it. Edmond,
The lover, her devout chagrin doth share;
Blanc-mange and absinthe are his penitent fare,
Till his pale aspect makes her over-fond:
So, to preclude fresh sin, he tries rosbif.
Meantime the husband is no more abused: 10
Auguste forgives her ere the tear is used.
Then hangeth all on one tremendous IF:—
If she will choose between them. She does choose;
And takes her husband, like a proper wife.
Unnatural? My dear, these things are life:
And life, some think, is worthy of the Muse.

XXVI

Love ere he bleeds, an eagle in high skies,
Has earth beneath his wings: from reddened eve
He views the rosy dawn. In vain they weave
The fatal web below while far he flies.
But when the arrow strikes him, there 's a change.
He moves but in the track of his spent pain,
Whose red drops are the links of a harsh chain,
Binding him to the ground, with narrow range.
A subtle serpent then has Love become.
I had the eagle in my bosom erst: 10
Henceforward with the serpent I am cursed.
I can interpret where the mouth is dumb.
Speak, and I see the side-lie of a truth.
Perchance my heart may pardon you this deed:
But be no coward:—you that made Love bleed,
You must bear all the venom of his tooth!

XXVII

Distraction is the panacea, Sir!
I hear my oracle of Medicine say.
Doctor! that same specific yesterday
I tried, and the result will not deter
A second trial. Is the devil's line
Of golden hair, or raven black, composed?
And does a cheek, like any sea-shell rosed,
Or clear as widowed sky, seem most divine?
No matter, so I taste forgetfulness.
And if the devil snare me, body and mind,   *10*
Here gratefully I score:—he seeméd kind,
When not a soul would comfort my distress!
O sweet new world, in which I rise new made!
O Lady, once I gave love: now I take!
Lady, I must be flattered. Shouldst thou wake
The passion of a demon, be not afraid.

XXVIII

I must be flattered. The imperious
Desire speaks out. Lady, I am content
To play with you the game of Sentiment,
And with you enter on paths perilous;
But if across your beauty I throw light,
To make it threefold, it must be all mine.
First secret; then avowed. For I must shine
Envied,—I, lessened in my proper sight!
Be watchful of your beauty, Lady dear!
How much hangs on that lamp you cannot tell.   *10*
Most earnestly I pray you, tend it well:
And men shall see me as a burning sphere;
And men shall mark you eyeing me, and groan
To be the God of such a grand sunflower!
I feel the promptings of Satanic power,
While you do homage unto me alone.

XXIX

Am I failing? For no longer can I cast
A glory round about this head of gold.
Glory she wears, but springing from the mould;
Not like the consecration of the Past!
Is my soul beggared? Something more than earth
I cry for still: I cannot be at peace
In having Love upon a mortal lease.
I cannot take the woman at her worth!
Where is the ancient wealth wherewith I clothed
Our human nakedness, and could endow   *10*
With spiritual splendour a white brow
That else had grinned at me the fact I loathed?
A kiss is but a kiss now! and no wave
Of a great flood that whirls me to the sea.
But, as you will! we 'll sit contentedly,
And eat our pot of honey on the grave.

XXX

What are we first? First, animals; and next
Intelligences at a leap; on whom
Pale lies the distant shadow of the tomb,
And all that draweth on the tomb for text
Into which state comes Love, the crowning sun:
Beneath whose light the shadow loses form
We are the lords of life, and life is warm.
Intelligence and instinct now are one.
But nature says: 'My children most they seem
When they least know me: therefore I decree   *10*
That they shall suffer.' Swift doth young Love flee,
And we stand wakened, shivering from our dream.
Then if we study Nature we are wise.
Thus do the few who live but with the day:
The scientific animals are they.—
Lady, this is my sonnet to your eyes.

XXXI

This golden head has wit in it. I live
Again, and a far higher life, near her.
Some women like a young philosopher;
Perchance because he is diminutive.
For woman's manly god must not exceed
Proportions of the natural nursing size.
Great poets and great sages draw no prize
With women: but the little lap-dog breed,
Who can be hugged, or on a mantel-piece
Perched up for adoration, these obtain   10
Her homage. And of this we men are vain?
Of this! 'Tis ordered for the world's increase!
Small flattery! Yet she has that rare gift
To beauty, Common Sense. I am approved.
It is not half so nice as being loved,
And yet I do prefer it. What's my drift?

XXXII

Full faith I have she holds that rarest gift
To beauty, Common Sense. To see her lie
With her fair visage an inverted sky
Bloom-covered, while the underlids uplift,
Would almost wreck the faith; but when her mouth
(Can it kiss sweetly? sweetly!) would address
The inner me that thirsts for her no less,
And has so long been languishing in drouth,
I feel that I am matched; that I am man!
One restless corner of my heart or head,   10
That holds a dying something never dead,
Still frets, though Nature giveth all she can.
It means, that woman is not, I opine,
Her sex's antidote. Who seeks the asp
For serpents' bites? 'Twould calm me could I clasp
Shrieking Bacchantes with their souls of wine!

XXXIII

'In Paris, at the Louvre, there have I seen
The sumptuously-feathered angel pierce
Prone Lucifer, descending. Looked he fierce,
Showing the fight a fair one? Too serene!
The young Pharsalians did not disarray
Less willingly their locks of floating silk:
That suckling mouth of his upon the milk
Of heaven might still be feasting through the fray.
Oh, Raphael! when men the Fiend do fight,
They conquer not upon such easy terms.   10
Half serpent in the struggle grow these worms.
And does he grow half human, all is right.'
This to my Lady in a distant spot,
Upon the theme: *While mind is mastering clay,
Gross clay invades it.* If the spy you play,
My wife, read this! Strange love-talk, is it not?

XXXIV

Madam would speak with me. So, now it comes:
The Deluge or else Fire! She 's well; she thanks
My husbandship. Our chain on silence clanks.
Time leers between, above his twiddling thumbs.
Am I quite well? Most excellent in health!
The journals, too, I diligently peruse.
Vesuvius is expected to give news:
Niagara is no noisier. By stealth
Our eyes dart scrutinizing snakes. She 's glad
I 'm happy, says her quivering under-lip.   10
'And are not you?' 'How can I be?' 'Take ship!
For happiness is somewhere to be had.'
'Nowhere for me!' Her voice is barely heard.
I am not melted, and make no pretence.
With commonplace I freeze her, tongue and sense.
Niagara or Vesuvius is deferred.

XXXV

It is no vulgar nature I have wived.
Secretive, sensitive, she takes a wound
Deep to her soul, as if the sense had swooned,
And not a thought of vengeance had survived.
No confidences has she: but relief
Must come to one whose suffering is acute.
O have a care of natures that are mute!
They punish you in acts: their steps are brief.
What is she doing? What does she demand
From Providence or me? She is not one   *10*
Long to endure this torpidly, and shun
The drugs that crowd about a woman's hand.
At Forfeits during snow we played, and I
Must kiss her. 'Well performed!' I said: then she:
' 'Tis hardly worth the money, you agree?'
Save her? What for? To act this wedded lie!

XXXVI

My lady unto Madam makes her bow.
The charm of women is, that even while
You 're probed by them for tears, you yet may smile,
Nay, laugh outright, as I have done just now.
The interview was gracious: they anoint
(To me aside) each other with fine praise:
Discriminating compliments they raise,
That hit with wondrous aim on the weak point:
My Lady's nose of Nature might complain.
It is not fashioned aptly to express   *10*
Her character of large-browed steadfastness.
But Madam says: Thereof she may be vain!
Now, Madam's faulty feature is a glazed
And inaccessible eye, that has soft fires,
Wide gates, at love-time, only. This admires
My Lady. At the two I stand amazed.

XXXVII

Along the garden terrace, under which
A purple valley (lighted at its edge
By smoky torch-flame on the long cloud-ledge
Whereunder dropped the chariot) glimmers rich,
A quiet company we pace, and wait
The dinner-bell in prae-digestive calm.
So sweet up violet banks the Southern balm
Breathes round, we care not if the bell be late:
Though here and there grey seniors question Time
In irritable coughings. With slow foot   10
The low rosed moon, the face of Music mute,
Begins among her silent bars to climb.
As in and out, in silvery dusk, we thread,
I hear the laugh of Madam, and discern
My Lady's heel before me at each turn.
Our tragedy, is it alive or dead?

XXXVIII

Give to imagination some pure light
In human form to fix it, or you shame
The devils with that hideous human game:—
Imagination urging appetite!
Thus fallen have earth's greatest Gogmagogs,
Who dazzle us, whom we can not revere:
Imagination is the charioteer
That, in default of better, drives the hogs.
So, therefore, my dear Lady, let me love!
My soul is arrowy to the light in you.   10
You know me that I never can renew
The bond that woman broke: what would you have?
'Tis Love, or Vileness! not a choice between,
Save petrifaction! What does Pity here?
She killed a thing, and now it 's dead, 'tis dear.
Oh, when you counsel me, think what you mean!

XXXIX

She yields: my Lady in her noblest mood
Has yielded: she, my golden-crownëd rose!
The bride of every sense! more sweet than those
Who breathe the violet breath of maidenhood.
O visage of still music in the sky!
Soft moon! I feel thy song, my fairest friend!
True harmony within can apprehend
Dumb harmony without. And hark! 'tis nigh!
Belief has struck the note of sound: a gleam
Of living silver shows me where she shook   *10*
Her long white fingers down the shadowy brook,
That sings her song, half waking, half in dream.
What two come here to mar this heavenly tune?
A man is one: the woman bears my name,
And honour. Their hands touch! Am I still tame?
God, what a dancing spectre seems the moon!

XL

I bade my Lady think what she might mean.
Know I my meaning, I? Can I love one,
And yet be jealous of another? None
Commits such folly. Terrible Love, I ween,
Has might, even dead, half sighing to upheave
The lightless seas of selfishness amain:
Seas that in a man's heart have no rain
To fall and still them. Peace can I achieve,
By turning to this fountain-source of woe,
This woman, who 's to Love as fire to wood?   *10*
She breathed the violet breath of maidenhood
Against my kisses once! but I say, No!
The thing is mocked at! Helplessly afloat,
I know not what I do, whereto I strive.
The dread that my old love may be alive
Has seized my nursling new love by the throat.

XLI

How many a thing which we cast to the ground,
When others pick it up becomes a gem!
We grasp at all the wealth it is to them;
And by reflected light its worth is found.
Yet for us still 'tis nothing! and that zeal
Of false appreciation quickly fades.
This truth is little known to human shades,
How rare from their own instinct 'tis to feel!
They waste the soul with spurious desire,
That is not the ripe flame upon the bough.   *10*
We two have taken up a lifeless vow
To rob a living passion: dust for fire!
Madam is grave, and eyes the clock that tells
Approaching midnight. We have struck despair
Into two hearts. O, look we like a pair
Who for fresh nuptials joyfully yield all else?

XLII

I am to follow her. There is much grace
In women when thus bent on martyrdom.
They think that dignity of soul may come,
Perchance, with dignity of body. Base!
But I was taken by that air of cold
And statuesque sedateness, when she said
'I 'm going'; lit a taper, bowed her head,
And went, as with the stride of Pallas bold.
Fleshly indifference horrible! The hands
Of Time now signal: O, she 's safe from me!   *10*
Within those secret walls what do I see?
Where first she set the taper down she stands:
Not Pallas: Hebe shamed! Thoughts black as death
Like a stirred pool in sunshine break. Her wrists
I catch: she faltering, as she half resists,
'You love . . . ? love . . . ? love . . . ?' all on an in-
      drawn breath.

XLIII

Mark where the pressing wind shoots javelin-like
Its skeleton shadow on the broad-backed wave!
Here is a fitting spot to dig Love's grave;
Here where the ponderous breakers plunge and strike,
And dart their hissing tongues high up the sand:
In hearing of the ocean, and in sight
Of those ribbed wind-streaks running into white.
If I the death of Love had deeply planned,
I never could have made it half so sure,
As by the unblest kisses which upbraid   *10*
The full-waked sense; or failing that, degrade!
'Tis morning: but no morning can restore
What we have forfeited. I see no sin:
The wrong is mixed. In tragic life, God wot,
No villain need be! Passions spin the plot:
We are betrayed by what is false within.

XLIV

They say, that Pity in Love's service dwells,
A porter at the rosy temple's gate.
I missed him going: but it is my fate
To come upon him now beside his wells;
Whereby I know that I Love's temple leave,
And that the purple doors have closed behind.
Poor soul! if, in those early days unkind,
Thy power to sting had been but power to grieve,
We now might with an equal spirit meet,
And not be matched like innocence and vice.   *10*
She for the Temple's worship has paid price,
And takes the coin of Pity as a cheat.
She sees through simulation to the bone:
What 's best in her impels her to the worst:
Never, she cries, shall Pity soothe Love's thirst,
Or foul hypocrisy for truth atone!

XLV

It is the season of the sweet wild rose,
My Lady's emblem in the heart of me!
So golden-crownëd shines she gloriously,
And with that softest dream of blood she glows:
Mild as an evening heaven round Hesper bright!
I pluck the flower, and smell it, and revive
The time when in her eyes I stood alive.
I seem to look upon it out of Night.
Here 's Madam, stepping hastily. Her whims
Bid her demand the flower, which I let drop.   *10*
As I proceed, I feel her sharply stop,
And crush it under heel with trembling limbs.
She joins me in a cat-like way, and talks
Of company, and even condescends
To utter laughing scandal of old friends.
These are the summer days, and these our walks.

XLVI

At last we parley: we so strangely dumb
In such a close communion! It befell
About the sounding of the Matin-bell,
And lo! her place was vacant, and the hum
Of loneliness was round me. Then I rose,
And my disordered brain did guide my foot
To that old wood where our first love-salute
Was interchanged: the source of many throes!
There did I see her, not alone. I moved
Toward her, and made proffer of my arm.   *10*
She took it simply, with no rude alarm;
And that disturbing shadow passed reproved.
I felt the pained speech coming, and declared
My firm belief in her, ere she could speak.
A ghastly morning came into her cheek,
While with a widening soul on me she stared.

XLVII

We saw the swallows gathering in the sky,
And in the osier-isle we heard them noise.
We had not to look back on summer joys,
Or forward to a summer of bright dye:
But in the largeness of the evening earth
Our spirits grew as we went side by side.
The hour became her husband and my bride.
Love, that had robbed us so, thus blessed our dearth!
The pilgrims of the year waxed very loud
In multitudinous chatterings, as the flood   10
Full brown came from the West, and like pale blood
Expanded to the upper crimson cloud.
Love, that had robbed us of immortal things,
This little moment mercifully gave,
Where I have seen across the twilight wave
The swan sail with her young beneath her wings.

XLVIII

Their sense is with their senses all mixed in,
Destroyed by subtleties these women are!
More brain, O Lord, more brain! or we shall mar
Utterly this fair garden we might win.
Behold! I looked for peace, and thought it near.
Our inmost hearts had opened, each to each.
We drank the pure daylight of honest speech.
Alas! that was the fatal draught, I fear.
For when of my lost Lady came the word,
This woman, O this agony of flesh!   10
Jealous devotion bade her break the mesh,
That I might seek that other like a bird.
I do adore the nobleness! despise
The act! She has gone forth, I know not where.
Will the hard world my sentience of her share?
I feel the truth; so let the world surmise.

XLIX

He found her by the ocean's moaning verge.
Nor any wicked change in her discerned;
And she believed his old love had returned,
Which was her exultation, and her scourge.
She took his hand, and walked with him, and seemed
The wife he sought, though shadow-like and dry.
She had one terror, lest her heart should sigh,
And tell her loudly she no longer dreamed.
She dared not say, 'This is my breast: look in.'
But there 's a strength to help the desperate weak.   *10*
That night he learned how silence best can speak
The awful things when Pity pleads for Sin.
About the middle of the night her call
Was heard, and he came wondering to the bed.
'Now kiss me, dear! it may be, now!' she said.
Lethe had passed those lips, and he knew all.

L

Thus piteously Love closed what he begat:
The union of this ever-diverse pair!
These two were rapid falcons in a snare,
Condemned to do the flitting of the bat.
Lovers beneath the singing sky of May,
They wandered once; clear as the dew on flowers:
But they fed not on the advancing hours:
Their hearts held cravings for the buried day.
Then each applied to each that fatal knife,
Deep questioning, which probes to endless dole.   *10*
Ah, what a dusty answer gets the soul
When hot for certainties in this our life!—
In tragic hints here see what evermore
Moves dark as yonder midnight ocean's force,
Thundering like ramping hosts of warrior horse,
To throw that faint thin line upon the shore!

(1862)

MINOR PRE-RAPHAELITE POETS

WILLIAM MICHAEL ROSSETTI

(1829–1919)

Editor of *The Germ,* William Michael Rossetti was in effect both secretary and publicist for the PRB, the faithful recorder of the group's objectives and activities. Throughout a long life he issued journals, diaries, reminiscences, editions of Dante Gabriel's poems and Christina's—a great many of the primary sources upon which all students of Pre-Raphaelitism must depend. Though employed for nearly fifty years in the service of the Inland Revenue Board, he found time, apart from his self-imposed familial duties, to edit Shelley, Blake, and Whitman, to write a good deal of practical art criticism and reviews for periodicals, and to concern himself (as his brother refused to do) with liberal causes in society. His verses, as here, are aesthetically uneven and inadequate, but characteristically modest, and interesting as attempts to explain or to illustrate Pre-Raphaelite principles.

SONNET

(*for the cover of* The Germ)

When whoso merely hath a little thought
    Will plainly think the thought which is in him,—
    Not imaging another's bright or dim,
Not mangling with new words what others taught;
When whoso speaks, from having either sought
    Or only found,—will speak, not just to skim
    A shallow surface with words made and trim,
But in that very speech the matter brought:
Be not too keen to cry—"So this is all!—
    A thing I might myself have thought as well,   *10*
    But would not say it, for it was not worth!"
    Ask: "Is this truth?" For is it still to tell
    That, be the theme a point or the whole earth,
Truth is a circle, perfect, great or small?

                                                    (1850)

Fancies at Leisure

I IN SPRING

The sky is blue here, scarcely with a stain
Of grey for clouds: here the young grasses gain
A larger growth of green over this splinter
Fallen from the ruin. Spring seems to have told Winter
He shall not freeze again here. Tho' their loss
Of leaves is not yet quite repaired, trees toss
Sprouts from their boughs. The ash you called so stiff
Curves, daily, broader shadow down the cliff.

II IN SUMMER

How the rooks caw, and their beaks seem to clank!
    Let us just move out there,—(it might be cool   *10*

Under those trees,) and watch how the thick tank
  By the old mill is black,—a stagnant pool
Of rot and insects. There goes by a lank
  Dead hairy dog floating. Will Nature's rule
Of life return hither no more? The plank
  Rots in the crushed weeds, and the sun is cruel.

V THE FIRE SMOULDERING

I look into the burning coals, and see
    Faces and forms of things; but they soon pass,
    Melting one into other: the firm mass
Crumbles, and breaks, and fades gradually,   20
Shape into shape as in a dream may be,
    Into an image other than it was:
    And so on till the whole falls in, and has
Not any likeness,—face, and hand, and tree,
All gone. So with the mind: thought follows thought,
  This hastening, and that pressing upon this,
    A mighty crowd within so narrow room:
    And then at length heavy-eyed slumbers come,
  The drowsy fancies grope about, and miss
Their way, and what was so alive is nought.   30

                    (1850)

THE EVIL UNDER THE SUN

How long, oh Lord?—The voice is sounding still,
    Not only heard beneath the altar stone,
    Not heard of John Evangelist alone
In Patmos. It doth cry aloud and will
Between the earth's end and earth's end, until
    The day of the great reckoning, bone for bone,
    And blood for righteous blood, and groan for
      groan:
Then shall it cease on the air with a sudden thrill;

Not slowly growing fainter if the rod
   Strikes one or two amid the evil throng,
      Or one oppressor's hand is stayed and numbs,—
      Not till the vengeance that is coming comes:
For shall all hear the voice excepting God?
   Or God not listen, hearing?—Lord, how long?

                             (*1849*)

THOMAS WOOLNER

(1825–1892)

A member of the original PRB, Thomas Woolner aspired to be both sculptor and poet. Disheartened by his immediate prospects in either art in London, he sailed off in 1852 to seek his fortune in the Australian gold fields—his departure providing Ford Madox Brown the occasion for his dramatic painting "The Last of England." In his subsequent career (he was back in England within two years) Woolner achieved some success as a maker of portrait busts (his first was of Tennyson) and monumental statues, though little of his work in stone bears the impress of any great creative intensity. He also continued to write, but his late volumes—*Pygmalion* (1881), *Silenus* (1884), and *Tiresias* (1886)—no longer in any sense Pre-Raphaelite, are scarcely more animated than his sculptures. His most memorable poem remains "My Beautiful Lady," which he contributed to the first issue of *The Germ,* a piece still striking in its naive detail and its awkward angularity, its self-conscious "truth to nature."

MY BEAUTIFUL LADY

I love my lady; she is very fair;
Her brow is white, and bound by simple hair;

Her spirit sits aloof, and high,
Altho' it looks thro' her soft eye
Sweetly and tenderly.

As a young forest, when the wind drives thro',
My life is stirred when she breaks on my view.
Altho' her beauty has such power,
Her soul is like the simple flower
Trembling beneath a shower.   10

As bliss of saints, when dreaming of large wings,
The bloom around her fancied presence flings,
I feast and wile her absence, by
Pressing her choice hand passionately—
Imagining her sigh.

My lady's voice, altho' so very mild,
Maketh me feel as strong wine would a child;
My lady's touch, however slight,
Moves all my senses with its might,
Like to a sudden fright.   20

A hawk poised high in air, whose nerved wing-tips
Tremble with might suppressed, before he dips,—
In vigilance, not more intense
Than I; when her word's gentle sense
Makes full-eyed my suspense.

Her mention of a thing—august or poor,
Makes it seem nobler than it was before:
As where the sun strikes, life will gush,
And what is pale receive a flush,
Rich hues—a richer blush.   30

My lady's name, if I hear strangers use,—
Not meaning her—seems like a lax misuse.
I love none but my lady's name;
Rose, Maud, or Grace, are all the same,
So blank, so very tame.

Illustration by Holman Hunt of Thomas Woolner's
"My Beautiful Lady" in The Germ, *1850*

My lady walks as I have seen a swan
Swim thro' the water just where the sun shone.
    There ends of willow branches ride,
    Quivering with the current's glide,
    By the deep river-side.   40

Whene'er she moves there are fresh beauties stirred;
As the sunned bosom of a humming-bird
    At each pant shows some fiery hue,
    Burns gold, intensest green or blue:
    The same, yet ever new.

What time she walketh under flowering May,
I am quite sure the scented blossoms say,
    "O lady with the sunlit hair!
    "Stay, and drink our odorous air—
    "The incense that we bear: 50

"Your beauty, lady, we would ever shade;
"Being near you, our sweetness might not fade."
    If trees could be broken-hearted,
    I am sure that the green sap smarted,
    When my lady parted.

This is why I thought weeds were beautiful;—
Because one day I saw my lady pull
    Some weeds up near a little brook,
    Which home most carefully she took,
    Then shut them in a book.   60

A deer when startled by the stealthy ounce,—
A bird escaping from the falcon's trounce,
    Feels his heart swell as mine, when she
    Stands statelier, expecting me,
    Than tall white lilies be.

The first white flutter of her robe to trace,
Where binds and perfumed jasmine interlace,

Expands my gaze triumphantly:
Even such his gaze, who sees on high
His flag, for victory.   70

We wander forth unconsciously, because
The azure beauty of the evening draws:
    When sober hues pervade the ground,
    And life in one vast hush seems drowned,
    Air stirs so little sound.

We thread a copse where frequent bramble spray
With loose obtrusion from the side roots stray,
    (Forcing sweet pauses on our walk):
    I'll lift one with my foot, and talk
    About its leaves and stalk.   80

Or may be that the prickles of some stem
Will hold a prisoner her long garment's hem;
    To disentangle it I kneel,
    Oft wounding more than I can heal;
    It makes her laugh, my zeal.

Then on before a thin-legged robin hops,
Or leaping on a twig, he pertly stops,
    Speaking a few clear notes, till nigh
    We draw, when quickly he will fly
    Into a bush close by.   90

A flock of goldfinches may stop their flight,
And wheeling round a birchen tree alight
    Deep in its glittering leaves, until
    They see us, when their swift rise will
    Startle a sudden thrill.

I recollect my lady in a wood,
Keeping her breath and peering—(firm she stood
    Her slim shape balanced on tiptoe—)
    Into a nest which lay below,
    Leaves shadowing her brow.   100

I recollect my lady asking me,
What that sharp tapping in the wood might be?
    I told her blackbirds made it, which,
    For slimy morsels they count rich,
    Cracked the snail's curling niche:

She made no answer. When we reached the stone
Where the shell fragments on the grass were strewn,
    Close to the margin of a rill;
    "The air," she said, "seems damp and chill,
    "We'll go home if you will."   *110*

"Make not my pathway dull so soon," I cried,
"See how those vast cloudpiles in sun-glow dyed,
    "Roll out their splendour: while the breeze
    "Lifts gold from leaf to leaf, as these
    "Ash saplings move at ease."

Piercing the silence in our ears, a bird
Threw some notes up just then, and quickly stirred
    The covert birds that startled, sent
    Their music thro' the air; leaves lent
    Their rustling and blent,   *120*

Until the whole of the blue warmth was filled
So much with sun and sound, that the air thrilled.
    She gleamed, wrapt in the dying day's
    Glory: altho' she spoke no praise,
    I saw much in her gaze.

Then, flushed with resolution, I told all;—
The mighty love I bore her,—how would pall
    My very breath of life, if she
    For ever breathed not hers with me;—
    Could I a cherub be,   *130*

How, idly hoping to enrich her grace,
I would snatch jewels from the orbs of space;—
    Then back thro' the vague distance beat,

Glowing with joy her smile to meet,
And heap them round her feet.

Her waist shook to my arm. She bowed her head,
Silent, with hands clasped and arms straightened:
    (Just then we both heard a church bell)
    O God! It is not right to tell:
    But I remember well   *140*

Each breast swelled with its pleasure, and her whole
Bosom grew heavy with love; the swift roll
    Of new sensations dimmed her eyes,
    Half closing them in ecstacies,
    Turned full against the skies.

The rest is gone; it seemed a whirling round—
No pressure of my feet upon the ground:
    But even when parted from her, bright
    Showed all; yea, to my throbbing sight
    The dark was starred with light.   *150*

                    (1850)

EMBLEMS

I lay through one long afternoon,
  Vacantly plucking the grass.
I lay on my back, with steadfast gaze
  Watching the cloud-shapes pass;
Until the evening's chilly damps
  Rose from the hollows below,
  Where the cold marsh-reeds grow.

I saw the sun sink down behind
  The high point of a mountain;
Its last light lingered on the weeds   *10*
  That choked a shattered fountain,

Where lay a rotting bird, whose plumes
   Had beat the air in soaring.
   On these things I was poring:—

The sun seemed like my sense of life,
   Now weak, that was so strong;
The fountain—that continual pulse
   Which throbbed with human song:
The bird lay dead as that wild hope
   Which nerved my thoughts when young.   *20*
   These symbols had a tongue,

And told the dreary lengths of years
   I must drag my weight with me;
Or be like a mastless ship stuck fast
   On a deep, stagnant sea.
A man on a dangerous height alone,
   If suddenly struck blind,
   Will never his home path find.

When divers plunge for ocean's pearls,
   And chance to strike a rock,   *30*
Who plunged with greatest force below
   Receives the heaviest shock.
With nostrils wide and breath drawn in,
   I rushed resolved on the race;
   Then, stumbling, fell in the chase.

Yet with time's cycles forests swell
   Where stretched a desert plain:
Time's cycles make the mountains rise
   Where heaved the restless main:
On swamps where moped the lonely stork,   *40*
   In the silent lapse of time
   Stands a city in its prime.

I thought: then saw the broadening shade
   Grow slowly over the mound,

That reached with one long level slope
    Down to a rich vineyard ground:
The air about lay still and hushed,
    As if in serious thought:
    But I scarcely heeded aught,

Till I heard, hard by, a thrush break forth,   50
    Shouting with his whole voice,
So that he made the distant air
    And the things around rejoice.
My soul gushed, for the sound awoke
    Memories of early joy:
    I sobbed like a chidden boy.

(1850)

ELIZABETH SIDDAL ROSSETTI

(1834–1862)

Discovered as a milliner's assistant by Walter Deverell early in the 1850s, Elizabeth Siddal seemed to all the Pre-Raphaelites a perfect "stunner," the ideal model for painting, the exciting type of a new beauty. To Dante Gabriel Rossetti, who immediately made her his own protégée, she was all this and far more, the very incarnation of his troubled dreams, the woman prefigured by his imagination—his Blessed Damozel and his Beata Beatrix. In less solemn terms, she soon became The Sid, Guggums, or Ida (for she had the dignity of Tennyson's Princess). Under Rossetti's tutelage and with Ruskin's encouragement she began to draw and to write verse; and her work, concerned all with love and death and hopeless yearning, suggests both a fragile talent and a strange sad submission to the will of her master. After a long courtship during much of which she was a semi-invalid, Rossetti married Elizabeth in May, 1860. Less than two years later, she died—ill and neurotic—from a deliberate overdose of sedative. Rossetti's art, which had anticipated her beauty, remained until the end haunted by the memory of her presence.

"Beata Beatrix," crayon drawing by Dante Gabriel Rossetti, 1869, an idealized memory-portrait of Elizabeth Siddal Rossetti. Courtesy of the Fogg Art Museum, Harvard University, Grenville L. Winthrop Bequest

DEAD LOVE

Oh never weep for love that's dead,
   Since love is seldom true,
But changes his fashion from blue to red,
   From brightest red to blue,
And love was born to an early death
   And is so seldom true.

Then harbour no smile on your loving face
   To win the deepest sigh;
The fairest words on truest lips
   Pass off and surely die;   *10*
And you will stand alone, my dear,
   When wintry winds draw nigh.

Sweet, never weep for what cannot be,
   For this God has not given:
If the merest dream of love were true,
   Then, sweet, we should be in heaven;
And this is only earth, my dear,
   Where true love is not given.

                            (1855–1857?)

SPEECHLESS

Many a mile o'er land and sea
Unsummoned my Love returned to me;
I remember not the words he said,
But only the trees mourning overhead.
And he came ready to take and bear
The cross I had carried for many a year:
But my words came slowly one by one
From frozen lips that were still and dumb.
How sounded my words so still and slow
To the great strong heart that loved me so?   *10*
Ah I remember, my God, so well,

How my brain lay dumb in a frozen spell;
And I leaned away from my lover's face
To watch the dead leaves that were running a race.
I felt the spell that held my breath,
Bending me down to a living death—
As if hope lay buried when he had come
Who knew my sorrows all and some.

(1855–1857?)

SHEPHERD TURNED SAILOR

Now Christ thee save, thou bonny Shepherd,
    Sailing on the sea;
Ten thousand souls are sailing there
    But I belong to thee.
If thou art lost then all is lost
    And all is dead to me.

My love should have a grey head-stone
    And green moss at his feet,
And clinging grass above his breast
    Whereon his lambs could bleat;   10
And I should know the span of earth
    Where one day I might sleep.

(1855–1857?)

A YEAR AND A DAY

Slow days have passed that make a year,
    Slow hours that make a day,
Since I could take my first dear love,
    And kiss him the old way:
Yet the green leaves touch me on the cheek,
    Dear Christ, this month of May.

I lie among the tall green grass
    That bends above my head,

And covers up my wasted face,
   And folds me in its bed   *10*
Tenderly and lovingly
   Like grass above the dead.

Dim phantoms of an unknown ill
   Float through my tiring brain:
The unformed visions of my life
   Pass by in ghostly train;
Some pause to touch me on the cheek,
   Some scatter tears like rain.

The river ever running down
   Between its grassy bed,   *20*
The voices of a thousand birds
   That clang above my head,
Shall bring to me a sadder dream
   When this sad dream is dead.

A silence falls upon my heart,
   And hushes all its pain.
I stretch my hands in the long grass,
   And fall to sleep again,
There to lie empty of all love,
   Like beaten corn of grain.   *30*

(1857?)

AT LAST

O mother, open the window wide
   And let the daylight in;
The hills grow darker to my sight,
   And thoughts begin to swim.

And, mother dear, take my young son
   (Since I was born of thee),
And care for all his little ways,
   And nurse him on thy knee.

And, mother, wash my pale, pale hands,
 And then bind up my feet;   *10*
My body may no longer rest
 Out of its winding-sheet.

And, mother, take a sapling twig
 And green grass newly mown,
And lay them on my empty bed,
 That my sorrow be not known.

And, mother, find three berries red
 And pluck them from the stalk,
And burn them at the first cockcrow,
 That my spirit may not walk.   *20*

And, mother dear, break a willow wand,
 And if the sap be even,
Then save it for my lover's sake,
 And he'll know my soul's in heaven.

And, mother, when the big tears fall
 (And fall, God knows, they may),
Tell him I died of my great love,
 And my dying heart was gay.

And, mother dear, when the sun has set,
 And the pale church grass waves,   *30*
Then carry me through the dim twilight
 And hide me among the graves.

           (1862?)

WILLIAM ALLINGHAM

(1824–1889)

Introduced to the first Pre-Raphaelite group by Coventry
Patmore, William Allingham, Irish civil servant, poet, and
dramatist, wrote most of his best lyrics during the period
of his close friendship with Rossetti. His 1855 volume of
verses, *The Music Master,* enjoyed the distinction of carry-
ing nine Pre-Raphaelite illustrations, among them Ros-
setti's drawing for "The Maids of Elfin-Mere." On the
whole, however, his work is scarcely Pre-Raphaelite, ex-
cept perhaps in its recurrent nostalgia for a lost time, its
celebration of meaningful moments and impressions, and
its rigid rejection of overt didactic purpose. And most
of his later pieces, including the long narrative poem
Laurence Bloomfield in Ireland (1864), bear no relation
at all to the poetic practice of the Brotherhood.

THE FAIRIES

Up the airy mountain,
    Down the rushy glen,
We daren't go a-hunting
    For fear of little men;
Wee folk, good folk,
    Trooping all together;

Green jacket, red cap,
　And white owl's feather!

Down along the rocky shore
　Some make their home,　　　　　　　　　*10*
They live on crispy pancakes
　Of yellow tide-foam;
Some in the reeds
　Of the black mountain lake,
With frogs for their watch-dogs,
　All night awake.

High on the hill-top
　The old King sits;
He is now so old and gray
　He's nigh lost his wits.　　　　　　　　　*20*
With a bridge of white mist
　Columbkill he crosses,
On his stately journeys
　From Slieveleague to Rosses;

Or going up with music
　On cold starry nights,
To sup with the Queen
　Of the gay Northern Lights.

They stole little Bridget
　For seven years long;　　　　　　　　　*30*
When she came down again
　Her friends were all gone.
They took her lightly back,
　Between the night and morrow,
They thought that she was fast asleep,
　But she was dead with sorrow.
They have kept her ever since
　Deep within the lake,
On a bed of flag-leaves,
　Watching till she wake.　　　　　　　　　*40*

By the craggy hill-side,
   Through the mosses bare,
They have planted thorn-trees
   For pleasure here and there.
Is any man so daring
   As dig them up in spite,
He shall find their sharpest thorns
   In his bed at night.

Up the airy mountain,
   Down the rushy glen,   50
We daren't go a-hunting
   For fear of little men;
Wee folk, good folk,
   Trooping all together;
Green jacket, red cap,
   And white owl's feather.

                                (1850)

THE WITCH-BRIDE

A fair witch crept to a young man's side,
And he kiss'd her and took her for his bride.

But a Shape came in at the dead of night,
And fill'd the room with snowy light.

And he saw how in his arms there lay
A thing more frightful than mouth may say.

And he rose in haste, and follow'd the Shape
Till morning crown'd an eastern cape.

And he girded himself, and follow'd still
When sunset sainted the western hill.   10

But, mocking and thwarting, clung to his side,
Weary day!—the foul Witch-Bride.

                                (1855)

FOUR DUCKS ON A POND

Four ducks on a pond,
A grass-bank beyond,
A blue sky of spring,
White clouds on the wing;
What a little thing
To remember for years—
To remember with tears!

(1854)

EVERYTHING PASSES

Everything passes and vanishes;
  Everything leaves its trace;
And often you see in a footstep
  What you could not see in a face.

(1889)

THE MAIDS OF ELFIN-MERE

When the spinning-room was here,
Came Three Damsels, clothed in white,
With their spindles every night;
One and two and three fair Maidens,
Spinning to a pulsing cadence,
Singing songs of Elfin-Mere;
Till the eleventh hour was toll'd,
Then departed through the wold.
    Years ago, and years ago;
    And the tall reeds sigh as the wind doth blow.   *10*

Three white Lilies, calm and clear,
And they were loved by every one;
Most of all, the Pastor's Son,
Listening to their gentle singing,

Illustration by Dante Gabriel Rossetti of William Allingham's "The Maids of Elfin-Mere"

Felt his heart go from him, clinging
To these Maids of Elfin-Mere;
Sued each night to make them stay,
Saddened when they went away.
      Years ago, and years ago;
      And the tall reeds sigh as the wind doth blow.   20

Hands that shook with love and fear
Dared put back the village clock,—
Flew the spindle, turned the rock,
Flowed the song with subtle rounding,
Till the false "eleven" was sounding;
Then these Maids of Elfin-Mere
Swiftly, softly left the room,
Like three doves on snowy plume.
      Years ago, and years ago;
      And the tall reeds sigh as the wind doth blow.   30

One that night who wandered near
Heard lamentings by the shore,
Saw at dawn three stains of gore
In the waters fade and dwindle.
Never more with song and spindle
Saw we Maids of Elfin-Mere.
The Pastor's Son did pine and die;
Because true love should never lie.
      Years ago, and years ago;
      And the tall reeds sigh as the wind doth blow.   40
                                        (1855)

RICHARD WATSON DIXON

(1833–1900)

Richard Watson Dixon was a Pre-Raphaelite both by association and, in his early work, by practice. Edward Burne-Jones was his classmate at school in Birmingham, and William Morris became his close friend at Oxford. With Morris and Burne-Jones he projected the Pre-Raphaelite *Oxford and Cambridge Magazine* and joined Rossetti's crew in painting the murals of the Oxford Union. He was ordained a curate in 1858, and in the next year he officiated at the marriage of Morris to Jane Burden. His first two volumes, *Christ's Company and Other Poems* (1861) and *Historical Odes* (1864), were distinctly Pre-Raphaelite in tone, explicit in sharply etched detail, possessed of a troubled wonder. Most of his later energies went into his vocation as clergyman (as a minor canon of Carlisle Cathedral and as a country vicar) and his painstaking research on Anglicanism, which culminated in his six-volume *History of the Church of England from the Abolition of the Roman Jurisdiction.* But in 1878 he opened a remarkable correspondence with Gerard Manley Hopkins, whom he had tutored years before in London; and with the stimulus of Hopkins' criticism he wrote several new books of verse, each scholarly and conscientious but all lacking in the old Pre-Raphaelite intensity.

ST. MARY MAGDALENE

Kneeling before the altar step,
   Her white face stretched above her hands;
In one great line her body thin
Rose robed right upwards to her chin;
Her hair rebelled in golden bands,
     And filled her hands;

Which likewise held a casket rare
   Of alabaster at that tide;
Simeon was there and looked at her,
Trancedly kneeling, sick and fair;   *10*
Three parts the light her features tried,
     The rest implied.

Strong singing reached her from within,
   Discordant, but with weighty rhymes;
Her swaying body kept the stave;
Then all the woods about her wave,
She heard, and saw, in mystic mimes,
     Herself three times.

Once, in the doorway of a house,
   With yellow lintels painted fair,   *20*
Very far off, where no men pass,
Green and red banners hung in mass
Above scorched woodwork wormed and bare,
     And spider's snare.

She, scarlet in her form and gold,
   Fallen down upon her hands and knees,
Her arms and bosom bare and white,
Her long hair streaming wild with light,
Felt all the waving of the trees,
     And hum of bees.   *30*

A rout of mirth within the house,
   Upon the ear of madness fell,

Stunned with its dread, yet made intense;
A moment, and might issue thence
Upon the prey they quested well,
    Seven fiends of hell.

She grovelled on her hands and knees,
   She bit her breath against that rout;
Seven devils inhabited within,
Each acting upon each his sin,   40
Limb locked in limb, snout turning snout,
    And these would out.

Twice, and the woods lay far behind,
   Gold corn spread broad from slope to slope;
The copses rounded in faint light,
Far from her pathway gleaming white,
Which gleamed and wound in narrow scope,
    Her narrow hope.

She on the valley stood and hung,
   Then downward swept with steady haste;   50
The steady wind behind her sent
Her robe before her as she went;
Descending on the wind, she chased
    The form she traced.

She, with her blue eyes blind with flight,
   Rising and falling in their cells,
Hands held as though she played a harp,
Teeth glistening as in laughter sharp,
Flew ghostly on, a strength like hell's,
    When it rebels.   60

Behind her, flaming on and on,
   Rushing and streaming as she flew;
Moved over hill as if through vale,
Through vale as if o'er hill, no fail;
Her bosom trembled as she drew
    Her long breath through.

Thrice, with an archway overhead,
  Beneath, what might have seemed a tomb;
White garments fallen fold on fold,
As if limbs yet were in their hold,   70
Drew the light further in the gloom,
    Of the dark room.

She, fallen without thought or care,
  Heard, as it were, a ceaseless flow
Of converse muttered in her ear,
Like waters sobbing wide and near,
About things happened long ago
    Of utter woe.

                            (1861)

EUNICE

When her holy life was ended
  Eunice lay upon her side;
When her holy death was ended
  Eunice died.

Then a spirit raised her spirit
  From the urn of dripping tears;
And a spirit from her spirit
  Soothed the fears.

And upon her spirit lightly—
  Spirit upon spirit wrote;   10
And she rose to worlds eternal,
  Taking note.

First she joined the world eternal
  Which is never seen of men;
Through its climes she wandered lightly,
  Happy then.

Then she learned a song of comfort
   For the loves she left behind,
Children kissing one another,
   Husband kind.   *20*

I have joined the world of spirit,
   Which the flesh does never see;
But to you a realm is open
   As to me.

World invisible of spirit
   Doth invisible remain
Not less certainly to angels
   Than to men.

As you see it not on earth
   I behold it not in heaven;   *30*
Yet to both of us alike
   It is given.

For we both may walk within it,
   And meet blindfolded above;
'Tis the world of thought and feeling
   And of love.

Enter then this world of spirit;
   It is yours by right of birth,
Mine by death: let heaven possess it,
   And let earth.   *40*

(1861)

DREAM

I

With camel's hair I clothed my skin,
   I fed my mouth with honey wild;

And set me scarlet wool to spin,
   And all my breast with hyssop filled;
Upon my brow and cheeks and chin
   A bird's blood spilled.

I took a broken reed to hold,
   I took a sponge of gall to press;
I took weak water-weeds to fold
   About my sacrificial dress.   *10*

I took the grasses of the field,
   The flax was bolled upon my crine;
And ivy thorn and wild grapes healed
   To make good wine.

I took my scrip of manna sweet,
   My cruse of water did I bless;
I took the white dove by the feet,
   And flew into the wilderness.

11

The tiger came and played;
Uprose the lion in his mane;   *20*
The jackal's tawny nose
And sanguine dripping tongue
Out of the desert rose
And plunged its sands among;
The bear came striding o'er the desert plain.

Uprose the horn and eyes
And quivering flank of the great unicorn,
And galloped round and round;
Uprose the gleaming claw
Of the leviathan, and wound   *30*
In steadfast march did draw
Its course away beyond the desert's bourn.

I stood within a maze
Woven round about me by a magic art,

And ordered circle-wise:
The bear more near did tread,
And with two fiery eyes,
And with a wolfish head,
Did close the circle round in every part.

III

With scarlet corded horn,   40
With frail wrecked knees and stumbling pace,
The scapegoat came:
His eyes took flesh and spirit dread in flame
At once, and he died looking towards my face.

                                                    (1861)

DAWNING

Over the hill I have watched the dawning,
I have watched the dawn of morning light,
Because I cannot well sleep by night,
Every day I have watched the dawning.
And to-day very early my window shook
With the cold wind fresh from the ghastly brook,
And I left my bed to watch the dawning.
Very cold was the light, very pale, very still,
And the wind blew great clouds over the hill
Towards the wet place of the dying dawning;   10
It blew them over towards the east
In heavier charge as the light increased,
From the very death of the dying dawning.
Whence did the clouds come over the hill?
I cannot tell, for no clouds did fill
The clear space opposite the dawning
Right over the hill, long, low, and pearl-grey,
Set in the wind to live as it may;
And as the light increased from the dawning,
The cold, cold brook unto my seeming   20
Did intermit its ghastly gleaming
And ran forth brighter in the dawning.

The wall-fruit stretched along the wall,
The pear-tree waved its banners tall;
Then close beside me in the dawning,
I saw thy face so stonily grey,
And the close lips no word did say,
The eyes confessed not in the dawning.
I saw a man ride through the light
Upon the hill-top, out of sight   30
Of me and thee and all the dawning.

(1861)

WAITING

By the ancient sluice's gate
Here I wait, here I wait;
Here is the sluice with its cramped stone,
Which the shadows dance upon.
                    Here I wait.

Stone, with time-blots red and blue,
And white, the shadows tremble through,
When the sun strikes out through the poplars tall,
And the sun strikes out upon the wall.
                    Here I wait.   10

From the sluice the stream descends
A bowshot; then its running ends
In flags and marsh flowers; then it runs
Bright and broad beneath the suns.
                    Here I wait.

And to one side of it come down
The walls and roofs of our good town;
The other side for miles away
The willows prick it short and grey.
                    Here I wait.   20

Any moment I might see
My lady in her majesty
Moving on from tree to tree
Where the river runs from me.
                    Here I wait.

Any moment she might rise
From the hedgerow, where my eyes
Wait for her without surprise,
While the first bat starts and flies.
                    Here I wait.   30

Here I lie along the trunk
That swings the heavy sluice-door sunk
In the water, which outstreams
In little runlets from its seams.
                    Here I wait.

The last yellowhammer flits,
The winds begin to shake by fits;
More coldly swing the mists and chase:
Thinking of my lady's face
                    Here I wait.   40

Like a tower so standeth she,
Built of solid ivory;
Her sad eyes well opened be,
Her wide hair runs darkly free.
                    Here I wait.

Her eyes are like to water-birds
On little rivers, and her words
As little as the lark, which girds
His wings to measure out his words.
                    Here I wait.   50

Here the crows come flying late—
One flies past me; past the gate

Of the old sluice another flies;
Heavily upwards they do rise.
>   Here I wait.

I am growing thoughtful now;
Will she never kiss my brow?
Solemnly I sit and feel
The edge upon my sword of steel.
>   Here I wait.   60

If she come, her feet will sound
Not at all upon the ground;
I think upon thy feet, my love,
Red as feet of any dove.
>   Here I wait.

Here my face is white and cold,
Here my empty arms I fold;
Here float down the beds of weeds,
With the fly that on them feeds.
>   Here I wait.   70

>   (1861)

SONG

The feathers of the willow
Are half of them grown yellow
>   Above the swelling stream;
And ragged are the bushes,
And rusty now the rushes,
>   And wild the clouded gleam.

The thistle now is older,
His stalk begins to moulder,
>   His head is white as snow;
The branches all are barer,   10
The linnet's song is rarer,
>   The robin pipeth now.

>   (1864)

ARTHUR O'SHAUGHNESSY

(1848–1881)

A shy, silent herpetologist in the British Museum, Arthur O'Shaughnessy surprised his associates in 1870 by issuing his passionate *Epic of Women*. The volume at once won the approval of Rossetti and Swinburne, both of whom were obvious influences on its manner and matter. *Lays of France* (1872) and *Music and Moonlight* (1874) established O'Shaughnessy's reputation as a minor Pre-Raphaelite, and marriage to a fragile beauty, Eleanor Marston, sister of the blind poet Philip Bourke Marston, linked him personally to the third Pre-Raphaelite circle. Though his own verse was severely limited in range, his knowledge of contemporary French writers, especially Baudelaire, brought a new note into English poetry of the seventies, and his sympathy with the doctrine of art for art's sake, which is clearly evident in his posthumously published *Songs of a Worker* (1881), anticipated the new concerns of the Aesthetic Movement of the eighties.

ODE

We are the music makers,
   And we are the dreamers of dreams,
Wandering by lone sea-breakers,
   And sitting by desolate streams;—

World-losers and world-forsakers,
  On whom the pale moon gleams:
Yet we are the movers and shakers
  Of the world for ever, it seems.

With wonderful deathless ditties
We build up the world's great cities,   *10*
  And out of a fabulous story
  We fashion an empire's glory:
One man with a dream at pleasure,
  Shall go forth and conquer a crown;
And three with a new song's measure
  Can trample a kingdom down.

We, in the ages lying
  In the buried past of the earth,
Built Nineveh with our sighing,
  And Babel itself in our mirth;   *20*
And o'erthrew them with prophesying
  To the old of the new world's worth;
For each age is a dream that is dying,
  Or one that is coming to birth.

A breath of our inspiration
Is the life of each generation;
  A wondrous thing of our dreaming
  Unearthly, impossible seeming—
The soldier, the king, and the peasant
  Are working together in one,   *30*
Till our dream shall become their present,
  And their work in the world be done.

They had no vision amazing
Of the goodly house they are raising;
  They had no divine foreshowing
  Of the land to which they are going:
But on one man's soul it hath broken,
  A light that doth not depart;

And his look, or a word he hath spoken,
  Wrought flame in another man's heart.   *40*

And therefore to-day is thrilling
With a past day's late fulfilling;
  And the multitudes are enlisted
  In the faith that their fathers resisted,
And, scorning the dream of to-morrow,
  Are bringing to pass, as they may,
In the world, for its joy or its sorrow,
  The dream that was scorned yesterday.

But we, with our dreaming and singing,
  Ceaseless and sorrowless we!   *50*
The glory about us clinging
  Of the glorious futures we see,
Our souls with high music ringing:
  O men! it must ever be
That we dwell, in our dreaming and singing,
  A little apart from ye.

For we are afar with the dawning
  And the suns that are not yet high,
And out of the infinite morning
  Intrepid you hear us cry—   *60*
How, spite of your human scorning,
  Once more God's future draws nigh,
And already goes forth the warning
  That ye of the past must die.

Great hail! we cry to the comers
  From the dazzling unknown shore;
Bring us hither your sun and your summers,
  And renew our world as of yore;
You shall teach us your song's new numbers,
  And things that we dreamed not before: *70*
Yea, in spite of a dreamer who slumbers,
  And a singer who sings no more.

                                              (1874)

THE CYPRESS

O Ivory bird, that shakest thy wan plumes,
    And dost forget the sweetness of thy throat
    For a most strange and melancholy note—
That wilt forsake the summer and the blooms
    And go to winter in a place remote!

The country where thou goest, Ivory bird!
    It hath no pleasant nesting-place for thee;
    There are no skies nor flowers fair to see,
Nor any shade at noon—as I have heard—
    But the black shadow of the Cypress tree.   *10*

The Cypress tree, it groweth on a mound;
    And sickly are the flowers it hath of May,
    Full of a false and subtle spell are they;
For whoso breathes the scent of them around,
    He shall not see the happy Summer day.

In June, it bringeth forth, O Ivory bird!
    A winter berry, bitter as the sea;
    And whoso eateth of it, woe is he—
He shall fall pale, and sleep—as I have heard—
    Long in the shadow of the Cypress tree.   *20*

                  (1870)

TO A YOUNG MURDERESS

Fair yellow murderess, whose gilded head
    Gleaming with deaths; whose deadly body white,
Writ o'er with secret records of the dead;
    Whose tranquil eyes, that hide the dead from sight
Down in their tenderest depth and bluest bloom;
    Whose strange unnatural grace, whose prolonged youth,
Are for my death now and the shameful doom
    Of all the man I might have been in truth,

Your fell smile, sweetened still, lest I might shun
   Its lingering murder, with a kiss for lure,   *10*
Is like the fascinating steel that one
   Most vengeful in his last revenge, and sure
The victim lies beneath him, passes slow,
   Again and oft again before his eyes,
And over all his frame, that he may know
   And suffer the whole death before he dies.

Will you not slay me? Stab me; yea, somehow,
   Deep in the heart: say some foul word to last,
And let me hate you as I love you now.
   Oh, would I might but see you turn and cast   *20*
That false fair beauty that you e'en shall lose,
   And fall down there and writhe about my feet,
The crooked loathly viper I shall bruise
   Through all eternity:—
                    Nay, kiss me, Sweet!

                           (1874)

THE GREAT ENCOUNTER

Such as I am become, I walked one day
Along a sombre and descending way,
Not boldly, but with dull and desperate thought:
Then one who seemed an angel—for 'twas He,
My old aspiring self, no longer *Me*—
Came up against me terrible, and sought
To slay me with the dread I had to see
His sinless and exalted brow. We fought;
And, full of hate, he smote me, saying, "Thee
I curse this hour: go downward to thine hell."   *10*
And in that hour I felt his curse and fell.

                           (1874)

SONG

When the Rose came I loved the Rose,
  And thought of none beside,
Forgetting all the other flowers,
  And all the others died;
And morn and noon, and sun and showers,
And all things loved the Rose,
  Who only half returned my love,
Blooming alike for those.

I was the rival of a score
  Of loves on gaudy wing,   10
The nightingale I would implore
  For pity not to sing;
Each called her his; still I was glad
  To wait or take my part;
I loved the Rose—who might have had
  The fairest lily's heart.

(1881)

EDEN

Weary and wandering, hand in hand,
  Through ways and cities rough,
And with a law in every land
  Written against our love,
We set our hearts to seek and find,
Forgotten now and out of mind,
  Lost Eden garden desolate,
Hoping the angel would be kind,
  And let us pass the gate.

We turned into the lawless waste   10
  Wild outer gardens of the world—
We heard awhile our footsteps chased,
  Men's curses at us hurled;

But safe at length, we came and found,
Open with ruined wall all round,
   Lost Eden garden desolate;
No angel stood to guard the ground
   At Eden garden gate.

We crossed the flower-encumbered floor,
   And wandered up and down the place,   20
And marvelled at the open door
   And all the desolate grace
And beast and bird with joy and song
That broke man's laws the whole day long;
   For all was free in Eden waste:
There seemed no rule of right and wrong,
   No fruit we might not taste.

Our hearts, o'erwhelmed with many a word
   Of bitter scathing, human blame,
Trembled with what they late had heard,   30
   And fear upon us came,
Till, finding the forbidden tree,
We ate the fruit, and stayed to see
   If God would chide our wickedness;
No God forbade my love and me
   In Eden wilderness.

The rose has overgrown the bower
   In lawless Eden garden waste,
The eastern flower and western flower
   Have met and interlaced;   40
The trees have joined above and twined
And shut out every cruel wind
   That from the world was blown:
Ah, what a place for love to find
   Is Eden garden grown!

The fair things exiled from the earth
   Have found the way there in a dream;

The phoenix has its fiery birth
  And nests there in the gleam;
Love's self, with draggled rainbow wings,   50
At rest now from his wanderings,
  In Eden beds and bowers hath lain
So long, no wealth of worldly kings
  Will win him back again.

And now we need not fear to kiss;
  The serpent is our playfellow,
And tempts us on from bliss to bliss,
  No man can see or know.
Love was turned out of Eden first
By God, and then of man accurst;   60
  And fleeing long from human hate,
And counting man's hard laws the worst,
  Returned to Eden gate.

Now every creature there obeys
  Exuberantly his lawless power;
The wall is overthrown, the ways
  Ruined by bird and flower;
The nuptial riot of the rose
Runs on for centuries and grows;
  The great heart of the place is strong—   70
It swells in overmastering throes
  Of passionate sigh and song.

And while we joy in Eden's state,
  Outside men serve a loveless lord;
They think the angel guards the gate
  With burning fiery sword!
Ah, fools! he fled an age ago,
The roses pressed upon him so,
  And all the perfume from within,
And he forgot or did not know;   80
  Eden must surely win.

                                    (1881)

PHILIP BOURKE MARSTON

(1850–1887)

Philip Bourke Marston was the son of the spasmodic poet-
dramatist J. Westland Marston and the godson of "Festus"
Bailey. Blind from early childhood, he found relief in
literature from the burdens of an unhappy life marked
by many deprivations. Befriended by both Rossetti and
Swinburne and encouraged by Arthur O'Shaughnessy,
who became his brother-in-law, Marston published three
volumes of verse, *Song-Tide* (1871), *All in All* (1874),
and *Wind-Voices* (1883), and composed a number of other
pieces issued posthumously. Many of his poems were son-
nets, heavily indebted in both style and substance to Ros-
setti's *House of Life*.

IN MEMORY OF D. G. ROSSETTI

What wreath have I above thy rest to place,
   What worthy song-wreath, Friend,—nay, more than
      friend?
   For so thou didst all other men transcend
That the pure, fiery worship of old days—
That of the boy, content to hear, to gaze—
   Burned on most brightly; though as lamps none tend
   The lights on other shrines had made an end,

And darkness reigned where was the festal blaze.

Far from us now thou art; and never again
   Thy magic voice shall thrill me, as one thrills   *10*
When noblest music storms his heart and brain.
   The sea remembers thee,—the woods, the hills,
   Sunlight and moonlight, and the hurrying rills,—
And Love saith, "Surely this man leads my train!"

                       (1883)

LOVE'S LOST PLEASURE-HOUSE

Love built for himself a Pleasure-house,—
   A Pleasure-house fair to see:
The roof was gold, and the walls thereof
   Were delicate ivory.

Violet crystal the windows were,
   All gleaming and fair to see;
Pillars of rose-stained marble upbore
   That house where men longed to be.

Violet, golden, and white and rose,
   That Pleasure-house fair to see   *10*
Did show to all; and they gave Love thanks
   For work of such mastery.

Love turned away from his Pleasure-house,
   And stood by the salt, deep sea:
He looked therein, and he flung therein
   Of his treasure the only key.

Now never a man till time be done
   That Pleasure-house fair to see
Shall fill with music and merriment,
   Or praise it on bended knee.   *20*

                 (1891)

HER IN ALL THINGS

Unto mine ear I set a faithful shell,
  That as of old it might rehearse to me
  The very music of the far-off sea,
And thrill my spirit with its fluctuant spell:
But not the sea's tones there grew audible,
  But Love's voice, whispering low and tenderly,
  Of things so dear that they must ever be
Unspoken, save what heart to heart may tell:

And hearing in the shell those tones divine,—
  Where once I heard the sea's low sounds confer,—   *10*
I said unto myself, "This life of thine
  Holds nothing then which is not part of Her;
  And all sweet things that to men minister
Come but from Love, who makes Her heart his shrine."

(1891)

HERE IN THIS SUNSET SPLENDOUR
DESOLATE

Here in this sunset splendour desolate,
  As in some Country strange and sad, I stand;
  A mighty sadness broods upon the land,—
The gloom of some unalterable Fate.
O Thou whose love dost make august my state,
  A little longer leave in mine thy hand:
  Night birds are singing, but the place is banned
By stern gods whom no prayers propitiate.

Seeking for bliss supreme, we lost the track:
  Shall we then part, and parted try to reach   *10*
    A goal like that we two sought day and night,
    Or shall we sit here, in the sun's low light,
  And see, it may be through Death's twilight breach,
A new path to the old way leading back?

(1891)

THEODORE WATTS-DUNTON

(1834–1914)

Theodore Watts-Dunton is remembered first of all as the London solicitor who in 1879 rescued the sadly debilitated Swinburne and for the next thirty years gave him shelter and care at The Pines in Putney. In his time he was an active journalist, critic, and reviewer for the *Athenæum,* the author of innumerable literary obituaries, and a poet of more or less Pre-Raphaelite derivations. He was on close terms with Rossetti from the early seventies till Rossetti's death, and he commemorated his friend in the following sonnet and as Darcy in his popular novel *Aylwin* (1898).

A DEAD POET

Thou knewest that island, far away and lone,
   Whose shores are as a harp, where billows break
   In spray of music and the breezes shake
O'er spicy seas a woof of colour and tone,
While that sweet music echoes like a moan
   In the island's heart, and sighs around the lake,
   Where, watching fearfully a watchful snake,
A damsel weeps upon her emerald throne.
Life's ocean, breaking round thy senses' shore,

Struck golden song, as from the strand of Day: *10*
  For us the joy, for thee the fell foe lay—
Pain's blinking snake around the fair isle's core,
  Turning to sighs the enchanted sounds that play
Around thy lovely island evermore.

                         (1882?)

POLEMIC, PARODY,
CRITICISM

As a group in protest against existing conditions in art, the Pre-Raphaelites from the beginning provoked much antagonism, misunderstanding and ridicule. John Ruskin —perhaps too readily—regarded their work as inspired by the same doctrine of integrity that he had advanced in *Modern Painters*. The first considerable champion of their unlikely cause, Ruskin sent two letters to *The Times* attempting to reverse negative assessments of Millais and Hunt, and he issued the longer pamphlet *Pre-Raphaelitism* (1851), which compared and contrasted the young artists with the great Turner. Rossetti escaped attack by refusing to exhibit his pictures and by withholding his poems. Over the years he saw the reputations of his literary associates and disciples grow more and more assured —the success of his sister's *Goblin Market* and of Morris' long narratives, and the triumph (despite thunderous opposition) of Swinburne's *Poems and Ballads*. It appeared that his own *Poems,* published at last in 1870, had been respectfully received until Robert Buchanan in "The Fleshly School of Poetry" viciously assailed Pre-Raphaelite principle and practice. Buchanan cloaked his identity in the pseudonym Thomas Maitland, for his malice was largely personal in origin, prompted by old quarrels with Swinburne and William Michael Rossetti. Incensed by the assault and outraged by its deviousness, Rossetti replied with "The Stealthy School of Criticism," one of his rare pieces in prose, a reasonable defense of work that in truth needed no apology. Buchanan returned with an expanded pamphlet, *The Fleshly School of Poetry and Other Phenomena of the Day,* only to find himself demolished by Swinburne's deadly counterblast, *Under the Microscope.*

Far better-tempered than Buchanan and correspondingly more effective in their gibes at the Pre-Raphaelites were the satirists and parodists. In his "Legend of Camelot," which appeared in *Punch* (March, 1866), George Du Maurier by caricature drawings and verses poked fun at such long-haired passionate women as Morris' Guenevere. In *Everyman His Own Poet, or the Inspired Singer's Recipe Book,* W. H. Mallock, a young Oxford wit, offered his directions "How to Make a Modern Pre-Raphaelite Poem," in which Rossetti's verse is the object of derision. Writers of light verse, notably A. C. Hilton and C. S. Calverley, parodied the simplicities and extravagances of Christina Rossetti, Morris, and Swinburne. H. D. Traill, a political journalist, proved his adeptness at catching two of Rossetti's modes, the ballad and the sonnet, in "After Dilettante Concetti," but his parody is scarcely more telling than Swinburne's "Sonnet for a Picture," written with the insight of an initiate. Gilbert and Sullivan's popular comic opera *Patience* (1881) lightly lampooned some of the more obvious Pre-Raphaelite "props." Best of all are Max Beerbohm's caricatures in *Rossetti and His Circle* (1922), which though drawn from the distance of half a century, recapture with amused sympathy and a hint of nostalgia "the silver thread of lunacy" woven through the Pre-Raphaelite tapestry.

Among the literary defenders of Pre-Raphaelitism in the eighties, two deserve our attention. In "The English Renaissance of Art," Oscar Wilde related the PRB to the larger context of the Romantic movement and suggested its importance in creating and maintaining an aesthetic component in Victorian culture. In his belated review of

Morris' *Defence of Guenevere* and in his essay on Rossetti, both included in *Appreciations* (1889), Walter Pater memorably described "aesthetic poetry" as "the desire of beauty quickened by the sense of·death" and explored the relation between a sensuous intensity and a mystical apprehension. Mallock in *The New Republic* (1877) had satirized Pater as "Mr. Rose the Pre-Raphaelite." Whether or not the label was wholly appropriate, Pater seemed better able than any other Victorian critic to perceive and define a Pre-Raphaelite quality, a principle broad enough to embrace both the poetry and the painting, both the early startling naïveté and the late aggregations of ornate detail.

JOHN RUSKIN

FROM PRE-RAPHAELITISM

[*In his characteristically digressive defense of the Pre-Raphaelites, Ruskin insists on the importance of aesthetic "truth to nature," the resolute will "to render nature as she is." He continues, in the paragraphs here extracted, to explain the Pre-Raphaelite defiance of stereotyped rules in the rigorous and sometimes awkward effort to achieve an honest "naturalism." He then compares the literal vision of the young Millais and the bolder imagination of Turner.*]

But is there to be no place left, it will be indignantly asked, for imagination and invention, for poetical power, or love of ideal beauty? Yes; the highest, the noblest place —that which these only can attain when they are all used in the cause, and with the aid of truth. Wherever imagination and sentiment are, they will either show themselves without forcing, or, if capable of artificial development, the kind of training which such a school of art would give them would be the best they could receive. The infinite absurdity and failure of our present training consists mainly in this, that we do not rank imagination and invention high enough, and suppose that they *can* be taught. Throughout every sentence that I ever have written, the reader will find the same rank attributed to these powers,—the rank of a purely divine gift, not to be attained, increased, or in any wise modified by teaching, only in various ways capable of being concealed or quenched. Understand this thoroughly; know once for all, that a poet on canvas is exactly the same species of creature as a poet in song; and nearly every error in our methods of teaching will be done away with. For who among us now thinks of bringing men up to be poets?—of producing poets by any kind of general recipe or method of cultivation? Suppose even that we see in youth that which we hope may, in its development, become a power of this kind, should we instantly, supposing that we wanted to make a poet of him, and nothing else, forbid him all quiet, steady, rational labor? Should we force him to perpetual spinning of new crudities out of his boyish brain, and set before him, as the only objects of his study, the laws of versification which criticism has supposed itself to discover in the works of previous writers? Whatever gifts the boy had, would much be likely to come of them so treated? unless, indeed they were so great as to break through all such snares of falsehood and vanity and build their own foundation in spite of us; whereas if, as in cases numbering millions against units, the natural gifts were too weak to do this, could any thing come of such training but utter inanity and spuriousness of the whole man? But if we had sense, should we not rather restrain and bridle the first flame of invention in early youth, heaping material on it as one would on the first sparks and tongues of a fire which we desired to feed into greatness? Should we not educate the whole intellect into general strength, and all the affections into warmth and honesty, and look to heaven for the rest? This, I say, we should have sense enough to do, in order to produce a poet in words: but, it being required to produce a poet on canvas, what is our way of setting to work? We begin, in all probability, by telling the youth of fifteen or sixteen, that Nature is full of faults, and that he is to improve her; but that Raphael is perfection, and that the more he copies Raphael the better; that after much copying of Raphael, he is to try what he can do himself in a Raphaelesque, but yet original, manner: that is to say, he is to try to do something very clever, all out of his own head, but yet this clever something is to be properly subjected to Raphaelesque rules, is to have a principal light occupying one-seventh of its space, and a principal shadow occupying one-third of the same; that no two people's heads in the picture are to be turned the same way, and that all the personages represented are to possess ideal beauty of the highest order, which ideal beauty consists partly in a Greek outline of nose, partly in proportions expressible in decimal fractions between the lips and chin; but partly also in that degree of improvement which the youth of sixteen is to bestow upon God's work in general. This I say is the kind of teaching which through various channels, Royal Academy lecturings, press criticisms, public enthusiasms, and not least by solid weight of gold, we give to our young men. And we wonder we have no painters!

But we do worse than this. Within the last few years some sense of the real tendency of such teaching has appeared in some of our younger painters. It only *could* appear in the younger ones, our older men having become familiarised with the false system, or else having passed through it and forgotten it, not well knowing the degree of harm they had sustained. This sense appeared, among our youths,—increased,—matured into resolute action. Necessarily, to exist at all, it needed the support both of strong instincts and of considerable self-confidence, otherwise it must at once have been borne down by the weight of general authority and received canon law. Strong instincts are apt to make men strange, and rude; self–confidence, however well founded, to give much of what they do or say the appearance of impertinence. Look at the self–confidence of Wordsworth, stiffening every other sentence of his prefaces into defiance; there is no more of it than was needed to enable him to do his work, yet it is not a little ungraceful here and there. Suppose this stubborness and self-trust in a youth, labouring in an art of which the executive part is confessedly to be best learnt from masters, and we shall hardly wonder that much of his work has a certain awkwardness and stiffness in it, or that he should be regarded with disfavor by many, even the most temperate, of the judges trained in the system he was breaking through, and with utter contempt and reprobation by the envious and the dull. Consider, farther, that the particular system to be overthrown was, in the present case, one of which the main characteristic was the pursuit of beauty at the expense of manliness and truth; and it will seem likely, *à priori,* that the men intended successfully to resist the influence of such a system should be endowed with little natural sense of beauty, and thus rendered dead to the temptation it presented. Summing up these conditions, there is surely little cause for surprise that pictures painted, in a temper of resistance, by exceedingly young men, of stubborn instincts and positive self-trust, and with little natural perception of beauty, should not be calculated, at the first glance, to win us from works enriched by plagiarism, polished by convention, invested with all the attractiveness of artificial grace, and recommended to our respect by established authority.

We should, however, on the other hand, have anticipated, that in proportion to the strength of character required for the effort, and to the absence of distracting sentiments, whether respect for precedent, or affection for ideal beauty, would be the energy exhibited in the pursuit of the special objects which the youths proposed to themselves, and their success in attaining them.

All this has actually been the case, but in a degree which it would have been impossible to anticipate. That two youths of the respective ages of eighteen and twenty, should have conceived for themselves a totally independent and sincere method of study, and enthusiastically persevered in it against every kind of dissuasion and opposition, is strange enough; that in the third or fourth year of their efforts they should have produced works in many parts not inferior to the best of Albert Dürer, this is perhaps not less strange. But the loudness and universality of the howl which the common critics of the press have raised against them, the utter absence of all generous help or encouragement from those who can both measure their toil and appreciate their success, and the shrill, shallow laughter of those who can do neither the one nor the other,—these are strangest of all—unimaginable unless they had been experienced.

And as if these were not enough, private malice is at work against them, in its own small, slimy way. The very day after I had written my second letter to the *Times* in the defence of the Pre-Raphaelites, I received an anonymous letter respecting one of them, from some person apparently hardly capable of spelling, and about as vile a specimen of petty malignity as ever blotted paper. I think it well that the public should know this, and so get some insight into the sources of the spirit which is at work against these men—how first roused it is difficult to say, for one would hardly have thought that mere eccentricity in young artists could have excited an hostility so determined and so cruel;—hostility which hesitated at no assertion, however impudent. That of the "absence of perspective" was one of the most curious pieces of the hue and cry which began with the *Times,* and died away in feeble maundering in the Art Union; I contradicted it in the *Times*—I here contradict it directly for the second time. There was not a single error in perspective in three out of the four pictures in question. But if otherwise, would it have been anything remarkable in them? I doubt if, with the exception of the pictures of David Roberts, there were one architectural drawing in perspective on the walls of the Academy; I never met but with two men in my life who knew enough of perspective to draw a Gothic arch in a retiring plane, so that its lateral dimensions and curvatures might be calculated to scale from the drawing. Our architects certainly do not, and it was but the other

day that, talking to one of the most distinguished among
them, the author of several most valuable works, I found
he actually did not know how to draw a circle in per-
spective. And in this state of general science our writers
for the press take it upon them to tell us, that the forest
trees in Mr. Hunt's *Sylvia,* and the bunches of lilies in
Mr. Collins's *Convent Thoughts,* are out of perspective.

It might not, I think, in such circumstances, have been
ungraceful or unwise in the Academicians themselves to
have defended their young pupils, at least by the contradic-
tion of statements directly false respecting them* and the

---

* These false statements may be reduced to three principal heads, and
directly contradicted in succession.

The first, the current fallacy of society as well as the press, was, that
the Pre-Raphaelites imitated the *errors* of early painters.

A falsehood of this kind could not have obtained credence anywhere
but in England, few English people, comparatively, having ever seen a
picture of early Italian Masters. If they had, they would have known that
the Pre-Raphaelite pictures are just as superior to the early Italian in
skill of manipulation, power of drawing, and knowledge of effect, as
inferior to them in grace of design; and that in a word, there is not a
shadow of resemblance between the two styles. The Pre-Raphaelites
imitate no pictures: they paint from nature only. But they have opposed
themselves as a body to that kind of teaching above described, which
only began after Raphael's time: and, they have opposed themselves as
sternly to the entire feeling of the Renaissance schools; a feeling com-
pounded of indolence, infidelity, sensuality, and shallow pride. Therefore
they have called themselves Pre-Raphaelites. If they adhere to their
principles, and paint nature as it is around them, with the help of
modern science, with the earnestness of the men of the thirteenth and
fourteenth centuries, they will, as I said, found a new and noble school
in England. If their sympathies with the early artists lead them into
mediævalism or Romanism, they will of course come to nothing. But I
believe there is no danger of this, at least for the strongest among them.
There may be some weak ones, whom the Tractarian heresies may touch;
but if so, they will drop off like decayed branches from a strong stem.
I hope all things from the school.

The second falsehood was, that the Pre-Raphaelites did not draw well.
This was asserted, and could have been asserted only by persons who had
never looked at the pictures.

The third falsehood was, that they had no system of light and shade.
To which it may be simply replied that their system of light and shade
is exactly the same as the Sun's; which is, I believe, likely to outlast that
of the Renaissance, however brilliant. [Ruskin's note]

direction of the mind and sight of the public to such real merit as they possess. . . . But as I cannot hope for this, I can only ask the public to give their pictures careful examination, and look at them at once with the indulgence and the respect which I have endeavored to show they deserve.

Yet let me not be misunderstood. I have adduced them only as examples of the kind of study which I would desire to see substituted for that of our modern schools, and of singular success in certain characters, finish of detail, and brilliancy of color. What faculties, higher than imitative, may be in these men, I do not yet venture to say; but I do say, that if they exist, such faculties will manifest themselves in due time all the more forcibly because they have received training so severe.

For it is always to be remembered that no one mind is like another, either in its powers or perceptions; and while the main principles of training must be the same for all, the result in each will be as various as the kinds of truth which each will apprehend; therefore, also, the modes of effort, even in men whose inner principles and final aims are exactly the same. Suppose, for instance, two men, equally honest, equally industrious, equally impressed with a humble desire to render some part of what they saw in nature faithfully; and, otherwise, trained in convictions such as I have above endeavored to induce. But one of them is quiet in temperament, has a feeble memory, no invention, and excessively keen sight. The other is impatient in temperament, has a memory which nothing escapes, an invention which never rests, and is comparatively near sighted.

Set them both free in the same field in a mountain valley. One sees everything, small and large, with almost the same clearness; mountains and grasshoppers alike; the leaves on the branches, the veins in the pebbles, the bubbles in the stream: but he can remember nothing, and invent nothing. Patiently he sets himself to his mighty task; abandoning at once all thoughts of seizing transient effects, or giving general impressions of that which his eyes present to him in microscopical dissection, he chooses some small portion out of the infinite scene, and calculates with courage the number of weeks which must elapse before he can do justice to the intensity of his perceptions, or the fulness of matter in his subject.

Meantime, the other has been watching the change of the clouds, and the march of the light along the mountain sides; he beholds the entire scene in broad, soft masses of true gradation, and the very feebleness of his sight is in some sort an advantage to him, in making him more sensible of the aerial mystery of distance, and hiding from him the multitudes of circumstances which it would have been impossible for him to represent. But there is not one change in the casting of the jagged shadows along the hollows of the hills, but it is fixed on his mind for ever; not a flake of spray has broken from the sea of cloud about their bases, but he has watched it as it melts away, and could recall it to its lost place in heaven by the slightest effort of his thoughts. Not only so, but thousands and thousands of such images, of older scenes, remain congregated in his mind, each mingling in new associations with those now visibly passing before him, and these again confused with other images of his own ceaseless, sleepless imagination, flashing by in sudden troops. Fancy how his paper will be covered with stray symbols and blots, and undecipherable short-hand:—as for his sitting down to "draw from Nature," there was not one of the things which he wished to represent that stayed for so much as five seconds together: but none of them escaped, for all that: they are sealed up in that strange storehouse of his; he may take one of them out, perhaps, this day twenty years, and paint it in his dark room, far away. Now, observe, you may tell both of these men, when they are young, that they are to be honest, that they have an important function, and that they are not to care what Raphael did. This you may wholesomely impress on them both. But fancy the exquisite absurdity of expecting either of them to possess any of the qualities of the other.

I have supposed the feebleness of sight in the last, and

of invention in the first painter, that the contrast between them might be more striking; but, with very slight modification, both the characters are real. Grant to the first considerable inventive power, with exquisite sense of color; and give to the second, in addition to all his other faculties, the eye of an eagle; and the first is John Everett Millais, the second Joseph Mallard William Turner.

They are among the few men who have defied all false teaching, and have, therefore, in great measure, done justice to the gifts with which they were intrusted. They stand at opposite poles, marking culminating points of art in both directions; between them, or in various relations to them, we may class five or six more living artists who, in like manner, have done justice to their powers. I trust that I may be pardoned for naming them, in order that the reader may know how the strong innate genius in each has been invariably accompanied with the same humility, earnestness, and industry in study. . . .

(1851)

ROBERT BUCHANAN

THE FLESHLY SCHOOL OF POETRY:
MR. D. G. ROSSETTI

If, on the occasion of any public performance of Shake-spere's great tragedy, the actors who perform the parts of Rosencranz and Guildenstern were, by a preconcerted arrangement and by means of what is technically known as "gagging," to make themselves fully as prominent as the leading character, and to indulge in soliloquies and business strictly belonging to Hamlet himself, the result would be, to say the least of it, astonishing; yet a very similar effect is produced on the unprejudiced mind when the "walking gentlemen" of the fleshly school of poetry, who bear precisely the same relation to Mr. Tennyson as Rosencranz and Guildenstern do to the Prince of Denmark in the play, obtrude their lesser identities and parade their smaller idiosyncrasies in the front rank of leading performers. In their own place, the gentlemen are interesting and useful. Pursuing still the theatrical analogy, the present drama of poetry might be cast as follows: Mr. Tennyson supporting the part of Hamlet, Mr. Matthew Arnold that of Horatio, Mr. Bailey that of Voltimand, Mr. Buchanan that of Cornelius, Messrs. Swinburne and Morris, the parts of Rosencranz and Guildenstern, Mr. Rossetti that of Osric, and Mr. Robert Lytton that of "A Gentleman." It will be seen that we have left no place for Mr. Browning, who may be said, however, to play the leading character in his own peculiar fashion on alternate nights.

This may seem a frivolous and inadequate way of opening our remarks on a school of verse-writers which some people regard as possessing great merits; but in good truth, it is scarcely possible to discuss with any seriousness the pretensions with which foolish friends and small critics have surrounded the fleshly school, which, in spite of its spasmodic ramifications in the erotic direction, is merely one of the many sub-Tennysonian schools expanded to supernatural dimensions, and endeavouring by affectations all its own to overshadow its connection with the great original. In the sweep of one single poem, the weird and doubtful "Vivien," Mr. Tennyson has concentrated all the epicene force which, wearisomely expanded, constitutes the characteristic of the writers at present under consideration; and if in "Vivien" he has indicated for them the bounds of sensualism in art, he has in "Maud," in the dramatic person of the hero, afforded distinct precedent for the hysteric tone and overloaded style which is now so familiar to readers of Mr. Swinburne. The fleshliness of "Vivien" may indeed be described as the distinct quality held in common by all the members of the last sub-Tennysonian school, and it is a quality which becomes unwholesome when there is no moral or intellectual quality to temper and control it. Fully conscious of this themselves, the fleshly gentlemen have bound themselves by solemn league and covenant to extol fleshliness as the distinct and supreme end of poetic and pictorial art; to aver that poetic expression is greater than poetic thought, and by inference that the body is greater than the soul, and sound superior to sense; and that the poet, properly to develop his poetic faculty, must be an intellectual hermaphrodite, to whom the very facts of day and night are lost in a whirl of æsthetic terminology. After Mr. Tennyson has probed the depths of modern speculation in a series

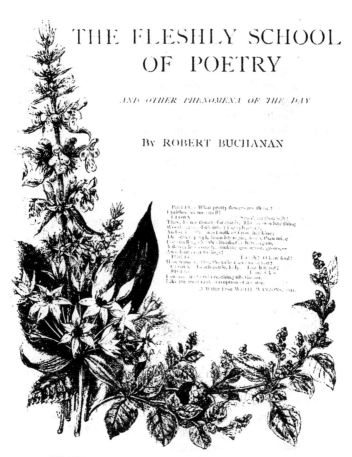

THE FLESHLY SCHOOL OF POETRY

AND OTHER PHENOMENA OF THE DAY

By ROBERT BUCHANAN

STRAHAN & CO., 56, LUDGATE HILL, LONDON.

The title page of Robert Buchanan's pamphlet,
The Fleshly School of Poetry

of commanding moods, all right and interesting in him as the reigning personage, the walking gentlemen, knowing that something of the sort is expected from all leading performers, bare their roseate bosoms and aver that *they* are creedless; the only possible question here being, if any disinterested person cares twopence whether Rosencranz, Guildenstern, and Osric are creedless or not—their self-revelation on that score being so perfectly gratuitous. But having gone so far, it was and is too late to retreat. Rosencranz, Guildenstern, and Osric, finding it impossible to risk an individual bid for the leading business, have arranged all to play leading business together, and mutually to praise, extol, and imitate each other; and although by these measures they have fairly earned for themselves the title of the Mutual Admiration School, they have in a great measure succeeded in their object—to the general stupefaction of a British audience. It is time, therefore, to ascertain whether any of these gentlemen has actually in himself the making of a leading performer. When the *Athenæum*—once more cautious in such matters—advertised nearly every week some interesting particular about Mr. Swinburne's health, Mr. Morris's holiday-making, or Mr. Rossetti's genealogy, varied with such startling statements as "We are informed that Mr. Swinburne dashed off his noble ode *at a sitting*," or "Mr. Swinburne's songs have already reached a second edition," or "Good poetry seems to be in demand; the first edition of Mr. O'Shaughnessy's poems is exhausted;" when the *Academy* informed us that "During the past year or two Mr. Swinburne has written several novels" (!) and that some review or other is to be praised for giving Mr. Rossetti's poems "the attentive study which they demand"—when we read these things we might or might not know pretty well how and where they originated; but to a provincial eye, perhaps, the whole thing really looked like leading business. It would be scarcely worth while, however, to inquire into the pretensions of the writers on merely literary grounds, because sooner or later all literature finds its own level, whatever criticism may say or do in the matter; but it unfortunately happens in the present case that the fleshly school of verse-writers are, so to speak, public offenders, because they are diligently spreading the seeds of disease broadcast wherever they are read and understood. Their complaint too is catching, and carries off many young persons. What the complaint is, and how it works, may be seen on a very slight examination of the works of Mr. Dante Gabriel Rossetti, to whom we shall confine our attention in the present article.

Mr. Rossetti has been known for many years as a painter of exceptional powers, who, for reasons best known to himself, has shrunk from publicly exhibiting his pictures, and from allowing anything like a popular estimate to be formed of their qualities. He belongs, or is said to belong, to the so-called Pre-Raphaelite school, a school which is generally considered to exhibit much genius for colour, and great indifference to perspective. It would be unfair to judge the painter by the glimpses we have had of his works, or by the photographs which are sold of the principal paintings. Judged by the photographs, he is an artist who conceives unpleasantly, and draws ill. Like Mr. Simeon Solomon, however, with whom he seems to have many points in common, he is distinctively a colourist, and of his capabilities in colour we cannot speak, though we should guess that they are great; for if there is any good quality by which his poems are specially marked, it is a great sensitiveness to hues and tints as conveyed in poetic epithet. These qualities, which impress the casual spectator of the photographs from his pictures, are to be found abundantly among his verses. There is the same thinness and transparency of design, the same combination of the simple and the grotesque, the same morbid deviation from healthy forms of life, the same sense of weary, wasting, yet exquisite sensuality; nothing virile, nothing tender, nothing completely sane; a superfluity of extreme sensibility, of delight in beautiful forms, hues, and tints, and a deep-seated indifference to all agitating forces and agencies, all tumultuous griefs and sorrows, all the thunderous stress of life, and all the straining storm of speculation. Mr. Morris is often pure, fresh, and wholesome as his own great model; Mr. Swinburne startles us more than once by some fine flash of insight; but the mind of Mr. Rossetti is like a glassy mere, broken only by the dive of some water-bird or by the hum of winged insects, and brooded over by an atmosphere of insufferable closeness, with a light blue sky above it, sultry depths mirrored within it, and a surface so thickly sown with water-lilies that it retains its glassy smoothness even in the strongest wind. Judged relatively to his poetic associates, Mr. Rossetti must be pronounced inferior to either. He cannot tell a pleasant story like Mr. Morris, nor forge alliterative thunderbolts like Mr. Swinburne. It must be conceded, nevertheless, that he is neither so glibly imitative as the one, nor so transcendently superficial as the other.

Although he has been known for many years as a poet as well as a painter—as a painter and poet idolized by his own family and personal associates—and although he has once or twice appeared in print as a contributor to magazines, Mr. Rossetti did not formally appeal to the public until rather more than a year ago, when he published a copious volume of poems, with the announcement that the book, although it contained pieces composed at intervals during a period of many years, "included nothing which the author believes to be immature." This work was inscribed to his brother, Mr. William Rossetti, who, having written much both in poetry and criticism, will perhaps be known to bibliographers as the editor of the worst edition of Shelley which has yet seen the light. No sooner had the work appeared than the chorus of eulogy began. "The book is satisfactory from end to end," wrote Mr. Morris in the *Academy*; "I think these lyrics, with all their other merits, the most complete of their time; nor do I know what lyrics of any time are to be called *great,* if we are to deny the title to these." On the same subject Mr. Swinburne went into a hysteria of admiration: "golden affluence," "jewel-coloured words," "chastity of form," "harmonious nakedness," "consummate fleshly sculpture," and so on in Mr. Swinburne's well-known manner when reviewing his friends. Other critics, with a singular similarity of phrase followed suit. Strange to say, moreover, no one accused Mr. Rossetti of naughtiness. What had been heinous in Mr. Swinburne was majestic exquisiteness in Mr. Rossetti. Yet we question if there is anything in the unfortunate "Poems and Ballads" quite so questionable on the score of thorough nastiness as many pieces in Mr. Rossetti's collection. Mr. Swinburne was wilder, more outrageous, more blasphemous, and his subjects were more atrocious in themselves; yet the hysterical tone slew the animalism, the furiousness of epithet lowered the sensation; and the first feeling of disgust at such themes as "Laus Veneris" and "Anactoria" faded away into comic amazement. It was only a little mad boy letting off squibs; not a great strong man, who might be really dangerous to society. "I *will* be naughty!" screamed the little boy; but, after all, what did it matter? It is quite different, however, when a grown man, with the self-control and easy audacity of actual experience, comes forward to chronicle his amorous sensations, and, first proclaiming in a loud voice his literary maturity, and consequent responsibility, shamelessly prints and publishes such a piece of writing as this sonnet on "Nuptial Sleep":—

At length their long kiss severed, with sweet smart:
And as the last slow sudden drops are shed
From sparkling eaves when all the storm has fled,
So singly flagged the pulses of each heart.
Their bosoms sundered, with the opening start
Of married flowers to either side outspread
From the knit stem; yet still their mouths, burnt red,
Fawned on each other where they lay apart.

Sleep sank them lower than the tide of dreams,
    And their dreams watched them sink, and slid away.

Slowly their souls swam up again, through gleams
  Of watered light and dull drowned waifs of day;
Till from some wonder of new woods and streams
  He woke, and wondered more: for there she lay.

This, then, is "the golden affluence of words, the firm out-
line, the justice and chastity of form." Here is a full-grown
man, presumably intelligent and cultivated, putting on
record for other full-grown men to read, the most secret
mysteries of sexual connection, and that with so sickening
a desire to reproduce the sexual mood, so careful a choice
of epithet to convey mere animal sensations, that we merely
shudder at the shameless nakedness. We are no purists in
such matters. We hold the sensual part of our nature to
be as holy as the spiritual or intellectual part, and we be-
lieve that such things must find their equivalent in all;
but it is neither poetic, nor manly, nor even human, to
obtrude such things as the themes of whole poems. It is
simply nasty. Nasty as it is, we are very mistaken if many
readers do not think it nice. English society of one kind
purchases the *Day's Doings*. English society of another
kind goes into ecstasy over Mr. Solomon's pictures—pretty
pieces of morality, such as "Love dying by the breath of
Lust." There is not much to choose between the two ob-
jects of admiration, except that painters like Mr. Solomon
lend actual genius to worthless subjects, and thereby pro-
duce veritable monsters—like the lovely devils that danced
round Saint Anthony. Mr. Rossetti owes his so-called suc-
cess to the same causes. In poems like "Nuptial Sleep,"
the man who is too sensitive to exhibit his pictures, and
so modest that it takes him years to make up his mind to
publish his poems, parades his private sensations before
a coarse public, and is gratified by their applause.

It must not be supposed that all Mr. Rossetti's poems are
made up of trash like this. Some of them are as noteworthy
for delicacy of touch as others are for shamelessness of
exposition. They contain some exquisite pictures of na-
ture, occasional passages of real meaning, much beautiful

phraseology, lines of peculiar sweetness, and epithets chosen with true literary cunning. But the fleshly feeling is everywhere. Sometimes, as in "The Stream's Secret," it is deliciously modulated, and adds greatly to our emotion of pleasure at perusing a finely-wrought poem; at other times, as in the "Last Confession," it is fiercely held in check by the exigencies of a powerful situation and the strength of a dramatic speaker; but it is generally in the foreground, flushing the whole poem with unhealthy rose-colour, stifling the senses with overpowering sickliness, as of too much civet. Mr. Rossetti is never dramatic, never impersonal—always attitudinizing, posturing, and describing his own exquisite emotions. He is the "Blessed Damozel," leaning over the "gold bar of heaven," and seeing

> Time like a pulse shake fierce
> Thro' all the worlds;

he is "heaven-born Helen, Sparta's queen" whose "each twin breast is an apple sweet"; he is Lilith, the first wife of Adam; he is the rosy Virgin of the poem called "Ave," and the Queen in the "Staff and Scrip"; he is "Sister Helen" melting her waxen man; he is all these, just as surely as he is Mr. Rossetti soliloquizing over Jenny in her London lodging, or the very nuptial person writing erotic sonnets to his wife. In petticoats or pantaloons, in modern times or in the middle ages, he is just Mr. Rossetti, a fleshly person, with nothing particular to tell us or teach us, with extreme self-control, a strong sense of colour, and a careful choice of diction. Amid all his "affluence of jewel-coloured words," he has not given us one rounded and noteworthy piece of art, though his verses are all art; not one poem which is memorable for its own sake, and quite separable from the displeasing identity of the composer. The nearest approach to a perfect whole is the "Blessed Damozel," a peculiar poem, placed first in the book, perhaps by accident, perhaps because it is a key to the poems which follow. This poem appeared in a rough

shape many years ago in the *Germ,* an unwholesome pe-
riodical started by the Pre-Raphaelites, and suffered, after
gasping through a few feeble numbers, to die the death of
all such publications. In spite of its affected title, and of
numberless affectations throughout the text, the "Blessed
Damozel" has great merits of its own, and a few lines of
real genius. We have heard it described as the record of
actual grief and love, or, in simple words, the apotheosis
of one actually lost by the writer; but, without having any
private knowledge of the circumstance of its composition,
we feel that such an account of the poem is inadmissible.
It does not contain one single note of sorrow. It is a "com-
position," and a clever one. Read the opening stanzas:—

> The blessed damozel leaned out
>   From the gold bar of Heaven;
> Her eyes were deeper than the depth
>   Of water stilled at even;
> She had three lilies in her hand,
>   And the stars in her hair were seven.
>
> Her robe, ungirt from clasp to hem,
>   No wrought flowers did adorn,
> But a white rose of Mary's gift,
>   For service meetly worn;
> Her hair that lay along her back
>   Was yellow like ripe corn.

This is a careful sketch for a picture, which, worked into
actual colour by a master, might have been worth seeing.
The steadiness of hand lessens as the poem proceeds, and
although there are several passages of considerable power,
—such as that where, far down the void,

> this earth
> Spins like a fretful midge,

or that other, describing how

> the curled moon
> Was like a little feather
> Fluttering far down the gulf,—

the general effect is that of a queer old painting in a missal, very affected and very odd. What moved the British critic to ecstasy in this poem seems to us very sad nonsense indeed, or, if not sad nonsense, very meretricious affectation. Thus, we have seen the following verses quoted with enthusiasm, as italicised—

> And still she bowed herself and stooped
>   Out of the circling charm;
> *Until her bosom must have made*
>   *The bar she leaned on warm,*
> And the lilies lay as if asleep
>   Along her bended arm.

> From the fixed place of Heaven she saw
>   *Time like a pulse shake fierce*
> *Thro' all the worlds.* Her gaze still strove
>   Within the gulf to pierce
> Its path; and now she spoke as when
>   The stars sang in their spheres.

It seems to us that all these lines are very bad, with the exception of the two admirable lines ending the first verse, and that the italicized portions are quite without merit, and almost without meaning. On the whole, one feels disheartened and amazed at the poet who, in the nineteenth century, talks about "damozels," "citherns," and "citoles," and addresses the mother of Christ as the "Lady Mary,"—

> With her five handmaidens, whose names
>   Are five sweet symphonies,
> Cecily, Gertrude, Magdalen,
>   Margaret and Rosalys.

A suspicion is awakened that the writer is laughing at us. We hover uncertainly between picturesqueness and namby-pamby, and the effect, as Artemus Ward would express it, is "weakening to the intellect." The thing would have been almost too much in the shape of a picture, though the workmanship might have made amends. The truth is that literature, and more particularly poetry, is in a very bad way when one art gets hold of another, and imposes upon it its conditions and limitations. In the first few verses of the "Damozel" we have the subject, or part of the subject, of a picture, and the inventor should either have painted it or left it alone altogether; and had he done the latter, the world would have lost nothing. Poetry is something more than painting; and an idea will not become a poem because it is too smudgy for a picture.

In a short notice from a well-known pen, giving the best estimate we have seen of Mr. Rossetti's powers as a poet, the *North American Review* offers a certain explanation for affectation such as that of Mr. Rossetti. The writer suggests that "it may probably be the expression of genuine moods of mind in natures too little comprehensive." We would rather believe that Mr. Rossetti lacks comprehension than that he is deficient in sincerity; yet really, to paraphrase the words which Johnson applied to Thomas Sheridan, Mr. Rossetti is affected, naturally affected, but it must have taken him a great deal of trouble to become what we now see him—such an excess of affectation is not in nature.* There is very little writing in the volume spontaneous in the sense that some of Swinburne's verses are spontaneous; the poems all look as if they had taken a great deal of trouble. The grotesque mediævalism of "Stratton Water" and "Sister Helen," the mediæval classicism of "Troy-Town," the false and shallow mysticism of "Eden Bower," are one and all essentially imitative and must have cost the writer much pains. It is time, indeed,

---

* "Why, sir, Sherry is dull, *naturally* dull; but it must have taken him *a great deal of trouble* to become what we now see him—such an excess of stupidity is not in nature."—Boswell's *Life*. [Buchanan's note]

to point out that Mr. Rossetti is a poet possessing great powers of assimilation and some faculty for concealing the nutriment on which he feeds. Setting aside the "Vita Nuova" and the early Italian poems, which are familiar to many readers by his own excellent translation, Mr. Rossetti may be described as a writer who has yielded to an unusual extent to the complex influences of the literature surrounding him at the present moment. He has the painter's imitative power developed in proportion to his lack of the poet's conceiving imagination. He reproduces to a nicety the manner of an old ballad, a trick in which Mr. Swinburne is also an adept. Cultivated readers, moreover, will recognize in every one of these poems the tone of Mr. Tennyson broken up by the style of Mr. and Mrs. Browning, and disguised here and there by the eccentricities of the Pre-Raphaelites. The "Burden of Nineveh" is a philosophical edition of "Recollections of the Arabian Nights"; "A Last Confession" and "Dante at Verona" are, in the minutest trick and form of thought, suggestive of Mr. Browning; and that the sonnets have been largely moulded and inspired by Mrs. Browning can be ascertained by any critic who will compare them with the "Sonnets from the Portuguese." Much remains, nevertheless, that is Mr. Rossetti's own. We at once recognize as his own property such passages as this:—

I looked up
And saw where a brown-shouldered harlot leaned
Half through a tavern window thick with vine.
Some man had come behind her in the room
And caught her by her arms, and she had turned
With that coarse empty laugh on him, as now
He *munched her neck with kisses, while the vine
Crawled in her back.*

Or this:—

As I stopped, her own lips rising there
Bubbled with brimming kisses at my mouth.

Or this:—

> Have seen your lifted silken skirt
> Advertise dainties through the dirt!

Or this:—

> "What more prize than love to impel thee,
> *Grip* and *lip* my limbs as I tell thee!"

Passages like these are the common stock of the walking gentleman of the fleshly school. We cannot forbear expressing our wonder, by the way, at the kind of women whom it seems the unhappy lot of these gentlemen to encounter. We have lived as long in the world as they have, but never yet came across persons of the other sex who conduct themselves in the manner described. Females who bite, scratch, scream, bubble, munch, sweat, writhe, twist, wriggle, foam, and in a general way slaver over their lovers, must surely possess some extraordinary qualities to counteract their otherwise most offensive mode of conducting themselves. It appears, however, on examination, that their poet-lovers conduct themselves in a similar manner. They, too, bite, scratch, scream, bubble, munch, sweat, writhe, twist, wriggle, foam, and slaver, in a style frightful to hear of. Let us hope that it is only their fun, and that they don't mean half they say. At times, in reading such books as this, one cannot help wishing, that things had remained forever in the asexual state described in Mr. Darwin's great chapter on Palingenesis. We get very weary of this protracted hankering after a person of the other sex; it seems meat, drink, thought, sinew, religion for the fleshly school. There is no limit to the fleshliness, and Mr. Rossetti finds in it its own religious justification much in the same way as Holy Willie:—

> Maybe thou let'st this fleshly thorn
> Perplex thy servant night and morn.
>   'Cause he's so gifted.

> If so, thy hand must e'en be borne,
> Until thou lift it.

Whether he is writing of the holy Damozel, or of the Virgin herself, or of Lilith, or of Helen, or of Dante, or of Jenny the streetwalker, he is fleshly all over, from the roots of his hair to the tip of his toes; never a true lover merging his identity into that of the beloved one; never spiritual, never tender; always self-conscious and æsthetic. "Nothing," says a modern writer, "in human life is so utterly remorseless—not love, not hate, not ambition, not vanity—as the artistic or æsthetic instinct morbidly developed to the suppression of conscience and feeling;" and at no time do we feel more fully impressed with this truth than after the perusal of "Jenny," in some respects the finest poem in the volume, and in all respects the poem best indicative of the true quality of the writer's humanity. It is a production which bears signs of having been suggested by Mr. Buchanan's quasi-lyrical poems, which it copies in the style of title, and particularly by "Artist and Model"; but certainly Mr. Rossetti cannot be accused, as the Scottish writer has been accused, of maudlin sentiment and affected tenderness. The first two lines are perfect:—

> Lazy, laughing languid Jenny,
> Fond of a kiss and fond of a guinea;

And the poem is a soliloquy of the poet—who has been spending the evening in dancing at a casino—over his partner, whom he has accompanied home to the usual style of lodgings occupied by such ladies, and who has fallen asleep with her head upon his knee, while he wonders, in a wretched pun—

> Whose person or whose purse may be
> The lodestar of your reverie?

The soliloquy is long, and in some parts beautiful, despite a very constant suspicion that we are listening to an emasculated Mr. Browning, whose whole tone and gesture, so to speak, is occasionally introduced with startling fidelity; and there are here and there glimpses of actual thought and insight, over and above the picturesque touches which belong to the writer's true profession, such as that where, at daybreak—

> lights creep in
> Past the gauze curtains half drawn-to,
> And *the lamp's doubled shade grows blue*.

What we object to in this poem is not the subject, which any writer may be fairly left to choose for himself; nor anything particularly vicious in the poetic treatment of it; nor any bad blood bursting through in special passages. But the whole tone, without being more than usually coarse, seems heartless. There is not a drop of piteousness in Mr. Rossetti. He is just to the outcast, even generous; severe to the seducer; sad even at the spectacle of lust in dimity and fine ribbons. Notwithstanding all this, and a certain delicacy and refinement of treatment unusual with this poet, the poem repels and revolts us, and we like Mr. Rossetti least after its perusal. We are angry with the fleshly person at last. The "Blessed Damozel" puzzled us, the "Song of the Bower" amused us, the love-sonnet depressed and sickened us, but "Jenny," though distinguished by less special viciousness of thought and style than any of these, fairly makes us lose patience. We detect its fleshliness at a glance; we perceive that the scene was fascinating less through its human tenderness than because it, like all the others, possessed an inherent quality of animalism. "The whole work," ("Jenny"), writes Mr. Swinburne, "is worthy to fill its place forever as one of the most perfect poems of an age or generation. There is just the same lifeblood and breadth of poetic interest in this episode of a London street and lodging as in the song of 'Troy Town' and the song of 'Eden Bower'; just as much, and no jot more,"—to which last statement we cordially assent;

for there is bad blood in all, and breadth of poetic interest in none. "Vengeance of Jenny's case," indeed!—when such a poet as this comes fawning over her, with tender compassion in one eye and æsthetic enjoyment in the other!

It is time that we permitted Mr. Rossetti to speak for himself, which we will do by quoting a fairly representative poem entire:—

LOVE-LILY

Between the hands, between the brows,
  Between the lips of Love-Lily,
A spirit is born whose birth endows
  My blood with fire to burn through me;
Who breathes upon my gazing eyes,
  Who laughs and murmurs in mine ear,
At whose least touch my colour flies,
  And whom my life grows faint to hear.

Within the voice, within the heart,
  Within the mind of Love-Lily,
A spirit is born who lifts apart
  His tremulous wings and looks at me;
Who on my mouth his finger lays,
  And shows, while whispering lutes confer,
That Eden of Love's watered ways,
  Whose winds and spirits worship her.

Brows, hands, and lips, heart, mind, and voice,
  Kisses and words of Love-Lily,—
Oh! bid me with your joy rejoice
  Till *riotous longing rest in me!*
Ah! let not hope be still distraught,
  But find in her its gracious goal,
Whose speech Truth knows not from her thought,
  Nor Love her body from her soul.

With the exception of the usual "riotous longing," which seems to make Mr. Rossetti a burthen to himself, there is nothing to find fault with in the extreme fleshliness of these verses, and to many people who live in the country they may even appear beautiful. Without pausing to criticize a thing so trifling—as well might we dissect a cobweb or anatomize a medusa—let us ask the reader's attention to a peculiarity to which all the students of the fleshly school must sooner or later give their attention—we mean the habit of accenting the last syllable in words which in ordinary speech are accented on the penultimate:—

> Between the hands, between the brows,
> Between the lips of Love-Lil*ee!*

which may be said to give to the speaker's voice a sort of cooing tenderness just bordering on a loving whistle. Still better as an illustration are the lines:—

> Saturday night is market night
> Everywhere, be it dry or wet,
> And market night in the Haymar-*ket!*

which the reader may advantageously compare with Mr. Morris's

> Then said the king
> Thanked be thou; *neither for nothing*
> Shalt thou this good deed do to me;

or Mr. Swinburne's

> In either of the twain
> Red roses full of rain;
> She hath for bondwo*men*
> All kinds of flowers.

It is unnecessary to multiply examples of an affectation which disfigures all these writers—Guildenstern, Rosen-

cranz, and Osric; who, in the same spirit which prompts
the ambitious nobodies that rent London theatres in the
"empty" season to make up for their dulness by fearfully
original "new readings," distinguish their attempt at lead-
ing business by affecting the construction of their grand-
fathers and great-grandfathers, and the accentuation of
the poets of the court of James I. It is in all respects a sign
of remarkable genius, from this point of view, to rhyme
"was" with "grass," "death" with "lièth," "love" with "of,"
"once" with "suns," and so on *ad nauseam*. We are far
from disputing the value of bad rhymes used occasionally
to break up the monotony of verse, but the case is hard
when such blunders become the rule and not the exception,
when writers deliberately lay themselves out to be as ar-
chaic and affected as possible. Poetry is perfect human
speech, and these archaisms are the mere fiddlededeeing
of empty heads and hollow hearts. Bad as they are, they
are the true indication of falser tricks and affectations
which lie far deeper. They are trifles, light as air, showing
how the wind blows. The soul's speech and the heart's
speech are clear, simple, natural, and beautiful, and reject
the meretricious tricks to which we have drawn attention.

It is on the score that these tricks and affectations have
procured the professors a number of imitators, that the
fleshly school deliver their formula that great poets are
always to be known because their manner is immediately
reproduced by small poets, and that a poet who finds few
imitators is probably of inferior rank—by which they mean
to infer that they themselves are very great poets indeed.
It is quite true that they are imitated. On the stage, twenty
provincial "stars" copy Charles Kean, while not one copies
his father; there are dozens of actors who reproduce Mr.
Charles Dillon, and not one who attempts to reproduce
Macready. When we take up the poems of Mr. O'Shaugh-
nessy, we are face to face with a second-hand Mr. Swin-
burne; when we read Mr. Payne's queer allegories, we
remember Mr. Morris's early stage; and every poem of Mr.
Marston's reminds us of Mr. Rossetti. But what is really

most droll and puzzling in the matter is that these imitators seem to have no difficulty whatever in writing nearly, if not quite, as well as their masters. It is not bad imitations they offer us, but poems which read just like the originals; the fact being that it is easy to reproduce sound when it has no strict connection with sense, and simple enough to cull phraseology not hopelessly interwoven with thought and spirit. The fact that these gentlemen are so easily imitated is the most damning proof of their inferiority. What merits they have lie with their faults on the surface, and can be caught by any young gentleman as easily as the measles, only they are rather more difficult to get rid of. All young gentlemen have animal faculties, though few have brains; and if animal faculties without brains make poems, nothing is easier in the world. A great and good poet, however, is great and good irrespective of manner, and often in spite of manner; he is great because he brings great ideas and new light, because his thought is a revelation; and, although it is true that a great manner generally accompanies great matter, the manner of great matter is almost inimitable. The great poet is not Cowley, imitated and idolized and reproduced by every scribbler of his time; nor Pope, whose trick of style was so easily copied that to this day we cannot trace his own hand with any certainty in the *Iliad*; nor Donne, nor Sylvester, nor the Della Cruscans. Shakspere's blank verse is the most difficult, and Jonson's the most easy to imitate, of all the Elizabethan stock; and Shakspere's verse is the best verse, because it combines the great qualities of all contemporary verse, with no individual affectations; and so perfectly does this verse, with all its splendour, intersect with the style of contemporaries *at their best,* that we would undertake to select passage after passage which would puzzle a good judge to tell which of the Elizabethans was the author—Marlowe, Beaumont, Dekker, Marston, Webster, or Shakspere himself. The great poet is Dante, full of the thunder of a great Idea; and Milton, unapproachable in the serene white light of thought and sumptuous wealth of style; and Shakspere, all poets by turns, and all men in succession; and Goethe, always innovating, and ever indifferent to innovation for its own sake; and Wordsworth, clear as crystal and deep as the sea; and Tennyson, with his vivid range, far-piercing sight, and perfect speech; and Browning, great, not by virtue of his eccentricities, but because of his close intellectual grasp. Tell "Paradise Lost," the "Divine Comedy," in naked prose; do the same by *Hamlet, Macbeth,* and *Lear*; read Mr. Hayward's translation of "Faust"; take up the "Excursion," a great poem, though its speech is nearly prose already; turn the "Guinevere" into a mere story; reproduce Pompilia's last dying speech without a line of rhythm. Reduced to bald English, all these poems, and all great poems lose much; but how much do they not retain? They are poems to the very roots and depths of being, poems born and delivered from the soul, and treat them as cruelly as you may, poems they will remain. So it is with all good and thorough creations, however low in their rank; so it is with the "Ballad in a Wedding" and "Clever Tom Clinch," just as much as with the "Epistle of Karsheesh," or Goethe's torso of "Prometheus"; with Shelley's "Skylark," or Alfred de Musset's "À la Lune," as well as Racine's "Athalie," Victor Hugo's "Parricide," or Hood's "Last Man." A poem is a poem first as to the soul, next as to the form. The fleshly persons who wish to create form for its own sake are merely pronouncing their own doom. But *such* form! If the Pre-Raphaelite fervour gains ground, we shall soon have popular songs like this;—

> When winds do roar, and rains do pour,
> Hard is the life of a sail*or;*
> He scarcely as he reels can tell
> The side-lights from the binna*cle;*
> He looketh on the wild wa*ter,* etc.,

and so on, till the English speech seems the speech of raving madmen. Of a piece with other affectations is the de-

vice of a burthen, of which the fleshly persons are very
fond for its own sake, quite apart from its relevancy. Thus
Mr. Rossetti sings:—

> Why did you melt your waxen man,
>> Sister Helen?
> To-day is the third since you began.
> The time was long, yet the time ran,
>> Little brother.
>> (*O mother, Mary mother,*
> *Three days to-day between Heaven and Hell.*)

This burthen is repeated, with little or no alteration,
through thirty-four verses, and might with as much music,
and far more point, run as follows:—

> Why did you melt your waxen man,
>> Sister Helen?
> To-day is the third since you began.
> The time was long, yet the time ran,
>> Little Brother.
>> (*O Mr. Dante Rossetti*
> *What stuff is this about Heaven and Hell?*)

About as much to the point is a burthen of Mr. Swin-
burne's something to the following effect:—

> We were three maidens in the green corn
>> *Hey chickaleerie, the red cock and gray,*
> Fairer maidens were never born,
>> *One o'clock, two o'clock, off and away.*

We are not quite certain of the words, as we quote from
memory, but we are sure our version fairly represents the
original and is quite as expressive. Productions of this sort
are "silly sooth" in good earnest, though they delight some
newspaper critics of the day, and are copied by young
gentlemen with animal faculties morbidly developed by

too much tobacco and too little exercise. Such indulgence, however, would ruin the strongest poetical constitution; and it unfortunately happens that neither masters nor pupils were naturally very healthy. In such a poem as "Eden Bower" there is not one scrap of imagination, properly so-called. It is a clever grotesque in the worst manner of Callot, unredeemed by a gleam of true poetry or humour. No good poet would have wrought into a poem the absurd tradition about Lilith; Goethe was content to glance at it merely, with a grim smile, in the great scene in the Brocken. We may remark here that poems of this unnatural and morbid kind are only tolerable when they embody a profound meaning, as do Coleridge's "Ancient Mariner" and "Cristabel." Not that we would insult the memory of Coleridge by comparing his exquisitely conscientious work with this affected rubbish about "Eden Bower" and "Sister Helen," though his influence in their composition is unmistakable. Still more unmistakable is the influence of that most unwholesome poet, Beddoes, who, with all his great powers, treated his subjects in a thoroughly insincere manner, and is now justly forgotten.

The great strong current of English poetry rolls on, ever mirroring in its bosom new prospects of fair and wholesome thought. Morbid deviations are endless and inevitable; there must be marsh and stagnant mere as well as mountain and wood. Glancing backward into the shady places of the obscure, we see the once prosperous nonsense-writers each now consigned to his own little limbo— Skelton and Gower still playing fantastic tricks with the mother-tongue; Gascoigne outlasting the applause of all, and living to see his own works buried before him; Sylvester doomed to oblivion by his own fame as a translator; Carew the idol of courts, and Donne the beloved of schoolmen, both buried in the same oblivion; the fantastic Fletchers winning the wonder of collegians and fading out through sheer poetic impotence; Cowley shaking all England with his pindarics, and perishing with them; Waller, the famous, saved from oblivion by the natural note of

one single song—and so on, through league after league of
a flat and desolate country, which once was prosperous,
till we come again to these fantastic figures of the fleshly
school, with their droll mediæval garments, their funny
archaic speech, and the fatal marks of literary consump-
tion in every pale and delicate visage. Our judgment on
Mr. Rossetti, to whom we in the meantime confine our
judgment, is substantially that of the *North American
Reviewer,* who believes that "we have in him another
poetical man, and a man markedly poetical, and of a kind
apparently, though not radically, different from any of our
secondary writers of poetry, but that we have not in him
a new poet of any weight"; and that he is "so affected,
sentimental, and painfully self-conscious, that the best to
be done in his case is to hope that this book of his, having
unpacked his bosom of so much that is unhealthy, may
have done him more good than it has given others pleas-
ure." Such, we say, is our opinion, which might very well
be wrong, and have to undergo modification, if Mr. Ros-
setti was younger and less self-possessed. His "maturity"
is fatal.

Thomas Maitland.
(1871)

DANTE GABRIEL ROSSETTI

THE STEALTHY SCHOOL OF CRITICISM

(*from* THE ATHENÆUM, 1871)

Your paragraph, a fortnight ago, relating to the pseudonymous authorship of an article, violently assailing myself and other writers of poetry, in the *Contemporary Review* for October last, reveals a species of critical masquerade which I have expressed in the heading given to this letter. Since then, Mr. Sidney Colvin's note, qualifying the report that he intends to "answer" that article, has appeared in your pages; and my own view as to the absolute forfeit, under such conditions, of all claim to honourable reply, is precisely the same as Mr. Colvin's. For here a critical organ, professedly adopting the principle of open signature, would seem, in reality, to assert (by silent practice, however, not by enunciation,) that if the anonymous in criticism was—as itself originally inculcated—but an early caterpillar stage, the nominate too is found to be no better than a homely transitional chrysalis, and that the ultimate butterfly form for a critic who likes to sport in sunlight and yet to elude the grasp, is after all the pseudonymous. But, indeed, what I may call the "Siamese" aspect of the entertainment provided by the *Review* will elicit but one verdict. Yet I may, perhaps, as the individual chiefly attacked, be excused for asking your assistance now in giving a specific denial to specific charges which, if unrefuted, may still continue, in spite of their author's strategic *fiasco,* to serve his purpose against me to some extent.

The primary accusation, on which this writer grounds all the rest, seems to be that others and myself "extol flesh-liness as the distinct and supreme end of poetic and pictorial art; aver that poetic expression is greater than poetic thought; and, by inference, that the body is greater than the soul, and sound superior to sense."

As my own writings are alone formally dealt with in the article, I shall confine my answer to myself; and this must first take unavoidably the form of a challenge to prove so broad a statement. It is true, some fragmentary pretence at proof is put in here and there throughout the attack, and thus far an opportunity is given of contesting the assertion.

A Sonnet entitled *Nuptial Sleep* is quoted and abused at page 338 of the *Review,* and is there dwelt upon as a "whole poem," describing "merely animal sensations." It is no more a whole poem, in reality, than is any single stanza of any poem throughout the book. The poem, written chiefly in sonnets, and of which this is one sonnet-stanza, is entitled *The House of Life*; and even in my first published instalment of the whole work (as contained in the volume under notice) ample evidence is included that no such passing phase of description as the one headed *Nuptial Sleep* could possibly be put forward by the author of *The House of Life* as his own representative view of the subject of love. In proof of this, I will direct attention (among the love-sonnets of this poem) to Nos. 2, 8, 11, 17, 28, and more especially 13, which, indeed, I had better print here.

LOVE-SWEETNESS

"Sweet dimness of her loosened hair's downfall
 About thy face; her sweet hands round thy head
 In gracious fostering union garlanded;
Her tremulous smiles; her glances' sweet recall
Of love; her murmuring sighs memorial;
 Her mouth's culled sweetness by thy kisses shed
 On cheeks and neck and eyelids, and so led
Back to her mouth which answers there for all:—
"What sweeter than these things, except the thing
 In lacking which all these would lose their sweet:—
 The confident heart's still fervour; the swift beat
And soft subsidence of the spirit's wing
Then when it feels, in cloud-girt wayfaring,
 The breath of kindred plumes against its feet?"

Any reader may bring any artistic charge he pleases against the above sonnet; but one charge it would be impossible to maintain against the writer of the series in which it occurs, and that is, the wish on his part to assert that the body is greater than the soul. For here all the passionate and just delights of the body are declared—somewhat figuratively, it is true, but unmistakably—to be as naught if not ennobled by the concurrence of the soul at all times. Moreover, nearly one half of this series of sonnets has nothing to do with love, but treats of quite other life-influences. I would defy any one to couple with fair quotation of Sonnets 29, 30, 31, 39, 40, 41, 43, or others, the slander that their author was not impressed, like all other thinking men, with the responsibilities and higher mysteries of life; while Sonnets 35, 36, and 37, entitled *The Choice,* sum up the general view taken in a manner only to be evaded by conscious insincerity. Thus much for *The House of Life,* of which the sonnet *Nuptial Sleep* is one stanza, embodying, for its small constituent share, a beauty of natural universal function, only to be reprobated in art if dwelt on (as I have shown that it is not here) to the exclusion of those other highest things of which it is the harmonious concomitant.

At page 342, an attempt is made to stigmatize four short quotations as being specially "my own property," that is, (for the context shows the meaning,) as being grossly sensual; though all guiding reference to any precise page or poem in my book is avoided here. The first of these unspecified quotations is from the *Last Confession*; and is the description referring to the harlot's laugh, the hideous character of which, together with its real or imagined resemblance to the laugh heard soon afterwards from the lips of one long cherished as an ideal, is the immediate cause which makes the maddened hero of the poem a murderer. Assailants may say what they please; but no poet or poetic reader will blame me for making the incident recorded in these seven lines as repulsive to the reader as it was to the hearer and beholder. Without this, the chain of motive and result would remain obviously incomplete. Observe also that these are but seven lines in a poem of some five hundred, not one other of which could be classed with them.

A second quotation gives the last two lines *only* of the following sonnet, which is the first of four sonnets in *The House of Life* jointly entitled *Willowwood*:—

"I sat with Love upon a woodside well,
   Leaning across the water, I and he;
   Nor ever did he speak nor looked at me,
But touched his lute wherein was audible
The certain secret thing he had to tell:
   Only our mirrored eyes met silently
   In the low wave; and that sound seemed to be
The passionate voice I knew; and my tears fell.

"And at their fall, his eyes beneath grew hers;
  And with his foot and with his wing-feathers
   He swept the spring that watered my heart's drouth.

Then the dark ripples spread to waving hair,
And as I stooped, her own lips rising there
  Bubbled with brimming kisses at my mouth."

The critic has quoted (as I said) only the last two lines, and he has italicized the second as something unbearable and ridiculous. Of course the inference would be that this was really my own absurd bubble-and-squeak notion of an actual kiss. The reader will perceive at once, from the whole sonnet transcribed above, how untrue such an inference would be. The sonnet describes a dream or trance of divided love momentarily re-united by the longing fancy; and in the imagery of the dream, the face of the beloved rises through deep dark waters to kiss the lover. Thus the phrase, "Bubbled with brimming kisses," etc., bears purely on the special symbolism employed, and from that point of view will be found, I believe, perfectly simple and just.

A third quotation is from *Eden Bower,* and says,

  "What more prize than love to impel thee?
  Grip and lip my limbs as I tell thee!"

Here again no reference is given, and naturally the reader would suppose that a human embrace is described. The embrace, on the contrary, is that of a fabled snake-woman and a snake. It would be possible still, no doubt, to object on other grounds to this conception; but the ground inferred and relied on for full effect by the critic is none the less an absolute misrepresentation. These three extracts, it will be admitted, are virtually, though not verbally, garbled with malicious intention; and the same is the case, as I have shown, with the sonnet called *Nuptial Sleep* when purposely treated as a "whole poem."

The last of the four quotations grouped by the critic as conclusive examples consists of two lines from *Jenny.* Neither some thirteen years ago, when I wrote this poem, nor last year when I published it, did I fail to foresee impending charges of recklessness and aggressiveness, or to perceive that even some among those who could really *read* the poem, and acquit me on these grounds, might still hold that the thought in it had better have dispensed with the situation which serves it for framework. Nor did I omit to consider how far a treatment from without might here be possible. But the motive powers of art reverse the requirement of science, and demand first of all an *inner* standing-point. The heart of such a mystery as this must be plucked from the very world in which it beats or bleeds; and the beauty and pity, the self-questionings and all-questionings which it brings with it, can come with full force only from the mouth of one alive to its whole appeal, such as the speaker put forward in the poem,—that is, of a young and thoughtful man of the world. To such a speaker, many half-cynical revulsions of feeling and reverie, and a recurrent presence of the impressions of beauty (however artificial) which first brought him within such a circle of influence, would be inevitable features of the dramatic relations portrayed. Here again I can give the lie, in hearing of honest readers, to the base or trivial ideas which my critic labours to connect with the poem. There is another little charge, however, which this minstrel in mufti brings against *Jenny,* namely, one of plagiarism from that very poetic self of his which the tutelary prose does but enshroud for the moment. This question can, fortunately, be settled with ease by others who have read my critic's poems; and thus I need the less regret that, not happening myself to be in that position, I must be content to rank with those who cannot pretend to an opinion on the subject.

It would be humiliating, need one come to serious detail, to have to refute such an accusation as that of "binding oneself by solemn league and covenant to extol fleshliness as the distinct and supreme end of poetic and pictorial art"; and one cannot but feel that here every one will think it allowable merely to pass by with a smile the foolish fellow who has brought a charge thus framed against any reasonable man. Indeed, what I have said already is substantially enough to refute it, even did I not feel sure that a fair balance of my poetry must, of itself, do so in the eyes of every candid reader. I say nothing of my pictures; but those who know them will laugh at the idea. That I may, nevertheless, take a wider view than some poets or critics, of how much, in the material conditions absolutely given to man to deal with as distinct from his spiritual aspirations, is admissible within the limits of Art,—this, I say, is possible enough; nor do I wish to shrink from such responsibility. But to state that I do so to the ignoring or overshadowing of spiritual beauty, is an absolute falsehood, impossible to be put forward except in the indulgence of prejudice or rancour.

I have selected, amid much railing on my critic's part, what seemed the most representative indictment against me, and have, so far, answered it. Its remaining clauses set forth how others and myself "aver that poetic expression is greater than poetic thought . . . and sound superior to sense"—an accusation elsewhere, I observe, expressed by saying that we "wish to create form for its own sake." If writers of verse are to be listened to in such arraignment of each other, it might be quite competent to me to prove, from the works of my friends in question, that no such thing is the case with them; but my present function is to confine myself to my own defence. This, again, it is difficult to do quite seriously. It is no part of my undertaking to dispute the verdict of any "contemporary," however contemptuous or contemptible, on my own measure of executive success; but the accusation cited above is not against the poetic value of certain work, but against its primary and (by assumption) its admitted aim. And to this I must reply that so far, assuredly, not even Shakspeare himself could desire more arduous human tragedy for development in Art than belongs to the themes I venture to embody, however incalculably higher might be his power of dealing with them. What more inspiring for poetic effort than the terrible Love turned to Hate,—perhaps the deadliest of all passion-woven complexities,—which is the theme of *Sister Helen,* and, in a more fantastic form, of *Eden Bower*— the surroundings of both poems being the mere machinery of a central universal meaning? What, again, more so than the savage penalty exacted for a lost ideal, as expressed in the *Last Confession*;—than the outraged love for man and burning compensations in art and memory of *Dante at Verona*;—than the baffling problems which the face of *Jenny* conjures up;—or than the analysis of passion and feeling attempted in *The House of Life,* and others among the more purely lyrical poems? I speak here, as does my critic in the clause adduced, of *aim,* not of *achievement;* and so far, the mere summary is instantly subversive of the preposterous imputation. To assert that the poet whose matter is such as this aims chiefly at "creating form for its own sake," is, in fact, almost an ingenuous kind of dishonesty; for surely it delivers up the asserter at once, bound hand and foot, to the tender mercies of contradictory proof. Yet this may fairly be taken as an example of the spirit in which a constant effort is here made against me to appeal to those who either are ignorant of what I write, or else belong to the large class too easily influenced by an assumption of authority in addressing them. The false name appended to the article must, as is evident, aid this position vastly; for who, after all, would not be apt to laugh at seeing one poet confessedly come forward as aggressor against another in the field of criticism?

It would not be worth while to lose time and patience in noticing minutely how the system of misrepresentation is carried into points of artistic detail,—giving us, for example, such statements as that the burthen employed in the ballad of *Sister Helen* "is repeated with little or no alteration through thirty-four verses," whereas the fact is, that the alteration of it in every verse is the very scheme of the poem. But these are minor matters

quite thrown into the shade by the critic's more daring
sallies. In addition to the class of attack I have answered
above, the article contains, of course, an immense amount
of personal paltriness; as, for instance, attributions of my
work to this, that, or the other absurd derivative source;
or again, pure nonsense (which can have no real meaning
even to the writer) about "one art getting hold of another,
and imposing on it its conditions and limitations"; or,
indeed, what not besides? However, to such antics as this,
no more attention is possible than that which Virgil en-
joined Dante to bestow on the meaner phenomena of his
pilgrimage.

Thus far, then, let me thank you for the opportunity
afforded me to join issue with the Stealthy School of
Criticism. As for any literary justice to be done on this
particular Mr. Robert-Thomas, I will merely ask the
reader whether, once identified, he does not become mani-
festly his own best "sworn tormentor"? For who will
then fail to discern all the palpitations which preceded his
final resolve in the great question whether to be or not
to be his acknowledged self when he became an assailant?
And yet this is he who, from behind his mask, ventures
to charge another with "bad blood," with "insincerity,"
and the rest of it (and that where poetic fancies are alone
in question); while every word on his own tongue is
covert rancour, and every stroke from his pen perversion
of truth. Yet, after all, there is nothing wonderful in the
lengths to which a fretful poet-critic will carry such
grudges as he may bear, while publisher and editor can
both be found who are willing to consider such means
admissible, even to the clear subversion of first professed
tenets in the *Review* which they conduct.

In many phases of outward nature, the principle of
chaff and grain holds good,—the base enveloping the
precious continually; but an untruth was never yet the
husk of a truth. Thresh and riddle and winnow it as you
may,—let it fly in shreds to the four winds,—falsehood

only will be that which flies and that which stays. And thus the sheath of deceit which this pseudonymous undertaking presents at the outset insures in fact what will be found to be its real character to the core.

(*1871*)

WILLIAM HURRELL MALLOCK

HOW TO MAKE A MODERN
PRE-RAPHAELITE POEM

Take a packet of fine selected early English, containing
no words but such as are obsolete and unintelligible. Pour
this into about double the quantity of entirely new Eng-
lish, which must have never been used before, and
which you must compose yourself, fresh, as it is wanted.
Mix these together thoroughly till they assume a color
quite different from any tongue that was ever spoken,
and the material will be ready for use.

Determine the number of stanzas of which your poem
shall consist, and select a corresponding number of the
most archaic or most peculiar words in your vocabulary,
allotting one of these to each stanza; and pour in the
other words round them, until the entire poem is filled in.

This kind of composition is usually cast in shapes.
These, though not numerous—amounting, in all, to some-
thing under a dozen—it would take too long to describe
minutely here; and a short visit to Mr. ——'s shop, in
King Street, where they are kept in stock, would explain
the whole of them. A favourite one, however, is the
following, which is of very easy construction. Take three
damozels, dressed in straight night-gowns. Pull their hair-

pins out, and let their hair tumble all about their
shoulders. A few stars may be sprinkled into this with
advantage. Place an aureole about the head of each, and
give each a lily in her hand, about half the size of herself.
Bend their necks all different ways, and set them in a row
before a stone wall, with an apple-tree between each, and
some large flowers at their feet. Trees and flowers of the
right sort are very plentiful in church windows. When
you have arranged all these objects rightly, take a cast of
them in the softest part of your brain, and pour in your
word-composition as above described.

This kind of poem is much improved by what is called
a burden. This consists of a few jingling words, generally
of an archaic character, about which we have only to be
careful that they have no reference to the subject of the
poem they are to ornament. They are inserted without
variation between the stanzas.

In conclusion, we would remark to beginners that this
sort of composition must be attempted only in a perfectly
vacant atmosphere; so that no grains of common-sense
may injure the work whilst in progress.

(1872)

HENRY DUFF TRAILL

AFTER DILETTANTE CONCETTI

"Why do you wear your hair like a man,
                              Sister Helen?
This week is the third since you began."
"I'm writing a ballad; be still if you can,
                              Little brother.
          (*O Mother Carey, mother!*
What chickens are these between sea and heaven?)"

"But why does your figure appear so lean,
                              Sister Helen?
And why do you dress in sage, sage green?"   10
"Children should never be heard, if seen,
                              Little brother.
          (*O Mother Carey, mother!*
What fowls are a-wing in the stormy heaven!)"

"But why is your face so yellowy white,
                              Sister Helen?
And why are your skirts so funnily tight?"
"Be quiet, you torment, or how can I write,
                              Little brother?
          (*O Mother Carey, mother!*   20
How gathers thy train to the sea from the heaven!)"

"And who's Mother Carey, and what is her train,
          Sister Helen?
And why do you call her again and again?"
"You troublesome boy, why that's the refrain,
          Little brother.
     (*O Mother Carey, mother!*
What work is toward in the startled heaven?)"

"And what's a refrain? What a curious word,
          Sister Helen!   30
Is the ballad you're writing about a sea-bird?"
"Not at all; why should it be? Don't be absurd,
          Little brother.
     (*O Mother Carey, mother!*
Thy brood flies lower as lowers the heaven.)"

     (*A big brother speaketh:*)
"The refrain you've studied a meaning had,
          Sister Helen!
It gave strange force to a weird ballàd,
But refrains have become a ridiculous 'fad,'
          Little brother.   40
     And *Mother Carey, mother,*
Has a bearing on nothing in earth or heaven.

"But the finical fashion has had its day,
          Sister Helen.
And let's try in the style of a different lay
To bid it adieu in poetical way,
          Little brother.
     So Mother Carey, mother!
Collect your chickens and go to—heaven."

     (*A pause. Then the big brother singeth, accompany-*
     ing himself in a plaintive wise on the triangle:)

"Look in my face. My name is Used-to-was,*   50
    I am also called Played-out and Done-to-Death,
    And It-will-wash-no-more. Awakeneth
Slowly, but sure awakening it has,
The common-sense of man; and I, alas!
    The ballad-burden trick, now known too well,
    Am turned to scorn, and grown contemptible—
A too transparent artifice to pass.

"What a cheap dodge I am! The cats who dart
    Tin-kettled through the streets in wild surprise
    Assail judicious ears not otherwise;   60
And yet no critics praise the urchin's 'art,'
Who to the wretched creature's caudal part
    Its foolish empty-jingling 'burden' ties."

                                            (1882)

* A parody of *The House of Life*, Sonnet XCVII.

WILLIAM SCHWENCK GILBERT

FROM PATIENCE

[*Gilbert and Sullivan's operetta* Patience *mocked the Aesthetic Movement of the 1880's and especially the gestures of its leader Oscar Wilde. Bunthorne's song indicates the way in which the Aesthetes mingled Pre-Raphaelite attitudes and symbols with motifs from France, Japan, and the English eighteenth century.*]

BUNTHORNE'S RECITATIVE

Am I alone,
  And unobserved? I am!
Then let me own
  I'm an aesthetic sham!

This air severe
  Is but a mere
    Veneer!

This cynic smile
  Is but a wile
    Of guile!

This costume chaste
  Is but good taste
    Misplaced!

Let me confess!
A languid love for lilies does *not* blight me!
Lank limbs and haggard cheeks do *not* delight me!
    I do *not* care for dirty greens
      By any means.
     I do *not* long for all one sees
      That's Japanese.   20
     I am *not* fond of uttering platitudes
      In stained-glass attitudes.
     In short, my mediaevalism's affectation,
     Born of a morbid love of admiration!

BUNTHORNE'S SONG

If you're anxious for to shine in the high aesthetic line as
    a man of culture rare,
You must get up all the germs of the transcendental
    terms, and plant them everywhere.
You must lie upon the daisies and discourse in novel
    phrases of your complicated state of mind,
The meaning doesn't matter if it's only idle chatter of a
    transcendental kind.
    And everyone will say,
    As you walk your mystic way,
"If this young man expresses himself in terms too deep
    for *me,*
Why, what a very singularly deep young man this deep
    young man must be!"

Be eloquent in praise of the very dull old days which have
    long since passed away,
And convince 'em, if you can, that the reign of good
    Queen Anne was Culture's palmiest day.   10

Of course you will pooh-pooh whatever's fresh and new,
    and declare it's crude and mean,
For Art stopped short in the cultivated court of the
    Empress Josephine.
    And everyone will say,
    As you walk your mystic way,
"If that's not good enough for him which is good enough
    for *me,*
Why, what a very cultivated kind of youth this kind of
    youth must be!"

Then a sentimental passion of a vegetable fashion must
    excite your languid spleen,
An attachment *à la* Plato for a bashful young potato, or
    a not-too-French French bean!
Though the Philistines may jostle, you will rank as an
    apostle in the high aesthetic band,
If you walk down Piccadilly with a poppy or a lily in
    your mediaeval hand.   20
    And everyone will say,
    As you walk your flowery way,
"If he's content with a vegetable love which would cer-
    tainly not suit *me,*
Why, what a most particularly pure young man this pure
    young man must be!"

                                        (1881)

OSCAR WILDE

FROM THE ENGLISH RENAISSANCE
OF ART

Phidias and the achievements of Greek art are fore-shadowed in Homer: Dante prefigures for us the passion and colour and intensity of Italian painting: the modern love of landscape dates from Rousseau, and it is in Keats that one discerns the beginning of the artistic renaissance of England.

Byron was a rebel and Shelley a dreamer; but in the calmness and clearness of his vision, his perfect self-control, his unerring sense of beauty and his recognition of a separate realm for the imagination, Keats was the pure and serene artist, the forerunner of the pre-Raphaelite school, and so of the great romantic movement of which I am to speak.

Blake had indeed, before him, claimed for art a lofty, spiritual mission, and had striven to raise design to the ideal level of poetry and music, but the remoteness of his vision both in painting and poetry and the incomplete-ness of his technical powers had been adverse to any real influence. It is in Keats that the artistic spirit of this century first found its absolute incarnation.

And these pre-Raphaelites, what were they? If you ask

nine-tenths of the British public what is the meaning of
the word aesthetics, they will tell you it is the French for
affectation or the German for a dado; and if you inquire
about the pre-Raphaelites you will hear something about
an eccentric lot of young men to whom a sort of divine
crookedness and holy awkwardness in drawing were the
chief objects of art. To know nothing about their great
men is one of the necessary elements of English education.

As regards the pre-Raphaelites the story is simple
enough. In the year 1847 a number of young men in
London, poets and painters, passionate admirers of Keats
all of them, formed the habit of meeting together for dis-
cussions on art, the result of such discussions being that
the English Philistine public was roused suddenly from
its ordinary apathy by hearing that there was in its midst
a body of young men who had determined to revolu-
tionise English painting and poetry. They called them-
selves the pre-Raphaelite Brotherhood.

In England, then as now, it was enough for a man to
try and produce any serious beautiful work to lose all his
rights as a citizen; and besides this, the pre-Raphaelite
Brotherhood—among whom the names of Dante Rossetti,
Holman Hunt and Millais will be familiar to you—had
on their side three things that the English public never
forgives: youth, power and enthusiasm.

Satire, always as sterile as it is shameful and as impotent
as it is insolent, paid them that usual homage which
mediocrity pays to genius—doing, here as always, infinite
harm to the public, blinding them to what is beautiful,
teaching them that irreverence which is the source of all
vileness and narrowness of life, but harming the artist not
at all, rather confirming him in the perfect rightness of his
work and ambition. For to disagree with three-fourths of
the British public on all points is one of the first elements
of sanity, one of the deepest consolations in all moments
of spiritual doubt.

As regards the ideas these young men brought to the
regeneration of English art, we may see at the base of

their artistic creations a desire for a deeper spiritual value to be given to art as well as a more decorative value.

Pre-Raphaelites they called themselves; not that they imitated the early Italian masters at all, but that in their work, as opposed to the facile abstractions of Raphael, they found a stronger realism of imagination, a more careful realism of technique, a vision at once more fervent and more vivid, an individuality more intimate and more intense.

For it is not enough that a work of art should conform to the aesthetic demands of its age: there must be also about it, if it is to affect us with any permanent delight, the impress of a distinct individuality, an individuality remote from that of ordinary men, and coming near to us only by virtue of a certain newness and wonder in the work, and through channels whose very strangeness makes us more ready to give them welcome.

La personalité, said one of the greatest of modern French critics, *voilà ce qui nous sauvera.*

But above all things was it a return to Nature—that formula which seems to suit so many and such diverse movements: they would draw and paint nothing but what they saw, they would try and imagine things as they really happened. Later there came to the old house by Blackfriars Bridge, where this young brotherhood used to meet and work, two young men from Oxford, Edward Burne-Jones and William Morris—the latter substituting for the simpler realism of the early days a more exquisite spirit of choice, a more faultless devotion to beauty, a more intense seeking for perfection: a master of all exquisite design and of all spiritual vision. It is of the school of Florence rather than of that of Venice that he is kinsman, feeling that the close imitation of Nature is a disturbing element in imaginative art. The visible aspect of modern life disturbs him not; rather is it for him to render eternal all that is beautiful in Greek, Italian, and Celtic legend. To Morris we owe poetry whose perfect precision and clearness of word and vision has not been excelled in the literature of our country, and by the revival of the decorative arts he has given to our individualised romantic movement the social idea and the social factor also.

But the revolution accomplished by this clique of young men, with Ruskin's faultless and fervent eloquence to help them, was not one of ideas merely but of execution, not one of conceptions but of creations.

For the great eras in the history of the development of all the arts have been eras not of increased feeling or enthusiasm in feeling for art, but of new technical improvements primarily and specially. The discovery of marble quarries in the purple ravines of Pentelicus and on the little low-lying hills of the island of Paros gave to the Greeks the opportunity for that intensified vitality of action, that more sensuous and simple humanism, to which the Egyptian sculptor working laboriously in the hard porphyry and rose-coloured granite of the desert could not attain. The splendour of the Venetian school began with the introduction of the new oil medium for painting. The progress in modern music has been due to the invention of new instruments entirely, and in no way to an increased consciousness on the part of the musician of any wider social aim. The critic may try and trace the deferred resolutions of Beethoven to some sense of the incompleteness of the modern intellectual spirit, but the artist would have answered, as one of them did afterwards, "Let them pick out the fifths and leave us at peace."

And so it is in poetry also: all this love of curious French metres like the Ballade, the Villanelle, the Rondel; all this increased value laid on elaborate alliterations, and on curious words and refrains, such as you will find in Dante Rossetti and Swinburne, is merely the attempt to perfect flute and viol and trumpet through which the spirit of the age and the lips of the poet may blow the music of their many messages.

And so it has been with this romantic movement of ours: it is a reaction against the empty conventional work-

manship, the lax execution of previous poetry and paint-
ing, showing itself in the work of such men as Rossetti
and Burne-Jones by a far greater splendour of colour, a
far more intricate wonder of design than English imagina-
tive art has shown before. In Rossetti's poetry and the
poetry of Morris, Swinburne and Tennyson a perfect
precision and choice of language, a style flawless and
fearless, a seeking for all sweet and precious melodies and
a sustaining consciousness of the musical value of each
word are opposed to that value which is merely intellectual.
In this respect they are one with the romantic movement
of France of which not the least characteristic note was
struck by Théophile Gautier's advice to the young poet to
read his dictionary every day, as being the only book
worth a poet's reading.

While, then, the material of workmanship is being
thus elaborated and discovered to have in itself incom-
municable and eternal qualities of its own, qualities en-
tirely satisfying to the poetic sense and not needing for
their aesthetic effect any lofty intellectual vision, any deep
criticism of life or even any passionate human emotion at
all, the spirit and the method of the poet's working—
what people call his inspiration—have not escaped the
controlling influence of the artistic spirit. Not that the
imagination has lost its wings, but we have accustomed
ourselves to count their innumerable pulsations, to estimate
their limitless strength, to govern their ungovernable free-
dom.

(*1882*)

WALTER PATER

AESTHETIC POETRY

The "aesthetic" poetry is neither a mere reproduction of Greek or mediaeval poetry, nor only an idealisation of modern life and sentiment. The atmosphere on which its effect depends belongs to no simple form of poetry, no actual form of life. Greek poetry, mediaeval or modern poetry, projects, above the realities of its time, a world in which the forms of things are transfigured. Of that transfigured world this new poetry takes possession, and sublimates beyond it another still fainter and more spectral, which is literally an artificial or "earthly paradise." It is a finer ideal, extracted from what in relation to any actual world is already an ideal. Like some strange second flowering after date, it renews on a more delicate type the poetry of a past age, but must not be confounded with it. The secret of the enjoyment of it is that inversion of home-sickness known to some, that incurable thirst for the sense of escape, which no actual form of life satisfies, no poetry even, if it be merely simple and spontaneous.

The writings of the "romantic school," of which the aesthetic poetry is an afterthought, mark a transition not so much from the pagan to the mediaeval ideal, as from a lower to a higher degree of passion in literature. The end of the eighteenth century, swept by vast disturbing currents, experienced an excitement of spirit of which one note was a reaction against an outworn classicism severed not more from nature than from the genuine motives of ancient art; and a return to true Hellenism was as much a part of this reaction as the sudden preoccupation with things mediaeval. The mediaeval tendency is in Goethe's *Goetz von Berlichingen,* the Hellenic in his *Iphigenie.* At first this mediaevalism was superficial, or at least external. Adventure, romance in the frankest sense, grotesque individualism—that is one element in mediaeval poetry, and with it alone Scott and Goethe dealt. Beyond them were the two other elements of the mediaeval spirit: its mystic religion at its apex in Dante and Saint Louis, and its mystic passion, passing here and there into the great romantic loves of rebellious flesh, of Lancelot and Abelard. That stricter, imaginative mediaevalism which re-creates the mind of the Middle Age, so that the form, the presentment grows outward from within, came later with Victor Hugo in France, with Heine in Germany.

In the *Defence of Guenevere: and Other Poems,* published by Mr. William Morris now many years ago, the first typical specimen of aesthetic poetry, we have a refinement upon this later, profounder mediaevalism. The poem which gives its name to the volume is a thing tormented and awry with passion, like the body of Guenevere defending herself from the charge of adultery, and the accent falls in strange, unwonted places with the effect of a great cry. In truth these Arthurian legends, in their origin prior to Christianity, yield all their sweetness only in a Christian atmosphere. What is characteristic in them is the strange suggestion of a deliberate choice between Christ and a rival lover. That religion, monastic religion at any rate, has its sensuous side, a dangerously sensuous side, has been often seen: it is the experience of Rousseau as well as of the Christian mystics. The Christianity of the Middle Age made way among a people whose loss was in the life of the senses, partly by its aesthetic beauty, a thing so profoundly felt by the Latin hymn-writers, who for one moral or spiritual sentiment have a hundred sensuous images. And so in those imaginative loves, in their highest expression, the Provençal poetry, it is a rival religion with a new rival *cultus* that we see. Coloured through and through with Christian sentiment, they are rebels against it. The rejection of one worship for another is never lost sight of. The jealousy of that other lover, for whom these words and images and refined ways of sentiment were first devised, is the secret here of a borrowed, perhaps factitious colour and heat. It is the mood of the cloister taking a new direction, and winning so a later space of life it never anticipated.

Hereon, as before in the cloister, so now in the *château,* the reign of reverie set in. The devotion of the cloister knew that mood thoroughly, and had sounded all its stops. For the object of this devotion was absent or veiled, not limited to one supreme plastic form like Zeus at Olympia or Athena in the Acropolis, but distracted, as in a fever dream, into a thousand symbols and reflections. But then, the Church, that new Sibyl, had a thousand secrets to make the absent near. Into this kingdom of reverie, and with it into a paradise of ambitious refinements, the earthly love enters, and becomes a prolonged somnambulism. Of religion it learns the art of directing towards an unseen object sentiments whose natural direction is towards objects of sense. Hence a love defined by the absence of the beloved, choosing to be without hope, protesting against all lower uses of love, barren, extravagant, antinomian. It is the love which is incompatible with marriage for the chevalier who never comes, of the serf for the *châtelaine,* of the rose for the nightingale, of Rudel for the Lady of Tripoli. Another element of extravagance came in with the feudal spirit: Provençal love is full of the very forms of vassalage. To be the servant of love, to have offended, to taste the subtle luxury of chastisement, of reconciliation—the religious spirit, too, knows that, and meets just there, as in Rousseau, the delicacies of the

earthly love. Here, under this strange complex of condi-
tions, as in some medicated air, exotic flowers of senti-
ment expand, among people of a remote and unaccus-
tomed beauty, somnambulistic, frail, androgynous, the
light almost shining through them. Surely, such loves
were too fragile and adventurous to last more than for a
moment.

That monastic religion of the Middle Age was, in fact,
in many of its bearings, like a beautiful disease or disorder
of the senses: and a religion which is a disorder of the
senses must always be subject to illusions. Reverie, illusion,
delirium: they are the three stages of a fatal descent both
in the religion and the loves of the Middle Age. Nowhere
has the impression of this delirium been conveyed as by
Victor Hugo in *Notre Dame de Paris*. The strangest
creations of sleep seem here, by some appalling licence, to
cross the limit of the dawn. The English poet too has
learned the secret. He has diffused through *King Arthur's
Tomb* the maddening white glare of the sun, and tyranny
of the moon, not tender and far-off, but close down—the
sorcerer's moon, large and feverish. The colouring is in-
tricate and delirious, as of "scarlet lilies." The influence of
summer is like a poison in one's blood, with a sudden
bewildered sickening of life and all things. In *Galahad: a
Mystery,* the frost of Christmas night on the chapel stones
acts as a strong narcotic: a sudden shrill ringing pierces
through the numbness: a voice proclaims that the Grail
has gone forth through the great forest. It is in the *Blue
Closet* that this delirium reaches its height with a singular
beauty, reserved perhaps for the enjoyment of the few.

A passion of which the outlets are sealed begets a ten-
sion of nerve, in which the sensible world comes to one
with a reinforced brilliancy and relief—all redness is turned
into blood, all water into tears. Hence a wild, convulsed
sensuousness in the poetry of the Middle Age, in which
the things of nature begin to play a strange delirious part.
Of the things of nature the mediaeval mind had a deep
sense; but its sense of them was not objective, no real

escape to the world without us. The aspects and motions of nature only reinforced its prevailing mood, and were in conspiracy with one's own brain against one. A single sentiment invaded the world: everything was infused with a motive drawn from the soul. The amorous poetry of Provence, making the starling and the swallow its messengers, illustrates the whole attitude of nature in this electric atmosphere, bent as by miracle or magic to the service of human passion. . . .

One characteristic of the pagan spirit the aesthetic poetry has, which is on its surface—the continual suggestion, pensive or passionate, of the shortness of life. This is contrasted with the bloom of the world, and gives new seduction to it—the sense of death and the desire of beauty: the desire of beauty quickened by the sense of death. But that complexion of sentiment is at its height in another "aesthetic" poet of whom I have to speak next, Dante Gabriel Rossetti.

(1889)

DANTE GABRIEL ROSSETTI

It was characteristic of a poet who had ever something about him of mystic isolation, and will still appeal perhaps, though with a name it may seem now established in English literature, to a special and limited audience, that some of his poems had won a kind of exquisite fame before they were in the full sense published. *The Blessed Damozel,* although actually printed twice before the year 1870, was eagerly circulated in manuscript; and the volume which it now opens came at last to satisfy a long-standing curiosity as to the poet, whose pictures also had become an object of the same peculiar kind of interest. For those poems were the work of a painter, understood to belong to, and to be indeed the leader, of a new school then rising into note; and the reader of today may observe already, in *The Blessed Damozel,* written at the age of eighteen, a prefiguration of the chief characteristics of that school, as he will recognise in it also, in proportion as he really knows Rossetti, many of the characteristics which are most markedly personal and his own. Common to that school and to him, and in both alike of primary significance, was the quality of sincerity, already felt as one of the charms of that earliest poem—a perfect sincerity, taking effect in the deliberate use of the most direct and unconventional expression, for the conveyance of a poetic sense which recognised no conventional standard of what poetry was called upon to be. At a time when poetic originality in England might seem to have had its utmost play, here was certainly one new poet more, with a structure and music of verse, a vocabulary, an accent, unmistakably novel, yet felt to be no mere tricks of manner adopted with a view to forcing attention—an accent which might rather count as the very seal of reality on one man's own proper speech; as that speech itself was the wholly natural expression of certain wonderful things he really felt and saw. Here was one, who had a matter to present to his readers, to himself at least, in the first instance, so valuable, so real and definite, that his primary aim, as regards form or expression in his verse, would be but its exact equivalence to those *data* within. That he had this gift of transparency in language—the control of a style which did but obediently shift and shape itself to the mental motion, as a well-trained hand can follow on the tracing-paper the outline of an original drawing below it, was proved afterwards by a volume of typically perfect translations from the delightful but difficult "early Italian poets": such transparency being indeed the secret of all genuine style, of all such style as can truly belong to one man and not to another. His own meaning was always personal and even recondite, in a certain sense learned and casuistical, sometimes complex or obscure; but the term was always, one could see, deliberately chosen from many competitors, as the just transcript of that peculiar phase of soul which he alone knew, precisely as he knew it.

One of the peculiarities of *The Blessed Damozel* was a

definiteness of sensible imagery, which seemed almost
grotesque to some, and was strange, above all, in a theme
so profoundly visionary. The gold bar of heaven from
which she leaned, her hair yellow like ripe corn, are but
examples of a general treatment, as naively detailed as
the pictures of those early painters contemporary with
Dante, who has shown a similar care for minute and
definite imagery in his verse; there, too, in the very midst
of profoundly mystic vision. Such definition of outline is
indeed one among many points in which Rossetti re-
sembles the great Italian poet, of whom, led to him at
first by family circumstances, he was ever a lover—a
"servant and singer," faithful as Dante, "of Florence and
of Beatrice"—with some close inward conformities of
genius also, independent of any mere circumstances of
education. It was said by a critic of the last century, not
wisely though agreeably to the practice of his time, that
poetry rejoices in abstractions. For Rossetti, as for Dante,
without question on his part, the first condition of the
poetic way of seeing and presenting things is particularisa-
tion. "Tell me now," he writes, for Villon's

> Dictes-moy où, n'en quel pays,
> Est Flora, la belle Romaine—
>
> Tell me now, in what hidden way is
> Lady Flora the lovely Roman:

—"way," in which one might actually chance to meet her;
the unmistakably poetic effect of the couplet in English
being dependent on the definiteness of that single word
(though actually lighted on in the search after a difficult
double rhyme) for which every one else would have
written, like Villon himself, a more general one, just
equivalent to place or region.

   And this delight in concrete definition is allied with
another of his conformities to Dante, the really imagina-
tive vividness, namely, of his personifications—his hold

upon them, or rather their hold upon him, with the force of a Frankenstein, when once they have taken life from him. Not Death only and Sleep, for instance, and the winged spirit of Love, but certain particular aspects of them, a whole "populace" of special hours and places, "the hour" even "which might have been, yet might not be," are living creatures, with hands and eyes and articulate voices.

> Stands it not by the door—
> Love's Hour—till she and I shall meet;
> With bodiless form and unapparent feet
> That cast no shadow yet before,
> Though round its head the dawn begins to pour
> The breath that makes day sweet?—
>
> Nay, why
> Name the dead hours? I mind them well:
> Their ghosts in many darkened doorways dwell
> With desolate eyes to know them by.

Poetry as a *mania*—one of Plato's two higher forms of "divine" mania—has, in all its species, a mere insanity incidental to it, the "defect of its quality," into which it may lapse in its moment of weakness; and the insanity which follows a vivid poetic anthropomorphism like that of Rossetti may be noted here and there in his work, in a forced and almost grotesque materialising of abstractions, as Dante also became at times a mere subject of the scholastic realism of the Middle Age.

In *Love's Nocturn* and *The Stream's Secret*, congruously perhaps with a certain feverishness of soul in the moods they present, there is at times a near approach (may it be said?) to such insanity of realism—

> Pity and love shall burn
> In her pressed cheek and cherishing hands;
> And from the living spirit of love that stands
> Between her lips to soothe and yearn,

> Each separate breath shall clasp me round in turn
> And loose my spirit's bands.

But even if we concede this; even if we allow, in the very
plan of those two compositions, something of the literary
conceit—what exquisite, what novel flowers of poetry, we
must admit them to be, as they stand! In the one, what
a delight in all the natural beauty of water, all its details
for the eye of a painter; in the other, how subtle and fine
the imaginative hold upon all the secret ways of sleep
and dreams! In both of them, with much the same attitude
and tone, Love—sick and doubtful Love—would fain in-
quire of what lies below the surface of sleep, and below
the water; stream or dream being forced to speak by
Love's powerful "control"; and the poet would have it
foretell the fortune, issue, and event of his wasting passion.
Such artifices, indeed, were not unknown in the old
Provençal poetry of which Dante had learned something.
Only, in Rossetti at least, they are redeemed by a serious
purpose, by that sincerity of his, which allies itself readily
to a serious beauty, a sort of grandeur of literary work-
manship, to a great style. One seems to hear there a really
new kind of poetic utterance, with effects which have
nothing else like them; as there is nothing else, for in-
stance, like the narrative of Jacob's Dream in *Genesis,* or
Blake's design of the Singing of the Morning Stars, or
Addison's Nineteenth Psalm.

With him indeed, as in some revival of the old
mythopoeic age, common things—dawn, noon, night—
are full of human or personal expression, full of sentiment.
The lovely little sceneries scattered up and down his
poems, glimpses of a landscape, not indeed of broad open-
air effects, but rather that of a painter concentrated upon
the picturesque effect of one or two selected objects at a
time—the "hollow brimmed with mist," or the "ruined
weir," as he sees it from one of the windows, or reflected
in one of the mirrors of his "house of life" (the vignettes
for instance seen by Rose Mary in the magic beryl)

attest, by their very freshness and simplicity, to a pictorial or descriptive power in dealing with the inanimate world, which is certainly also one half of the charm, in that other, more remote and mystic, use of it. For with Rossetti this sense of lifeless nature, after all, is translated to a higher service, in which it does but incorporate itself with some phase of strong emotion. Every one understands how this may happen at critical moments of life; what a weirdly expressive soul may have crept, even in full noon-day, into "the white-flower'd elder-thicket," when Godiva saw it "gleam through the Gothic archways in the wall," at the end of her terrible ride. To Rossetti it is so always, because to him life is a crisis at every moment. A sustained impressibility towards the mysterious conditions of man's everyday life, towards the very mystery itself in it, gives a singular gravity to all his work: those matters never became trite to him. But throughout, it is the ideal intensity of love—of love based upon a perfect yet peculiar type of physical or material beauty—which is enthroned in the midst of those mysterious powers; Youth and Death, Destiny and Fortune, Fame, Poetic Fame, Memory, Oblivion, and the like. Rossetti is one of those who, in the words of Mérimée, *se passionnent pour la passion,* one of Love's lovers.

And yet, again as with Dante, to speak of his ideal type of beauty as material, is partly misleading. Spirit and matter, indeed, have been for the most part opposed, with a false contrast or antagonism by schoolmen, whose artificial creation those abstractions really are. In our actual concrete experience, the two trains of phenomena which the words *matter* and *spirit* do but roughly distinguish, play inextricably into each other. Practically, the church of the Middle Age by its aesthetic worship, its sacramentalism, its real faith in the resurrection of the flesh, had set itself against that Manichean opposition of spirit and matter, and its results in men's way of taking life; and in this, Dante is the central representative of its spirit. To him, in the vehement and impassioned heat of his conceptions, the material and the spiritual are fused and blent: if the spiritual attains the definite visibility of a crystal, what is material loses its earthiness and impurity. And here again, by force of instinct, Rossetti is one with him. His chosen type of beauty is one,

Whose speech Truth knows not from her thought,
Nor Love her body from her soul.

Like Dante, he knows no region of spirit which shall not be sensuous also, or material. The shadowy world, which he realises so powerfully, has still the ways and houses, the land and water, the light and darkness, the fire and flowers, that had so much to do in the moulding of those bodily powers and aspects which counted for so large a part of the soul, here.

For Rossetti, then, the great affections of persons to each other, swayed and determined, in the case of his highly pictorial genius, mainly by that so-called material loveliness, formed the great undeniable reality in things, the solid resisting substance, in a world where all beside might be but shadow. The fortunes of those affections—of the great love so determined; its casuistries, its languor sometimes; above all, its sorrows; its fortunate or unfortunate collisions with those other great matters; how it looks, as the long day of life goes round, in the light and shadow of them: all this, conceived with an abundant imagination, and a deep, a philosophic, reflectiveness, is the matter of his verse, and especially of what he designed as his chief poetic work, "a work to be called *The House of Life*," towards which the majority of his sonnets and songs were contributions.

The dwelling-place in which one finds oneself by chance or destiny, yet can partly fashion for oneself; never properly one's own at all, if it be changed too lightly; in which every object has its associations—the dim mirrors, the portraits, the lamps, the books, the hair-tresses of the dead and visionary magic crystals in the secret drawers, the names and words scratched on the windows, windows open upon prospects the saddest or the sweetest; the house one must quit, yet taking perhaps, how much of its quietly active light and colour along with us!—grown now to be a kind of raiment to one's body, as the body, according to Swedenborg, is but the raiment of the soul—under that image, the whole of Rossetti's work might count as a *House of Life,* of which he is but the "Interpreter." And it is a "haunted" house. A sense of power in love, defying distance, and those barriers which are so much more than physical distance, of unutterable desire penetrating into the world of sleep, however "lead-bound," was one of those anticipative notes obscurely struck in *The Blessed Damozel,* and, in his later work, makes him speak sometimes almost like a believer in mesmerism. Dream-land, as we said, with its "phantoms of the body," deftly coming and going on love's service, is to him, in no mere fancy or figure of speech, a real country, a veritable expansion of, or addition to, our waking life; and he did well perhaps to wait carefully upon sleep, for the lack of it became mortal disease with him. One may even recognise a sort of morbid and over-hasty making-ready for death itself, which increases on him, thoughts concerning it, its imageries, coming with a frequency and importunity, in excess, one might think, of even the very saddest, quite wholesome wisdom.

And indeed the publication of his second volume of *Ballads and Sonnets* preceded his death by scarcely a twelvemonth. That volume bears witness to the reverse of any failure of power, or falling-off from his early standard of literary perfection, in every one of his then accustomed forms of poetry—the song, the sonnet, and the ballad. The newly printed sonnets, now completing *The House of Life,* certainly advanced beyond those earlier ones, in clearness; his dramatic power in the ballad, was here at its height; while one monumental, gnomic piece, *Soothsay,* testifies, more clearly even than the *Nineveh* of his first volume, to the reflective force, the dry reason, always at

work behind his imaginative creations, which at no time
dispensed with a genuine intellectual structure. For in
matters of pure reflection also, Rossetti maintained the
painter's sensuous clearness of conception; and this has
something to do with the capacity, largely illustrated by
his ballads, of telling some red-hearted story of impas-
sioned action with effect.

Have there, in very deed, been ages, in which the ex-
ternal conditions of poetry such as Rossetti's were of more
spontaneous growth than in our own? The archaic side of
Rossetti's work, his preferences in regard to earlier poetry,
connect him with those who have certainly thought so,
who fancied they could have breathed more largely in
the age of Chaucer, or of Ronsard, in one of those ages,
in the words of Stendhal—*ces siècles de passions où les
âmes pouvaient se livrer franchement à la plus haute
exaltation, quand les passions qui font la possibilité comme
les sujets des beaux arts existaient.* We may think, perhaps,
that such old time as that has never really existed except
in the fancy of poets; but it was to find it, that Rossetti
turned so often from modern life to the chronicle of the
past. Old Scotch history, perhaps beyond any other, is
strong in the matter of heroic and vehement hatreds and
love, the tragic Mary herself being but the perfect blossom
of them; and it is from that history that Rossetti has taken
the subjects of the two longer ballads of his second
volume: of the three admirable ballads in it, *The King's
Tragedy* (in which Rossetti has dexterously interwoven
some relics of James's own exquisite early verse) reaching
the highest level of dramatic success, and marking per-
fection, perhaps, in this kind of poetry; which, in the
earlier volume, gave us, among other pieces, *Troy Town,
Sister Helen,* and *Eden Bower.*

Like those earlier pieces, the ballads of the second
volume bring with them the question of the poetic value
of the "refrain"—

> Eden bower's in flower:
> And O the bower and the hour!

—and the like. Two of those ballads—*Troy Town* and *Eden Bower,* are terrible in theme; and the refrain serves, perhaps, to relieve their bold aim at the sentiment of terror. In *Sister Helen* again, the refrain has a real, and sustained purpose (being here duly varied also) and performs the part of a chorus, as the story proceeds. Yet even in these cases, whatever its effect may be in actual recitation, it may fairly be questioned, whether, to the mere reader their actual effect is not that of a positive interruption and drawback, at least in pieces so lengthy; and Rossetti himself, it would seem, came to think so, for in the shortest of his later ballads, *The White Ship*—that old true history of the generosity with which a youth, worthless in life, flung himself upon death—he was contented with a single utterance of the refrain, "given out" like the keynote or tune of a chant.

In *The King's Tragedy,* Rossetti has worked upon motive, broadly human (to adopt the phrase of popular criticism) such as one and all may realise. Rossetti, indeed, with all his self-concentration upon his own peculiar aim, by no means ignored those general interests which are external to poetry as he conceived it; as he has shown here and there, in this poetic, as also in pictorial, work. It was but that, in a life to be shorter even than the average, he found enough to occupy him in the fulfilment of a task, plainly "given him to do." Perhaps, if one had to name a single composition of his to readers desiring to make acquaintance with him for the first time, one would select: *The King's Tragedy*—that poem so moving, so popularly dramatic, and lifelike. Notwithstanding this, his work, it must be conceded, certainly through no narrowness or egotism, but in the faithfulness of a true workman to a vocation so emphatic, was mainly of the esoteric order. But poetry, at all times, exercises two distinct functions: it may reveal, it may unveil to every eye, the ideal aspects of common things, after Gray's way (though Gray too, it is well to remember, seemed in his own day, seemed even to Johnson, obscure) or it may actually add to the number of motives poetic and uncommon in themselves, by the imaginative creation of things that are ideal from their very birth. Rossetti did something, something excellent, of the former kind; but his characteristic, his really revealing work, lay in the adding to poetry of fresh poetic material, of a new order of phenomena, in the creation of a new ideal.

(*1883*, 1889)

INDEX OF AUTHORS

INDEX OF TITLES

INDEX OF FIRST LINES

CPSIA information can be obtained
at www.ICGtesting.com
Printed in the USA
BVHW090924250123
657012BV00010B/741